After Forty Years

Other Titles in the Series

AFTER FORTY YEARS
VATICAL COUNCIL II'S DIVERSE LEGACY

Proceedings from the 28th Annual Convention of the Fellowship
of Catholic Scholars, September 23–25, 2005
Charlotte, North Carolina

Edited by Kenneth D. Whitehead

ST. AUGUSTINE'S PRESS
South Bend, Indiana
2007

Manufactured in the United States of America.

1 2 3 4 5   12 11 10 09 08 07

Library of Congress Cataloging in Publication Data
Fellowship of Catholic Scholars. Convention
(28th: 2005: Charlotte, N.C.)
After 40 years: Vatican Council II's diverse legacy
proceedings from the 28th Annual Convention of the Fellowship of
Catholic Scholars, Charlotte, North Carolina, September 23–25, 2005
Kenneth D. Whitehead, editor
p. cm.
ISBN 978-1-58731-016-4 (paperbound: alk. paper)
1. Catholic Church – Doctrines – Congresses. 2. Vatican Council
(2nd : 1962–1965) – Congresses. I. Whitehead, K. D. II. Title.

BX1747.F45 2005
262'.52 – dc22

∞ *The paper used in this publication meets the minimum requirements of the
American National Standard for Information Sciences – Permanence of Paper
for Printed Materials, ANSI Z39.48-1984.*

St. Augustine's Press
www.staugustine.net

CONTENTS

Introduction

KENNETH D. WHITEHEAD

Subtitling this volume "Vatican Council II's Diverse Legacy" was not only not meant to imply any claim that *the* legacy of the epochal and historic event that Vatican Council II was could be summed up in a single volume such as this; on the contrary, it was meant, precisely, to signal that only a part, perhaps even only a small part, of the Council's rich legacy could be covered in the course of the customary weekend annual convention of the Fellowship of Catholic Scholars – and then subsequently be presented in the volume which each year issues from our annual conventions.

When the FCS Board of Directors decided that the 40th anniversary of the close of the Second Vatican Council needed to be suitably commemorated by our association of scholars which is particularly interested in and focused upon the magisterium of the Catholic Church, it was clear from the beginning that any attempt to cover all of the sixteen documents of the Council could result only in superficial coverage at best, and, indeed, was surely an impossibility in any case.

It was also immediately clear that the Council document which has had the greatest impact on Catholic life and worship since the Council, namely, the Constitution on the Sacred Liturgy, *Sacrosanctum Concilium*, could not adequately be treated at a single session of any convention. It was accordingly decided, in view of the importance of the subject – and, especially, in view of the obvious mixed results forty years after the Council's unprecedented decision to mandate a comprehensive reform and renewal of the entire liturgy of the Roman rite – that the entire 2006 convention next year would be devoted exclusively to *Sacrosanctum Concilium* and to the sacred liturgy: this year we would focus on the Council apart from the question of the reform of the sacred liturgy.

Even with the question of the liturgical reform decreed by Vatican II deferred, however, the territory covered by the remaining fifteen Council documents still remained much too vast to be covered at a single convention. As explained by Professor William May, who was named program chairman by the Board of Directors, it was therefore decided to try to cover only the major documents issued by the Council, namely: the two great Constitutions on the Church, and the equally significant Constitution on divine revelation (and hence, very importantly, on Scripture), plus the Declaration on Religious Liberty and the Decree on Ecumenism. Professor May describes how these subjects were divided up and speakers chosen.

It soon became evident, however, that one of the particular special interests of the scholars who were approached was in what may be styled the "Christian anthropology" of *Gaudium et Spes*, the Pastoral Constitution of the Church in the Modern World. As a result, no less than three sessions of the convention ended up being devoted to various aspects of *Gaudium et Spes*, while the other documents treated rated only one session each. It will be recalled that GS was perhaps the favorite Vatican II document of Pope John Paul II (who as a Polish bishop had a hand in its drafting); and so the special emphasis on it here reflects the continuing interest in and preoccupation with some of its themes during the pontificate of Pope John Paul II.

Thus, this is a book which, while dealing with the *diverse* legacy of Vatican II, focuses quite deliberately on aspects of the Council deemed to be of special interest forty years later. Nevertheless, readers will find that all of the documents covered here have been given careful, in-depth attention by scholars who – to judge only by the copious endnotes generally provided by them – are only too well aware of the great importance of Vatican II in the teaching and life of the Church; and, if anything, have been able to enhance that importance by bringing it out in ways which go well beyond the superficiality with which the Second Vatican Council and its aftermath have unfortunately all too often been treated today.

Placing such emphasis on the Council's major documents, however, has unavoidably meant neglecting some of the other aspects of the Council which, it is fully realized, remain important nonetheless. Thus there is nothing here, for example, on all the *ad intra* decrees on bishops, priests (two separate decrees!), religious, laity, and Eastern-rite Catholics which have motivated so many of the efforts at reform and renewal in the post-conciliar era (some of which have gone astray as a result of the particular conciliar decree *not* being followed as carefully as it should have been!). The Council's beautifully written Decree on the Church's Missionary Activity, *Ad Gentes* – parts of which were based on a draft originally prepared by the influential *peritus*, Father Yves M.-J.

Congar, O.P., and the young Father Joseph Ratzinger, the *peritus* of Cardinal Joseph Frings of Cologne – is similarly not treated here as it would normally deserve to be, especially in view of the fact that the Church's missionary impulse has for a number of reasons flagged somewhat in the post-conciliar era – *Ad Gentes* remains among those conciliar documents yet to be fully carried out.

Again, the Council's Declaration on Christian Education, *Gravissimum Educationis*, which presciently emphasized the special rights of both parents and the Church in education – as if the Council Fathers had foreseen the crisis of educational institutions at all levels which has characterized the post-conciliar era – is not really touched upon in these pages. The same thing is true of the document which, in view of the prominent attention given to the Jews and to the Nazi holocaust against the Jews in the post-conciliar era, has probably attracted more attention in the public arena than almost any other Vatican II document, namely, the Declaration on the Relation of the Church to Non-Christian Religions, *Nostra Aetate*; but it was one more of the Vatican II documents that we were unable to treat here. Nor, in today's age of the media is Vatican II's solid principle-based Decree on the Means of Social Communication, *Inter Mirifica,* dealt with here.

In short, the 2005 FCS convention in Charlotte found itself obliged to pick and choose from among the Council's diverse legacy those issues which, while they certainly did count among the more important issues within the Council's enormous output, were also issues which Fellowship scholars were more interested in and felt competent to deal with as our contribution to the commemoration of the Council forty years after its close. The result, we believe, should be of great interest to everyone who realizes what the 21st general council of the Catholic Church has meant and still means in her life and practice as we move further into the Third Millennium of Christianity.

Convention Program Chairman's Introduction

WILLIAM E. MAY

The program of the 28th Annual Convention of the Fellowship of Catholic Scholars held in Charlotte, North Carolina, on September 23-25, 2005, celebrated the 40th anniversary of the close of Vatican Council II. Since the meeting next year will focus entirely on the liturgy of the Church, this year's meeting did not consider the Constitution on the Sacred Liturgy, *Sacrosanctum Concilium*. It centered attention rather on the Council's other major documents, namely, the Dogmatic Constitution on the Church, *Lumen Gentium,* the Pastoral Constitution on the Church in the Modern World, *Gaudium et Spes*, the Dogmatic Constitution on Divine Revelation, *Dei Verbum,* the Declaration on Religious Liberty, *Dignitatis Humanae*, and the Decree on Ecumenism, *Unitatis Redintegratio.*

With the great help of Kenneth Whitehead, who himself gave a splendid presentation on the significance of *Unitatis Redintegratio*, as well as sound advice from Monsignor William B. Smith, the convention program committee of which I was in charge was fortunate in being able to line up a terrific roster of speakers. Father Thomas Weinandy, O.F.M. Cap., gave a masterful keynote address. He noted that confusion did indeed reign for a time after the Council because too many theologians and others focused on the Council's alleged "spirit" – which to a great extent consisted of hot air – rather than upon what the Council actually said. Thanks to the leadership of Pope John Paul II the Great, as well as that of Cardinal Ratzinger-Pope Benedict XVI, however, much progress has been made since by dedicated scholars to present in depth not only the authentic teaching of the Council but its great significance for our day.

Several presentations focused on the moral and anthropological vision of the Council, particularly the vision at the heart of *Gaudium et Spes,* contrasting it with the pseudo-personalism of some contemporary dualistic anthropologies, and with the metaphysics of a "virtual reality," which regards the human body not as integral to the personhood of living men and women, but as a datum of information to be manipulated according to desire. These presentations included the stimulating sessions featuring Mark Latkovic's and Father Paul deLadurantaye's probing analyses of the moral vision of *Gaudium et Spes,* Sister Mary Timothy Prokes' remarkable overview of the challenges to Catholic faith and theology raised by some features of "virtual reality" today, and Peter Casarella's insightful comments on her presentation. Monsignor Stuart Swetland contributed another response to the presentation of Sister Prokes on the subject of "Encountering the 'Really Real.'"

Then there was a session featuring the marvelous discussions of contemporary psychological studies in the light of the Christian vision of man, especially as set forth in *Gaudium et Spes.* These discussions featured presentations by Gladys Sweeney, Paul Vitz, and E. Christian Brugger, all faculty members of the new Institute for Psychological Sciences in Northern Virginia, a very important new institution on the Catholic higher education scene. Father John Harvey, O.S.F.S., also contributed brief remarks.

Fathers John McDermott, S.J., and Matthew Lamb gave excellent talks on the great and continuing significance of *Lumen Gentium*, showing how it corrected an overly formalistic and defensive view of the Church that had emerged from the Council of Trent in the wake of the Protestant Reformation. This correction was very importantly the result of a return to the sources – Scripture, the Fathers, the great Scholastics – and a deepening of a grasp of the mystery of the one true, holy, Catholic, apostolic Church.

An excellent discussion of *Dei Verbum* was offered by three outstanding Scripture scholars: Father William Kurz, S.J., Stephen Miletic, and Joseph Atkinson. Father Kurz helped us all to see how the Dogmatic Constitution on Divine Revelation sets forth key principles of Catholic biblical theology, challenging scholars to go beyond textual criticism in order to probe the deep *theological* meaning of Sacred Scripture; Dr. Miletic illustrated what Father Kurz was talking about by giving us an absorbing exegesis of the opening verses of the Gospel according to Mark, while Dr. Atkinson focused on the always difficult question of the inerrancy of Scripture.

Thomas Farr and Kevin Hasson gave stimulating talks on the meaning of *Dignitatis Humanae*, the Council's important Declaration on Religious Liberty, and, in particular, on the difficulties of integrating its teaching on the immunity from coercion persons should have concerning issues of their religious faith in those states that are today governed by Islamic law. Dr. Farr, formerly of the State Department's Office of

International Religious Freedom, spoke as a practitioner with very recent experience in the field. Kevin Hasson, a man with the happy knack of putting matters humorously as well as accurately, is suffering from Parkinson's disease, he and his family (wonderful wife and seven children) thus have need of our prayers. (Unfortunately, no text of his stimulating talk was furnished to us in written form and hence it is not included in this volume.)

As noted earlier, in the final session of the convention Kenneth Whitehead gave a thoughtful address on *Unitatis Redintegratio* and on the new Catholic ecumenism that has issued from Vatican II. We had planned on having a response to this talk but the scholar selected for this was unable to make it to the convention.

I am very grateful to all these splendid speakers, and I am particularly happy that three of them are former students of mine: Mark Latkovic and Paul deLadurantaye at the John Paul II Institute, and Peter Casarella at St. Anselm's Abbey School, where for many years I taught "upper school" religion to help pay the cost of tuition for my own four sons. I taught all of these students sexual ethics, and all of them, I am happy to say, deserved the "A's" they received. Peter also took a course called "Readings in Christian Classics," and I like to think that his introduction to Saints Augustine, Anselm, Bonaventure, and Thomas Aquinas may have stimulated him to major in theology when he went to Yale. Some of his classmates told me that they thought that Augustine and Anselm had poor "self images" because they considered themselves "nothing" before God, miserable sinners, etc. I told them that, on the contrary, having a low "self image" was definitely not their problem.

I also want to thank all those who served as chairpersons for the different sessions of the convention: Father Peter Ryan, S.J., Monsignor Stuart Swetland, John Haas, Kenneth Whitehead, Father John Harvey, O.S.F.S., Christopher Wolfe, and E. Christian Brugger. Here too was a case where two former students of mine, Monsignor Swetland and Dr. John Haas, came to our aid.

This 28th Annual Convention saw former Fellowship president Gerard V. Bradley receive the Cardinal Wright Award that he so richly deserved both for his scholarship and his leadership; and it also saw the remarkable Helen Hitchcock being given the Cardinal O'Boyle Award for her continuing outstanding work for the Church, both as the founding head of the Women for Faith and Family organization and as the editor of the respected *Adoremus Bulletin*. Along with her husband, longtime FCS notable, accomplished scholar and author, and history professor at St. Louis University, James Hitchcock, Helen is chairing the program committee for next year's convention focusing on Vatican II's reform of the sacred liturgy as mandated by *Sacrosanctum* Concilium.

This year our Fellowship President, Dean Bernard Dobranski of the Ave Maria Law School, did a marvelous job presiding over all the various sessions and meetings, while Jack and Marlene Rook, as usual, competently made all the arrangements with the hotel, the local diocese, the travel of all the speakers, etc. We also want to extend our warm thanks and gratitude to the Most Reverend Peter J. Jugis, D.D., J.C.D., bishop of Charlotte, who graciously celebrated our Sunday Mass for us.

All in all, this 28th Annual Convention was a great success. It is a blessing to be a member of this wonderful Fellowship!

Professor William E. May has since 1991 been the Michael J. McGivney Professor of Moral Theology at the John Paul II Institute for Studies on Marriage and the Family located at the Catholic University of America in Washington, D.C. Prior to that he taught moral theology at CUA itself from 1971 through 1991. Besides being almost a legend as a teacher, he is one of the most distinguished and productive of Catholic theologians working today.

Dr. May is the author of more than a dozen books, and is the co-author, editor, co-editor, or translator of a number others; he is also the author of hundreds of articles and essays in both scholarly and popular publications. His books include such notable titles as *An Introduction to Moral Theology* (OSV, 1994) as well as *Marriage: The Rock on which the Family Is Built* (Ignatius Press, 1995). In addition, he has authored a plethora of other titles such as *Sex, Marriage, and Chastity* (Franciscan Herald Press, 1981) and *Human Existence, Medicine, and Ethics* (Franciscan Herald Press, 1977). The book *Catholic Sexual Ethics* (OSV, 1985), co-authored by him with the late Father Ronald Lawler, O.F.M. Cap., and Joseph M. Boyle, Jr., is virtually the standard general published work on this subject. In his lectures, articles, and reviews, as well as in the book *The Teaching of Humanae Vitae: A Defense* (Ignatius Press, 1988), which he co-authored with Father John C. Ford, S.J., Germain Grisez, Joseph Boyle, and John Finnis, Dr. May has proved to be one of the most effective defenders of the teaching of Pope Paul VI's famous controverted encyclical. Among other books, he also edited the seminal volume, *Catholic Moral Life* (Franciscan Herald Press, 1980). He has even ventured into the translation field, having translated from the Italian Ramon Garcia de Haro's *Marriage and the Family in the Documents of the Magisterium* (Ignatius Press, 1993).

Professor May earned a B.A. and M.A. in philosophy at the Catholic

University of America and a Ph.D. in philosophy from Marquette University in Milwaukee. He served on the International Theological Commission from 1986 through 1997. He received the *Pro Ecclesia et Pontifice* Medal in 1991, He currently serves as a consultor to the Congregation for the Clergy in Rome. A past president of the Fellowship of Catholic Scholars, and still a member of the organization's Board of Directors, he received the FCS's Cardinal Wright Award in 1980. He is married to Patricia Keck May, and they are the parents of seven children and a growing number of grandchildren.

Keynote Address
Vatican II: Forty Years Later
Struggles and Initiatives

REVEREND THOMAS G. WEINANDY, O.F.M. CAP.

I was a young college seminarian during the years of the Second Vatican Council, just beginning my life as a Capuchin friar. At that time it never entered into my consciousness how radically Vatican II would affect my life as a Capuchin priest and as a Catholic theologian. And the major effects of the Council upon my life have not come merely from what the Council actually taught, though, obviously, the changes within the liturgy had the most immediate practical impact. What has most profoundly affected my priestly ministry and theological life over these past forty years is from the unexpected fallout and unintended consequences of the Council.

The Council was called by Pope John XXIII for renewal and *aggiornamento*, to allow the Holy Spirit to breath fresh life within the Church, empowering it to live more faithfully the Gospel and so become a more powerful and effective witness to the Kingdom of God. The Council Fathers rightly perceived their task in this light, and the Council documents that they forged testify to their ardent desire to enhance the Church's own spiritual life and its impact upon the larger world. As The Constitution on the Sacred Liturgy, *Sacrosanctum Concilium*, the very first document to be promulgated (on December 4, 1963) states at its onset: "The sacred Council has set out to impart an ever-increasing vigor to the Christian life of the faithful; to adapt more closely to the needs of our age those institutions which are subject to change; to foster whatever can promote union among all who believe in Christ; to strengthen whatever can help to call all mankind into the Church's fold" (SC #1).

The renewal of the liturgy, especially the celebration of the Eucharist, was to allow the faithful to enter more fully into and so appropriate more completely the redemptive work of Christ; and thus be better able "to express in their lives and manifest to others the mystery of

Christ and the real nature of the true Church" (SC #2). The Council Fathers desired, as stated in the Council's foundational document, the Dogmatic Constitution on the Church, *Lumen Gentium*, promulgated on November 26, 1964, "to bring to all men the light of Christ which shines out visibly from the Church" (LG# 1). By articulating the true nature of the Church, the Council Fathers hoped to draw all peoples into a common humanity for "it still remains for them to achieve full unity in Christ"(LG #1). Sharing in "the joy and hope, the grief and anguish of the men of our time" the Council Fathers, in the Council's Pastoral Constitution on the Church in the Modern World, *Gaudium et Spes*, promulgated December 7, 1965, identified the Church as "a community of men, of men who, united in Christ and guided by the Holy Spirit, press onwards towards the kingdom of the Father and are bearers of a message of salvation intended for all men" (GS #1).

At the very heart of the Council resides the Gospel truth that, since Christ, as its all-holy head, makes the Church, his body, holy, so all of its members are called to become holy. The Council identified the fostering of this holiness as its primary task and goal (see *Lumen Gentium* #39). These few quotations from three significant documents that span the four years of the Council demonstrate the unfolding of common themes. The Fathers are urgently advocating a renewed vibrancy within the members of the Church through a deeper appropriation of the salvation of Christ in the holiness of the Spirit. This deepening of Gospel life among all of the faithful would not only benefit the Church itself, but would also enhance its divine mission within the world – to be the universal sacrament of salvation for all of humankind. This was the vision and, indeed, the spirit of Vatican II.

Inherent within this call for renewal was the realization that the Church not only needed to update its various ecclesial structures but also, and more importantly, it needed to transpose the conception and articulation of the Gospel so as to enhance the Catholic life of the faithful and to proclaim the Gospel more effectively within the contemporary world. This was not a call, however, for a radical redefining or altering of the Church's unchanging faith, for it is precisely this perennial Gospel that was seen by the Council Fathers as the message the Church and the world needed to hear anew.

While the Council Fathers probably did not fully realize it at the time, this call for a renewed presentation, theologically and pastorally, of the unchanging Gospel contained an inbuilt tension as well as a complementary relationship. What changes were needed for creating a truly renewed articulation and presentation of the Gospel, and, simultaneously, what could not be altered so as to insure that it is actually the Gospel that is being renewed? The struggles within the post-Vatican II Church have been over maintaining the proper balance and interrelationship between these two concerns.

Historically, this balance was frequently not maintained. Ostensibly, this very same vision of renewal and aggiornamento gave rise to an irresistible ecclesial, theological, and pastoral mind-set that generated a whirlwind of changes or proposed changes, bearing upon every aspect of Catholic life. Many of these changes were, and often continue to be, either contrary to the Council itself, or bear little relationship to its stated intentions. Because of this, my life over the past forty years, beginning with my theological education in preparation for ordination, has been one long relentless struggle, and it has been a struggle not only for me, but also for most, if not all, of those present here at this convention, not to mention the countless faithful Catholics around the world, who have, in various ways, taken up the task of recovering the true intentions and teachings of Vatican II. The struggles in which we have been engaged have often been fought at close quarters – within the very institutions where we work, the dioceses in which we live, and the parishes where we worship. We are all too aware, after forty years, in what these conflicts and tensions consist.

What made and continues to make these encounters so critical is that the very heart of the Gospel and the very life of the Church are at stake. It is ultimately a struggle to ensure that what Vatican II envisioned and taught becomes a reality. What has complicated the post-Vatican II situation, and still continues to do so, is that the engagement has so many different forms and expressions, making it difficult – at least it was so in the early days – to mobilize dedicated groups of faithful Catholics to address and focus on any one issue adequately and consistently. Moreover, if the battles that beset the post-Vatican II Church were merely against a secular world that had abandoned Christianity and had raised its voice and exercised its power against it, the conflict would have been simpler and more clear cut. (It definitely would have been more fun!)

However, what has made these struggles so fierce and prolonged, and, at times, so confusing and often frustrating, is that not a few of the adversaries of an authentic implementation of Vatican II were themselves baptized Catholics. Being "Catholic," they were able to camouflage their intentions and actions by weaving themselves tightly into the very fabric of the Church's life. In so doing they sought to reconfigure the theological and pastoral design of already existing Catholic institutions, universities, seminaries, religious orders, chanceries, parishes, societies, journals, etc. Their goal was to alter radically what the Church professed and taught, how the Church worshipped and prayed, and, ultimately, how the Church lived out the Gospel. They did all of this, having woven themselves into everything Catholic, under the guise and pretext of implementing the vision and the teaching of Vatican II. Thus, when voices were raised in opposition, the response often seemed to appear in the form of rhetorical questions. How could a Catholic university not be Catholic? How could a Catholic seminary not be Catholic? How could a Catholic theological society not be Catholic? How could a Catholic parish not be Catholic? How could priests ordained by Catholic bishops not be Catholic? How could some members of Catholic orders of women and men religious not be Catholic? The implication was that those who were opposed to what was happening in many situations throughout the Church were suggesting something that just could not possibly be true. Yet, we all know that some "Catholic" men and women – clerics, religious and lay – who were and are associated with many Catholic institutions, lost their doctrinal, moral, and pastoral way in the post-Vatican II Church, often aligning themselves with the contemporary and frequently anti-Christian and anti-Catholic agenda of today's secular intellectual elites. Thus, what they often said and did under the aegis and in the name of being "Catholic" – thus claiming it to be in accordance with Vatican II – was not truly or authentically Catholic. Rather, such words and actions were an exploitation of the sacred Council.

However, it would be false to conclude that since Vatican II the struggles in which we have been and are engaged were and are merely negative, that is, have been solely opposed to what is contrary to Church's authentic teaching and sound pastoral practice. Yes, we have frequently said "no" in the past forty years: to interpretations of Scripture that are contrary to Catholic doctrine and moral teaching; to the denial of the full divinity of Jesus and his bodily resurrection; to abortion, artificial contraception, and euthanasia; to assertions that forms of sexual activity other than those within the marriage of a man and a woman are morally permissible; to catechetical programs and texts that did not adequately reflect the fullness of the Catholic faith; to turning our Catholic schools, colleges and universities into clones of their secular counterparts. But our goal in all these things has not merely been, or even solely, to stop the evils that were undermining our Catholic faith and heritage. Our goal has been to put an end to what is evil and in so doing ensure that the changes that had to be made, and were often in desperate need of being made, were changes that would bring about a true and authentic renewal of the life of the Church in all is facets.

We were not and are not "nay-sayers," for we were and are, ultimately, saying "yes" to the authentic vision of Vatican II, and especially as that vision has been embodied and articulated by Pope John Paul the Great and by Joseph Cardinal Ratzinger, now Pope Benedict XVI. The conflicts in which we have been engaged during the past forty years have been conflicts to protect and promote what is true, good, and, therefore, what is beautiful – nothing less than the Gospel of Jesus Christ.

It is often assumed that the proposals offered by what the media so easily labels the progressive or liberal Catholics are the most life-giving. In actual fact, such proposals are often destructive of life, since they are frequently old heresies or causes that uncritically reflect a secular and non-Christian agenda. What has often been forgotten is the truth, stated in Vatican II and often repeated by John Paul II, that it is "only in the mystery of the Word made flesh that the mystery of man truly becomes clear" (*Gaudium et Spes* #22). This truth profoundly affects not only Catholic Christology, but Catholic anthropology as well. It is those who have been loyal to this Vatican II vision of the Incarnate Son as the revelation of all that is truly human who have demonstrated, over the past forty years, that Catholic moral teaching enhances our human dignity as men and women, that Catholic doctrine expresses the foundational realities of our salvation, and that Catholic liturgy allows us to enter into communion with the very mystery of the triune God.

It was in this spirit that those who were loyal to Vatican II marshaled their spiritual and intellectual strength to initiate and foster creative alternatives that have since had a huge impact upon the present-day Church. Significant ground has been reclaimed in some institutions that appeared to have lost their Catholic identity – such as in some Catholic universities. This is to be welcomed and applauded because it was achieved by the hard work and steadfast integrity of men and women who did not give up the cause for Catholic truth and goodness.

Moreover, in these past forty years, we have seen the rise of many new endeavors that are authentically Catholic even if they are sometimes rough on the edges or embody aspects that do not appeal to all. For example, the teaching and spirit of Vatican II has spawned a whole host of movements and institutes of renewal which have enlivened the faith of many people, enabling them to live the Gospel with greater commitment and joy. There are also a variety of new religious orders of men and women, many of which have enthusiastically taken up the challenges of

Vatican II and have become vibrant communities of an authentic Gospel life. Many of these movements and orders have become instruments of evangelization, especially among the young. The Church's great hope is that those young people who have come alive in their Catholic faith have not aligned themselves with those who promote and embody a false and sterile vision of Vatican II, but with those who have been loyal to the doctrinal and moral tradition of the Church and to its liturgical heritage. This is the John Paul II generation that is now being carried on in a new Benedict XVI generation.

Having said all of that, it must also be stated that some conservative elements within the Church have not been entirely faithful to Vatican II. In their desire to preserve the unchanging truth of the Gospel they have, in some ways, turned their backs upon renewal and have insisted instead upon simply returning to elements that the Council intended to correct by offering fuller dimensions and connections of the whole mystery of Christ and the Church. Their appeal, though, has been enhanced by the unwarranted changes enacted in the name of Vatican II, and by the often virulent but dubious doctrinal, moral, and liturgical environment that developed in its wake.

During the past forty years, while Catholic educational institutions have closed or struggled to keep their genuine Catholic identity, we have simultaneously witnessed the founding of promising Catholic schools, colleges and universities, and other institutes of Catholic higher education. These new educational adventures were initiated precisely to advance the vision of Vatican II, especially to provide an education that demonstrated that in Christ all that is truly human – the intellectual and the moral – can be sanctified and made new in Christ. It is to these institutions that many of the most talented young Catholics are applying.

Furthermore, while many of the pre-Vatican II theological journals, popular magazines, and Catholic newspapers tended not only to cater to but also actually to promote the theological, moral, liturgical and cultural whims of the day, over the past forty years there have appeared numerous new Catholic publications which, in various ways, have taken up the cause of promoting authentic Catholic theology and providing a genuine Catholic voice within the ecclesial and public square. Many of these periodicals, newsletters, and papers sprang from new and vibrant associations and societies – not least of which would be the Fellowship of Catholic Scholars and its *Quarterly*.

After years of concern and sometimes frustration, we are also beginning to see as well the improvement in the catechetical situation within the Church. This is due not only to the *Catechism of the Catholic*

Church, but also to the enduring faithfulness of many men and women – bishops, priests, women and men religious and laity – who have initiated and fostered creative catechetical programs and have written attractive texts which are faithful to the teaching of the Church.

Even within the liturgy there are signs of hope. This new confidence was, again, born amidst years of committed and long-suffering labor, often performed by loyal and persistent lay men and women who were, at times, dismissed or ignored by their pastors. Nonetheless, after the liturgical shenanigans that have plagued many parishes and religious orders for so many years, it appears that this banal phase of Catholic worship is finally coming to an end. In spite of much trivialization of the liturgy the faithful of the United States have come, on the whole, to participate actively in the Eucharist in a manner that far exceeds most of my experiences in Great Britain and the European continent. This should not be taken lightly, for it demonstrates that, in the midst of all the turmoil, the faithful do have a desire to give glory and praise to God at the Eucharistic liturgy. Another hopeful sign is the restoration and even resurgence of Eucharistic adoration within parishes. This will have tremendous benefits on how Catholics perceive the Eucharistic liturgy theologically and participate in it.

Two events will further this genuine renewal of the liturgy. The first is the new translation of the *Ordo Missae*, which will be, hopefully, an improvement over what we presently possess, though some will probably still find some legitimate flaws. The second is that the men being trained and ordained to the priesthood today are, on the whole, more open to the teachings of Vatican II and its program for renewal than many of those in the more proximate post-Vatican II era. They possess that Vatican II vision that indeed Christ is the revelation of all that is truly life-giving and authentically human, a vision that many involved in the recent-revealed scandals did not possess. This new vintage of priests is the result not only of the change in the ecclesial climate during the course of John Paul II's pontificate, but also to the salutary affects that many of the renewal movements have had upon young men. Equally, after the scandalous state of many seminaries immediately after Vatican II, many of the seminaries in the United States are now academically and spiritually sound. This is due to better trained and spiritual aware rectors and teachers who are committed both to training priests for the twenty-first century and to passing on to them the living heritage of the Catholic faith. One concern I have is that while most of the newly ordained are serious about their faith and truly love the Church, some appear to have once more donned the cloak of clericalism.

The front line where many of us here have been stationed over the past forty years has been within the academy, especially in the area of theology. At times, especially in the late 60s and the 70s, it often appeared that theology had degenerated to such a state that there was little hope for its authentic renewal. Yet, we continued at our appointed stations and there we worked tirelessly to provide theological alternatives that would not only counter much of the literature that was being published, but also to formulate arguments and positions that were theologically sound, creative and appealing. This is especially the case within moral theology, which continues to be the scene of major engagements.

Over the past forty years, what are now some of our old war horses authored many books and articles. They have done so out of love for the Church and with a vision that to live humanly is to live the mystery of the Incarnate Christ. They have provided the Church with an arsenal of rigorous moral arguments and positions that address all the major ethical issues of our day. Their devoted work will probably not have its full impact until after they have received their heavenly reward. Moreover, their teaching has given birth to a whole new generation of moral theologians who have taken up the ethical challenges that face the contemporary Church and society. While a great many contests still loom on the ethical horizon, we can have confident hope in the intellectual ability of those who are now defending and promoting the Catholic cause.

The past forty years have also witnessed the rise of a new generation of solid and creative Catholic scholars in other areas of theology. They have taken seriously the call for a renewed theology, and they have realized that such theological renewal must find its wellspring in the ancient Christian sources such as the Fathers of the early Church. Moreover, when it appeared that the writings of Thomas Aquinas would only be found on the dusty shelves of Dominican or antiquarian libraries or in the remote corners of eccentric second hand books stores, we are now witnessing a Thomistic revival of both philosophy and theology that could easily make its pre-Vatican II predecessor appear as a prelude to the real thing. This present Thomistic resurgence is not only in Aquinas' philosophical and ethical teaching, as in the past, but also in his doctrinal teaching within his great *Summae* and now even within his Biblical commentaries. While the old heresies are still with us being paraded about bedecked in the latest politically correct fashion and festooned with banners announcing their revolutionary theological potential, it is not the younger generation of Catholic scholars who are leaping about in enthusiasm mesmerized by the glitter, but those whose leaps have long ago lost a great deal of their youthful spring. Catholic systematic theology forty years after Vatican II looks to a promising future and it is those who have remained true to its vision of renewal who are producing the imaginative theological tracts founded upon the wellspring of the Catholic faith and tradition.

I have attempted to provide a reading of the post-Vatican II era that takes into account both some of the past and present struggles as well as some of the hopeful initiatives that have come to exist over the past forty years. I believe that we would not have been as resourceful, as creative, as hard working and as productive as we have been over these years if the Father, in his wisdom, had not allowed the post-Vatican II mischief to take place. Hopefully, we are becoming holy in the process.

I would like to conclude this address by briefly enumerating two items that I believe still need to be tackled if the implementation of Vatican II is to succeed fully. My twosome may not be the most important, but they are two concerns that I do have. The first is primarily pastoral and the second is more academic.

First, the issue of Catholic men has not been fully addressed. If there is one group that has been largely dis-enfranchised in the post-Vatican II Church it is ordinary lay men. I am saddened that John Paul II, one of the most manly of men ever to have sat on the Chair of Peter, never addressed any statement, in all of his voluminous writings, specifically to men. Reams have been written on the importance of women and their genuine roles and charisms within the Church. As we all know, much of what has been written is actually destructive of women's dignity, even while much has also been articulated that is true and right, and needed to be said.

Nonetheless, the significance and the roles of lay men within the Church still go unaddressed, even though adult men are less likely to attend Sunday Mass on a regular basis, and they are also less likely to be active in serving the Church, not only within the parish but in other ways as well. Until we address the needs of men – their vocations as husbands and fathers, their apostolic responsibility within the world – and until they become once more a vibrant force within the Church, providing much needed leadership, the Church itself will remain weak and so be unable adequately to bear a full witness to the Gospel in our contemporary world. A faithful body of lay men is absolutely essential for protecting Catholic family life, for evangelizing the young, especially boys, and, as fellow brother workers in Christ, for supporting bishops and priests and so bolstering their sometimes flagging courage.

Secondly, over the past forty years, while great strides have been made to free Catholic moral and doctrinal theology from a secular and faithless agenda, the Bible still languishes within the dungeons of the Biblical scholars, chained by interpretative protocols that deprive it of life and by philosophical presuppositions that subvert its message. If theology and the whole of Catholic academic life, and of Catholic thought and prayer, is to flourish truly anew, an academic and pastoral crusade must be waged so as to allow the Bible to breathe freely, once more, its life-giving truth of the Spirit – the Gospel of Jesus Christ. The Bible should not be a book jealously guarded by an elitist academy whose members sometimes do not actually believe the message it contains, but it must become what it truly is – a Catholic book, a book of the Church. As such, it must be recognized that, as Vatican II's Dogmatic Constitution on Divine Revelation, *Dei Verbum*, truly stated: "Sacred Tradition and sacred Scripture make up a single sacred deposit of the Word of God, which is entrusted to the Church" (DV #10). The truth of Scripture can only be rightfully interpreted and so fully known from within the living tradition of the Church, for both have been entrusted to it. Only within the Church does the Bible truly become the Word of truth, revealing to us the mystery of our life in Christ.

There are, presently, some hopeful signs within biblical studies. Interest in patristic and medieval exegesis is blossoming and such exegesis, while in some ways inadequate, nonetheless allows Scripture the freedom to breathe life into doctrinal and moral theology, into preaching, and into one's spiritual life. Moreover, a number of Catholic, Orthodox, and Protestant scholars, sometimes in disciplines other than strictly biblical interpretation, are moving beyond what has become an often stale and sterile exegesis. As St. Paul himself said: "The word of God is not chained" (II Tm 2:9).

Over the past forty years, many of us have fought what we believe to be the good fight of faith. It may not have been pleasant, but it has been good precisely because it has been a struggle to preserve the faith – the faith articulated by Vatican II and the faith that the Council hoped would bring new life to the Church and to the world. The conflicts are not over, and never will be, but I have attempted to demonstrate that our efforts have not been in vain, and thus we must resist all cynicism, resentment, and self-pity. The most encouraging thing about the good fight of faith is that one absolutely knows, from the very onset, that one will ultimately obtain victory. The contest will not be lost because it resides within the providential care of the Father. Moreover, we are armed with the sword of the Spirit, and we serve the invincible King – our Lord Jesus Christ. Lastly, in the midst of all that has taken place over the past forty years, many of us have grown in our love for the Church, the Church that was so much at the heart of the Second Vatican Council. May we continue to serve that Church in the wisdom, courage, fortitude, joy and love of the Spirit, and so give praise to our Lord Jesus Christ to the glory of God the Father.

Thomas G. Weinandy, O.F.M., Cap., Ph.D., is Executive Director of the Secretariat for Doctrine and Pastoral Practices of the United States Conference of Catholic Bishops (USCCB). A native of Ohio, he is a Capuchin Franciscan friar ordained to the priesthood in 1972. In 1975, he obtained a Doctorate in Historical Theology from King's College, University of London, England. He has taught theology at a number of colleges and universities in the United States, including Mount Saint Mary's College in Emmitsburg, Maryland, and the Franciscan University of Steubenville in Steubenville, Ohio. In 1991-2004, Father Weinandy served as Warden of Greyfriars Hall, Oxford, and was a tutor and lecturer in history and doctrine at the University of Oxford.

Father Weinandy has written or edited some seventeen books, including *Does God Change? The Word's Becoming in the Incarnation* (1985); *In the Likeness of Sinful Flesh: An Essay on the Humanity of Christ* (1993); and *Jesus the Christ* (2003). He is a member of the Catholic Theological Society of America (CTSA), the Catholic Theological Association of Great Britain, the Fellowship of Catholic Scholars, and the North American Patristics Society.

Gaudium Et Spes's Vision of the Moral Life

MARK S. LATKOVIC

Introduction

My paper addresses, on the 40th anniversary of this wide-ranging Council document – at once ground-breaking, but also rooted in the Tradition (*nova et vetera*) – the first part of Vatican II's *Gaudium et Spes*[1] and its vision of the moral life, set in the context of the "new evangelization" called for by recent popes, in particular John Paul II. At the heart of the Council's call for the renewal of the Church – and indeed of the world – is the very core message of our Catholic faith: the mystery of Jesus Christ and his body, the Church.

Thus, I whole-heartedly agree with Walter Cardinal Kasper when he writes of the Council's plan for renewing the Church: "According to the New Testament, [the term] mystery signifies the eternal salvific decision of God which became a reality in history through Jesus Christ...and which now, through all ages and across all boundaries is to be made present by the Holy Spirit through the Church. The message of this mystery of God in Jesus Christ through the Holy Spirit is the Church's true good news of salvation, it constitutes her true identity."[2] Therefore, Kasper continues, the Church must be "anchored firmly in the mystery of God in Jesus Christ. She must proclaim Jesus as the crucified and risen Lord and testify that he is the life of the world. For it is in Christ that man finds his ultimate and most profound destiny. Searching and questioning humanity expects and awaits no less and nothing else from the Church than this saving mystery."[3] The Council Fathers hoped that every Catholic would appropriate this "Good News" and find new but faithful ways of spreading it in word and deed, thereby bringing about the sanctification of men as well as the renewal of the temporal order.[4]

The late Pope John Paul II echoes the Council's teaching, for example, in his 1993 encyclical on moral theology, *Veritatis Splendor*, where he makes the following key lines from *Gaudium et Spes* # 22 his own: "It is only in the mystery of the Word incarnate that light is shed on the mystery of man...It is Christ, the last Adam, who fully discloses man to himself and unfolds his noble calling by revealing the mystery of the Father and the Father's love."[5] These often quoted words, which have stimulated no small measure of theological comment, are in fact at the heart of the Pope's theological anthropology, as they were for the Council Fathers – the future John Paul II among them – who authored *Gaudium et Spes*. I will return to these words in part two.

Specifically, this paper will attempt to articulate what *Gaudium et Spes* was calling all Catholics to do, or rather, *to be*[6] – namely, *other Christs in the midst of the modern world*[7] – given its strong Christological focus.[8] Hence I focus chiefly on part one of the document ("The Church and Man's Calling," ##11–45), which concerns the general principles of the Church's mission in the modern world. My focus is therefore not on the second part ("Some Problems of Special Urgency," ## 46–93), which concentrates on specific questions such as marriage, culture, social life, economics, politics, and war and peace.[9]

Although *Gaudium et Spes* has been the subject of many polemics – indeed, it has stood at the center of the conflicting interpretations of Vatican II over the last 40 years[10] – I will strive for an objective exegesis of the text itself and leave, with a few exceptions, the disputed questions and other matters in the endnotes.[11]

I will proceed first by summarizing *Gaudium et Spes's* brief "Preface" (GS ##1–3) and "Introduction" (GS ## 4–10). Here I will need to discuss the themes of the "signs of the times," the question of whether human nature changes and the moral implications of that, the universal call to holiness, and personal vocations – even though the latter two themes are treated in part one of *Gaudium et Spes*. Second, I will examine the first four chapters of part one, with special attention given to the text's anthropology. This will involve also describing the Pastoral Constitution's view of morality, its understanding of life in Christ, and the role of the Church in the world, among other themes. Third, I will reflect on some of the implications that this famous conciliar document has for what Pope John Paul II has called the "new evangelization." Finally, in a brief conclusion, will reflect on the significance of *Gaudium et Spes* for our times.

I. The "Signs of the Times," Change in Human Nature, the Universal Call to Holiness, and Personal Vocations

The "Signs of the Times"

Vatican Council II indicates its fundamental *pastoral* intention (although not as opposed to *doctrine*, as footnote 1 of the document makes clear) from the famous opening words of *Gaudium et Spes's*

"Preface" – words which announce in no uncertain terms that the Church is firmly on the side of the world and of the goods that perfect it, and against everything (such as sin) that hinders this perfection: "The joy and hope, the grief and anguish of the men of our time, especially of those who are poor or afflicted in any way are the joy and hope, the grief and anguish of the followers of Christ as well. Nothing that is genuinely human fails to find an echo in their hearts" (GS #1). For the Council, the reason for this deep solidarity with the human family is no mere philanthropic sentiment, but is clearly *theological*: because the Church is a community of persons joined to Christ, who firmly believes that God wills all human persons to be saved.[12] Although human persons are free to reject God's gift of salvation, there is not a single living human person who stands outside this offer of salvation; not a single living human person who stands outside this call to reconciliation and to eternal life in fellowship with God the Father, God the Son, and God the Holy Spirit. There never was such a person and there never will be one.[13]

Pope Benedict XVI, then Cardinal Joseph Ratzinger, noted in a commentary on this "Preface," that when the Council uses the term "world" it means "the counterpart of the Church."[14] The purpose of the text, according to Ratzinger, is to bring "the two into a relationship of cooperation, the goal of which is the reconstruction of the 'world.'" The vision that characterizes the text therefore is one of the Church cooperating "with the world in order to build up the world…"[15] The Church hopes in this way, writes Cardinal Ratzinger, "'to carry on the work of Christ'…namely, 'to bear witness to the truth,' 'to serve and not be served.'"[16]

Following the "Preface," the "Introduction" to *Gaudium et Spes* then paints a portrait of man's contemporary situation. It begins with the human condition today because the human person is the point at which culture, politics, and religion intersect. Hence, the Council declares, that under the light of faith, "the focal point of [its] presentation will be man himself, whole and entire, body and soul, heart and conscience, mind and will" (GS #3). In their description of the "signs of the times," the Council Fathers speak of the many deep-seated changes in the social order, the changes in attitudes, morals, religion, the family, and so on.[17] Some of these changes are to be welcomed, yet others rejected. Our situation is primarily characterized, say the Council Fathers, by a shift from a static to a dynamic world view (see GS #5) – a situation, it is important to note, was neither celebrated nor condemned, but simply described by them – and by what they refer to as "the dichotomy of a world that is at once powerful and weak, capable of doing what is noble and what is base, disposed to freedom and slavery, progress and decline, brotherhood and hatred. Man is growing conscious that the forces that he has unleashed are in his own hands and that it is up to him to control them or be enslaved by them. Here lies the modern dilemma" (GS #9). "Will man, with God's help, take responsibility for his actions or will he not?" the Council Fathers seem to ask of this morally ambiguous situation.

The conflict within the human person and between human persons that *Gaudium et Spes* identifies creates profound discord throughout the world and in our own society. Yet the Church believes that Christ is the One who can heal these divisions, reveal to man his true identity and destiny as a child of God, and empower him to be worthy of this destiny and reach it.[18] This is precisely why the Council reflects on the "signs of the times" and interprets "them in the light of the Gospel" (GS # 4): not as an end in itself but for the sake of offering better service to mankind. To serve man, the Church needs to be aware of those situations – war, poverty, advanced forms of communication, scientific, technological, and economic progress – that affect him for either weal or woe. But its desire to overcome human problems is stimulated not by merely this-worldly concerns, but by *Christian faith*, for it is faith that "manifests God's design for man's total vocation" and "directs the mind to solutions which are fully human" (GS #11).

Christ, Morality, and the Question of Changing Human Nature

Thus, centered in this faith, *Gaudium et Spes* declares that "the key, the center and the purpose of the whole of man's history" is to be found in faith's object – "its Lord and Master," Jesus Christ (see GS #10; see also GS # 45). In a world characterized by "rapid changes" (GS, no. 4), Christ can be counted as the "ultimate foundation" of those "many realities [that] do not change" (GS, no. 10).[19] This point has great anthropological and moral significance for the argument against those revisionist theologians who have commonly asserted in the years after the Council, that because human nature itself changes and in fact has changed,[20] there can be no unchanging and objective morality, or at least no absolute (i.e., exceptionless) moral norms. Human historicity in this view implies the relativity of moral truth.[21] I would like now to dwell briefly on this important matter, since the Council's thought is often interpreted in this way or used to justify positions of this sort.

From a theological perspective, we can respond by observing, as Germain Grisez does, that human nature, in its "historical actuality" under the influence of sin and grace, can be changed for better or worse (e.g., human persons can go the way of virtue or vice). Thus, he notes, Vatican II taught that Christ, "the perfect man, reveals to human persons what human nature *can and should be*. All human persons can be united to him and *perfected in him* (see GS ## 22, 29, 41, 45; LG ##13, 40)."[22] Hence, according to Grisez, the standard of morality is not "a formal essence and a set of invariant relationships," as it was for what he calls scholastic natural law theory,[23] but "the basic possibilities of human individuals as bodily creatures, endowed with intelligence, able to engage in fruitful work and creative play, psychically complex, capable of more or less reasonable action, in need of companionship, capable of love, and open to friendship with God in whose image they are made. If these possibilities in their basic givenness are what is meant by 'human nature,' then human nature does not change."[24]

In fact, Grisez argues, that when "nature" is understood in terms of basic human possibilities, that is, basic human goods, "the very notion that human nature could change is logically absurd, for 'change' not only in respect to actuality but also in respect to basic possibility would no longer be change but simple *loss of identity*."[25] To support the notion of radical moral change, one would have to show how the basic goods of human existence such as life, knowledge, friendship, etc., are *not* basic goods for at least some human persons.[26] Of course, the revisionists who make this claim have never done this. The same goods, which, for example, fulfilled Jesus' own sinless human nature, are the same goods that fulfill ours today. This shared human nature makes possible man's looking to Christ as, according to *Gaudium et Spes, the* model of the "perfect man" (see GS ##22, 38, 41, and 45), in whom "human nature is assumed, not annulled" (GS #22), and who "sanctified" all human realities (see GS ##32 and 41) and fully revealed man's "high calling" or vocation (see GS #22).[27]

But if human nature and the natural law do not change, how are we to make room for moral development and ongoing growth of insight into human possibilities? Again, Grisez is insightful here. He notes that in acting for a good, "one gradually comes to perceive its possibilities more and more fully. Thus, human nature and natural-law morality are both stable and changing (cf. S.t., 1–2. q. 94, aa. 4–5)." Stable, Grisez argues, "in that the givenness and fundamental unalterability of natural inclinations account for the unalterability of the principles of the natural law; but also changing, in that the dynamism of the inclinations, their openness to continuing and expanding fulfillment, accounts for the openness of natural law to authentic development."

The Universal Call to Holiness and Personal Vocation

Before examining part one of *Gaudium et Spes*, we need first to deal with the question of the "form" or "shape" that the Christian vocation takes in the Council's vision. For, while our supreme calling is union with the Triune God and the Blessed in heaven, our vocation in this life takes the form of "the universal call to holiness." Thus, we see that the view of the Church as "mystery" that I articulated earlier is not merely a theoretical concept, but truly discloses what all baptized members of the Church are (to be) – the the people of God, the body of Christ – and how they are to act consistent with that great identity. The Council's Dogmatic Constitution on the Church, *Lumen Gentium*, teaches: "Christians in any state or walk of life are called to the fullness of Christian life and to the perfection of love" (LG # 40). This concern for holiness, however, as Cardinal Kasper notes, is not some stale or ossi-fied program focusing "only" on personal perfection. "As illustrated by Jesus' command of love, the 'fullness of Christian life' must be directed toward God as well as one's fellow human beings..."[28] In short, the Church and Her members "must become more devout. This is the pre-requisite and the source of strength she will need in order to face con-temporary problems in the right way."[29]

In addressing the call to holiness to everyone in the Church, the Council Fathers, as Hans Urs Von Balthasar and others have noted,[30] dealt a death blow to the notion that there was a two-tiered system of morality in the Church, that is, the notion that living the fullness of the Christian life was a concern for the clergy and religious alone, with the laity expected merely to avoid mortal sin but not to attain the heights of Christian perfection.[31] Vatican II called all baptized persons to holiness (see LG ##39–41)[32] just as Jesus called all of his disciples to be "per-fect, as [their] heavenly Father is perfect" (see Matthew 5:48).

Thus, even the laity is exhorted to live a holy life, fully and com-pletely, within whatever particular state of life or vocation they have cho-sen. This would include living the evangelical counsels of Christ's and Mary's poverty, chastity, and obedience, according to the particular state of life they are in.[33] By virtue of their baptism and as "called by God to carry out their apostolate in the world" (*Apostolicam Actuositatem* # 2), as *the presence of Christ to it*, the laity are directed to recognize the "close connection between secular activity and religion to which many of our contemporaries seem to object" (GS #36), since in fact "the trans-formation of the world" belongs "to the new commandment of love" (GS #38). The call to holiness must be made concrete "in the promotion of justice" and must lead "toward the civilization of love."[34]

Therefore, every layperson "should stand before the world as a wit-ness to the resurrection and life of the Lord Jesus and as a sign that God lives" (LG #38). This standing-before-the-world-as-witness "can inspire others to ask themselves: What is it that motivates these people?"[35] What is it about these Christians that attract one to their way of life?

The conciliar "apologetic" for the truth of the Catholic Church, therefore, was the universal call to holiness, or what we can call "testimony" or "witness" of life – one of the major and privileged themes of Vatican II. According to the Council, "to bear witness" or "to testify" means "to confirm, by a life lived in accordance with the gospel, that the gospel is indeed true and the way to human salvation."[36] All men and women are called to live the life of Christian witness, that is, all are called to be models of sanctity, to be saints of God. Hence, the message of the Council is no mere abstraction, but a concrete and compelling proposal for faithfully living the gospel today and engaging in evangelization.

René Latourelle has written that Vatican II's way of proposing the traditional call to holiness in terms of "testimony" or "witness," as a sign that God's salvation is present, "seems to be the one most attractive to our contemporaries."[37] For example, he says, to persons "highly developed technologically but underdeveloped morally and showing a surprising psychological fragility, witnesses appear as healthy beings, people who are at peace with themselves and who radiate joy and peace despite suffering and death. A meeting with such people can rouse the desire to share in this kind of full life."[38]

Vatican II, however, was calling not only individual Christians to witness or give testimony to Jesus Christ, but also the whole Church. Indeed, it is the calling of every parish, Church group, and ecclesial movement. The norm for this evangelical witness on the part of the Church must be whether it radiates "the spirit of Christ to all who draw near to [her]…For, in the final analysis, it is the image that the Church presents to the world that turns it into either an expressive, attractive sign [of salvation] or a negative sign of the salvation it preaches."[39]

Moreover, the Church as a whole, and each of us *as members of Christ's Church,* are called to be a sign of Christ's love, not only in the larger specific vocations that are ours (i.e., priesthood, religious life, marriage, and the single life) but also in terms of responding to a "personal vocation," which, as Germain Grisez describes it, "embraces the whole" of one's life, and "not merely part of it, for God calls each believer to love and serve him" with the whole of his or her being.[40] Personal vocation is the uniquely responsive way through which we will follow Christ and help carry out his redemptive work in the world.[41]

In the climate of the contemporary secular culture, however, with so many options available to us which are often incompatible with faith's requirements, and no longer having the "option" as in past cultures of "passively accepting roles and responsibilities," Christians must "reflect critically on culturally defined roles, examine their gifts and opportunities in the light of faith, discern what God asks of them, and commit themselves to doing it."[42] By emphasizing an integral understanding of vocation, Vatican II proposes to better integrate "faith and daily life, whose bifurcation, the Council teaches, 'deserves to be counted among the more serious errors of our age.'"[43]

Hence, it is precisely by reason of the supernatural vocation given to man, that human persons do in fact involve themselves with "contingent realities," working in all areas (e.g., politics, culture, business, etc.) for the temporal improvement of the world. As the Council Fathers inform us: "Far from diminishing our concern to develop this earth, the expectancy of a new earth should spur us on, for it is here that the body of a new human family grows, foreshadowing in some way the age which is to come" (GS #39). Although we must not blur the difference between earthly progress and God's kingdom, "such progress is of vital concern to the kingdom...insofar as it can contribute to the better ordering of human society" (GS #39).

Far from a merely instrumental view of work in the world, the Council views work (and not only "religious work") as having an intrinsic value of its own in contributing to man's perfection and sanctification (see GS ##34–35). In the Council's dynamic theological vision of renewal, all the fruits of our nature and good works – for example, the goods of "human dignity, brotherly communion, and freedom" – are the building blocks of the heavenly kingdom, to be found "once again, cleansed this time from the stain of sin, illuminated and transfigured..."(GS #39). "Mysteriously present" now, says *Gaudium et Spes*, the kingdom "'of truth and life...of holiness and grace...of justice, love and peace'" will be perfected when the Lord returns in final glory (see GS #39).[44]

At this point, having spoken of the Church in terms of "mystery," and its corresponding embodiment in the call to holiness or witness, we have also noted how this call to holiness is *specified* in the notion of "personal vocation." Having done so, we are now ready to look more explicitly at *Gaudium et Spes's* very general understanding of "man and his vocation." Again, I will treat in synthetic fashion the first four chapters of *Gaudium et Spes* (but not always in a linear way), given their direct bearing on how they can help "to create a society in which all human beings of whatever age, race, condition, or sex are loved as God loves them and are, thus, wanted."[45] That is, how they can help create a "civilization of love," with a "culture of life" at its heart.

II. Philosophical and Theological Anthropology, Moral Principles, Life in Christ, and the Church-World Relationship

Each of the first four chapters of part one of *Gaudium et Spes* attempts to answer a particular question: "What does the Church think of man? (Ch. 1). What measures are to be recommended for building up society today? (Ch. 2). What is the meaning of man's activity in the universe?" (Ch. 3; GS #11). And how should the Church relate to the world (Ch. 4)? The Council Fathers teach that "the mission of the Church will show itself to be supremely human *by the very fact of being religious*" (GS #11, emphasis added).

Philosophical and Theological Anthropology

The first chapter of *Gaudium et Spes*, "The Dignity of the Human Person" (GS ##12–22), provides a Christian anthropology.[46] In fact, this is the first time that a council has done so as a subject in its own right.[47] Indeed, as Cardinal Ratzinger has observed, the entire document is "a kind of *summa* of Christian anthropology and of the central problems of the Christian ethos."[48] The Council Fathers tell us, citing the books of Genesis and Wisdom, that it is man who is made in the "image of God" (GS #12; cf. Gn 1:26; Wis 2:23). Man is created with an intellect to know God and with a will to love him; and he is endowed with freedom to do the truth in love (see Eph 4:15). Indeed this power of free choice "is an exceptional sign of the divine image in man" (GS #17).

Yet at the dawn of history, tempted by the Devil, man "abused his freedom." This abuse, that is, his original sin, has ruptured the peace and harmony "that should reign within himself as well as between himself and other men and all creatures" (GS #13).

Since the source of man's dignity "lies in [his] call to communion with God" (GS #19), when man rejects God as his "beginning," he also disrupts his proper relationship to his own ultimate goal..." (GS #13). Concupiscence as well as sin – original and personal – explains this internal disharmony that man forever experiences. In sum, it explains, in language that recalls Blaise Pascal's *Pensées*,[49] his "call to grandeur and the depths of his misery..." (GS #13).[50]

Moreover, *Gaudium et Spes* proclaims that man, who as an individual person is a *unity* of a living body and an immortal soul (see GS #14), is also a *social* being who finds himself, as his "certain likeness" to the divine Trinitarian communion of Persons implies, only in the "sincere gift of himself," since indeed, "man is the only creature on earth that God has wanted for its own sake" (see GS #24; cf. Lk 17:33). Further, from the beginning, God creates man as *male and female* (see Gn 1:27); and their complementary companionship "produces the primary form of interpersonal communion" – marriage and family (GS #12).

In affirming these truths about man, the Council rubs against the grain of much modern and post-modern thought on the nature of the human person. For one thing, in teaching that man is a composite of both matter and spirit, the Council Fathers manifest not only their disagreement with materialism, but also with anthropological dualism – the very anthropology that underlies the "culture of death" – which makes a sharp distinction between being a *human being* (i.e., a living member of the human species) and being a *human person* (i.e., having minimal exercisable cognitive abilities, incipient autonomy, an awareness of self over time, etc.).[51]

Second, in affirming the communal nature of man, the Fathers of Vatican II make it abundantly clear that society is not, as it is for many modern thinkers, a necessary evil or artificial construct,[52] but an intrinsic good of his nature, something that he is naturally inclined to seek. "Man is a social being," *Gaudium et Spes* affirms (GS #12). Therefore, the human person achieves his integral fulfillment only in the family, social life, and the political community (see GS #29).

And third, in teaching that men and women are *complementary* body persons (i.e., identical yet different) created for communion, the Council Fathers take issue with any ideology (e.g., certain strands of radical feminism) that either denies that there are fundamental differences between men and women (the "sex unity" view) or emphasizes these differences to such a degree that the sexes are radically divided (the "sex polarity" view).[53] *Gaudium et Spes*, however, sees male and female, not as culturally constructed "gender roles," but as natural created realities that are part of God's design as well as one way in which this design is revealed, for example, in the sacrament of marriage (cf. GS #. 50).

At the heart of *Gaudium et Spes's* anthropology, of course, is Paragraph #22. Here the relationship between anthropology and Christology is spelled out, although not in detail. In saying that the mystery of man is revealed only in the mystery of the Incarnate Word, it proclaims, as Cardinal Kasper writes, that Jesus Christ is "the origin and end of true humanity."[54] This perspective entitles us to call Vatican II's anthropology not only "Christian," but also "Christological."[55]

In placing Jesus the God-man at the forefront of its teaching, the Council proposes, says Henri Cardinal de Lubac, "an effort of the understanding of reality *by way of faith*."[56] This is a reading of reality that "is in the service of an anthropology, and the anthropology is inspired by a vision of humanity in Jesus Christ, a vision of the new human being."[57] Indeed, the question that man is to himself can only be answered by showing that "the Christian vocation [in Christ] is the final reason – and the only fully satisfying one – of the…terrestrial activity of man."[58]

Substantively, *Gaudium et Spes* #22 teaches that "man's call or vocation is made known most fully in the person of Jesus Christ….[Thus], [t]he hallmark of a *Christian* anthropology is its Christological character…"[59] Indeed, we can say that in *Gaudium et Spes*, anthropology is "surpassed by Christology, which defines man's purpose and goal as his *humanization through a divinization* which man himself cannot realize."[60] At the center of this anthropology, then, lies "the fact that Christ reveals both *who man is* and *who man is called to be*. Christ reveals man and man's vocation. The two are intimately related (according to *Gaudium et Spes*) if for no other reason because his vocation specifies man's very existence. Man is called 'as soon as he comes into being' (GS #19) to converse with God, and man can be called to such a 'high calling' (GS #22) because of who he is, because he has been created in the image of God, because he is rational and free and can love."[61]

Moral Principles, Moral Truth, and Moral Action

To give of himself rightly in personal and social life, thus realizing his dignity, man needs to follow certain fundamental moral principles that are mediated by God to him through his conscience ("man's most secret core and sanctuary," GS #16) or his ability to know the truth of the moral law revealed by God and "written on [the] heart" (see Rom 2:15).[62] In fact, *Gaudium et Spes* teaches, "the more a correct conscience prevails, the more do persons and groups turn aside from blind choice and try to be guided by objective standards of moral conduct" (GS #16). Therefore, man is truly free and realizes his dignity only when his freedom is rooted in and conformed to the truth about the human person and human action.[63] This is made clear later in GS #51, where it is stated that with respect to marital sexual ethics, sexual activity in the area of birth regulation does not depend only on "a sincere intention and a consideration of motives," but must be based on "objective criteria," and these in turn should be based on the "*nature* of the human person and his acts,"[64] as well as the eternal life that each human person is called to share with God (see GS #51).[65] But because man's freedom – an essential aspect of his nature – "has been weakened by sin," it is only with the aid of "God's grace" that man can perform moral acts which will truly order him to his final end – God (see GS #17).[66]

At this point in our examination of *Gaudium et Spes*, we see the need for a general overarching moral principle, that is, a "first principle of morality," that will help *guide* each man to exercise his gift of freedom – which, as we know, can be exercised to choose either moral good or moral evil – by conforming it to the truth about the human person, so as to help him achieve his authentic good and acquire the kind of dignity that he gives to himself by exercising virtuous free action. To be in conformity with this truth means to be in conformity with God's moral law – a law ultimately revealed to the Christian in the person of Christ, who himself, as Pope John Paul II says, "becomes a living and personal law" for the disciple to follow.[67]

Chapter 2, titled "The Community of Mankind" (GS ##23–32), provides a compelling biblical answer to the question of how man is to act if he is to be in conformity to his dignity and build up society, thus treating some of the most "basic truths" of Christian teaching about human social life (see GS #23). In a word, it offers a "first principle of morality" to guide human activity. In GS #24 the Council teaches that *the twofold and inseparable commandment to love God above all else and one's neighbor as oneself* is "the first and greatest commandment." This truth is of "paramount importance,"[68] especially in a world marked by increasing "socialization," that is, growth in mutual interdependence between people (see GS #25). And later in GS #38, the Council declares that Christ's new law of love is "the basic law of human perfection and hence of the world's transformation." This law includes even the love of enemies (see GS #28; cf. Mt 5:43–44).

The love commandments are actually one of two foundation stones in *Gaudium et Spes*'s defense of human rights, the other being its holistic Christian anthropology. Indeed, unlike many modern secular liberal theories of rights, that are not based on God's moral law (e.g., as found in the Decalogue) and a sound anthropology, the Pastoral Constitution grounds the "universal and inviolable" rights *and* duties of human persons on the following: their imaging of God, who is the Creator and goal of all (see GS #24), their "exalted dignity" (see GS #26; see also ##27–31), their shared humanity (see GS #29), their solidarity and love (see GS ##24, 26–28, and 32), and on the "common good," which itself follows from the "need to transcend an individualistic morality" (GS #30).

In sum, the Council Fathers teach that "since all men possess a rational soul and are created in God's likeness, since they have the same nature and origin, have been redeemed by Christ and enjoy the same divine calling and destiny, the basic equality of all must receive increasingly greater recognition"(GS #29).[69] This perspective explains why, for the Council, "any kind of social or cultural discrimination in basic personal rights on the grounds of sex, race, color, social conditions, language or religion, must be curbed and eradicated as incompatible with God's design"(GS #29).

In Chapter 3 ("Man's Activity on the Universe," GS ##33–39), the Council Fathers provide us with a more technical – and we might add, less biblical and Christological – formulation of the "first principle of morality" than the commandment to "love God and neighbor" or the exhortation to "imitate Christ."[70] They teach that the first principle of morality or most basic moral norm is the following: human action is "to harmonize with the authentic good[71] of the human race, in accordance with God's will and design, and to enable men as individuals and as members of society to pursue and fulfill their total vocation"(GS #35).[72] That is, in making good moral choices, *Gaudium et Spes* teaches, human persons "are to choose in such a way that they reverence and respect, in each and every choice and action, whatever is really a good of human persons."[73] In addition to its centrality in guiding man's free choices to the good, this universal and objective norm is important, because, as John Paul II observes, it is "on the path of the moral life that the way of salvation" becomes a possibility for all human persons whether Christian or not.[74]

This norm also guides how the relationship between human activity and religion is to be conceived: man is given the task of exploring, investigating, and unlocking the secrets of nature,[75] but this search for knowledge must be rooted in *God's loving and wise plan for human existence*. Thus, man's rightful autonomy (in secular endeavors) cannot mean that he is *independent* of God, that he has no relation to his Creator (see GS ##36 and 41). For when man divorces his technological achievements from God's design – for example, as happens with atheism (see GS ##19–21; see also GS #41) – it leads not to his liberation, but rather to his enslavement, as we are seeing now with various forms of biotechnology such as cloning and embryonic stem cell research. To avoid this sorry state of affairs, man's activity "must be purified and perfected by the power of Christ's cross and resurrection" (GS#37).

Convinced of the soundness of this teaching, John Paul II, in *Veritatis Splendor*, speaks of man's "genuine moral autonomy" as an assent to God's moral law; so much so that we can see that "human freedom and God's law meet and are called to intersect…"[76] The Pope refers to this obedience to God as "participated theonomy," and thus in effect underlines, in good Thomistic fashion, the fact that human beings rationally participate or actively share in God's providential plan for human existence.[77]

Moral Life in Christ Jesus

As both Vatican II and John Paul II make clear,[78] man's reasoned participation in God's wisdom, that is, *natural law*, and the fundamental norm of human activity, are situated in the context of the "Word made flesh" who "fully reveals man to himself" (see GS #22). With these words of *Gaudium et Spes*, the Council, John Paul says, "expresses the anthropology that lies at the heart of the entire conciliar Magisterium. Christ not only teaches us the ways of the interior life, but he proposes himself as the 'Way' to be followed in order to arrive at our goal. He is the 'Way' because he is the Word made flesh, the perfect Man."[79] In this regard, the theologian David L. Schindler has argued that "the natural law – the Ten Commandments – the morality common to all men – is not eliminated by the call to follow Jesus Christ; but it remains intrinsically ordered to this discipleship, and indeed to living out the spirit of the Beatitudes and the Sermon on the Mount."[80] In other words, the natural moral law in the Council's vision is completed and perfected in Christ's new law of love (see Jn 13:34).

We can say then that the Christian moral life is, as Msgr. Lorenzo Albacete expresses it, a matter of "the capacity to live according to that personal configuration of mind, body, and spirit that conforms to the creative plan of God in Christ…Thinking in accordance with the natural law is thinking within creative Wisdom, but creative Wisdom is a very concrete Person. It is Jesus of Nazareth. *Thinking in accordance with the natural law is thinking with Jesus Christ*; it is 'co-judging' reality with Christ. It is, therefore, being taken up into his concrete personal presence."[81] We should, I believe, understand the absolute moral norms proposed by the Church in Christ's name from within this Christological perspective, when it teaches that certain acts (e.g. murder, genocide, abortion, infanticide, euthanasia, suicide, torture, slavery, and total war) are never to be done because they are incapable of being ordered either to the good of the human person or to the love of God (cf. GS ##27, 51, and 79–80).[82]

The Church and the World

The teaching of Chapter 4, "The Role of the Church in the Modern World" (GS ##40–45), presupposes the teaching of the previous three chapters and what the Council has already said about the Church (e.g., in *Lumen Gentium*), thus laying the foundation for the relationship between the Church and the world and for their dialogue (see GS #40). Although its subject is the Church and society, Chapter 4 contains rich moral and anthropological orientations rooted in Christ and the mystery of the Church. Thus, I will summarize its teaching, paying particular attention to this morality and anthropology.[83]

To begin, the Church – which is of Trinitarian origins – has, in the Council's mind, a soteriological and eschatological mission that can be fully realized only in the next world. But she is already present in this world, in history, and composed of men who are called "to form the family of God's children" on earth until Christ's second coming in glory (see GS #40).

Moreover, in carrying out the saving purpose given to her by Christ, the Church, according to *Gaudium et Spes*, communicates divine life to men but in some way also casts "the reflected light of that life over the entire earth, most of all by its healing and elevating impact on the dignity of the person, by the way in which it strengthens the seams of human society and imbues the everyday activity of men with a deeper meaning and importance" (GS #40).[84]

The Council goes on to articulate some general principles for "the proper fostering" of the "mutual exchange and assistance in concerns which are in some way common to the world and the Church"(GS #40).[85] To these I now turn.

First, the Church proclaims the fundamental *rights* of the human person. The Council Fathers again note that while the Church's primary mission is to lead men to God as their ultimate end, in doing so She also sheds light on man's true fulfillment and the deepest yearnings of his heart: the Church proclaims, in echoes of St. Augustine's "restless heart"[86] language, that only God will satisfy man's spiritual hunger for meaning. For, by nature, man is a searching being who wants to know the "meaning of his life, of his activity, of his death" (GS #41). However, only God, who made man in his own image and redeemed him, provides the most adequate answer to these existential questions. "He does this," says *Gaudium et Spes*, "through what He has revealed in Christ His Son, Who became man. *Whoever follows after Christ, the perfect man, becomes himself more of a man.* For by His incarnation the Father's Word assumed, and sanctified through His cross and resurrection, the whole of man, body and soul, and through that totality the whole of nature created by God for man's use"(GS #41, emphasis added). Hence, it is in the *imitatio Christi* that man finds the surest guide to his true good and perfection.

This revealed truth enables the Church to "anchor the dignity of human nature" against the shifting sands of opinion, for example, those which "undervalue the human body or idolize it" – both views common in the "culture of death." The Gospel proclaims the freedom of the children of God and rejects the bondage that ultimately results from sin (cf. Rom 8:14–17). It also has a sacred reverence for the dignity of conscience and its authentic freedom of choice; it counsels that human talents are be used to serve God and man; and, finally, it "commends all to the charity of all"(cf. Mt 22:39; see GS #41). Thus, in preaching the Gospel, the Church safeguards and protects the unsurpassable dignity of the human person.

"Christ, to be sure, gave His Church no proper mission in the political, economic or social order. The purpose which He set before her is a religious one. But out of this religious mission itself come a function, a light and an energy which can serve to structure and consolidate the human community according to the divine law." With these words of GS #42, the Council teaches us that when the Church – as sacramental sign and instrument of union with God (see LG #1) – promotes unity, she is being true to Her very own identity and offering Her greatest gift to a world beset by various divisions (see GS #42). Because the Church is tied to no particular cultural, political, economic, or social system, she has (or should have if it is being denied to her) the freedom to be a force (an "honest broker" as we say) for unity in the world among all peoples, nations, and groups (see GS #42).

Paragraph # 43 reminds us that we should not divorce faith from morality, faith from life. Religion includes more than worship; it involves every aspect of human existence. This is why the "split between the faith which many profess and their daily lives deserves to be counted among the more serious errors of our age" (GS #43). Thus, the Christian who neglects his temporal duties, say the Council Fathers, is really also neglecting his duties toward his neighbor and even God, and *jeopardizing his eternal salvation*. Hence, Christians must be about the work of bringing their worldly activities into "one vital synthesis with religious values, under whose supreme direction all things are harmonized unto God's glory"(GS #43).

The remaining content of GS #43 deals with the proper and distinctive role of the laity. That is, how, given their "secular" character, it belongs to them to work in the world and transform it from within with faith, hope, and love. "Since they have an active role to play in the whole life of the Church, laymen are not only bound to penetrate the world with a Christian spirit, but are also called to be witnesses to Christ in all things in the midst of human society"(GS #43).

Paragraph #44 lays out some general principles for evangelization that I will take up in part three. And finally, GS #45 reiterates that the Church's mission and message remains the same religious one given to her by Christ two thousand years ago: just as Christ "was Himself made flesh so that as perfect man He might save all men and sum up all things in Himself," so too does the Church solely exist to bring about God's kingdom and the integral salvation of the whole human race. Her "entire function," says theologian David Bohr, is to serve God's saving plan "by proclaiming the gospel both in word and deed, for 'by thus giving witness to the truth, we will share with others the mystery of the heavenly Father's love' (GS 93)."[87]

III. The Church, Evangelization, and the "New Evangelization"

If we are to renew our Church, evangelize this society, and turn it around for the better, we must take to heart the Council's words that call each Christian to live out personally the call to holiness in their daily lives. We must, as the Council exhorts us, "make ourselves the neighbor of every man" (GS #27) and see to it that "public and private organizations" are "at the service of the dignity and destiny of man"(GS #29). We must work therefore towards a social order that is "founded in truth, built on justice, and enlivened by love…"(GS #26). As the Catholic Campaign for America once expressed it, we must strive "to be *consistent*, integrating our [Christian] faith into every aspect of our lives…seeing our faith as the foundational element of our professional, family and public lives."[88]

The Catholic Church has, of course, a great role to play in addressing the moral and spiritual crisis that profoundly affects our country and affluent Western countries in general. If the Church is to be a more effective evangelizing presence in American society, however, it will, I believe, have to do or do better at least three things (among many others). Here I mention some very general suggestions from theologian René Latourelle, but they are also firmly rooted in what *Gaudium et Spes* teaches about evangelization as I will show.

First, says Latourelle, the Church must "show respect" for the *sound* "human values acknowledged in the secular world, e.g., professional competence, efficiency in work [etc.]…"[89] A similar idea is expressed in *Gaudium et Spes*: "This council exhorts Christians, as citizens of two cities, to strive to discharge their earthly duties conscientiously and in response to the Gospel spirit. They are mistaken who, knowing that we have here no abiding city but seek one which is to come [cf. Heb 13:14], think that they may therefore shirk their earthly responsibilities. For they are forgetting that by the faith itself they are more obliged than ever to measure up to these duties, each according to his proper vocation"(GS #43; cf. 2 Th 3:6–13; Eph 4:28). The idea here is to show the compatibility between a good *human* life and the Christian faith. The Council's "Christian humanism," so marvelously expressed by *Gaudium et Spes*, has pointed us in the right direction to do this.

As Germain Grisez has noted, Vatican II, and especially this Pastoral Constitution, taught that when Christians accept the gifts of faith and divine life they "need not set aside anything of their human lives; and to live fully human lives, they cannot aim at anything less than lives of the highest holiness (see LG ##39–41; GS ##1, 11, 21, 22, 32, 34, 92; AA #7). The call to intimacy with God who definitively reveals himself in Jesus is also a call to protect and promote the flourishing of human persons and societies in the goods which fulfill human nature (see GS ##34–35)."[90] Hence, the name "Christian humanism" best captures the Council's teaching.[91]

Second, Latourelle argues, because of our increasingly "smaller world," captured in such a term as "globalization,"[92] all Catholics need to be humble missionaries bearing witness to the teaching and love of Christ to the "foreigner" in our own backyard or wherever we may find him or her[93] (cf. GS #27). This would include the *re-evangelization* of those formerly Christian Western countries that have now largely abandoned the faith or those Catholics in our own country who have for various reasons stopped practicing the faith.

In fact, the Church has always tried to adapt the Gospel, as *Gaudium et Spes* explains, "to the grasp of all as well as to the needs of the learned, insofar as such was appropriate. Indeed this accommodated preaching of the revealed word ought to remain *the law of all evangelization*"(GS #45, emphasis added). Thus, say the Council Fathers, "the ability to express Christ's message in its own way is developed in each nation, and at the same time there is fostered a living exchange between the Church and the diverse cultures of people"(GS #45). This evangelization effort will involve the Church seeking out "the special help of those who live in the world, are versed in different institutions and specialties, and grasp their innermost significance in the eyes of both believers and unbelievers"(GS #45).

Third, says Latourelle, the Church must also "show itself to be an especially fervent communion in the Spirit."[94] As *Gaudium et Spes* reminds us: "In his preaching [Christ] clearly taught the sons of God to treat one another as brothers" (GS #32; see also GS #92). If Catholics are unable or unwilling to radiate an ardent love for *each other*, in imitation of their Lord, their *witness* in the name of Christ on behalf of the world will be seriously hampered, and its efforts on behalf of specific moral issues in the public square will be rendered ineffective. As St. Paul begs, "in the name of the Lord Jesus Christ," we must "agree in what [we] say." There must "be no factions [among us]…but united in mind and judgment" (see I Cor 1:10).

Conclusion

The "new evangelization" does not propose a Gospel different than the one we have known for two thousand years. It does however propose a deeper *appropriation* of this same Gospel by Christians and, among other things, the use of media unimagined by previous generations of Christians.[95] As Latourelle has written: "The people of our day want to find in the Church, in Christian communities, and in every Christian a reflection of Christ's love – that pure and unshadowed, ardent and faithful love by which he gave himself completely," even unto death to save us. "If, " he continues, "thanks to the testimony of committed Christians, the people of our day can encounter this love of human beings for their own sake, a love with no slightest hint of rejection, they will have discovered a new world and will desire to share in this fullness, for they will have discovered that God is love."[96]

Following the lead of the Council and of our late Holy Father, Pope John Paul II, let us be hopeful, "confident that our faith is capable of transforming ourselves and the contemporary culture."[97] There is much work to be done on behalf of the "new evangelization" and many obstacles that stand in the way! Yet the Council, especially in *Gaudium et Spes*, has given us the theological "blueprint" or what John Paul II has described as the "'Magna Charta' of *human dignity* to be safeguarded and promoted."[98] At its heart it is really neither pessimistic nor optimistic regarding the future of the Church and humanity, but rather, it is full of Christian *hope*. Thus, I hope that I have shown that this most celebrated Council document is indeed still relevant, forty years later, to the great challenges we face. As Pedro Morandé has argued, we must continue to listen to *Gaudium et Spes* because it presents "a Church open to dialogue with all cultures and all social systems – a Church that is optimistic, but without any trace of naiveté, because she is convinced that the truth of man revealed to him in Christ has the necessary power to enable every human being to discover his deepest vocation to the freedom that comes from self-giving in love."[99]

The author would like to thank Professors William E. May, Janet E.

Smith, and Richard S. Myers for helpful comments on earlier drafts of this paper.

Dr. Mark S. Latkovic is a Professor of Moral and Systematic Theology at Sacred Heart Major Seminary in Detroit, Michigan, where since 1990 he has taught courses on fundamental moral theology, bioethics, marriage, family, and sexuality. He holds a B.A. from Cleveland State University, and an M.A. from the Catholic University of America. In addition, he holds both a Licentiate (*Summa cum Laude*) and a Doctorate in Sacred Theology (S.T.D.) from the John Paul II Institute for Studies on Marriage and the Family.

His articles and reviews have appeared in a wide variety of publications, both popular, such as *The Michigan Catholic* and *The National Catholic Register*, and scholarly, such as *Nova et Vetera* and *The National Catholic Bioethics Quarterly*. He was co-editor and contributor to the 2004 volume entitled *St. Thomas Aquinas and the Natural Law Tradition: Contemporary Perspectives* (CUA Press). In 2001 he was named book review editor of the bioethics journal *Linacre Quarterly*. He has also served on Cardinal Adam Maida's Detroit Archdiocesan Medical-Moral Committee. He is a frequent speaker, panelist, and guest on radio and T.V. on the subject of contemporary moral issues. In 2005 he was elected to the Board of Directors of the Fellowship of Catholic Scholars. Dr. Latkovic is married and is the father of four children.

ENDNOTES

1   The Pastoral Constitution on the Church in the Modern World, *Gaudium et Spes*, was promulgated on December 7, 1965. It was promulgated on the same day as The Declaration on Religious Liberty, *Dignitatis Humanae*, a document with a significant teaching of its own on the dignity of the human person, moral truth, and conscience. *Gaudium et Spes* was the only pastoral constitution promulgated by the Council. It was also the longest document issued by the Council. For commentary on the documents of Vatican II, see e.g., Herbert Vorgrimler, *et al.* (eds.), *Commentary on the Documents of Vatican II* (Herder and Herder, 1969). See particularly Joseph Ratzinger's commentary ("*Gaudium et Spes*, Articles 11–22") on paragraphs 11–22, in Vol. 5, pp. 115–163. See also, for the social and ecclesial context of the document, including a commentary on it (with which I am not always in agreement) by David Hollenbach, S.J., "Commentary on *Gaudium et Spes* (Pastoral Constitution in the Modern World)," in Kenneth R. Himes, O.F.M. (ed.), *Modern Catholic Social Teaching* (Georgetown University Press, 2005), pp. 266–291; and Giuseppe Alberigo and Joseph A. Komonchak (eds.), *History of Vatican II*, Vols. 1–3 (Orbis, 1995, 1997, 2000). For the Council documents themselves, see Austin Flannery, O.P. (ed.), *Vatican*

Council II: The Conciliar and Post Conciliar Documents, New Revised Edition (Costello Publishing Co., 1984), whose translations I generally follow, unless otherwise indicated. My use of "non-inclusive" language in most cases should not be taken in any way to exclude women. Here I am simply being consistent with the practice of the Council documents themselves.

2   Walter Kasper, "The Council's Vision for a Renewal of the Church," *Communio* Vol. 17, No. 4 (Winter 1990): 474–493, at 479.

3   *Ibid.*

4   This is one reason why the Council Fathers called for a renewal of the theological disciplines, including a renewed moral theology, whose central features would include among others a greater focus on the person of Christ, more emphasis on Sacred Scripture, and the illumination of the relationship between the Christian vocation of charity in this life and in the world to come (see *Optatam Totius* #16).

5   Pope John Paul II, *VeritatisSplendor* #2, quoting *Gaudium et Spes* #22, to cite but one place where the pope quotes these words (see also, especially, his first encyclical *RedemptorHominis*, March 4, 1979). Both encyclicals are available on the Holy See's web page. One of the things that Christ sheds light on is how "the riddles of sorrow and death" can "grow meaningful…[For] Christ has risen, destroying death by His death; He has lavished life upon us…" (GS #22; see also GS #18).

6   The essential message of the Council, says Hans Urs Von Balthasar, "is expressed with this double and inexorable principle: the *being* of the Church is (as mission) inseparably her *activity*, and the love of God proclaimed and lived by her is the principle of the unification of humanity in the spirit of brotherhood" (Von Balthasar, "The Council of the Holy Spirit," in Von Balthasar, *Explorations in Theology*, Vol. III: *Creator Spirit* [Ignatius Press, 1993], pp. 245–267, at 246).

7   "By suffering for us [Christ] not only gave us an example *so that we might follow in his footsteps* [cf. 1 Pet 2:21; Mt 16:24; Lk 14–27], *but he also opened up a way. If we follow this path, life and death are made holy and acquire a new meaning"* (GS #22, emphasis added).

8   Obviously, with a profound document like *Gaudium et Spes*, I cannot do so in a comprehensive fashion. Much has already been written on *Gaudium et Spes* and so I will reference but a fraction of this literature to help interpret its teaching. I will also make only occasional reference to other Vatican Council II documents. These documents will be treated by other speakers at the Fellowship of Catholic Scholars Convention (2005).

9   Some of these specific questions (i.e., those treated in ## 46–93 will be briefly treated by Fr. Paul deLadurantaye, the respondent to this paper at the Fellowship of Catholic Scholars' Convention.

10   These debates over the proper understanding of the Council over the last four decades (e.g., between the theologians of secularity and the liberation theologians in the years immediately after the Council) are, in many ways,

a continuation of those between the eschatological theologians, the theological humanists (or incarnational theologians), and the integralist Catholics on the eve of the Council's opening, especially in the French-speaking *milieux* mainly responsible for *Gaudium et Spes*. See Aidan Nichols, O.P., *Catholic Thought Since the Enlightenment: A Survey* (Gracewing, 1998), pp. 146–148, 151–158.

11   For some of the criticisms leveled against *Gaudium et Spes*, see Lois Ann Lorentzen, "Gaudium Et Spes," in Judith Dwyer (ed.), *The New Dictionary of Catholic Social Thought* (The Liturgical Press, 1994), pp. 406–416. In contrast, see the favorable view of the document offered by Mary Eberstadt, "Modernity and Its Discontents: *Gaudium et Spes* (1965)," in George Weigel and Robert Royal (eds.), *Building the Free Society: Democracy, Capitalism, and Catholic Social Thought* (Eerdmans/Ethics and Public Policy Center, 1993), pp. 89–105. For criticisms brought against the Council as a whole and sound response to it, see Alan Schreck, *Vatican II: The Crisis and the Response* (Servant Books, 2005).

12   "God...wants all men to be saved and to come to know the truth" (1 Timothy 2:3; cf. 4:10); cf. GS #22.

13   On the question of the relationship between the orders of nature and grace in *Gaudium et Spes*, see e.g., David L. Schindler, *Heart of the World, Center of the Church: Communio Ecclesiology, Liberalism, and Liberation* (Eerdmans, 1996), pp. 1–40, and Henri De Lubac, *A Brief Catechesis on Nature and Grace* (Ignatius Press, 1984), pp. 177–190. See also Germain Grisez, *The Way of the Lord Jesus*, Vol. 1: *Christian Moral Principles* (Franciscan Herald Press, 1983), Chapter 1, Question G and Chapter 34, among others.

14   Joseph Cardinal Ratzinger, *Principles of Catholic Theology: Building Stones for a Fundamental Theology*, trans., Sister Mary Frances McCarthy, S.N.D. (Ignatius Press, 1987), p. 379. Cf. GS #2.

15   *Ibid.* Ratzinger notes a certain ambiguity in the use of the term "world." It is not clear he says "whether the world that cooperates and the world that is to be built up are one and the same world; it is not clear what meaning is intended by the word 'world' in every instance" (*Ibid.*, p. 379). He goes on to speak of the "astonishing optimism" that characterized the relationship between humanity and the Church, including the great hope expected from the text's basic formal classification – "dialogue" (*Ibid.*, p. 380).

16   *Ibid.*, p. 381. The internal quotes are from the Preface of GS #3. The Church therefore "dialogues" with the world in order to "transform" the world for Christ (see GS #92).

17   On the new perspectives of Vatican II on the "signs of the times," see Rino Fisichella, "Signs of the Times," in René Latourelle and Rino Fisichella (eds.), *Dictionary of Fundamental Theology* (Crossroad Publishing, 1994), pp. 995–1001. Interestingly, Fr. Charles E. Curran has noted that the earlier drafts of *Gaudium et Spes* employed the term "signs of the times" quite often, but when some Council Fathers objected that the term is a biblical

one that refers to the eschatological signs of the last day, references in the final draft were made more sparse (see Charles E. Curran, *Catholic Social Teaching: 1891 – Present: A Historical, Theological, and Ethical Analysis* [Georgetown University Press, 2002)] p. 59, note omitted). He notes further that each of the five chapters of its second part begin with an overview of the "signs of the times" rather than with laws inscribed in human nature, as older Church documents were wont to do. Curran claims that this shows the Council giving greater emphasis to historical consciousness and an inductive methodology over a classicist and deductive approach (see pp. 54–60). This may be true, but it is clear that the Council does not in any way abandon objective moral principles and truths (see e.g., GS #79) that speak of the binding force of the natural law's "universal principles," as I think Curran himself would admit. The "signs of the times" language is used in a *pastoral* Constitution, it seems to me, in order to better speak to modern man; but it is always in the service of a dialogue whose goal is *Christian conversion*. Also, as Curran acknowledges, the kinds of issues addressed in part two of *Gaudium et Spes* lend themselves more to this type of inductive approach. With the social teaching of the Church, for example, one needs first to survey the present cultural landscape and then offer a theologically based moral analysis of this landscape, as the Council Fathers (and subsequent magisterial documents) do.

18　"But to all who received him, who believed in his name, he gave power to become children of God" (John 1:12).

19　The Council quotes Hebrews 13:8 to the effect that Christ is "the same yesterday, today, and forever."

20　As William E. May notes, those, like Karl Rahner, S.J., who assert this, say that while "transcendental" human nature does not change, "concrete" human nature does (see May, *An Introduction to Moral Theology*, Second Edition [Our Sunday Visitor, 2003], pp. 256–257).

21　Among authors who have made (and continue to make) this argument, Fr. Charles E. Curran is among the most prominent in the United States (see e.g., Charles E. Curran, *Contemporary Problems in Moral Theology* [Fides Publishers, 1970], pp. 116–136). See also Curran's *The Moral Theology of Pope John Paul II* (Georgetown University Press, 2005), pp. 106–109 and 117–119 for criticism that the pope's moral theology is not informed by historical consciousness. The essay that lies behind Curran's thinking and others on this matter is Bernard Lonergan, S.J.'s, "The Transition from a Classicist World-View to Historical-Mindedness," in W.F.J. Ryan, S.J., and B.J. Tyrrell, S.J., (eds.), *A Second Collection* (Westminster Press, 1974), pp. 1–9. An essay which thoroughly demolishes this influential way of thinking is John Finnis, "'Historical Consciousness' and Theological Foundations," The Etienne Gilson Lecture (Pontifical Institute for Medieval Studies, 1992).

22　Germain Grisez, *Christian Moral Principles*, p. 183, emphasis added.

23   See *Ibid.*, Question F, pp. 103–105, for a description of this theory, not to
      be confused with St. Thomas Aquinas' understanding of natural law. In
      brief, scholastic natural law theory's basic normative proposal is as follows:
      those actions which conform to human nature as given are morally good
      and those which do not conform to it are morally bad.

24   *Ibid.* See also endnote #21 on p. 202. On the many ways in which historic-
      ity and social change *can* affect moral judgment, see John Finnis, *Moral
      Absolutes: Tradition, Revision, and Truth* (The Catholic University of
      America Press, 1991), pp. 25–26.

25   *Ibid.*, emphasis added.

26   *Ibid.* See also the excellent essay by John Finnis, "The Natural Law,
      Objective Morality, and Vatican II," in William E. May (ed.), *Principles of
      Catholic Moral Life* (Franciscan Herald Press, 1981), pp. 113–149, espe-
      cially pp. 139–142, that superbly treat historicity and the natural law; and
      William E. May, *An Introduction to Moral Theology*, Second Edition, pp.
      87–91, on the Council's understanding of natural law and pp. 150, 157–158
      on the historicity of human existence.

27   As *Gaudium et Spes* #22 teaches: "By his Incarnation the Son of God has
      united himself in some fashion with *every man*. He worked with *human*
      hands, he thought with a *human* mind, acted by *human* choice, and loved
      with a *human* heart" (emphasis added). Except for being sinless, Christ was
      like us in all things, including our *human nature*. With this knowledge, we
      can be sure that the human nature that Christ redeemed on Calvary is the
      same human nature that he continues to redeem today.

28   Kasper, "The Council's Vision for the Renewal of the Church," p. 480.

29   *Ibid.*, p. 481.

30   "Once and for all, the fatal wound is dealt to the mentality that holds that
      one can be Catholic, too, alongside one's status as a good citizen, guaran-
      teeing one's own private salvation by the keeping of some religious obliga-
      tions while otherwise leaving the concern for Christianity to the specialists,
      the clergy" (Von Balthasar, "The Council of the Holy Spirit," p. 245).

31   Of course, it was always expected that the "average" Christian layperson
      was called to lead a morally good Christian life. However, scholars such as
      Servais Pinckaers, O.P., have argued, in modern times, that the heights of
      Christian perfection were often seen as reserved for a spiritual elite. In
      speaking of the universal call to holiness, the Council Fathers were in fact
      simply retrieving an idea that was lost in the more recent Tradition. As
      Pinckaers notes with respect to the Fathers of the Church, there is no sepa-
      ration of morality from spirituality. "In their view, all Christians have been
      called to 'live in the Spirit,' according to the vocations to which they have
      been called" (Servais Pinckaers, O.P., *Morality: The Catholic View* [St.
      Augustine's Press, 2001], p. 20). Such medieval theologians as St. Thomas
      Aquinas held the same view.

32   See also Pope John Paul II, *Veritatis Splendor* #16.

33   See David S. Crawford, "Consecration and Human Action: The Moral Life as Response," *Communio* Vol. 31, No. 3 (Fall 2004): 378–403.

34   Editorial in *New Oxford Review*, October 1994, p. 2.

35   René Latourelle, "Testimony II: Motive of Credibility," in Latourelle and Fisichella (eds.), *Dictionary of Fundamental Theology*, pp. 1051–1060, at p. 1053.

36   *Ibid.*, p. 1052.

37   *Ibid.*, p. 1053.

38   *Ibid.*

39   *Ibid.*, p. 1055.

40   Germain Grisez, *The Way of the Lord Jesus*, Vol. 2: *Living a Christian Life* (Franciscan Press, 1993), p. xii. Pope John Paul II likewise insists on the importance of personal vocation in many documents. See e.g., *Christifideles Laici* ##28 and 58.

41   On personal vocation, see Germain Grisez and Russell Shaw, *Personal Vocation: God Calls Everyone By Name* (Our Sunday Visitor, 2003), especially chapter 4.

42   Grisez, *Living a Christian Life*, p. xiii.

43   *Ibid.*, p. xii, quoting *Gaudium et Spes* #43, that also speaks of a person's "proper vocation." See also the Congregation for the Doctine of the Faith, Doctrinal Note on Some Questions Regarding the Participation of Catholics in PoliticalLife, November 24, 2002, available at: http://www.vatican.va/roman_curia/congregations/cfaith/documents/rc_con_cfaith_doc_2 0021124_politica_en.html. For Vatican II's understanding of personal vocation and vocation in general, see Grisez and Shaw, *Personal Vocation*, pp. 70–75.

44   The internal quote is from the Preface for the Feast of Christ the King.

45   William E. May, "Contraception: A Catholic Response," *Loyola of Los Angeles International and Comparative Law Journal* Vol. 16, No. 1 (November 1993): 75–79, at 79.

46   For some general overviews of the Council's anthropology, with particular attention to *Gaudium et Spes*, see e.g., Donald Asci, *The Conjugal Act as a Personal Act: A Study of the Catholic Concept of the Conjugal Act in the Light of Christian Anthropology* (Ignatius Press, 2002), pp. 61–66; and Paulinus Ikechukwu Odozor, C.S.Sp., *Moral Theology in an Age of Renewal: A Study of the Catholic Tradition since Vatican II* (University of Notre Dame Press, 2003), pp. 27–31; see also pp. 31–43 on the moral theology of Vatican II.

47   See Walter Kasper, "The Theological Anthropology of *Gaudium et Spes*," *Communio* Vol. 23, No. 1 (Spring 1996): 129–140, at 129.

48   Ratzinger, *Principles of Catholic Theology*, p. 379. See also the rich reflections on the anthropology of *Gaudium et Spes* offered by Pope John Paul II in *Memory and Identity: Conversations at the Dawn of the Millennium* (Rizzoli International Publications, 2005), pp. 109–114.

49   See Latourelle, "Gaudium et Spes," in Latourelle and Fisichella (eds.), *Dictionary of Fundamental Theology*, pp. 339–341, at p. 340. Pascal wrote: "The greatness of man is great insofar as he realizes that he is wretched" (*Pascal's Pensées*, Martin Turnell, trans. [Harper and Row, 1962], p. 94).

50   Some (e.g., Gregory Baum) have accused *Gaudium et Spes* of ignoring *social sin*; but a reading of GS #25 makes clear that the reality of social sin is clearly recognized even if the term itself is not used.

51   This last expression is from John Harris, "Euthanasia and the Value of Life," in John Keown (ed.), *Euthanasia Examined: Ethical, Clinical, and Legal Perspectives* (Cambridge University Press, 1997), pp. 6–22, see 9. The Pontifical Council for Justice and Peace's *Compendium of the Social Doctrine of the Church* (USCCB, 2004) speaks of the two characteristics of man: "*he is a material being, linked to this world by his body, and he is a spiritual being, open to transcendence* and the discovery of 'more penetrating truths,' thanks to his intellect, by which 'he shares in the light of the divine mind' [GS #15]…Neither the spiritualism that despises the body nor the materialism that considers the spirit a mere manifestation of the material do justice to the complex nature, to the totality or to the unity of the human being" (p. 57, no. 129).

52   As *Gaudium et Spes* expresses it, social life is not something "added on to man" (GS #25). And political community and public authority it says are "founded on human nature" (GS #75). On *society* as either an "artificial creation" or as "natural development," see Servais Pinckaers, O.P., *The Sources of Christian Ethics*, trans., Sr. Mary Thomas Noble, O.P. (The Catholic University of America Press, 1995), pp. 38–39, 432–436.

53   For these typologies, see Jean Bethke Elshtain, "Ethical Equality in the New Feminism," in Michelle M. Schumacher (ed.), *Women in Christ: Toward a New Feminism* (Eerdmans, 2003), pp. 285–296, in particular pp. 287–290. Elshtain follows Sr. Prudence Allen, R.S.M., in this threefold typology. See also Dale O'Leary, "Commentary: The Problem of Gender Feminism: Currents of Thought Running Counter to True Advancement," *L'Osservatore Romano* (November 17, 2004): 6–7.

54   Walter Kasper, "The Theological Anthropology of *Gaudium et Spes*," p. 137.

55   *Ibid.* Kasper's article provides a good discussion of the drafting of *Gaudium et Spes*, its anthropology, and some friendly criticism of this anthropology, e.g., the "tension" that is in the content of the *imago Dei*. As expressed by David L. Schindler, this tension involves using Genesis 1:26 ("Then God said: 'Let us make man in our image, after our likeness.'") in paragraph #12 as the context for understanding man as image of God, whereas it involves using Colossians 1:15 ("[Christ] is the image of the invisible God, the first-born of all creatures.") in paragraph #22, which concludes the first chapter, as the context. The tension that arises is thus "between a potentially 'theistically-colored and to a large extent non-historical view' of man, which can

result from article 12's omission of Christology from its theology of creation, and the more concrete view of man which results from article 22's christological integration of the orders of creation and redemption-eschatology" (David L. Schindler, "Christology and the *Imago Dei*: Interpreting *Gaudium et Spes*," *Communio* Vol. 23, No. 1 [Spring 1996]: 156–184, at 158; cf. Ratzinger, "*Gaudium et Spes*, Articles 11–22"). The distinct emphases in the two contexts, Schindler continues, "if left unintegrated, can lead to significant differences in anthropology – indeed, to the sorts of differences which, one might argue, have lain at the source of much of the ecclesial controversy and unrest since the Council" (p. 158).

56   Henri de Lubac, "The Total Meaning of Man and of the World: Two Interrelated Problems," *Communio* Vol. 17, No. 4 (Winter 1990): 613–616, at 615.

57   René Latourelle, "Gaudium et Spes," p. 340.

58   De Lubac, "The Total Meaning of Man and of the World," p. 616.

59   Asci, *The Conjugal Act as a Personal Act*, p. 65.

60   Kasper, "The Theological Anthropology of *Gaudium et Spes*," p. 140, emphasis added.

61   Asci, *The Conjugal Act as a Personal Act*, pp. 65–66.

62   *Dignitatis Humanae* # 3 teaches that the "highest norm of human life is God's divine law – eternal, objective, universal – whereby God orders, directs, and governs the entire universe and all the ways of the human community according to a plan conceived in wisdom and in love." It notes also that man was created "by God to participate in this law" (DH #3). This participation is precisely what is meant by the natural law (see also endnote 78 below). Here we have another example of where the Council does not use a particular term (in this case "natural law" in DH #3), but describes its reality well.

63   For the Council's understanding of human dignity as a search for moral truth, and free choice in accordance with that truth, see William E. May, *An Introduction to Moral Theology*, Second Edition, pp. 42–43.

64   Emphasis added. The Latin text reads: "*objectiva criteria ex personae eiusdemque actuum natura desumpta*"). The Council immediately specifies this norm of marital morality by saying that sexual acts must "preserve the full sense of mutual self-giving and human procreation in the context of true love." So, the goods of both love and life must be respected in each and every exercise of genital sexual activity. For commentary, see Ramón García de Haro, *Marriage and Family in the Documents of the Magisterium: A Course in the Theology of Marriage*, trans. William E. May (Ignatius Press, 1993), pp. 257–262.

65   "*That* is what human dignity demands: an objective (i.e., real) relationship to basic human goods, basic aspects of human personality as they are inevitably involved in certain sorts of human acts" (Finnis, "The Natural Law, Objective Morality, and Vatican II," p. 121).

66   Once again, it is interesting to note here that, although *Gaudium et Spes*

does not use the word *virtue* in paragraph #17, the text describes its reality very well: "Man achieves [his proper] dignity when, emancipating himself from all captivity to passion, he pursues his goal in a spontaneous choice of what is good, and procures for himself through effective and skillful action, apt helps to that end."

67   Pope John Paul II, *Veritatis Splendor* #15. "Jesus' way of acting and his words, his deeds and his precepts constitute the moral rule of Christian life" (*Ibid.*, no. 20). Christ in turn gives us the norm of all moral activity, namely the "New Law," i.e. the grace of the Holy Spirit given through faith in Christ (see *Ibid.*, nos. 23–24).

68   In *Gaudium et Spes* ##26–32, we find the practical implications of this norm for social life. Human beings not only are the bearers of certain inalienable rights in common (see GS #26), they are not to be treated in certain ways – given *who* they are – which would violate their God-given dignity (see GS #27).

69   Note the reference to the "same nature," contra Lonergan's "historical consciousness and changing human nature" argument (see endnote 21 above).

70   In explaining this difference in formulations of the first moral principle, it is helpful to keep in mind that the question "whether Christology determines anthropology or vice versa," as Walter Kasper observes, "concentrates and focuses the dilemma of the identity and relevance of the Christian reality, with which the Council Fathers had to struggle" in the drafting of *Gaudium et Spes* ("The Theological Anthropology of *Gaudium et Spes*," p. 136). Put another way, the question is whether Jesus Christ or the natural law is the starting-point for morality. Kasper states that although anthropology is the Council's starting-point, "Christology is nevertheless the criterion of all its statements about anthropology and remains the horizon in which they are to be understood" (*Ibid.*, p. 137). We must also remember that in part one, chapter three, where the Council begins with reflection on the value of human activity (see #34), its regulation (see #35), and autonomy (see #36), it is addressing "the whole human race" and is "eager to associate the light of revelation with the experience of mankind in trying to clarify the course upon which mankind has just entered" (GS #33). Later, in an explicitly Christian context, the Council will show how human activity is infected by sin (see GS #37) but is also fulfilled in the Paschal mystery (see GS ##38–39). Moreover, *Gaudium et Spes* # 2 states that it will address itself "to all men without distinction, in order to explain to all how [the Council] understands the presence and activity of the Church in the world of today."

71   The Flannery edited edition of the documents of Vatican II uses the term "interests" here instead of "good." William E. May has drawn my attention to the fact that this is a bad translation given by Flannery. The Latin speaks of "*bono autentico*" in the singular: action in harmony with the "authentic *good*" of the human person.

72   For discussion, see Grisez, *Christian Moral Principles*, pp. 183–184.

Grisez believes that Vatican II's formulation of the first principle of morality, as well as St. Thomas' formulation (i.e., the precepts of charity), is good,
but not entirely satisfactory for purposes of ethical reflection and moral theology. "To serve as a basic standard for practical judgment," he writes, "a
formulation must refer to the many basic goods which generate the need for
choice and moral guidance" (*Ibid.*, p. 184; originally in boldface type). As
a single principle, Grisez says, it "will give unity and direction to a morally good life. At the same, it must not exclude ways of living which might
contribute to a complete human community" (*Ibid*). For Grisez's own more
adequate formulation of the first moral principle, understood as willing in
full accord with integral human fulfillment, see *Ibid*. pp. 184–189.

73 William E. May, *An Introduction to Moral Theology*, Second Edition, p. 89.
It is in this way, May adds, "that human beings fulfill the command to love,
for by doing so they manifest (a) their love of God, who is the author of the
goods of human existence, and (b) their love of neighbor, in whom these
God-given goods are meant to flourish" (*Ibid*).

74 Pope John Paul II, *Veritatis* Splendor # 3. Cf. *Lumen* Gentium #16.

75 Recall that *Gaudium et Spes* affirms that man is given *dominion* over the
earth by God himself; but it is a dominion that implies a form of *worship*,
i.e. using created things "to God's glory" (see GS #12; see also GS #34).

76 Pope John Paul II, *Veritatis Splendor* # 41.

77 *Ibid*. Cf. St. Thomas Aquinas, *SummaTheolgiae*, I-II, q. 91, a. 2 where
Thomas defines natural law as "a participation of the eternal law in the
rational creature."

78 See Pope John Paul II, *Veritatis Splendor*, especially chapters 1–2.

79 Pope John Paul II, *Memory and Identity*, p. 111.

80 Interview with David Schindler, "The Culture of Love," in *The Catholic
World Report*, October 1994, p. 45. See also Schindler, "Christology and
the *Imago Dei*: Interpreting *Gaudium et Spes*."

81 Lorenzo Albacete, "The Relevance of Christ or the *Sequela Christi*?"
Communio Vol. 21, No. 2 (Summer 1994): 252–264, at 257–258, emphasis
added. See also Livio Melina, *Sharing in Christ's Virtues: For a Renewal of
Moral Theology in Light of Veritatis Splendor*, trans. William E. May (The
Catholic University of America Press, 2001), pp. 84–86 and chapter 5.

82 The Council Fathers describe these and other acts (e.g., prostitution) as
"crimes" against human persons and human life which "poison civilization;
and they debase their perpetrators more than their victims and militate
against the honor of the Creator" (GS #27). In John Paul II's *Veritatis
Splendor* #85, to take but one example, the pope says that it is "in the
Crucified Christ that the Church finds the answer" to the question as to why
we must obey "universal and unchanging norms." See also the discussion
in May, *An Introduction to Moral Theology*, Second Edition, pp. 89–90,
252–253.

83 See also my comments above on the "Preface" of *Gaudium et Spes*.

84 The Church is also "convinced that she can be abundantly and variously helped by the world in the matter of preparing the ground for the Gospel" (GS #40). But more often than not today, given the sorry state of the secular culture, the Church must be *against* the world in order to be *for* the world as Fr. Richard John Neuhaus has put it on occasion.

85 See Walter Kasper, "The Power of Christian Love to Transform the World: The Relationship between Christianity and Society," in Kasper, *Faith and the Future* (Crossroad, 1982), pp. 86–108. Citing *Lumen Gentium* ##21, 36–37 and *Gaudium et Spes* #43, he notes that the Council rejected the strategies of secularism as well as integralism and clericalism (p. 89).

86 See *Confessions*, I, 1.

87 David Bohr, *Evangelization in America: Proclamation, Way of Life, and the Catholic Church in America* (Paulist Press, 1977), p. 64.

88 The Catholic Campaign for America's "Principles of Public Catholicism," #7, quoted in Thomas V. Wykes, Jr., "Principles of Public Catholicism," in Thomas Patrick Melady (ed.), *Catholics in the Public Square* (Our Sunday Visitor, 1995), p. 16. See also the Congregation for the Doctrine of the Faith, Doctrinal Note on Some Questions Regarding the Participation of Catholics in Political Life.

89 Latourelle, "Testimony II," p. 1058.

90 Grisez, *Christian Moral Principles*, p. 17. Grisez also points out that in claiming that "human dignity 'is rooted and perfected in God,' the Council says it is the Church's teaching that Christian hope for eternal happiness with God 'does not lessen the importance of earthly duties, but rather adds new motives for fulfilling them (GS #21; translation supplied [by Grisez])" (*Ibid.*, p. 586).

91 Grisez argues that just as Jesus is both fully human and fully divine (as well as his entire life), so too is the Christian. While Jesus to be sure was divine by nature, our share in the divine nature is an adoptive one, but a share in divinity nonetheless. The underlying difficulty in moral theology, according to Grisez, "has been an inadequate understanding of how Christian life must be and can be at the same time completely human and divine (see GS ##22, 43, 45, 92)" [Grisez, *Christian Moral Principles*, p. 16; see pp. 16–17 and chapter 24 for the full discussion].

92 Once more, although the Council does not use the term, the reality of what we now call *globalization* is nicely captured in GS #26 when it speaks of growing "human interdependence" and the *universal* "common good."

93 Latourelle, "Testimony II," p. 1058.

94 *Ibid.*, p. 1059. Latourelle adds: "The place par excellence for the unity in love that constitutes personal and communal testimony is the Eucharist as assembly and as sacrifice" (*Ibid.*).

95 See e.g., Avery Dulles, S.J., *The New World of Faith* (Our Sunday Visitor, 2000), pp. 111–116, on the chief characteristics of the "new evangelization."

96 Latourelle, "Testimony II," p. 1059.

97 The Catholic Campaign for America's "Principles of Public Catholicism," #10, quoted in Wykes, "Principles of Public Catholicism," in Melady (ed.), *Catholics in the Public Square*, p. 17.

98 Pope John Paul II, "Only Christ Can Fulfill Man's Hopes," *Communio* Vol. 23, No. 1 (Spring 1996): 122–128, at 128. Originally given on November 8, 1995 to a Congress celebrating the 30th anniversary of *Gaudium et Spes*.

99 Pedro Morandé, "The Relevance of the Message of *Gaudium et Spes* Today: The Church's Mission in the Midst of Epochal Changes and New Challenges," *Commuunio* Vol. 23, No. 1 (Spring 1996): 141–155, at 155.

Response to Mark Latkovic
"At the Service of the Human Person"

REVEREND PAUL F. DELADURANTAYE

There can be little question that *Gaudium et Spes*[1] is a bold – some might say revolutionary – document. It marks a departure from the usual conciliar practice of addressing only Catholics in order to speak to "the whole of humanity," to whom "it longs to set forth the way it [the Second Vatican Council] understands the presence and function of the Church in the world of today"(GS #2).[2] In *Gaudium et Spes*, the Council Fathers consciously adopt a dialogic methodology, seeking to establish a kind of colloquium, a "speaking with" the world, in order to search mutually for solutions to the problems that press heavily upon contemporary man.[3] In this mutual search, the Church brings to bear her own particular contributions and hopes that with the contributions of others progress will be made. The contributions specific to the Church lie principally in the theological anthropology[4] – the vision of the human person – and the moral principles contained in Part One of the Pastoral Constitution and articulated so well for us by Dr. Latkovic in his presentation.

The fundamental presupposition of *Gaudium et Spes* is the unity of truth, that is, the unity of the natural and supernatural orders of knowledge, as this unity pertains to the human person. Hence, we read in the text of the constitution:

> The fact that it is the same God who is at once savior and creator, Lord of human history and of the history of salvation, does not mean that the autonomy of the creature, of man in particular, is suppressed; on the contrary, in the divine order of things all this redounds to the restoration and consolidation of this autonomy (GS #41).

> There is a truth about the human person that is accessible even to those without faith. *Gaudium et Spes* makes a fundamental assertion about man: by being faithful to himself in seeking the truth, he is in fact being faithful to God, Who is the Author of human nature and thus of man's inner drive and desire to pursue the

truth: "For God willed that man should 'be left in the hand of his
own counsel' (cf. Eccl 15:14) so that he might of his own accord
seek his creator and freely attain his full and blessed perfection by
cleaving to him" (GS #17).[5]

Thus, the Church's service to the world and to man involves the
proclamation of the essential truth about what it means to be a human
person created in the image of God, wounded by sin, but redeemed by
Christ Jesus, and destined for the loving vision of the Father, Son and
Holy Spirit in the life to come. Here, we can understand the character of
Gaudium et Spes as a "Pastoral" Constitution if we view it in light of
Pope John Paul II's words:

> Pastoral concern means the search for the true good of man, a
> promotion of the values engraved in his person by God. That is, it
> means observing that rule of understanding which is directed to the
> ever clearer discovery of God's plan for human love, in the certi-
> tude that the only true good of the human person consists in fulfill-
> ing this divine plan.[6]

Dr. Latkovic, in his presentation, has already indicated for us the
salient features of the anthropological and moral vision of *Gaudium et
Spes*. In summary, this vision is "a theological conception which
assumes the unity of the orders of creation and redemption in salvation
history."[7] Although *Gaudium et Spes* makes anthropology its starting
point, Christology remains the measure of all its statements about
anthropology and is the essential framework in which they are to be
understood. As the (justly) famous text of paragraph #22 puts it: "In reality it is only in the mystery of the Word made flesh that the mystery of
man truly becomes clear" (GS #22; see also GS ##10 and 45). In this
brief excerpt from paragraph #22, we discover the entire program of the
Pastoral Constitution. Hence, it is not surprising that, as Dr. Latkovic has
noted, the anthropology of *Gaudium et Spes* is not only a Christian, but
a Christocentric, anthropology. Thus, the Council Fathers address the
whole of humanity from a *theological* (not merely a philanthropic or fraternal) stance, convinced that the nature and destiny of humanity and of
the world can be definitively revealed only in the light of the crucified
and risen Christ.

The vision of the human person – his nature, destiny, activity, even
the fundamental questions that have always troubled the human heart (cf.
GS #10) – that is set forth in Part One of the document forms the foundation for all the considerations in the second part concerning the family, culture, economic and political order, war and peace, and international relations. Although tremendous changes have taken place in these

fields of human activity and endeavor over the past forty years – changes which, for the most part, no one could have foreseen in all their magnitude, rapidity, and complexity – nevertheless, the fundamental questions concerning the relationship of every human being to the collective work born of human inventiveness and industry remain essentially the same.[8] What concerned the Council Fathers forty years ago still concerns us today: the recognition of, and unconditional respect for, the dignity of the human person. *Gaudium et Spes* places this question at the center of its pastoral reflections.

Permit me to turn to Part Two of the Pastoral Constitution ("Some More Urgent Problems") in order to highlight, in a necessarily brief and panoramic way, how the Council's application of the anthropological and moral principles elaborated in Part One is reflected in the various spheres of social activity in which man is engaged.

With good reason, the Council begins its consideration of the "more urgent problems" of the day with a reflection upon marriage and the family. The family ("the primary vital cell of society"[9]) is threatened, as *Gaudium et Spes* has it, not only by "polygamy, the plague of divorce, so-called free love, and similar blemishes" (GS #47), but also by "an individualistic culture without solid ethical moorings, which misrepresents the very meaning of conjugal love and, challenging the co-natural need for stability, undermines the family unit's capacity for lasting communion and peace."[10] Since human dignity rests, according to *Gaudium et Spes*, on man's capacity (and thus his vocation) to enjoy communion with God (cf. GS #19), indissoluble marriage is one way (consecrated virginity being the other) of fulfilling the vocation to love. Therefore, the Council's charge to civil authorities that they should acknowledge and protect the true nature of marriage and the family (GS #52) aims at safeguarding the dignity of man and woman who, by their free and personal consent, enter into a permanent and faithful union, marked by mutual self-giving and ordered to the procreation and education of children.

How necessary it is to protect the dignity of marriage and family life as institutions, and the personal dignity of the spouses who form this unique partnership of the whole of life, has become ever more clear in the decades following the promulgation of the Pastoral Constitution. The past forty years have witnessed the worldwide commercialization of various forms of contraception, and the exaltation of sexual pleasure detached from the transmission of the gift of life. As a consequence, the very meaning of marriage and family life has been increasingly questioned, and divorce is now claimed as a right. Further attacks upon the dignity of marriage and family life include the widespread commercialization of pornography, the demand that homosexual acts be given the same legal protection as, and even the very name of, marriage, and the increasing recourse by couples to artificial forms of procreation. All of these moral ills affect not only the well-being of marriage and family life, but even the very health of society itself (cf. GS #47). Further, these ills are rooted in an anthropological dualism which separates the idea of human nature from that of human personhood: it is argued that a human individual can be biologically a member of the human species, but not be precisely a human person in the absence of a sense of personal autonomy, selfhood, consciousness, etc.

In its moral teaching on marriage and family, *Gaudium et Spes* places before us a unified, wholistic vision of the human person, a person who is capable of expressing his freedom by an act of self-giving, self-oblative, love on both the spiritual and bodily levels. *Gaudium et Spes* thus proclaims, as the anthropology developed in Part One of the document makes clear, that man who is made in God's image (GS #12; Gen 1:27), is made for communion, for relationships of mutual self-giving love founded on the truth.[11] Moreover, since from the beginning, God created man as male and female, their complementary partnership "constitutes the first form of communion between persons" (GS 12). Hence the Council teaches that fostering the dignity of marriage and the family is a duty incumbent upon all persons and institutions within society (GS #52).

Since man, by virtue of his being made in the image of God – that is, in the image pf the divine Trinitarian communion of Persons – is, for that very reason a social being (cf. GS ##24, 25), the same conception of human dignity and man's vocation to communion is evident in the Council's treatment of the cultural, economic, and political order.

Culture, *Gaudium et Spes* notes, is crucial in the development of the human person, for it is only through participating in a community that a person can come to a full and authentic humanity (cf. #GS 53). Social life is not external to the human person, but is an integral part of what it is to be human (GS #25). The many social relationships in which persons are involved give rise to duties and obligations and hence to actions of various types, and it is by means of these actions that human persons begin to develop their gifts, talents and capacities (cf. GS #32). The Council emphasizes culture as a perfection of man himself:

> [W]hen man works in the fields of philosophy, history, mathematics, and sciences and cultivates the arts, he can greatly contribute towards bringing the human race to a higher understanding of truth, goodness, and beauty, to points of view having universal

value...As a consequence, the human spirit, freed from the bondage of material things, can be more easily drawn to the worship and contemplation of the creator (GS #57).

Gaudium et Spes argues that the living conditions of modern life and the advances in the natural, human and social sciences have profoundly changed the way in which the human person is understood. Moreover, the document claims, various global forces are bringing about a greater uniformity of culture to the world – the idea of a "mass culture" which seemingly heralds a new age of human history (cf. GS #54).

While the Council recognizes some of the contradictions and dilemmas present in contemporary culture (GS #56), nevertheless its treatment remains quite positive and optimistic. However, in the wake of the Council, other documents of the Magisterium have adopted a different tone. In both *Evangelium Vitae*[12] and *Veritatis Splendor*[13] it is apparent that among the most serious problems of the modern world is a "culture of death" and a lack of concern for truth. While it may be the case that we have witnessed the birth of a new humanism, it is one with little, if any, sense of the sacred or any place for God.[14] In *Veritatis Splendor*, Pope John Paul II warned of modern currents of thought which discount the value of truth and so advocate moral relativism.[15] Reflection upon the state of contemporary culture forty years after the Council indicates a more sober assessment of the condition of the human person and of society than that expressed in the text of *Gaudium et Spes*. If the promise of *Gaudium et Spes* is to be fulfilled in regard to man's achievements in the cultural field, and if man is not to be a mere slave of the culture of the moment, then the Council's admonition that "culture must be subordinated to the integral development of the human person" (GS #59; cf. GS #26) will have to be a focal point in the new evangelization – the renewed and more intense appropriation of the Gospel – so ardently desired by the Church in the third millennium of Christianity.

Respect for the dignity of the person and the advancement of society, according to *Gaudium et Spes*, hinge on one another (GS #25). In economic and social life, therefore, the Pastoral Constitution argues that the dignity of the person and the welfare of society should be the source, center and end of all socio-economic activity (GS #63). Faced with the existence of two economic systems in the world at the time – the capitalist and the communist – *Gaudium et Spes* makes the point that too great a concentration on economic matters leads people to lose sight of the purpose of the economy, which is to serve human needs (cf. GS #63). The conciliar document reiterates the teaching contained in encyclicals both before and after it that economic activity is at the service of human beings, not the other way around.[16] For this reason, noting a growing contrast between economically advanced nations and those more disadvantaged, the Pastoral Constitution teaches that justice and equity require an end to excessive economic inequalities (GS ##63, 66); that society has a duty to see that citizens be able to find employment (GS #67); that wages should be just and provide a dignified livelihood for the worker and those who depend upon him or her for sustenance (GS #67). Likewise, man has the right to acquire and own property and material goods (GS #71), but this right is set within the Council's consideration of the common good, which is "based on the law of common destination of earthly goods" (GS #71).[17] The discussion of the common good, which frames much of the discussion of socio-economic problems which *Gaudium et Spes* addresses, yields several important themes.[18] There is, firstly, the idea that every person is entitled to the common good in which we all share and to which we all contribute in different ways. Secondly, there is the claim that we are all creatures made in the image of God and sharers, through Christ, in His divine life, responsible for one another. Third, the Pastoral Constitution argues that the sharing of our common goods should be directed towards helping others to develop themselves. Finally, the Council takes the view that it is consistent with human dignity that each person be encouraged to take responsibility for himself or herself. In these themes drawn from *Gaudium et Spes*, there can be seen a fundamental premise of the Church's social doctrine, namely, the primacy of ethics over economics (cf. GS #64). This premise is reflected throughout the Pastoral Constitution, as the point is made that technology, science, and efficiency are not, in themselves, adequate means to the realization of man's dignity; nor are they adequate means, in themselves, for addressing problems regarding the family, economics, politics, and questions of war and peace.[19]

"In its approach toward political life, *Gaudium et Spes* surveys modern public life in general terms, recalls the nature and purpose of the political community (cf. GS #74), and examines the necessity and conditions of the collaboration of all members of that community in its various tasks."[20] Participation in public life is regarded by the Council as both a right and a duty, and the Council Fathers note that the development of legal and political structures which give their citizens the chance to participate freely and actively – without any discrimination–in establishing the basis of the political community, governing the state, determining the scope and purpose of various institutions and electing leaders is in full accord with human dignity (GS #75). The Council therefore especially acknowledges those nations "whose systems permit the largest possible number of the citizens to take part in public life in a climate of genuine freedom" (GS #31). Such participation, *Gaudium et Spes* points out, permits citizens to "establish political life on a truly human basis...by encouraging an inward sense of justice, of good will, and of service to the common good, and by consolidating the basic convictions of men as to the true nature of the political community and the aim, proper exercise, and the limits of public authority" (GS #73).

The view of the world adopted by *Gaudium et Spes* builds on the autonomy of earthly realities. It is an autonomy that is "relative" or "right," that does not separate the created world from its Creator, yet nonetheless respects its inherent laws. When the Pastoral Constitution declares that "material being is endowed with its own stability, truth and excellence, its own order and laws [which] man must respect...because the things of the world and the things of faith derive from the same God" (GS #36), this is also valid for political life. Politics has to do with the construction of the common good, which is defined anthropocentrically as the sum total of societal conditions that serve the personal development of man (cf. GS ##26, 74). To attain the common good requires political authority, that is, power capable of asserting itself in a rightly ordered manner. It does not constitute "dirty business" to acquire and make use of such power, but when exercised properly it is rather a service to the citizen and indeed a distinct form of love of neighbor.[21]

This love of neighbor is concretized in the text of the Pastoral Constitution, which lays out a complex interrelationship of corresponding rights and duties governing the mutual interaction of leaders and citizens. Of particular significance is the document's recalling of the principle of subsidiarity, which incorporates both limiting as well as empowering dimensions. This principle rests on the anthropological premise that the successful shaping of human life is primarily dependent on the readiness and capacity of individuals to take initiatives, bear risks and deliver performances. Government must not curtail what citizens, families and smaller groups within society can attain on their own, but must extend its protective and supportive capacities when these groups are overwhelmed in order to restore them to their (rightful) autonomous activity. Once more, we can discern in the text of *Gaudium et Spes* "the basic need to promote a politics of life inspired by inalienable moral values in nations and between nations."[22] In so doing, the dignity of persons is enhanced and fostered.

The last important problem of the Church in the modern world, and perhaps the widest sphere of Christian responsibility, is dealt with in Part Two, Chapter Five of *Gaudium et Spes*, which is entitled, "Fostering of Peace and Establishment of a Community of Nations." The urgent need to address these issues lies in the Council's statement that "the whole human race faces a moment of supreme crisis in its advance toward maturity" and that mankind "will not succeed in accomplishing the task awaiting it, that is, the establishment of a truly human world for all men over the entire earth, unless everyone devotes himself to the cause of true peace with renewed vigor" (GS #77). After explaining the nature of peace in the light of the natural law and the truth of the Gospel (GS #78), the document analyzes in detail the moral problem of present-day warfare. This analysis is one of subtle balance. *Gaudium et Spes* affirms the right and duty of a nation to defend itself lawfully (cf. GS #79), but it also condemns the unjust and indiscriminate use of force (GS ##80–82). The document seeks to strike a balance between national and international points of view, between force and non-violence, and between principle and practical application.

Gaudium et Spes states that peace cannot be reduced merely to a balance of power. Peace is the fruit of both justice and love (GS #78). Hence, the Council calls for greater international cooperation, including the "establishment of a universally acknowledged public authority vested with the effective power to ensure security for all, regard for justice, and respect for law" (GS #82). If, in practice, this call has not been effectively realized to date, nonetheless it serves "as an upward pull on the thoughts and actions of the citizens of each nation."[23] This "upward pull" which serves to qualify the right and duty of a nation to self-defense is itself qualified by a sober realism. In its recognition that the work of peace extends beyond the order of justice and requires charity and love of neighbor (GS #78; cf. GS #83), the Council points to the root causes for violence and war: injustices on the economic and political levels, and at a deeper level, "envy, distrust, pride, and other selfish passions" (GS #83). Thus, the real problem identified by *Gaudium et Spes* is human sinfulness, and the solution is divine redemption. Therefore, the Pastoral Constitutions rightly states: "Insofar as men are sinners, the threat of war hangs over them and will so continue until the coming of Christ; but insofar as they can vanquish sin by coming together in charity, violence itself will be vanquished" (GS #78). In the view of the Council Fathers, the goal of true peace will be accomplished only in proportion to an advance of love.

Such an advance of love lies at the heart of the moral vision proposed by *Gaudium et Spes*. Throughout the text of the Pastoral Constitution, we see the continual assertion that all human activity has as its purpose the serving of human beings so that they may be fulfilled and that in this manner they may become more fully children of God. The successful outcome of human life is not dependent upon the right arrangement of social structures. Rather, the successful outcome of human life depends upon each person freely choosing to act in accord with the truth about God, the world and one's self. This will require (among other things) a life of virtue, the proper use of our freedom, the correct formation of our conscience, and the continual striving for holiness as the consummation of our personal vocation in Christ.

In its specific teachings regarding marriage and family, culture, economics, political life, and war and peace, *Gaudium et Spes* seeks (to adopt a phrase of Pope John Paul II) to protect and to serve the full good of the person by protecting and serving the various goods which characterize his identity as a spiritual and bodily being in relationship with God, with his neighbor, and with the material world.[24] The moral vision of *Gaudium et Spes* thus directs us to protect and enable to flourish all those goods that constitute the fulfillment of the human person in all the many activities and fields of endeavor that make up human life in the world. This task, proposed by the Council Fathers, is set within a Christocentric pattern of each person's life,[25] orienting us to a respect for the innate dignity of every person – a dignity we possess here and now, but which is still to be perfected in the life to come. As *Gaudium et Spes* notes,

> It is the Father's will that we should recognize Christ our brother in the persons of all men and love them with an effective love, in word and in deed, thus bearing witness to the truth; and it is his will that we should share with others the mystery of his heavenly love. In this way men all over the world will awaken to a lively hope (the gift of the Holy Spirit) that they will one day be admitted to the haven of surpassing peace and happiness in their homeland radiant with the glory of the Lord (GS 93).

Father Paul F. deLadurantaye holds the S.T.D. degree from the John Paul II Institute for Studies on Marriage and Family. Currently he serves as the Diocesan Secretary for Religious Education and the Sacred Liturgy in the diocese of Arlington, Virginia. He is also an Assistant Professor of Theology at the Notre Dame Graduate School of Christendom College, and an Adjunct Professor at Marymount University in Arlington. He is also pastor of the Queen of Apostles Church in Alexandria, Virginia.

ENDNOTES

1   *Gaudium et Spes* was promulgated on December 7, 1965. Its full title is rendered in English translation as the "Pastoral Constitution on the Church in the Modern World." The text is divided into two principal parts. In Part I

(##11–45), the Council develops its teaching on man, the world he inhabits and the Church's relationship to him. In Part II (## 46–93), the Council treats of various aspects of human society and turns its attention to some "more urgent" problems, chiefly marriage and family, culture, politics, economics, and questions of war, peace, and the international community. The relationship between these two parts may be considered as the application of principles (Part I) to specific concerns (Part II). This relationship may also be seen in a more complex sense as the justification, from the starting point of human reality, of the obligation that binds man to direct his path to the divine end that Jesus Christ reveals and promises through the mediation of the Church (Part I) and the justification, from the starting point of faith, of the interest that the Christian nonetheless attaches to the contingent realities of this world. For an elaboration of this point, see Henri de Lubac, S.J., "The Total Meaning of Man and of the World: Two Interrelated Problems," *Communio* Vol. 27, no. 4 (Winter 1990), 613–616.

2   References to *Gaudium et Spes* are taken from Austin Flannery, O.P., *Vatican Council II: The Conciliar and Post Conciliar Documents* (Northport, New York: Costello Publishing Company, 1975).

3   See *Gaudium et Spes* #3: "And so the Council…can find no more eloquent expression of its solidarity and respectful affection for the whole human family, to which it belongs, than to enter into dialogue with it about all these different problems." In regard to the term "world," Joseph Ratzinger notes an ambiguity present within the text of *Gaudium et Spes*. He observes: "By 'world' the Council means the counterpart of the Church. The purpose of the text is to bring the two into a relationship of cooperation…The Church cooperates with the world in order to build up the world…It is not clear, however, whether the world that cooperates and the world that is to be built up are one and the same world; it is not clear what meaning is intended by the word 'world' in every instance…By 'world,' it would seem, the document understands the whole scientific and technical reality of the present and all those who are responsible for it or who are at home in its mentality." See Joseph Cardinal Ratzinger, *Principles of Catholic Theology: Building Stones for a Fundamental Theology*, trans. by Sister Mary Frances McCarthy, S.N.D. (San Francisco: Ignatius Press, 1987), pp. 379–380.

4   In this regard, Walter Kasper, in his article, "The Theological Anthropology of *Gaudium et Spes*" (*Communio* Vol. 23, no. 1 [Spring 1996], 129–140), states, "*Gaudium et Spes* signals the first time that a council has consciously endeavored to set forth a systematic account of Christian anthropology in an independent thematic context…Prior to Vatican II no council had produced a 'general outline' of Christian anthropology. The Pastoral Constitution was the first attempt to do so" (p. 129).

5   See also the Declaration on Religious Liberty," *Dignitatis Humanae*, #2, in
  —   Flannery, p. 801: "It is in accordance with their dignity that all men, because they are persons, that is, beings endowed with reason and free will, and therefore bearing personal responsibility, are both impelled by their

nature and bound by a moral obligation to seek the truth, especially religious truth. They are also bound to adhere to the truth once they come to know it and direct their whole lives in accordance with the demands of truth." The same interior ordination to truth (and therefore to God) is repeated in *Dignitatis Humanae* #3 (Flannery, p. 801): "He is bound to follow this conscience faithfully in all his activity so that he may come to God, who is his last end."

6   Pope John Paul II, General Audience of July 25, 1984 in *The Theology of the Body: Human Love in the Divine Plan* (Boston: Pauline Books and Media, 1997), p. 392.

7   Walter Kasper, "The Theological Anthropology of *Gaudium et Spes*," p. 137.

8   Pedro Morandé, "The Relevance of the Message of *Gaudium et Spes* Today: The Church's Mission in the Midst of Epochal Changes and New Challenges," *Communio* Vol. 23, no. 1 (Spring 1996), p. 142.

9   Second Vatican Council, Decree on the Apostolate of Lay People, *Apostolicam Actuositatem* #11, in Flannery, p. 779.

10   Pope John Paul II, "Only Christ Can Fulfill Man's Hopes," *Communio* Vol. 23, no. 1 (Spring 1996), p. 125. This article was presented on November 8, 1995 in the Synod Hall of the Vatican to open a Congress celebrating the thirtieth anniversary of the Pastoral Constitution *Gaudium et Spes*. It originally appeared in the English edition of *L'Osservatore Romano* (November 15, 1995).

11   It is on this basis that the Council calls attention to the question of the means of the responsible transmission of human life and teaches that the moral evaluation of any such means must be based on objective criteria "drawn from the nature of the human person and human action, criteria which respect the total meaning of mutual self-giving and human procreation in the context of true love" (GS #51). It is on this point that differences, not only on matters of sexual ethics but also concerning Christian anthropology, between those moral theologians broadly termed "revisionists," and those who seek to defend the Church's teaching with regard to contraception become clear. For one illustration of such differences, see my article "'Irreconcilable Concepts of the Human Person' and the Moral Issue of Contraception: An Examination of the Personalism of Louis Janssens and the Personalism of Pope John Paul II," *Anthropotes* 13/2 (1997), 433–455.

12   Pope John Paul II, *Evangelium Vitae* (Vatican City State: Libreria Editrice Vaticana, 1995).

13   Pope John Paul II, *Veritatis Splendor* (Vatican City State: Libreria Editrice Vaticana, 1993).

14   On this point, see, for example, *Evangelium Vitae* #4: "…a new cultural climate is developing and taking hold, which gives crimes against life a new and – if possible – even more sinister character, giving rise to further grave concern: broad sectors of public opinion justify certain crimes against life

in the name of the rights of individual freedom, and on this basis they claim not only exemption from punishment but even authorization by the state, so that these things can be done with total freedom and indeed with the free assistance of health-care systems."

15   See *Veritatis Splendor* #4: "At the root of these presuppositions [anthropological and ethical] is the more or less obvious influence of currents of thought which end by detaching human freedom from its essential and constitutive relationship to truth."

16   See, for example, Pope Leo XIII, *Rerum Novarum* #48; Pope Pius XI, *Quadregesimo Anno* ##43 and 83 and Pope John Paul II, *Laborem Exercens* ##14, 15, in Michael Walsh and Brian Davies, eds., *Proclaiming Justice and Peace: Papal Documents from Rerum Novarum to Centesimus Annus* (Mystic, Connecticut: Twenty-third Publications, 1991).

17   On this point, see also Pope John XXIII, *Mater et Magistra* #119 in Michael Walsh and Brian Davies, eds., *Proclaiming Justice and Peace: Papal Documents from Rerum Novarum to Centesimus Annus* (Mystic, Connecticut: Twenty-third Publications, 1991).

18   For the themes that follow, I am indebted to John Ozolins, "Recurring Themes: Social Justice and *Gaudium et Spes*," *Australian Journal of Theology*, accessible at http://dlibrary.acu.edu/research/theology/ejournal/aet_1/Ozolins.htm.

19   See Douglas Bushman, "The Christ-centered Anthropology of *Gaudium et Spes* in Light of Developments in Pope John Paul II," accessible at http://www.catholic.net/rcc/Periodicals/Dossier/2000-08/article2.html.

20   Karol Wojtyla, *Sources of Renewal*, trans. by P. F. Falla (San Francisco: Harper and Row Publishers, 1980), p. 304.

21   Pope John Paul II, *Christifideles Laici* 42, 59 in J. Michael Miller, C.S.B., ed., *The Post-Synodal Apostolic Exhortations of John Paul II* (Huntington, Indiana: Our Sunday Visitor Publishing Division, 1998), pp. 423–426 and 451–452.

22   Pope John Paul II, "Only Christ Can Fulfill Man's Hopes," p. 126.

23   John P. Hittinger, "Cooperation with Evil in the Military Profession," in Kenneth D. Whitehead, ed., *The Catholic Citizen: Debating the Issues of Justice* (South Bend, Indiana: St. Augustine's Press, 2004), p. 173.

24   Pope John Paul II, *Veritatis Splendor* #13.

25   On this point, see *Gaudium et Spes* #22: "In reality it is only in the mystery of the Word made flesh that the mystery of man truly become clear…Christ, the new Adam, in the very revelation of the mystery of the Father and of his love, fully reveals man to himself and brings to light his most high calling."

The Christian Anthropology of Vatical II and Virtual Reality

SISTER M. TIMOTHY PROKES, F.S.E.

"May you live in interesting times." Whatever its derivation and intent, this saying applies to our times and to the events that clutch at the sleeves of our interest. It is a time of immense contrasts. In St. Peter's Square, a hundred thousand waited for a wisp of smoke over the Sistine, yet in many hands were cell phones, readied for immediate transmission of the ancient sign. In Wales, calligrapher Donald Johnson has guided an international team through the seven-year task of preparing *The St. John's Bible* – the first handwritten, illuminated Bible since the invention of the printing press. Meanwhile, nearby, children fret over the slow boot-up time of their computers. Feather quill and calfskin; computer mouse and fiberglass: a contrast of our times. More recently: it has been Hurricane water walls and slow death at the Superdome. Our times leap, detonate without warning, or seem too sluggish.

Jesus said: "In the evening you say 'It will be fine; there is a red sky,' and in the morning, 'Stormy weather today; the sky is red and overcast.' You know how to read the face of the sky, but you cannot read the signs of the times."'(Mt 16:2–3). *Gaudium et Spes* underscores these words of Christ: "At all times the Church carries the responsibility of reading the signs of the time and of interpreting them in the light of the Gospel, if it is to carry out its task."[1] What are the predominant signs of *our* time? Contrasts abound.

Forty years used to seem a "long time." As we commemorate the fortieth anniversary of the Second Vatican Council, we are aware that no other forty-year span of history has seen comparable changes in understanding what it means to be a human person – or to have a common cultural concern for the origin, nature, and destiny of humanity. This reflection juxtaposes two seemingly disparate things that sign our moment of time: the anthropology of Vatican II, and daily experience of all that is condensed in the term "virtual reality." It is my conviction that the interface between them constitutes one of the most challenging tasks of the Church in our time.

Twelve years ago, in his book *The Metaphysics of Virtual Reality*, Michael Heim asked:

> Will human nature itself change? Will we soon pass some point where we are so altered by our imaginations and inventions as to be unrecognizable to Shakespeare or the writers of the ancient Greek plays?
>
> No one knows, but many are trying to imagine such a world. They describe our children and grandchildren as no longer being like us. They call them trans-human or post-human.[2]

In laboratories, medical facilities, legislative and judicial chambers, and university lecture rooms, the meaning of "human" is hemorrhaging. Every serious discipline must grapple with the meaning of human life. The perspective here, however, is theological: faith seeking understanding – and, increasingly, faith seeking embodiment. In juxtaposing the anthropology of Vatican II and virtual reality, it is necessary to bracket manageable areas for reflection.

Virtual Reality

There is no univocal definition of virtual reality, but there are helpful descriptions. Marie-Laure Ryan traces root meanings of "virtual." In scholastic philosophy, she says, *actual* and *virtual* "exist in a dialectical relation rather than in one of radical opposition: the virtual is not that which is deprived of existence but that which possesses the potential, or force, of developing into actual existence."[3] "Nowadays," however, she writes, "we label virtual everything we experience or meet in 'cyberspace,' the imaginary place where computers take us when we log on to the Internet: virtual friends, virtual sex, virtual universities, virtual tours of virtual cities."[4] Ken Pimentel and Kevin Teixeira write that virtual reality is "interactive, immersive experience generated by a computer."[5]

Michael Heim's description is particularly helpful. "Virtual reality," he says, describes something that "*is real in effect but not in fact.*" These somewhat diverse descriptions loosely encompass the complexity of virtual reality. In 1993, Heim designated seven levels of virtual reality; these designations remain helpful:

> 1. *Simulation*, the first level, is the seeming degree of realism evoked by sharp audio and visual images. Examples include: computer graphics and images; and simulators used in flight training.
>
> 2. *Interaction*, the second level, describes any electronic representation with which we can interact; pharmaceutical companies and airlines, for example, respond to queries via computerized programs.

3. *Artificiality*, the third level, indicates imitation or some resemblance to what is real.

4. *Immersion*, a fourth level, requires specific hardware and software combinations (which are increasingly sophisticated and complex).

5. *Telepresence*, a fifth level, refers to *robotic presence*. This means to be somewhere, but to be there remotely (surgeons operating at a distance, for example).

6. *Full-Body Immersion,* sixth, utilizes equipment that projects a user's body in a manner that enables it to interact with graphic images and objects on a screen (attained without head-mounted or glove equipment).

7. *Networked Communication*, lastly, does not mean the Internet, but a new communications medium. Heim terms this "Post-Symbolic Communication," which is beyond verbal and even body language (somewhat alchemical and magical, he says). An example is RB2 (Reality Built for Two), which connects two virtual worlds[6]

To cite critical issues raised by this virtual reality is not to condemn it. Many aspects of the virtual enhance daily life, offer instant communication, and expedite routine tasks. If the electronic "net" is disconnected or virus-infected, normal activities can stop abruptly. From a faith perspective, it is not a question of reverting to an earlier technological era, but of "reading the signs of the times" with shrewd wisdom and love, and of discerning what promotes or destroys the human. My emphasis here is on theological issues evoked by virtual reality.

The Second Vatican Council

This conference opened with a focus on the moral vision and anthropology of *Gaudium et Spes*. How crucial these are for understanding *why* "the virtual" impacts on faith and its understanding? One can bracket five anthropological themes affirmed in the various Constitutions issued by the Council; these themes identify the human person as:

1. Centered in the Person of Jesus Christ.
2. Created in the image of God.
3. Privileged to be a unity of body and soul.
4. Called to holiness in terms of self-gift.
5. Destined for eternal Communion of Persons.

Article #22 of *Gaudium et Spes*, enunciates the *meaning* of humanity in Christ, "The New Man." This article reads as follows:

In reality it is only in the mystery of the Word made flesh that the mystery of man truly becomes clear...Christ the Lord, Christ the new Adam, in the very revelation of the mystery of the Father and of his love, fully reveals man to himself and brings to light his most high calling... Human nature, by the very fact that it was assumed, not absorbed, in him, has been raised in us also to a dignity beyond compare. For, by his incarnation, he, the son of God, has in a certain way united himself with each man. (GS #22).

Yet, the Constitution says, contemporary man often "either sets himself up as the absolute measure of all things, or debases himself to the point of despair."(GS #12). Scripture reveals that *creation in the image and likeness of God is the foundation of humanity's immense dignity.* The document cites the Psalm:

What is man that thou art mindful of him, and the son of man that thou dost care for him? Yet thou hast made him little less than God, and dost crown him with glory and honor. Thou hast given him dominion over the works of thy hands; thou hast put all things under his feet. (Ps 8:5–8).

Christ revealed that God, in whose image and likeness we are created, is a *communion of persons*. Each conciliar Constitution savors this from different perspectives. *Dei Verbum* quotes the First Letter of John: "We proclaim to you the eternal life which was with the Father and was made manifest to us – that which we have seen and heard we proclaim to you, so that you may have fellowship with us; and our fellowship is with the Father and with his Son Jesus Christ" (I Jn 1:3). *Dei Verbum* expands on this theme:

It pleased God, in his goodness and wisdom, to reveal himself and to make known the mystery of his will (cf. Eph 1:9). His will was that men should have access to the Father, through Christ, the Word made flesh, in the Holy Spirit, and thus become sharers in the divine nature...from this revelation, then, the invisible God...from the fullness of his love...addresses men as his friends...and moves among them."(DV #2).

Created *for* this intimacy, human persons, body and soul, hold a privileged position in regard to the rest of earthly creation. *Gaudium et Spes* affirms:

Man, though made of body and soul, is a unity. Through his very bodily condition he sums up in himself the elements of the material world. Through him they are thus brought to their highest perfection and can raise their voice in praise freely given to the creator. For this reason man may not despise his bodily life. Rather he is obliged to regard his body as good and to hold it in honor since

God has created it and will raise it up on the last day. Nevertheless, man has been wounded by sin. (GS #14).

Christic, Trinitarian, and corporeal-spiritual: from these flow a fourth anthropological characteristic: the universal vocation to holiness, enunciated in Chapter Five of *Lumen Gentium*. Jesus peached holiness of life "to each and every one of his disciples without distinction."(LG #40) "It is therefore quite clear," say the Council Fathers, "that all Christians in any state or walk of life are called to the fullness of Christian life and to the perfection of love, and by this holiness a more human life is fostered also in earthly society."(LG #40).

What does human *perfection* ultimately mean? In Christ, the Father and the Holy Spirit, it is *realized authentic self-gift*. In the Eucharist, Christ's self-gift in Body and Blood is offered as food and drink: the most radical expression of perfect love. *Gaudium et Spes* applies this self-gift to marriage:

> The intimate union of marriage, as a mutual self-giving of two persons, and the good of the children, demand total fidelity from the spouses and require an unbreakable unity between them...Just as of old God encountered his people with a covenant of love and fidelity, so our Savior, the spouse of the Church, now encounters Christian spouses through the sacrament of marriage. He abides with them in order that by their mutual self-giving spouses will love each other with enduring fidelity(GS #48).

From the beginning, the partnership of man and woman constitutes the first form of communion between persons, says *Gaudium et Spes*, "for by his inmost nature man is a social being."(GS #12). "There is a certain parallel between the union existing among the divine persons and the union of the sons of God in truth and love"(#24). From this it follows that "if man is the only creature on earth that God has wanted for his own sake, man can fully discover his true self only in a sincere giving of himself"(#24). Such self-gift requires a truthful, real presence. The Council Fathers were not being naive. Only in the risk of freedom can there be the possibility of perfect love, even though freedom has been a gift abused from "the very start of human history." There was a lifting up against God, a seeking to attain the goal of humanity apart from God. Article #13 says this very succinctly:

> Man therefore is divided in himself. As a result, the whole life of men, both individual and social, shows itself to be a struggle, and a dramatic one, between good and evil, between light and darkness. Man finds that he is unable of himself to overcome the assaults of evil successfully (GS #13).

A fifth characteristic of conciliar anthropology shows that human meaning does not terminate in this struggle: persons have an eternal destiny that endures beyond the assaults of evil. It is a destiny revealed and reopened to possibility through the self-gift of the Second Adam, Christ. While death is a reality, the seed of eternity in the human being means he cannot be reduced to mere matter. "All the aids made available by technology, however useful they may be, cannot set his anguished mind at rest. They may prolong his life-span; but this does not satisfy his heartfelt longing, one that cannot be stifled, for a life to come"(GS #18).

Sacrosanctum Concilium called for a renewed liturgical life that worthily celebrates Jesus Christ's enduring, effective self-gift and presence. On the very night of betrayal, Christ instituted the Eucharist, the sacrifice of his Body and Blood:

> This he did in order to perpetuate the sacrifice of the Cross throughout the ages until he should come again, and so to entrust to his beloved Spouse, the Church,a memorial of his death and resurrection: a sacrament of love, a sign of unity, a bond of charity, a paschal banquet in which Christ is consumed, the mind is filled with grace, and a pledge of future glory is given to us (SC #47).

There is a co-inherence among all these anthropological emphases. The Council not only claimed immense dignity for humanity, but explicated its *meaning*, no matter how disfigured through sin, hubris, or deception humanity may be. Through conscience, says *Gaudium et Spes*, man discovers a "law which he has not laid upon himself but which he must obey...Its voice, ever calling him to love...tells him inwardly: do this, shun that. For man has in his heart a law inscribed by God"(GS #16). Individualistic morality must be transcended, *Gaudium et Spes* cautions:

> The pace of change is so far reaching and rapid nowadays that no one can allow himself to close his eyes to the course of events or indifferently ignore them and wallow in the luxury of a merely individualistic morality. (*GS* #30).

At the Interface

There are five characteristics of virtual reality that contrast, but frequently interface in real life with a conciliar anthropology. They are: 1) the perception of body as an informational pattern, disposable, even irrelevant; 2) the technical creation of virtual persons, and worlds; 3) the simulation of food, sex, relationship; 4) the substitution of absence for real presence – destructive of self-gift; and 5) the blurring of boundaries between the natural and the supernatural (often outright denial of the supernatural). In highlighting these, I will give examples, so that discussion of the interface between theology and virtual reality does not remain an abstraction. It is common today to have our own time labeled "post-human." I would like to share an extended quotation from N. Katherine Hayles' book *How We Became Posthuman.* Hayles asks:

> What is the posthuman? Think of it as a point of view charac-
> terized by the following assumptions. I do not mean this list to be
> exclusive or definitive. Rather it names elements from a variety of
> sites. It is meant to be suggestive rather than prescriptive. First, the
> posthuman view privileges informational pattern over material
> instantiation, so that embodiment in a biological substrate is seen
> as an accident of history rather than the inevitability of life.
> Second, the posthuman view considers consciousness [emphasis
> mine] regarded as the seat of human identity in the Western tradi-
> tion long before Descartes thought he was mind thinking, as an
> epiphenomenon, as an evolutionary upstart, trying to claim it is the
> whole show when in actuality it is only a sideline. Third, the
> posthuman view thinks of the body as the original prostheses we all
> learn to manipulate, so that extending or replacing the body with
> other prostheses becomes a continuation of a process that began
> before we were born. Fourth, and most important, by these and
> other means, the posthuman view configures human being so that
> it can be seamlessly articulated with intelligent machines. In the
> posthuman, there are no essential differences or absolute demarca-
> tions between bodily existence and computer simulation, cybernet-
> ic mechanism and biological organism, robot technology and
> human goals.[7]

Deconstruction of the human person has been occurring since the Enlightenment, says Hayles. It has progressed in ways that lead to under-standing a human being as a *set of informational processes.* Then, if "information has lost its body" (something that Marshal McLuhan real-ized decades ago), embodiment itself is no longer seen as essential to human being. There has been a systematic downplaying, even erasing of embodiment in cybernetic construction of the posthuman. Hayles quotes William Gibson's book *Neuromancer*, where the narrator characterizes the posthuman body as "data made flesh."[8] It is not difficult, says Hayles, to see why the producers of *Star Trek* could imagine that the body could be dematerialized into an informational pattern and then rematerialized unchanged at a remote location: "Beam me up, Scotty."

The incarnational and sacramental implications of such disembodi-ment are obvious. If the human being is perceived basically as an infor-mational pattern, able to be materialized in various substrata, all that *Gaudium et Spes* #22 affirms about the centrality of the incarnate Christ for understanding the human person becomes irrelevant. John's awe that

"The Word became Flesh" can seem obsolete. Sacraments, which require specific matter and form for living, embodied persons may then be considered mere changeable, social rituals – if not as actually irrelevant.

Similarly, if the human body is only an informational pattern, why should there be concern if embryonic bodies are screened for their suitability in responding to the wants of prospective parents or researchers? Last summer, an advertisement in an airline magazine read "Donor Egg: Immediate Availability." The ad copy touted the merits of the "Genetics and IVF Institute" based in suburban Washington, D.C., saying it had long met the expectations of "sophisticated patients and medical specialists." The Institute promised availability of approximately 100 fully prescreened donors for matching patients, "including Doctoral Donors in advanced degree programs" as well as numerous donors with "special accomplishments, talents, or ethnicity." Those interested were invited to call the "Donor Egg Coordinator." The final line of the ad read "Life begins at the Genetics and IVF Institute."

Basically, virtual reality is not simply an aggregate of computers, electronic gear, competent programmers, and participants. *In the larger sense, virtual reality is a developing WORLDVIEW that encompasses the meaning of humanity, matter, the universe, and God. This worldview is permeating contemporary society.* Theological concern about it must respond at a depth worthy of the issues at stake, at a depth worthy of our colleagues and students. I recall a number of years ago seeing an agile Pope John Paul II disembark from a plane and kneeling to kiss the Canadian soil. Jeanne Sauvé, Governor General of Canada, in her brief but cogent welcoming words said to him: You will say some difficult things to us. Say them, and, like Jacob, we will wrestle with them after you have gone.

Our own wrestling with matters concerning the virtual and the human, needs to involve youth. As we realize, the hour is late for the present generation. Under the headline "'Sexual Chaos' at College," *The Washington Times* for August 9, 2005, reported that the Medical Institute for Sexual Health, in Austin, Texas, had claimed: "Almost 80 percent of college students, ages 18 to 24, have had sexual intercourse." When the body is viewed as a data instrument, an interchangeable possession, random sexual pleasure is of no importance.

Made, Not Begotten

A second characteristic of virtual reality is the technical creation of virtual persons, environments, and worlds. During the course of preparing this paper, I entered the phrase "virtual people" in Yahoo's search component. In an instant, 8,980,000 options were available. The first of the initial 10 listed was called "CVSSP: 3D-Vision Virtual People: Capturing realistic models of individual people to populate virtual worlds."

While some may pursue such activity as entertainment, there is an underlying quality of neo-gnosticism and docetism, of escape from reality. For example, *Second Life* is a current website describing itself as "an on-line digital world, built, shaped, and owned by its participants." There is an invitation to explore a changing and expanding world on over 100 servers, and participants are encouraged to buy and sell land, create a business, "exchange virtual for real currency...Fly through an ever-evolving 3D landscape and encounter wonderful places and things...all created by residents like you." Users are invited to "create your look from scratch," "change your appearance to look like anything...or change your surroundings." There is "infinite avatar customization." A website has flashing slogans. Among them: "Virtual worlds are the home of the future"; and: "For many the physical world is a prison – with the virtual we hand you the keys to that cell."

An extensive new vocabulary attends the development of virtual reality and some ordinary words take on extended meanings in virtual transactions. For example, the VWN Virtual Dictionary describes the meaning of "haptic" (literally, the sense of touch) in this way:

> It is the ability to feel something when it brushes up against you. Haptic is most frequently referred to as touch via the hands. This is because data gloves have captured the public imagination. While such gloves do exist, haptics can be applied to any part of the body, from gloves to bodysuits, vests and armbands.
>
> Haptics has been combined with the porn industry, to form the field of teledildonics, in which sex is enacted through a PC with devices at either end able to provide stimulation to the private areas of each party.[9]

I have contended that virtual reality expresses a worldview, and it involves the meaning of *truth*. Anthony Rizzi writes: "The purpose of the mind is to know reality, to conform to reality, and to find and hold onto truth."[10] In *Fides et Ratio*, Pope John Paul II noted "the more human beings know reality and the world, the more they know themselves in their uniqueness..." (#1).

Food

A changing understanding of the body relates to a changing understanding of food and eating. Changes in the production and consumption of human food in Western nations is significant. Already in the late 1960s, philosopher Alan Watts wrote of wheat that "is grown, unloved, by industrial farming over millions of featureless and treeless acres...sprayed by airplane with Flit and Bugdeath...shaved from the earth with immense mechanical clippers," ground, washed with detergents, and finally shipped out as "sleazy cushions."[11] More recently, many seeds for the production of food already contain insecticides and pesticides before they are sown in the earth. Many foods no longer are what they purport to be.

Why should that be of theological concern? Consider how the meaning of food pervades revelation and its transmission. The initial test of human love and creaturehood is described in terms of eating – that which nourishes, or that which brings death. When the time neared for making a covenant with a people, three mysterious visitors came to Abraham and Sarah and a meal was prepared to receive them. Notice the importance of food in other events of salvation history: the providential rescue from famine through Joseph in Egypt; the Exodus meal; the provision of manna, quail and water in the desert; and the promise of a land flowing with milk and honey. All of this was pointing to the Wedding Feast at Cana, the feeding of multitudes from a few loaves and fishes, and the revelatory "Bread of Life" discourse, foretaste of the Paschal Supper in which Christ instituted a Presence among us that will endure to the end of time: his own true Body and Blood given as Real Food and Drink.

Alterations of food and drink, and our manner of consuming them, are crucial signs of our times, often exemplifying one description of the virtual as "something that purports to be what it is not." Imitations are frequently praised as preferable to what is authentic, while real foods are sometimes labeled "dangerous, seductive," even "*sinfully* delicious." Store shelves are filled with products which are declared to look and taste real, which give the same pleasure as the real, but which do not contain unwanted aspects of the real. One ad has offered "no-fat-fat" and another recently promoted a product that would give the same pleasure as its real counterpart, but was designed to pass through the body without providing any nourishment – a form of "contraception eating"!

How deal with eating disorders and obesity in a society pressed to immediate gratification and its *virtual* assuaging? This is not a minor issue since it pertains to current challenges of faith regarding the reality of the Eucharist. Jesus assured that his Body is real food and his Blood real drink. In a culture so confused regarding the meaning and content of food, this is a vital concern. It impacts deeply on the reality of the

Eucharist, and the truth of the human body, as well as on daily food, and the care of the sick and needy.

Robotics, another area of the virtual, relates to the body and is becoming a burgeoning industry. Sherry Turkle of MIT has devoted over twenty years to observing how people interact with computers and other high tech products. The *Harvard Business Review* for September, 2003, published a "Conversation" with Turkle on "Technology and Human Vulnerability." She spoke of a "transformation" brought about through the computer. Along with its positive contributions of simulation and visualization, she said, the computer has the power "to change our habits of thought." Computer software changes how CEOs think about business, architects about buildings, surgeons about bodies.[12] From her studies on the effects of robots, Turkle said: "We are ill prepared for the new psychological world we are creating. We make objects that are emotionally powerful; at the same time, we say things such as 'technology is just a tool' that deny the power of our creation both on us as individuals and on our culture." In discussing robots that serve as companions to children and the elderly, Turkle said: "We create robots in our own image, we connect with them easily, and then we become vulnerable to the emotional power of that connection."[13] Turkle was questioned about moral responsibility for machines if we relate to them. She said that she knew a woman whose comments about AIBO, Sony's robot dog, were especially striking:

> [AIBO] is better than a real dog. It won't do dangerous things, and it won't betray you...Also, it won't die suddenly and make you feel very sad." The possibilities of engaging emotionally with creatures that will not die, whose loss we will never need to face, presents dramatic questions. The sight of children and the elderly exchanging tenderness with roboticpets brings philosophy down to earth. *In the end, the question is not whether children will come to love the toy robots more than their parents, but what will loving itself come to mean?* (Italics mine)[14]

Authentic Self-Gift

All this leads to a fourth concern regarding the virtual: indifference to real presence or absence and its effect on self-gift. The Christic and Trinitarian foundations of anthropology found in the Vatican II documents points to the fullness of human perfection as *self-gift.* Recall how *Gaudium et Spes,* in explicating the Communitarian nature of man's vocation, appeals to the prayer of Jesus at the Last Supper:

> ... the Lord Jesus, when praying to the Father "that they may all be one...even as we are one" (Jn 17:21–22), has opened up new

horizons closed to human reason by implying that there is a certain parallel between the union existing among the divine persons and the union of the sons of God in truth and love. It follows, then, that if man is the only creature on earth that God has wanted for its own sake, man can fully discover his true self only in a sincere giving of himself (GS #24).

That prayer is echoed from the heart of the Church in the Eucharistic canon: "May He [the Holy Spirit] make us an everlasting gift to you." In my earlier book on *Mutuality: The Human Image of Trinitarian Love*, I suggest that the first category of being is divine self-gift. The identity of each Person is that of relation, of giving and receiving in perfect love.

If human persons are to know a "certain parallel" to the union existing among the divine Persons, their own deepest identity is also to be relational self-gift. Their bodies become personal, *appropriate expressions of self-gift* (or its refusal), whatever their age, state of life, or material means. That is why pseudo-intercourse, by whatever means, is so devastating to human persons. Jesus Christ could find no more appropriate way of self-gift than offering himself as food and drink, perpetually: "This is my Body, This is my Blood, given for you."

Fashioning virtual people in virtual environments is more than a pastime. "The virtual" and its applications present a basic worldview, in which the human is radically changed – and, in the planning of some, surpassed in the near future. It seems such a brief time ago (just seven years after the close of Vatican II) that Joseph Fletcher's essay, "Indicators of Humanhood: A Tentative profile of Man," stunned many when it appeared in *The Hastings Report*. He said that many admit the need to explicate "humanness or humaneness," but fail to follow that admission with an inventory or profile by which to determine who should be considered human. Recall how Fletcher then presented a series of so-called positive and negative criteria. They still stun. He began his first "positive" criterion: "Any individual of the species *homo sapiens* who falls below the I.Q. 40-mark in a standard Stanford-Binet test, amplified if you like by other tests, is questionably a person; below the 20-mark, not a person."[15] There is no time here to elaborate on the way Fletcher interpreted his list of criteria. I will only quote his first "negative" criterion, since it applies to a technical/virtual estimation of human life and procreation:

> As Gaylin says, men are characterized by technique, and for a human being to oppose technology is "self-hatred." We are often confused on that score, attitudinally. A "test tube baby," for exam-

ple, although conceived and gestated *ex corpo*, would nonetheless be humanly reproduced and of human value. A baby made artificially by deliberate and careful contrivance, would be more *human* that one resulting from sexual roulette: the reproductive mode of the subhuman species.[16]

Fletcher was Visiting Professor of Medical Ethics at the University of Virginia School of Medicine when he wrote that. Those in the forefront of applying sophisticated aspects of the virtual world to business, industry, and economic ventures exceed Fletcher's reductions of the human person. For example, Dr. Yury P. Salamatov, is Director of the Institute of Innovative Design, Krasnoyarsk, Russia. His "Memorandum on New Field for TRIZ Applications and Development: TRIZ in Virtual World (Business Proposal for Years 2005–2020)" tells of contracts with large corporations from the United States, Japan, Germany, and Russia. The work of IID deals with innovative development and designing of new digital media technologies. While I have no competence to discuss their business developments and inventions, I cite portions from Salamatov's article that are pertinent here. He writes under the heading "Actuality of This Issue":

> In the years immediately ahead, all information, communication, and entertainment media systems would be integrated into a single Global Network, and a new virtual world will be created, in which absolutely unknown at present systems will rapidly get synthesized and progress.
>
> What existed previously? The human and the actual world. It was a small world, palpable, convenient and inhabited, a comfortable world. It included a family, acquaintances, work and city...
>
> What will exist in the future? The human, the actual world and the virtual world (a system shell over the society). This system shell over the society will gradually draw all people into the system and involve all people into mutual contact. It will bring an individual human into contact with the world community...the human will not be able to select. The human will be unable to live without interaction....
>
> The contact should be simple, intuitively understandable (consisting in a pointing gesture of a finger or a short utterance...)[17]

Salamatov writes that "the problem of human intellectual retardation as compared to AI of the virtual world will first become explicit in 2010–2015." Then, he writes:

> ... the number of people understanding what is going on in the virtual world will be decreasing gradually. The human will lose his

capacities "to do something himself." Engineering systems will act instead of him. A tremendous variety of functions and engineering systems will appear... A special system is required, which will identify what the human wants, what can be offered to him and what things require explanation. There should be a system of automatic advisors.[18]

Alan Turing, invented the "Turing Test" more than half a century ago, to ask what happens when a machine takes the place of a person in responding to questions. In proposing the Test, it was Turing himself who saw the first objection to it as "theological": thinking is a function of the immortal soul, so a machine could not think. Turing's reply to the objection: "...he sees no reason why it would not be possible for God to grant a computer a soul if he wished."[19]

The Supernatural

A fifth aspect of virtual reality, which can only be touched upon here, is the blurring of boundaries between the virtual and the supernatural. The *Catechism of the Catholic Church* describes "supernatural" as "surpassing the power of created beings, a result of God's gracious initiative. Our vocation is to eternal life as supernatural." This divinely-given destiny exceeds human ingenuity, no matter how brilliantly that ingenuity extends into biological nano-depths or outer-space.

There is a supposition that human genius can endlessly re-imagine and technically reproduce people and universes in ways that fulfill the inner longings of the human heart. We are created *for* transcendence every day of our lives. Jesus not only walked across dark, turbulent waters – he wanted Peter to join Him. Though he heard the invitation, "Come," Peter hesitated and then began to sink. How intense is the ache for transcendence – but on one's own terms, one's own making. (I am told that there is now a place on the Sea of Galilee where a ramp has been built, just under the surface of the water so that tourists can be photographed, seemingly "walking on water.") Benjamin Woolley describes "the West" as already immersed in "artificial reality," *preferring* the simulated and artificial to the real. He writes: "We are like cartoon characters who have walked off a cliff edge and, still suspended in air, have suddenly realized that there is nothing beneath us. This is the crisis of post-modernity, and it is technology that has produced it."[20]

Our Task

It is the task of theology to ask in every age: What is thrusting up anew from the depths of humanity? What is trying to break through that has potential for true human development, despite aberrations? In *The World is Flat: A Brief History of the Twenty-First Century,* Thomas L. Friedman describes existing "virtual global offices" where tasks are currently taken apart, distributed to remote locations of the world overnight and reassembled at a site unknown to workers the next day. "Boss" and workers never meet. "This is not a trivial revolution," says Friedman, and it "has happened in the twinkling of an eye – the span of two or three years."[21] Such a fragmentation is destructive of human person. But is there a way in which this technical potential could lead to ways of furthering communion of persons?

Like Pope John Paul II, we must ask over and over, what is the divine intent for humanity from the beginning? The roots of our trees are not coiled with cunning serpents; they are laced with fiberglass cables that can prompt an Eden-like message: *Who told you that there are limits? Be gods, creating new universes.* Neither the fiberglass cables nor the digital dexterity they enable are evil. What happens *in human interaction with them*, especially in the human heart: that is what is crucial.

Our task is immense and immediate. The Catholic Church in the United States has lost many young people and adults in the past few generations – often due to woefully inadequate catechesis and the use of reductionist resources. It amazes me how many scholars deeply involved in the study of virtual reality from a *secular* perspective write of its impact on anthropology and religious beliefs, while few within the Church express a *direct* concern.

Peter John Cameron, O.P., wrote in the August, 2005, issue of *Magnificat:* "A saying from the Middle Ages goes: 'A man is wise when all things taste to him as they really are.' The memory we taste in the meal of the Eucharist gives us just this taste toward reality." In an accompanying reflection, Father Raniero Cantalamessa, preacher to the papal household, comments on the meaning of *spousal communion* in Ephesians 5:31–32, and I Corinthians 7:4:

> "Applied to the Eucharist, this means that the incorruptible and life-giving flesh of the Incarnate Word become mine, and also that my flesh, my whole human reality, become Christ's truly his very own."[22]

Real body, real truth, real communion in self-gift…May we be so blessed!

Sister M. Timothy Prokes, Ph.D., a Franciscan Sister of the Eucharist, is Professor of Theology and Spirituality at the Notre Dame Graduate School of Christendom College in Alexandria, Virginia. She also teaches courses in the permanent diaconate program of the archdiocese of Washington, D.C. She earned her M.A. in theology at Marquette University in Milwaukee, and she has a Ph.D. from the Institute of Christian Thought at St. Michael's University in Toronto, Ontario, Canada. She has taught at Creighton University in Omaha, the Newman Theological College in Edmonton, Alberta, Canada, and the College of Notre Dame of Maryland in Baltimore.

She has published a number of books, including *Toward a Theology of the Body* (T &T Clark, Edinburgh, Scotland, and Wm. Eerdmans, Grand Rapids, Michigan 1996), *Mutuality: The Human Image of Trinitariana Love* (Paulist Press, 1993), and *Women's Challenge: Ministry in the Flesh* (Dimension Press, 1976). Her most recent book, on the subject of her stimulating talk to the Fellowship convention, is: *At the Interface: Theology and Virtual Reality* (Fenestra Books, Tucson, Arizona). Sister Prokes offers lectures and seminars in the areas of the theology of the body, pastoral care of the sick and dying, bioethical issues, and the spiritual life.

ENDNOTES

1   *Gaudium et Spes*, Pastoral Constitution on The Church in the Modern World, in *Vatican Council II: The Conciliar and Post Conciliar Documents*, Austin Flannery, gen. ed., new revised edition (Grand Rapids, Michigan: William B. Eerdmans Publishing Co., 1992), #4, p. 905. Unless indicated otherwise, all quotations cited from the Constitutions are from this translation.

2   Michael Heim, *The Metaphysics of Virtual Reality* (New York: Oxford University Press, 1993), p. 111.

3   Marie-Laure Ryan, *Narrative as Virtual Reality: Immersion and Interactivity in Literature and Electronic Media* (Baltimore: The Johns Hopkins University Press), pp. 26–27.

4   Ryan, *Ibid.,* p. 25.

5   Ken Pimentel and Kevin Teixeira, *Virtual Reality: Through the New Looking Glass* (New York: Intel/Windcrest McGraw Hill, 1993), p. 11.

6   See Heim, *The Metaphysics of Virtual Reality,* pp. 113–118.

7   N. Katherine Hayles, *How We Became Posthuman: Virtual Bodies in Cybernetics, Literature and Informatics* (University of Chicago press, 1999), pp. 2–3.

8   For further commentary, see Hayles, *How We Became Posthuman*, p. 5.

9   "Haptic," in *VWN Virtua Dictionary*,virtualworldlets.net/Resources/Dictionary.php?Term=haptics&Submit2=Fetch. Accessed July 29, 2005.

10   Anthony Rizzi, *The Science Before Science: A Guide for Thinking in the 21st Century* (Bloomington, Indiana: Press of the Institute for Advanced Physics, 2004), p. 137.

11   See Alan Watts, *Does It Matter: Essays on Man's Relationship to Materiality* (New York: Random House, 1970), p. 30.

12   See "A Conversation with Sherry Turkle," in *Harvard Business Review*, September, 2003, p. 44.

13   "A Conversation," p. 45.

14   "A Conversation," p. 46.

15   Joseph Fletcher, "Indicators of Humanhood: A Tentative Profile of Man," in *The Hastings Center Report* (November, 1972), p. 1.

16   Fletcher, "Indicators of Humanhood," p. 3.

17   Yury P. Salamatov, "Memorandum on New Field for TRIZ Application and Development: TRIZ in Virtual World (Business Proposal for Years 2005–2020," p. 2, ysal@siberianet.ru. Accessed August 18, 2005.

18   Salamatov, "Memorandum on New Field," p. 2.

19   "History," in "Turing Test," *Wikipedia: the Free Encyclopedia*, p. 1, http://en.wikipedia.org/wiki/Turing_test, accessed August 18, 2005.

20   Benjamin Woolley, *Virtual Worlds: A Journey in Hype and Hyperreality* (Oxford, UK and Cambridge, USA, 1992), p. 204.

21   Thomas L. Friedman, *The World is Flat: A Brief History of the Twenty-First Century* (New York: Farrar, Straus and Giroux, 2005), p. 80.

22   See *Magnificat*, August, 2005 (USA, LLC, Buffalo, New York), pp. 2–8.

The Christian Anthropology of Vatican II and Virtual Reality
A Response to Sister Mary Timothy Prokes F.S.E.

PETER CASARELLA

Our times leap, detonate without warning, or seem too sluggish."
This provocative sentence struck me when I read the presentation of
Sister Mary Timothy Prokes. The artfully combined image of imminent
progress, lethal landmines, and ingrained lethargy seemed like a good
description of the "modern world," as addressed by Vatican II's Pastoral
Constitution on the Modern World, *Gaudium et Spes*. What I have to add
to her presentation is intended not as critique but merely as supplemen-
tal reflection, for I find myself in fundamental agreement with the thrust
of her argument. My remarks will attempt to push the questioning that
she initiated further on two of the themes that she introduced, namely: 1)
the sense of an acceleration of time that accompanies modern technology and, especially, the phenomenon of a virtual reality; and 2) the question of embodied and disembodied interaction in our world today.

I.

There is little doubt that the final draft of *Gaudium et Spes*, in sharp
contrast to the draft submitted by the preparatory commission in 1962 to
the Council Fathers, situates the modern Christian at the very heart of a
highly technological world, a world whose progress has led to the unan-
ticipated pervasiveness of virtual reality only forty years later. In making this point, I do not intend either to bemoan or to exalt the recent
progress of modern technology. I am more interested in recalling the
precise language adopted in *Gaudium et Spes* regarding the nature of
such progress, and in using that language as a norm for evaluating the
phenomenon of virtual reality and the implicit norms for life that it carries with it. Some of the key phrases about technological progress have
already been cited in Sister Mary Timothy's presentation. Consider, for

example, the passage in paragraph 5, which with hindsight seems willy-nilly marked by the preparatory stages of the Apollo lunar space missions that were then underway:

> The spiritual uneasiness of today (*hodierna animorum commotio*) and the changing structure of life are part of a broader upheaval, whose symptoms are the increasing part played on the intellectual level by the mathematical and natural sciences (not excluding the sciences dealing with man himself) and on the practical level by their repercussions on technology (*in ordine vero agendi technicae artes ex illis scientiis profluentes*). The scientific mentality (*haec mens scientifica*) has wrought a change in the cultural sphere and on habits of thought, and the progress of technology is now reshaping the face of the earth and has its sights set on the conquest of space.[1]

Notice that the Fathers of the Council do not refer here to technology as a merely mechanical appendage to modern life. Instead they refer to *technicae artes* that issue from the new modern sciences and represent their application on the level of quotidian action. They speak of a mindset or worldview (*mens scientifica*) that has engendered a new cultural reality and in alluding to the race to reach the moon seem overwhelmed at the widening horizon of the modern world. Equally ebullient is the sentence that follows immediately thereafter:

> The human mind is, in a certain sense, broadening its mastery over time – over the past through the insights of history, over the future by foresight and planning.[2]

In this passage an explicit connection is drawn to the new conquered dominion over temporal duration that is garnered over the past through the *might* of historical knowledge (*ops cognitionis historicae*) and over the future by an even more formidable *ars technica*, one that looks into the future, takes notice of the manifold fruits of scientific progress, and makes plans that will exert influence on the social life of the planet (*in vitam societatum directe influxum exerceat*).[3] Taken by themselves, these passages could easily be interpreted as a capitulation to an Orwellian view of the future.

But these passages obviously are not meant to be read in isolation from other more realistic and biblically oriented passages in the document. Such a one-sided approach was what a thirty-nine year old theologian named Joseph Ratzinger criticized in his commentary on the evolving "Schema XIII" that was being debated during the last session of the Council. In a book that was completed just three months after the promulgation of *Gaudium et Spes*, Joseph Ratzinger says that more so than with any other conciliar decree *Gaudium et Spes* bears "the character of something unfinished, of a task, of a beginning."[4] Ratzinger, citing Hans Urs von Balthasar as his source, pointed to an attraction in some early drafts of Schema XIII to a mild "Teilhardism," a tendency that arose as an overreaction to an equally unacceptable Neo-scholastic formalism.[5] "Teilhardism," according to the young Ratzinger, has:

> ... with the aid of a cosmic Christology practically interpreted technological progress as Christological progress and thus called the Christian wholly into the service of technological progress. But even in the mild form given to it by Schema XIII, one could recognize the enormous re-invention (die ungeheuerliche Umdeutung) of what was Christian, a move that basically consisted of concocting here and there an artificial blend of the Christian expectation of the world to come with hope in technology.[6]

Joseph Ratzinger's criticism of Teilhardism was meant as the formulation of a theological problem within the emerging conciliar text, and, especially, in some of the drafts that immediately preceded it. It was *not* a rejection in any fashion of the final form of the Constitution. Inasmuch as he was able to formulate the problem as it arose in the conciliar discussions, he considered the still unresolved attitude towards technology as one of several problems recognized in Schema XIII that simultaneously handed over to the Church a summons for the future.[7]

Today we face, as Sister Mary Timothy has ably demonstrated, a dual challenge. Mild Teilhardism is indeed still present in the Church and texts of the Council such as the ones with which I began are used to legitimize its existence. Beyond that, there is today a much more virulent faith in technological progress that surpasses the most aggressive limits of the label "Teilhardism," and can only be considered as an outright eclipse of Christian hope. If we limit our perspective once again just to *Gaudium et Spes*, what can be said in response to these two undiminished challenges?

First, Sister Mary Timothy has given us wise counsel in interpreting the oft cited "reading the signs of the times" from *Gaudium et Spes* #4 in terms of Jesus' words in Matthew 16:3. The gospel highlights the distinction between a naturalist viewpoint and one directed at the coming of the Lord. Without adopting what Karl Rahner would term a false apocalypticism, one can still pursue the task of *aggiornamento as* a mode of Christian eschatology. The time against which progress is to be measured is neither a treasure of wisdom from the distant past nor a humanly planned future. God's time can and must be considered as *the* measure of our reading of the signs of the times. Second, the constitution interposes the mystery of death as a moment of decision in the Christian life.[8] "It is in regard to death that man's condition is most shrouded in doubt."[9] Such is the translation of Austin Flannery, O.P. A better translation of this passage would be: "In the face of death, the riddle of human existence reaches its highest point." The *aenigma* in question is not that of natural physical decay. The seed of eternity that man bears within himself instigates both a natural rebellion against mortality and an equal dissatisfaction with the prolongation of life promised by modern technology. The same paragraph notes God's call to human persons to join with one's whole nature in the perpetual divine communion of incorruptible life. In highlighting this invitation to partake of the Trinitarian communion, the Fathers use both the past and present tense: "God *called* and *calls*..." In this manner, the past of the God's covenant with his people is united to the present quest of technological man.

In light of the interposition on the part of the Council Fathers of our own interruptive mortality, one might characterize death as that authentic grasp of one's finite existence. Death is a human phenomenon that solidly resists all attempts at the virtualization of reality. The eschatological view of human existence that this entails provides the proper frame for considering the illusion of temporal enhancement most of us experience with virtual reality. I, for one, go on-line or correspond via e-mail because I sincerely believe that such tools are highly efficient means of communication. I find this truth hard to deny and even more difficult to resist. But what sort of theological reflection should accompany anyone who wishes to justify the grandiose claims made for the *worldview* of virtual reality on this basis? One need not be attracted to Luddite forms of resistance, I think, to realize the import of this question. In other words, the justification of the new media on the basis of good time management is itself a technological way of construing the issue. What has become, for example, of a living human voice in a world of purely virtual relations? Equally important, wherein lies the crux of the theological problem? In his treatment of the temporal ordering of creation in his *Systematic Theology*, Robert W. Jenson writes: "God takes time in his time for us. That is his act of creation."[10]

In this regard, it seems that the efficiency of virtual reality belies and suppresses the fullness of God's time. If God's time for us is palpably present in that act whereby he brings the harmony of the created order into existence, and if the Creator perpetually accompanies the music of creation through his covenantal love – two theses entirely consistent with *Gaudium et Spes* – then the pursuit of good time management *as a way of life* would be a truly splendid vice.

II.

Another central point raised by Sister Mary Timothy concerns the gnostic character of virtual reality. It is curious to me that the literature on virtual reality cited in her text accentuates "telepresence" and "full body immersion," but totally ignores the systematic elimination of human touch realized by the new technology. Some years ago I served as a faculty advisor in an undergraduate dormitory on the campus of The Catholic University of America. One evening in a discussion with the students about their favorite ways to avoid studying, they listed AIM as the chief culprit. Once the very concept was explained to me, it also dawned upon me how pervasively the new modes of communication had permeated their daily lives. In a relatively small community with virtu-ally uninhibited access to one another, their time was consumed with "instant messaging" and to that degree void of face-to-face encounters.

In terms of the theological anthropology already elaborated by Sister Mary Timothy, the disincarnate world of virtual reality calls our attention to two realities in their simultaneity: these two realities are: incarnation and body-soul unity. First, it highlights how the claim made in *Gaudium et Spes* #22 regarding the elucidation of the mystery of man through the mystery of the Word made flesh is truly a claim regarding the radicality of the Christian notion of the incarnation. The text goes on to state that the Incarnate Word:

> ... worked with human hands, he thought with a human mind. He acted with a human will, and with a human heart he loved. Born of the Virgin Mary, he has truly been made one of us, like to us in all things except sin.[11]

The Paschal mystery sheds light on the riddle of human suffering and death precisely because of the submission of Christ's human flesh to our condition. Out of this solidarity of Christ with us, we need to re-eval-uate the importance of touch to a Christian understanding of truth.[12] This re-evaluation is equally a problem for systematic theology as it is a task for Christian education.[13] The suggestion made by Sister Mary Timothy that the recourse to a human being as merely informational processes is surely an extension of the gnostic disembodiment of the human. On the other hand, I do wonder whether some form of complexity theory could be invoked in order to reconsider the unity of the soul with the body in terms of an information bearing pattern. Such a reconstrual of Thomistic hylomorphism in terms of the emergentist, complex processes studied in contemporary physics has been proposed by the scientist-theologian John Polkinghorne and merits, I think, further consideration in this con-text.[14]

Dr. Peter Casarella is an Associate Professor of Systematic Theology at the Catholic University of America, where he has taught since 1993. He has a Ph.D. in philosophy from Yale University and has also taught at the University of Dallas. He has co-edited two books, *Christian Spirituality and the Culture of Modernity: The Thought of Louis Dupré* (Eerdmans, 1998), and *Cuerpo de Cristo: The Hispanic Presence in the American Catholic Church (Crossroad, 1998)*; and he is the editor of another volume: *Cusanus: The Legacy of Learned Interest* (CUA Press, 2006). He is the author of the book *Word As Bread: Language and Theology in Nicholas of Cusa.* He was Director of the program of Medieval and Byzantine Studies at CUA in 1998–2001. As of June, 2005, he is president of the Academy of Catholic Hispanics in the U.S. His articles have appeared in *Communio, The Thomsit, Renascence, The American Catholic Philosophical Quarterly*, and elsewhere. In the Spring, 2005, issue of *Pro Ecclesia*, he contributed an article entitled "Contemplating Christ through the Eyes of Mary: The Apostolic Letter *Rosarium Virginis Mariae* and the New Mysteries of Light."

ENDNOTES

1   Unless otherwise noted, all English translations are taken from Austin Flannery, O.P., *Vatican Council II: The Conciliar and Post Conciliar Documents* (Northport, N.Y.: Costello, rev. ed., 1988), here at 906. Latin texts are cited from *Sacrosanctum Oecumenicum Concilium Vaticanum II Constitutiones Decreta Declarationes* (Vatican City: Typis Polyglottis Vaticanis, 1966), here at 686.

2   *Ibid.,*:"Super tempora quoque humanus intellectus dominium suum quodammodo dilatat: in praeteritum ope cognitionis historicae, in futurum arte prospectiva et planificatione."

3   *Sacrosanctum Oecumenicum Concilium Vaticanum II Constitutiones Decreta Declarationes*, 686–7, translation my own.

4   Joseph Ratzinger, *Die letzte Sitzungsperiode des Konzils* (Cologne: Bachem, 1966), 7.

5   *Ibid.,* 39–43. Ratzinger clearly indicates that the theology of Teilhard de Chardin itself militates against such an irenic view of modern progress.

6   *Ibid.,* 41.

7   *Ibid.,* 43.

8   *Gaudium et Spes*, #18.

9   *Ibid., "Coram morte aenigma condicionis humanae maximum evadit."* Cf. *Gaudium et Spes*, #13.

10   Robert W. Jenson, *Systematic Theology, II, The Works of God* (Oxford: Oxford University Press, 1999), 35.

11   *Gaudium et Spes, #22.*

12 See, for example, John Milbank and Catherine Pickstock, *Truth in Aquinas* (London: Routledge, 2001), 60–87.

13 See, for example, Sofia Cavalletti, *The Religious Potential of the Child* (Oak Park, IL: Catechesis of the Good Shepherd Publications, 1992), 158–67. The genial contribution by Dr. Gladys Sweeney to this volume considers the meaningfulness of touch to infants and seems to support the point being made here.

14 John Polkinghorne, *The God of Hope and the End of the World* (New Haven: Yale University Press, 2002), 206.

Another Response to the Thesis of Sister Mary Timothy Prokes
Encountering the "Really Real"
Realism, Sacraments, and Virtual Reality

MONSIGNOR STUART SWETLAND[1]

Sister M. Timothy's paper explores the theological anthropology promulgated in the documents of the Second Vatican Council, especially in *Gaudium et Spes*. She contrasts this with an emerging understanding of the human person influenced by the realm of "virtual reality," the latter being largely a product of computer and communications technologies. She prefaces her presentation by indicating that the "faith perspective" which she is pursuing is not aimed at a return to a simpler era. Rather, she wants to discern carefully those aspects of the employment of these virtual reality technologies which either enhance or diminish the human person.

Sister M. Timothy, drawing from Michael Heim's *The Metaphysics of Virtual Reality*, describes virtual reality as real in its effect but unreal in fact and outlines seven levels of virtual reality.[2] These seven levels proceed from less to more in terms of the realism of the experience and the integration of the various human senses, including tactile, into a disembodied interaction with a computationally generated environment that includes "virtual" persons. She then moves on to identify five anthropological themes which she draws from the conciliar documents. These themes are: 1) a Christocentric view of the human person; 2) man as created in the image of God; 3) a hylomorphic conception of the person (as a unity of body and soul); 4) the universal call to holiness as convertible with self-gift; and 5) man's destiny for eternal communion in the Trinitarian Communion of Persons.

Sister M. Timothy then evaluates virtual reality in the light of this conciliar anthropology. She identifies five characteristics of the former which contrast with, but also frequently interface with, the latter. The first is the tendency of those involved with virtual reality to view the body as a disposable, irrelevant, information pattern. In discussing this characteristic, she identifies the "transporter" from Gene Roddenberry's *Star Trek* as emblematic of extent to which deconstruction of the human person has proceeded since the Enlightenment. The transporter would dematerialize the person, store his "information pattern" in the transporter's computer, and then rematerialize the person in another location. Sister M. Timothy identifies the implications of this reductionist view for the incarnational and sacramental life of the Church. These include the irrelevance of the Incarnation and the reduction of the sacraments to passing social expressions. This dis-incarnational outlook similarly wreaks havoc on the moral life undermining any rationale for explaining the moral problematic associated with, for example, creating designer babies. She finds that virtual reality no longer means simply a technology but a developing world view affecting large segments of our society. This world view tends to undercut Christian anthropology, sacramental theology, and morality.

A second characteristic is the computational generation of virtual environments, worlds, and even persons. Sr. M. Timothy recognizes this can be entertainment for some people, but still cautions that it carries with it neo-gnostic undertones together with their antirealist implications. She shows real examples of web-based opportunities for users to escape into a world where everything conforms to their desires, including one's own appearance. She points to another case of tactile stimulus body suits which allow users to engage remotely in sexual encounters. Moral considerations aside, she cautions that this technology has the capacity to distort one's sense of reality. This distortion of reality actually warps the purpose of the mind which is to know and conform to reality and truth.

Sister M. Timothy's third virtual reality characteristic is the simulation of food, sex, and relationships. Here she shows how our ideas of food have changed as the way it is grown, processed, served, and consumed becomes less and less natural. She believes that this moves our understanding of food to be viewed less as sustenance and in ever more epicurean terms. She warns that the confusion over the meaning and content of food has seriously negative implications for the understanding of the reality of the Eucharist. As part of this third characteristic, she also discusses the way technology can subliminally change the way we think. She brings up the example of realistic robotics and the changes that they can influence in the way we view relationships and experience things like love. As an example, she cites the story of a woman who established a loving relationship with her Sony AIBO, a robot dog. The woman preferred the robot to a real dog because it was more reliable, would not betray her, and would not leave her alone by dying.

A fourth characteristic that sister identifies is the substitution of absence for real presence, creating an indifference for either real presence or absence. She finds this is destructive to the anthropological requirement of self-gift in order to achieve personal fulfillment. She provides several examples to illustrate the problem. However, her point is that the body expresses the soul and so the giving of the whole human person generally requires bodily presence. She indicates that is why Jesus in his self-gift to humanity offers himself as food and drink.

The fifth characteristic of virtual reality involves blurring the boundaries between the natural and the supernatural, often explicitly denying the latter. She describes the danger associated with virtual reality; it is that the innate human eros for the transcendent can be misdirected toward technological solutions which substitute illusion for God.

Sister M. Timothy concludes her paper by reiterating that neither the material technological developments themselves, nor the new capabilities that they engender are of themselves, evil. Rather, the danger arises when human interaction with them occurs. She says this is especially true with what happens in the human heart. Many young people have been lost to the siren song of technology driven confusion. She urges that this issue needs to be studied more by theologians and engaged pastorally by the leaders of the Church. The Second Vatican Council's anthropology, a theology of the body in which an incarnational self-gift is understood as the real approach to authentic communion; it is the way forward.

Dr. Peter Casarella provides a response to Sister M. Timothy's paper. Casarella takes no issue with Sister M. Timothy's thesis and so he devotes his response to further developing two themes broached in her presentation. The first was a tangential issue, the sense of the acceleration of time associated with technology and especially, with virtual reality. The second was the question of the contemporary person's embodied and disembodied interaction with the world.

Casarella takes the drafting process of *Gaudium et Spes* as the point of departure for his discussion of the first theme. He points to comments from Hans Urs von Balthasar and Joseph Ratzinger, the latter a *peritus* at the Council, on "Schema XIII," which would become *Gaudium et Spes*. These comments indicated that initial drafts of the document exhibited a mild "Teilhardism" arising in reaction to Neo-Scholastic formalism. This led to much debate and, as Ratzinger indicated, left the Church a yet unresolved task concerning her attitude toward technological progress. Casarella does not mention this, but in convoking the Council, John XXIII had indicated that the Church faced one of the gravest tasks she ever has, "as in the most tragic periods of its history."[3] He saw that modern society, having left God out of the equation, was headed toward catastrophe with its unparalleled technological progress without a commensurate progression in the moral field. Thus, the implication was that the Church had to develop the ability to dialogue with modernity and help it discern the good from the evil arising from the employment of new technologies.

Casarella says that the Church is still confronted with this issue of coming to terms with its own attitude toward technology. He sees this issue framed in terms of those, on the one hand, who still possess a mild Teilhardism, for which they find their justification in some of the passages of the final document. On the other hand, there are those who take this as their point of departure, but adopt such a virulent strain of Teilhardism, in which technological progress is viewed in almost salvific terms, that Casarella finds the endgame of their project to be nothing less than a total eclipse of Christian hope.[4] Casarella sees in Sister M. Timothy's article a way to address these two still present challenges. Limiting his scope to *Gaudium et Spes*, he finds that her admonition to read the signs of the times also leads to the Gospel's distinction between a purely naturalist perspective and one aimed at the *parousia*. Here Casarella suggests that we can avoid a false apocalypticism and "still pursue the task of *aggiornamento* as the Christian mode of eschatology." What he means is that it is not human wisdom or achievement that will bring about the eschaton; the latter will come only in God's time. We must discern how best to address contemporary circumstances in order to help sanctify the temporal sphere; but we must not think that we can hasten the eschaton by our own ingenuity.

Casarella goes on to point out, using his own translation of *Gaudium et Spes* #13, that the Council shows the way to a facet of life that is solidly resistant to the virtualization of reality. His translation of the relevant passage says that death brings man to the zenith of the mystery of human existence. Death contextualizes the illusion of temporal enhancement that one experiences with virtual reality technologies. I take this to mean that Casarella finds the reality of death a "wake up call" that should reveal to us our transient status in this life and the fact that virtual reality technologies, if we are not careful, can isolate us from the interpersonal relationships that are the means by which we help to carry out God's plan of love in time.

Casarella, in his second theme, looks at Sister M. Timothy's second point that deals with the gnostic character of virtual reality. He sees a gnostic dichotomy between body and soul in virtual reality's accentuation of "telepresence" and "full body immersion" divorced from human touch. The technology of "instant messaging" which results in a culture in many ways voided of face to face encounters is an example of this. Casarella suggests that the Paschal mystery, which reveals Christ's solidarity with man, should lead us to a re-appropriation of the importance of touch for understanding Christian truth. He agrees that Sister M. Timothy's appraisal that the reduction of the body to informational patterns is a symptom of gnostic disembodiment. However, he also wonders if there might be a way of re-introducing Thomistic hylomorphism into current thinking via John Polkinghorne's proposal of the "emergentist, complex processes" being studied by modern physics.

I find this topic quite intriguing, especially as virtual reality relates to the sacraments and the Real Presence. This issue directly touches my ministry to "millennial" college students at St. John's Catholic Newman Center at the University of Illinois at Urbana-Champaign. I have spoken on the issue of ministering to these millennials in different venues.[5] Sister M. Timothy's recognition of the dis-incarnational phenomena brought about by the omnipresent virtual reality technologies corresponds well with my own experiences with the millennial generation, which some have dubbed Generation Y. I have found that a common point of reference among them is their common experience of virtual presence via technologies such as the internet, cell phones, text messaging, instant messaging, remote gaming, etc. This leaves them with an experiential vacuum in terms of the nurturing presence of others. However, I find that there is another interesting phenomenon which seems to have arisen in response to the increasing dearth of interpersonal interaction.

We know that nature abhors a vacuum and that youthful human nature is no different. Generation Y is yearning for an incarnational faith. In contrast to their parents, they are searching for the "really real" in their spiritual and liturgical lives.[6] This is why they are attracted to traditional practices that emphasize the incarnational aspects of our faith. Thus, we have the return of the "new faithful" to traditions like the rosary, Stations of the Cross, icons, statues, incense, etc. They intuitively "get it." They are more able than their parents to recognize that God assumed human flesh because human flesh is good. They can appreciate that the Transcendent is most effectively, and really, mediated to us through matter. This incarnational truth is reflected in the Church's sacramental theology and discipline.

The Church has always recognized that sacramental action requires a physical presence which corresponds with the understanding that it is through matter that grace is mediated. Moral manualists uniformly assert the requirement for this physical presence.[7] Physical presence is presumed in magisterial teaching on the liturgy and Sacraments.[8] The Magisterium and its various organs of communication also constantly assert the requirement for this physical presence. For example, the United States Conference of Catholic Bishops' (USCCB) Committee on the Liturgy, in its June 1999 newsletter, states:

> The Secretariat for the Liturgy has received several inquiries concerning the celebration of the sacraments via various types of electronic communication. The celebration of the Sacrament of Penance via telephone, participation in Mass via television or the celebration of the Sacrament of Confirmation via video conference have on occasion been proposed. However, electronic communication via telephone, television, video conference or internet is not sufficient for the celebration of the sacraments. The celebration of the sacraments requires the physical and geographic presence of both the gathered faithful and the bishop, priest, deacon, or other presiding minister...The liturgy...requires a full, conscious, and active participation which demands the presence of the whole person in contact with the reality (not merely an image or concept) of the saving presence of Christ. A "live" telecast of an event allows a limited kind of "presence" for the viewer, but the viewer is very aware that he or she is not "really there" in the same manner as those physically present at the event. Effective participation and communication require that one be "present at" and "present to" the reality to be experienced.[9]

This document indicates that virtual reality's dis-embodied worldview is beginning to contend with the Church's sacramental life.

The Sacrament of Reconciliation, fallen as it has into disuse by a large segment of the faithful, is a prime target for the onslaught of virtual reality. Simultaneous with this decline, we see the proliferation of "confessions" of a different sort. For example we have confessionals on daytime talk shows of the Jerry Springer ilk, radio call-in programs such as Dr. Ruth's "Sexually Speaking," and even on-line confessions that are now proliferating all over the web. However, the Church has always recognized the requirement for a personal and integral confession for confession to be valid.[10] The Magisterium explicitly rules out telephone or internet confessions.[11] I believe that the rationale behind this can be found by looking at some of the other sacraments.

Marriage also normally requires the presence of both spouses along with the Church's representative.[12] For the marriage ceremony, the two who are to give their consent to be married must be physically present, or at least the physical presence is needed of one who can verify consent on behalf of one of the parties who cannot be present for some grave reason.[13] But marriage by proxy cannot be viewed as the virtual presence on the part of the missing party. Recall that consummation, which obviously requires the physical presence of husband and wife, is required in addition to ratification for the marriage to be indissoluble.[14] In other words, a sacramental, one-flesh union is not created without the physical presence of both spouses.

The Church recognizes that the very helpful proliferation of the televised Mass is a great tool for evangelization and can be a blessing for those who are homebound.[15] However, even in the early years of the explosion of homes with televisions, the Magisterium made it explicitly clear that a Mass via the radio or televised media was not equivalent to physical presence; it did not satisfy one's Sunday obligation.[16] Notably, Pius XII does not say that those viewing the Mass, who cannot attend for grave reasons, virtually participate in the Mass and so receive its grace. Rather he says, "valuable fruits for the strengthening of the Faith and the renewal of fervor can be obtained by all those who, for some reason, are unable to be actually present..."[17] The requirement for physical presence makes sense. Theologically, the Incarnation and the Real Presence of Christ in the Eucharist indicate that physical presence, for human beings, is the fullest sense of the term presence; it is a *substantial* presence.[18] The interpersonal communication of grace, a participation in the divine nature (cf. II Pt 1:4), between Christ and the recipient through the sacraments requires physical presence.

I believe that there is an anthropological explanation for the requirement of physical presence. I would start with the philosophical model of the human person that the Church employs – the soul is the substantial form of the human person.[19] This hylomorphic model carries with it implications for the human person and human interpersonal interactions. John Paul II's theology of the body articulates this emphasis on a psycho-somatic unity from a new perspective. One of these Sister M. Timothy mentioned; the body makes visible the soul and so it reveals and expresses the whole person who is a dual-unity of spirit and matter.[20]

Now let us look at this hylomorphism in the context of the Eucharist. In the Eucharist, the substance of the species of bread and wine actually becomes the substance of Christ's Body and Blood.[21] It would seem from this definition of transubstantiation that the substantial form of Christ, i.e., his soul, *informs* the matter of what was once bread and wine. Thus Holy Communion is *par excellence* a personal encounter with the living Christ. I do not believe it is too much to say that the one flesh union of marriage, the primordial sacrament as John Paul II has called it, is analogous to the flesh and blood union we experience with Christ in the Eucharist. This is what John Paul indicates in one of his Wednesday Audiences on his theology of the body when he says that marriage is the prototype of the entire sacramental system.[22] He bases this on Ephesians 5:21–23 which indicates that from the beginning marriage is man's proleptic participation in God's spousal union with His Church. Of course, then, the Eucharistic one-flesh union can happen only with the physical presence of the Bridegroom and His Bride.[23] This requirement for physical presence in all of the sacraments appears clear when looking at sacramental action from a metaphysical perspective.

Christ's form, mediated via sacramental matter, infuses grace into the substantial form of the recipient. St. Thomas refers to the resulting infusion as "created grace." By this he means that grace infuses an accidental form into the soul of the recipient.[24] While Christ is not present in the other sacraments the way he is in the Eucharist, it seems to me that the analogy applies. The form of the particular sacrament, mediated by the sacramental matter, is integral to the infusion of sacramental grace. With the Sacraments, the form is the words spoken by the minister of the sacrament and so the form is transmitted by the minister. In virtual reality, the form would be replaced by the form of the electro-mechanical apparatus used to modulate the air that produces the sound. Thus in virtual reality, not only is the matter missing, the form itself would be ontologically different from the form of the speaking minister. Philosophically speaking, one can see why virtual reality cannot mediate sacramental grace, which is the mystery of a personal encounter with Christ.

Virtual reality is a real concern for the Church. The Pontifical Council for Social Communications recognizes that it has some benefits even if it "cannot substitute for real interpersonal community, the incarnational reality of the sacraments and liturgy, or the immediate and direct proclamation of the gospel, it can complement them, attract people to a fuller experience of the life of faith, and enrich the religious lives of users."[25] However, they also warn that:

> ... the virtual reality of cyberspace has some worrisome implications for religion as well as for other areas of life. Virtual reality is no substitute for the Real Presence of Christ in the Eucharist, the

sacramental reality of the other sacraments, and shared worship in a flesh-and-blood human community. There are no sacraments on the Internet; and even the religious experiences possible there by the grace of God are insufficient apart from real-world interaction with other persons of faith.[26]

Sister M. Timothy's timely presentation echoes the Magisterium's concerns and hopefully awakens us to the challenges that we face as virtual reality technologies spawn virtual reality thought and culture. Without regressing to, as Dr. Casarella puts it, "Luddite forms of resistance," theologians, pastors, and laity ought to embrace the good, but must also recognize and address the dangers that virtual reality presents.

Real human relationship – be they with friends, spouse, or God – are still best carried-on in and through the "really real" of reality. No internet chat room can replace the dining room or living room where real friendships are entertained and deepened. No cyber-sex can bring people together in spousal intimacy. And no "virtual church" can substitute for the moral presence of God's people gathered around a common altar offering with a bishop or priest the Holy Sacrifice of the Mass.

Monsignor Stuart W. Swetland, S.T.D., was ordained a priest in 1991 for the diocese of Peoria, Illinois. He is a former naval officer and he earned his first undergraduate degree, in physics, from the U.S. Naval Academy in Annapolis. Then, in 1981, he was selected to be a Rhodes Scholar to study at Oxford University. He acquired both a B.A. and an M.A. in philosophy, politics, and economics there. Raised a Lutheran, he became a Catholic while studying at Oxford. He later earned an M.Div. and an M.A. from Mount Saint Mary's Seminary in Maryland; and, finally, he earned an S.T.L. and an S.T.D. from the John Paul II Institute for Studies on Marriage and the Family in Washington, D.C.

Currently Monsignor Swetland serves as Director of the Newman Foundation and is also Chaplain to Catholic Students at the University of Illinois at Urbana-Champaign; he is also an Adjunct Professor of Religious Studies there. In addition, he serves as Vicar for Social Justice in the diocese of Peoria – and as Executive Secretary of the Fellowship of Catholic Scholars as well. His conversion story was published in the well-known series *Surprised by Truth* 3 edited by Patrick Madrid.

ENDNOTES

1   I would like to acknowledge Dr. David Delaney's research and assistance in developing this manuscript.

2   Michael Heim's, *The Metaphysics of Virtual Reality* (New York: Oxford University Press, 1993).

3   John XIII, *Humanae Salutis*, Apostolic Exortation, 25 December, 1961, in *The Documents of Vatican II*, ed. Walter M. Abbot (New York: The America Press, 1966), 703. "Today the Church is witnessing a crisis under way within society. While humanity is on the edge of a new era, tasks of immense gravity and amplitude await the Church, as in the most tragic periods of its history. It is a question in fact of bringing the modern world into contact with the vivifying reality and perennial energies of the gospel, a world which exalts itself with its conquests in the technical and scientific fields, but which brings also the consequences of a temporal order which some have wished to reorganize excluding God. This is why modern society is earmarked by a great material progress to which there is not a corresponding advance in the moral field. Hence there is a weakening in the aspiration toward the values of the spirit. Hence an urge for the almost exclusive search for earthly pleasures, which progressive technology places with such ease within the reach of all. And hence there is a completely new and disconcerting fact: the existence of a militant atheism which is active on the world level" (*Ibid.*, 703–04).

4   Obviously Casarella's dichotomy leaves aside those who mildly or radically oppose technological progress, the latter of whom he refers to in terms of "Luddite forms of resistance."

5   Cf. e.g., Stuart W. Swetland, "Ministering to the Millennials: The Ethos and Culture of Generation Y," *Crossroads* XXXVIII No.1 (September 2005): 6–7,9.

6   Although it is always difficult to generalize about whole generations, many commentators (cf. e.g., William Strauss, Neil Howe, *The Fourth Turning: An American Prophecy* (New York: Broadway Books, 1997); *The Millennial Generation: Hearing God's Call* (Saint Meinrad School of Theology, 2000); and Robert Wuthnow, *After Heaven: Spirituality in America Since the 1950s*. (Los Angeles: University of California Press, 2000] have characterized the so-called "baby-boom generation," who experienced upheaval both in the Church (after the Council) and in the culture (with the sexual and counter-cultural revolution of the 1960s and 70s), as "totally modern." In other words, this generation, the Catholic parents of Gen Y, rejected traditional liturgical forms, art, and piety as "old fashioned" and "out of date superstition" without recognizing the inherent theological truths embedded within them or the real human needs that they met.

7   Cf. e.g., Karl H. Peschke, *Christian Ethics: Moral Theology in the Light of Vatican II*, Vol. 2, *Special Moral Theology* (Alcester, UK: C. Goodliffe Neale, 1985), 144f.; Francis J. Connell, *Father Connell Answers Moral Questions* (Washington, DC: The Catholic University of America Press, 1959), 75f.

8   Cf. e.g., Vatican Council II, Constitution on the Sacred Liturgy, *Sacrosanctum Concilium*, 26–27.

9   National Conference of Catholic Bishops, "The Sacraments via Electronic Communication," BCL Newsletter (June 1999) available on-line:

http://www.usccb.org/liturgy/innews/699.shtml, accessed on 29 September 2005.

10 Cf. 1983 *Codex Iuris Canonici (CIC)*, c. 960.

11 Apostolic Penitentiary, *Circular Letter*, Prot. N. 500/02, 23 October 2002.

12 Cf. *CIC*, c. 1104.

13 Cf. *CIC*, c. 1105.

14 Cf. *CIC*, cc. 1061 §1, 1141.

15 Cf. e.g., National Conference of Catholic Bishops (NCCB), Committee on the Liturgy, "Guidelines for Televising the Liturgy," November, 1997; available on-line: http://www.usccb.org/liturgy/current/tv.shtml.

16 Cf. Pius XII, *Miranda Prorsus*, Encyclical Letter, 8 September 1957, 4. Pope Pius XII explicitly states that physical presence is required for participation at Mass. He cites an earlier statement of his: *Sermo ad radiophonicae artis cultores conventum ex omnibus Nationibus participantes*: d. 5 Maii, a. 1950; *Discorsi e Radiomessaggi* di S S. Pio XII, vol. XII, pag. 75; available on-line: http://www.vatican.va/holy_father/pius_xii/encyclicals/ documents /hf_p-xii_enc_08091957_miranda-prorsus_en.html, accessed on 8 Nov 2005. One might argue that Pius XII himself is being inconsistent in requiring physical presence for the Mass because he decreed that one may receive the indulgence of a papal blessing over the radio (cf. AAS, XXXI [1939], 277). However, blessings are sacramentals which prepare one for grace. In sacramentals it is not the matter that mediates the grace as is the case for the sacraments. Sacramentals, further, are instituted by the Church and so the Church has the broad authority to establish the manner of administration – a power which she does not possess with regard to the Sacraments. While the dangers associated with virtual reality might recommend the reappraisal of broadcasting blessings because of its potentially negative pedagogical implications, it does not in any way contradict the necessity of physical presence for the actual bestowing of grace through the sacraments. Further, Pius XII's statement covers only papal blessings given over the radio as being valid for the indulgence. It is not at all evident that this validity extends beyond the papal blessing for the specific purpose of the indulgence. It is reasonable to believe that the universality of the pope combined with the discretion he has in applying indulgences makes this a singular situation.

17 Pius XII, *Miranda Prorsus*, 4.

18 Cf. Paul VI, *Mysterium Fidei*, Encyclical Letter, 3 September 1965, 39.

19 Cf. e.g., DS 902 (481) stated at the *Council of Vienne*, 1311–1312.

20 Cf. John Paul II, Wednesday General Audience, 31 October 1979,

21 Cf. *DS* 802 (430), 1640–1642 (876–877).

22 Cf. John Paul II, Wednesday General Audience, 20 October 1982. While the dimension of spousal unity in the Eucharist is implicit explicit in his Wednesday audience cited here, it is explicit in *Mane Nobiscum, Domine*, 31.

23 This spousal unity associated with the Eucharist is also found, sometimes

explicitly, in the Catholic mystical writers such as Sts. Bernard of Clairvaux in his *Sermons on the Song of Songs* 83 and 85, Teresa of Avila in her *Meditations on the Song of Songs*, 1, 31; and John of the Cross in *Ascent of Mt Carmel* XI, XII, *Living Flame of Love*, Stanza 1, and especially his *Spiritual Canticle of the Soul and the Bridegroom Christ*, Stanza 1.

24 Cf. *Summa Theologiae*, Ia IIae, Q. 110, a. 2, ad. 2. "Every substance is either the nature of the thing whereof it is the substance or is a part of the nature, even as matter and form are called substance. And because grace is above human nature, it cannot be a substance or a substantial form, but is an accidental form of the soul. Now what is substantially in God, becomes accidental in the soul participating the Divine goodness, as is clear in the case of knowledge. And thus because the soul participates in the Divine goodness imperfectly, the participation of the Divine goodness, which is grace, has its being in the soul in a less perfect way than the soul subsists in itself. Nevertheless, inasmuch as it is the expression or participation of the Divine goodness, it is nobler than the nature of the soul, though not in its mode of being" (*ST* vol 2, (Westminster, MD: Christian Classics,1948), 1133). This is not unlike the manner in which one comes to know an object by incorporating the object's form into one's soul (cf. *Summa Theologiae*, Ia, Q. 84, a. 1).

25 Pontifical Council for Social Communications, "The Church and the Internet," 22 February 2002, 5; available on-line: http://www.vatican.va/roman_curia/pontifical_councils/pccs/documents/rc _pc_pccs_doc_20020228_church-internet_en.html, accessed on 9 November 2005.

26 *Ibid.*, 9.

Panel on Christian Anthropology and Contemporary Psychological Studies

Introduction
The Integration of Psychological Wisdom into Moral Theology

REVEREND JOHN F. HARVEY, O.S.F.S.

Vatican Council II made a signal contribution to Christian anthropology. This was especially true of the Pastoral Constitution on the Modern World, *Gaudium et Spes*. Psychology, or the science of the mind, soul, or spirit, is a particularly important aspect of anthropology today, of course, and it is therefore important to examine how modern psychological studies relate to the Christian view of man and to Church teaching – and most especially how contemporary psychological wisdom can be integrated into moral theology. These are much needed inquiries.

When I was a student at Catholic University, I was influenced and impressed by the late Rudolph Allers, who, in my two years of philosophy, taught me in a course called Educational Psychology. As a result, I resolved that I would study for a Master's degree in psychology. My hope was that I might learn to integrate psychological knowledge and insights with theological and moral principles. After I had studied moral theology for several years with the late Father Francis J. Connell, C.Ss.R, I believed that I could profitably research the borderline between moral theology and psychological insights and data.

My first big opportunity along these lines came in 1956 when I addressed some thousand Notre Dame nuns in Maryland on the respective counseling approaches of Karl Rogers and St. Francis de Sales. Many similar opportunities followed in the ensuing years.

Meanwhile, as early as 1953, I had seen the need to study the data on homosexual behavior and how the Church should guide people with tendencies towards same-sex attractions in the practice of chastity. Before that I had had no particular interest in homosexuality as such – until my provincial called me into his office one day and asked me why my student-priests knew so little about homosexual behavior. This was in 1953. I responded: "Give them a break, Father." We were not going to discuss the subject until April, but then they took their examinations on hearing confessions in March, and did not do so well on this subject. "All right," my provincial said. "But see to it that your students know this next year."

I told myself that, most certainly, my students would know all about this subject the following year – and the years following that. As a result, I started to read many articles in psychological, psychiatric, and other professional journals, and I began to see how to deal with both the moral and the psychological aspects of homosexual behavior.

These were the beginnings of my own concern with and specialization on the subject of homosexuality. These beginnings led to the many years in which I have been engaged not only in teaching moral theology but also in the pastoral care of homosexual Christians. Little did I imagine at the time that I would end up writing or editing four books and many articles on the subject – not to speak of founding the organization Courage in order to assist persons with homosexual tendencies as well as those who help and counsel them. I thank God that, as a result, many have found healing and spiritual growth through acceptance of the Gospel.

In view of this special background and experience of my own, I was happy to hear a few years back about the founding of the Institute for Psychological Sciences in Northern Virginia. This was much needed development, in fact one long overdue. This new Institute strives as an institution of higher education to do what I have been trying to do for many years now, namely, to try to integrate sound psychological knowledge and insights with Catholic philosophy and theology and Church teaching – and not only on the subject of homosexuality (which happens to loom so large today) but across the board in what pertains to the Christian life generally.

We are fortunate at this convention to have Dean Gladys Sweeney and two professors from the Institute for Psychological Sciences, Doctors Paul Vitz and E. Christian Brugger, to give us three stimulating presentations on how various contemporary themes in psychological studies relate to important aspects of Catholic theology and the faith.

Father John H. Harvey, O.S.F.S., S.T.D., taught moral theology for more than forty years at the DeSales School of Theology. He is the founder of the organization Courage founded to help homosexuals wishing to live a chaste Christian life. For more than thirty years he has been engaged in the pastoral care of persons with homosexual tendencies. In the course of his work in this field, he has become one of the world's foremost authorities on the subject of homosexuality and the moral life. He is the author of more than 50 articles, as well as of the books: *The Homosexual Person: New Thinking in Pastoral Care* (Ignatius, 1987); and *The Truth about Homosexuality: The Cry of the Faithful* (Ignatius, 1996). With Notre Dame Law Professor Gerard V. Bradley, he authored the volume *Same-Sex Attraction: A Parent's Guide* (St. Augustine Press, 2003). Father Harvey was awarded the Fellowship's Cardinal Wright Award in 1988.

The Psychological Significance of "Touch"
A Concrete Manifestation of Man's Relationality

GLADYS A. SWEENEY

Introduction

Jesus' love touched all people. Literally. The Gospels are replete with illustrations of Jesus' use of touch to convey healing, forgiveness, compassion, and love.[1] Why touch? Certainly Jesus had the power to heal, forgive, and touch souls without physical contact. That He chose to use this human connection, this power of touch, is not at all surprising. Touch itself – and the psychological significance of touch – stand out as key indicators of man's relationality.

I speak to you today not as a theologian, but as a psychologist. The concepts of God as relational and of man as a relational being are important topics of discussion among theologians today.[2] My focus as a psychologist, however, will be on empirical data from the sciences demonstrating that man is meant to be relational. He not only needs to be in relationship with others in order to survive and to develop normally, he actually becomes himself most fully through his relationships with others.

"Relationality" means, *inter alia* , that we are not created in isolation but, on the contrary, that we are called to be in relationship with others from the first moment of our existence. And this relationship is not an abstract idea of relatedness but a very physical one. From conception, the unborn child – though a distinct person – is in the closest physical contact possible with another human being: he is literally inside his mother. As John Paul II noted: "On the human level, can there be any other *'communion'* comparable to that *between a mother and a child* whom she has carried in her womb and then brought to birth?"[3] From conception through birth and infancy, a child's close physical contact with his mother reveals much about the nature of touch.

The Nature of Touch

Touch develops early. In fact, one of the earliest sensory systems to develop in the human embryo is the somesthetic system – related to touch.[4] The nerve pathways in the skin develop first, followed by those related to movement, balance, hearing, and vision.[5] "[T]here is increasing evidence to indicate that the fetus experiences touch in utero,"[6] as unborn children as young as 13 ½ weeks move in response to stimuli in the uterine wall. Further, the parts of the brain necessary for self-awareness "are formed by twenty-eight to thirty-two weeks gestation...Thus intrauterine tactile experiences may provide the rudimentary foundations for perception of boundaries between one's own body and that of another."[7] The unborn child, then, begins to interpret the meaning of touch in a very basic way. As this paper will explore, touch "serves a multitude of purposes, ranging from maintaining an infant's state, to increasing weight gain and caloric intake in preterm infants, to providing comfort and warmth, to providing a means of social communication, to adjusting posture, to serving an important means of developing the early parent-infant relationship..."[8]

Most significantly, for our purposes, touch becomes the gateway to an infant's experience of relationships – particularly with his mother. One researcher expressed the connection between touch and man's relationality in this way: "Touch is inherently relational. The act of tickling is a good example...it is not possible to tickle oneself. The laughter evoked by tickling appears to depend entirely on the social situation....Similarly, to experience hugging demands a partner...Each of these examples makes clear the relational aspect" of touch.[9]

The Power of Touch: Infant Survival Depends on Human Contact

While touch has always been a natural part of human relationships, its significance was long underestimated. As modern society became better at safeguarding human life and health, especially through technology and medical innovation, for a time it overlooked the relational needs of the whole person. The consequences of such a one-sided view of the human person were disastrous.

Studies over the past 50 years have demonstrated that simply providing for an infant's physical needs is inadequate: it fails even to ensure his survival. Human touch – and all that it implies – is essential for survival. In the early 20th century, scientists observed the impact of institutional care on infants, both in Europe and in the United States. Though the institutions were sanitary and provided the food, care, and shelter infants needed, a huge percentage (31.7 to 75%) of the infants in the institutions studied died within the first year of life.[10] These figures supported anecdotal reports from medical doctors in several cities during the same time period. For example, the mortality rate in Baltimore institutions was estimated at over 90%; Albany reported one institution with an estimated death rate of nearly 100%.[11] These poor survival rates were not simply a function of inadequate medical care or neglect. Rather, they were the products of little or no interaction – even basic physical touch – with caring human beings. In particular, the absence of the mother or a loving substitute left the infant's emotional and developmental needs unmet. As a result, those infants were more prone to sickness and death and, as later studies showed, to psychological disturbances.

As a starting point, this early research on the value of touch points to an essential truth: the human person is a unity of body and soul. In addition to basic physical needs that must be met, he has emotional needs that can be met only in the context of relationship.

Lack of Touch (and by Implication, Relationship) Impairs Infant Development

Touch is significant not only in ensuring survival but also for a child's proper development. When caring, loving touch, offered in the context of a relationship, is absent, infants develop poorly. Studies in the 1930s in Europe noted that even as death rates among institutionalized children dropped, the rate of severe psychiatric illnesses soared. "Institutionalized children practically without exception developed subsequent psychiatric disturbances and became asocial, delinquent, feeble-minded, psychotic, or problem children."[12]

In short, institutionalization destroyed the very lives it meant to protect. The explanation was twofold: First, in institutional settings children were deprived of stimulation in an effort to sterilize the surroundings and make them germ-free. Yet even with hygienic environments, the infants in institutional care showed decreased resistance to illness and limited ability to regain health after illness. Second, the absence of the child's mother had a tremendously negative effect. "Stimulation by the mother will always be more intensive than even that of the best trained nursery personnel...Those institutions in which the mothers were present had better results than those where only trained child nurses were employed."[13] The mother's absence contributed to severe psychological damage, not just because mothers are better at providing stimulation but because a mother's touch frames the contours of a loving, human relationship.

A long-term, comprehensive study (the "Spitz study"), undertaken during the mid-century, honed in on the reasons why institutionalized children suffered psychiatric problems and developmental delays: the lack of human contact. It compared the developmental outcomes for infants in two different institutions with each other and with children in home environments. The Spitz study noted crucial differences between the two institutions – and very different outcomes. The first institution was a foundling home, which, while antiseptically clean, offered little stimulation and little contact with a mother or mother-substitute after the infant was weaned. The other institution, a home for delinquent girls and their infants, generally allowed the mothers to remain an active presence in their infant's lives. The children in the girls' home, while generally less gifted from birth, showed a steady developmental rate. The children in the foundling home began at a higher level developmentally but "spectacularly deteriorated,"[14] most notably after they were weaned. This developmental deterioration occurred even though the "nurses[at the Foundling home were]…unusually motherly, baby-loving women; but…the babies of Foundling Home nevertheless lack all human contact for most of the day [due to a ratio of one nurse to at least seven infants]."[15] In contrast, the home for delinquent girls, although an institutional setting, required the children's mothers or a consistent substitute to provide baby care. It "provides each child with a mother to the nth degree, a mother who gives the child everything a good mother does and, beyond that, everything else she has. Foundling Home does not give the child a mother, nor even a substitute mother, but only an eighth of a nurse."[16]

The benefit to the children who were with their mothers was expressed in this way by the Spitz study: "The interchange between mother and child is loaded with emotional factors and it is in this interchange that the child learns to play…In these emotional relations with the mother the child is introduced to learning and later to imitation. We have previously mentioned that the motherless children in the Foundling Home are unable to speak, to feed themselves, or to acquire habits of cleanliness: it is the security provided by the mother in the field of locomotion, the emotional bait offered by the mother calling to her child, that teaches him to walk. When this is lacking, even children two to three years cannot walk."[17]

A second study by Spitz noted that children who had been in the full-time care of their mothers, but who were then unavoidably separated from them (at ages 6 to 11 months) for a period of months responded with severe depression marked by weeping, withdrawal, and disconnect from their surroundings and others.[18] The infants regressed developmentally as well. In every case, however, when the relationship with the mother was restored, the depression evaporated and the child's developmental measures (which had fallen during the time of separation) jumped. Within just twelve hours after the mothers' return, the children scored up to 36.6 percent higher on developmental indices.[19]

More recent research has confirmed the emotional pathology that results when infants are deprived of touch in the pivotal first year of life. Children who were raised in institutions for the first three years of life suffered an impaired ability to establish deep relationships. "These children developed an 'isolation type of personality characterized by unsocial behavior, hostile aggression, lack of patterns for giving and receiving affection, inability to understand and accept limitations, much insecurity in adapting to environment."[20]

Another study yielded similar results: "The life histories tend to confirm the ...conclusion that infant deprivation results in a basic defect of total personality. This defect manifests itself in the spheres of intellect and feeling...suggesting that the institution child's personality is congealed at a level of extreme immaturity."[21] The lack of loving touch in an infant's first years creates a lasting legacy of impaired relationships. "From the start there is the dual problem of meeting his need for love and of molding his impulses and drives in accord with social requirements. His appetite for affection is insatiable and there is no appreciable development of the capacity for identifying with and loving others...The institution child...establishes no specific identification and engages in no meaningful reciprocal relationships with other people."[22] Ignoring the child's need for touch, for human relationships, in effect treats him as a material being – and damages his very humanity.

Healthy Development Requires Touch in the Context of Relationships

Not all studies focus on negative results for touch-deprived infants. Touch correlates with normal development because, as body-persons, we naturally relate to other human beings in a bodily way, not an abstract or theoretical way. More recent studies highlight the necessity of touch for optimal development; additional research also delineates the kinds and frequencies of touch, which make a difference in a child's life

One reason why touch is so essential to proper development is because it provides a vehicle for stimulation. Early studies that aimed to understand the nature and significance of touch relied on data from studies with rhesus monkeys: "Harlow's classic work with rhesus monkeys substantiated the importance of tactile stimulation by demonstrating that contact was more important than reducing the feeding drive for the development of social attachment."[23] In other words, monkeys developed a preference for a soft object over one that offered food but not comforting contact.

The studies of institutional care also support the view that lack of touch, and the resulting lack of stimulation, were primary causes of the infants' slow development. Other researchers, however, argued "the lack of intimate relationships is the factor responsible for institutionalized children's problems."[24]

In reality, the two factors are related. Touch provides stimulation, but touch also conveys meaning – meaning that grows out of the relationship between two people. An expanding field of research not only underscores the infant's need for human contact in order to develop properly, but also sheds light on the emotional value of touch in the context of relationships.

Every parent who has dealt with a newborn knows instinctively that holding, rocking, and caressing a fussy infant soothes him. Recent research supports that parental intuition: touch reduces crying, promotes healthy weight gain and consistent feeding, and even ameliorates failure to thrive syndrome.[25] Studies of pre-term infants shed further light on the value of touch. Because they are born early, pre-term infants are deprived of valuable *in utero* contact with the mother. Even in the womb, the unborn child benefits from physical contact with the mother, as studies reveal a "strong relationship between maternal sleep stages and intrauterine fetal activity."[26] One theory of why premature infants have a difficult time regulating temperature and breathing is that they "are deprived of the regulatory influences of maternal biological rhythms."[27] Touch, however, is an effective intervention for these vulnerable infants. "Body contact has been stressed as a most fundamentally important form of stimulation for early development."[28] Touch therapy, as well as specially designed waterbeds designed to simulate human contact, successfully compensate for the missing maternal contact, resulting in fewer instances of apnea (interrupted breathing) in these infants.[29]

For full-term infants, touch interventions produced improved health benefits as well, affecting "metabolism, intestinal motility and glandular, biochemical, and muscular changes."[30] Interestingly, infants who receive as little as an extra 20 minutes of handling a day showed greater visual attentiveness than those who did not receive the extra touching.[31]

But the power of touch goes beyond the physical benefits: it is necessary for emotional development as well. "The socialization of human newborns and their parents, that first relationship, begins early, even in the womb. Beyond its survival value, contact and affection between mother/father and infant are likely to serve the infant's developing social and emotional needs."[32] Most parents naturally touch their newborns in wonder and awe. Several studies confirm that "parents' first contacts with their newborns reveal the use of touch as integral and seemingly

central to those first communications."[33] Daily routines of touching
enhance bonding between parents and infant so that "positive effects
may be observed on the whole family system, rather than solely impact-
ing on the infant."[34]

Touch is instrumental not only in bonding the parent to the infant,
but also in creating an attachment relationship between them. But the
quality of touch matters – *what* the touch conveys is as important as the
touch itself. One noted researcher, Sandra Weiss, classified touch
according to duration, location, intensity, and sensation.[35] She noted
that, "Diverse qualities of touch may be viewed as symbols in a language of touch, just as word symbols create a verbal and written language for communication and shared meaning."[36] Touch conveys emotions, and "the type of touch conveys particular emotions. Emotions
(feeling states or messages) that might be communicated through touch
include: love and caring, sympathy, empathy, anger, and sense of security…"[37]

Another researcher pinpointed the two ways that touch conveys
meaning: "First, touch may transmit the caregiver's perceptions,
thoughts, and /or feelings to the infant….[or] the caregiver's touch may
influence that infant's perceptions, thoughts, feelings, or behaviors."[38]
Touch is "capable of communicating and eliciting positive emotions…as
well as modulating negative ones."[39] The emotions accompanying the
touch, experienced simultaneously, add to its meaning. "[P]ain, disgust,
fear, or tension, in contrast to feelings of closeness, comfort, relaxation,
or yielding which take place during a particular touch, give the tactile act
further meaning as it is carried to the CNS [Central Nervous System]."[40]
The kind of touch given affects the emotions felt by the infant.
Depressed mothers tended to engage in touch that elicited more negative
emotions from infants.[41] "[I]nfants who had received harsher and more
frequent touch demonstrated more aggressive and destructive behaviors
while infants who had received more nurturing touch had significantly
less depression and anxiety."[42] These results were measured over several years, suggesting long-term effects of touch as well as the short-term
emotional effect.[43]

"Attachment theorists have long regarded the quality of parent-
infant physical touch as a central feature of the responsive and available
care-giving environment that is necessary to foster an infant's sense of
security."[44] Meaningful touch between the mother (or mother-substitute)
and child helps strengthen the child's attachment to his mother, which in
turn creates a secure child. Attachment research highlights

> the importance of mothers' and infants' sensitivity to each
> other's behavior, and the role of touch in behavioral regulation.

Sensitivity and responsiveness have direct links to attachment, relationship quality and future interactions. Moreover, the amount and quality of physical contact (touching, proximity) are important to the mother-infant relationship...Contact behaviors have been found to be integral features of emotional communication between mothers and infants and higher levels of touch are related to secure positive attachment... Maternal sensitivity, considered a key contributor to synchronous and mutually reciprocal interactions, has been recently related to optimal patterns of attachment....The characteristics of maternal sensitivity and responsiveness often involves physical closeness and physical touching behaviors.[45]

However, when caregivers reject physical contact, especially ventral –central contact, with their infants,"[46] less secure attachment results.

Touch Contributes to the Child's Sense of Self (Self-Perception)

The human person becomes himself most fully through his relationships with others. We know this as a theological truth, but science also testifies that on the most basic level, the child's concept of himself as a person is shaped through his relationships with others. Specifically, how others touch him affects his perception of himself, his body and his sexuality. From birth onward, "body experiences are the primary means for relationship with others....[One study] has indicated that if a human infant is not given the handling necessary for integrating early undifferentiated bodily sensations, the effect could be a basic distortion of lack of perceptual integration of the body image."[47]

While this is a newer area of study, and warrants further research, preliminary results suggest that a child's self-perception is dependent, in part, on parental touch.

Under normal conditions, parents are the most significant people in the development of the child's body image, for the interaction with parents imparts an indelible impression on the child...From the initial tactile interaction with mother to those with father, children's perceptions of their bodies as meaningful objects begin to form....parents endure as those individuals whose touching offers the most available, consistent, and influential source of qualitative information...The body image develops against a background of differences in the qualities present in these tactile interactions between the child and the parents, an image that becomes integrated over time into a personal frame of reference for the child.[48]

A child's awareness of his own body, in turn, affects his larger sense of self. "A person's entire developing sense of self, although not limited

to sensations generated by the body, appears to be rooted in body awareness, body functions, and body activities…This assumption is supported by studies which show a significant correlation between one's feelings and perceptions regarding the body and one's concept of the total
self."[49]

In other words, the touches a child receives, particularly from his
parents, shape not only his basic perceptions of his body, but also his
perception of physical integrity itself, and ultimately the meaning he
attributes to his body. Those touches provide him both data and an interpretive context for the data. They help him begin to intuit who he is. In
short, a child's sense of how he is touched contributes directly to his
emerging sense of relationality and thus his personhood.

> The existence of a relationship and the nature of this relation-
> ship with the mother or parent are the cornerstone of developing
> identifications. They color the child's grasp of himself, his relation
> to people outside of the primary family group, his relation to the
> material world of things, his mode of solution of problems that may
> arise to meet him, his level of conceptualization, and probably even
> his simplest perceptions.[50]

Of course, a child's sense of who he is – and even who he can
become – depends in a concrete way on his relationships and on what
those relationships convey to him about himself. But in its fullest sense,
his relationality is far more than that. It becomes the framework for communicating meaning – significance, acceptance, and love – from one
person to another. In the process, the parent's message of love or lack of
love (communicated in part through the quality of touch) enables or
cripples the child as he begins to make sense of his existence, to understand himself and the meaning of his own life. He gives and receives
love and in turn is shaped by love, or not. And it is only in a love relationship that he discovers his true value and meaning. As John Paul II
reminded us in *Redemptor Hominis*, "Man remains a being incomprehensible to himself without love." He might have said a child remains
incomprehensible to himself without touch.[51]

The reality is that we are already in relationship with God because
we are created by Him and sustained by Him. Continuing contact with
Him as the source of love is essential for our growth as human persons;
in the same way, the love that is communicated by touch is essential to
normal human development. The relationship (initially that between
mother and child) that exists from the moment of conception sustains
and supports our essential human development. More importantly, it
helps us to know ourselves. In giving the gift of self, through loving

touch, the mother helps her infant to discover his significance, the fact that he is loved and created for love. We understand who we are by the sincere gift of self. It defines us, but the infant needs to receive it first.

In the *Letter to Women*,[52] John Paul II notes that the mother's joy – her smile – is "God's own smile upon the newborn child." In the same way, a mother's touches are God's own touches. It is the touch, first, of creation as the mother's touch participates in the unfolding of the child's sense of his divinely created personhood. And it is the touch of love – ultimately, the love of Jesus.

ENDNOTES

1   One of the most well known stories in the Gospels highlights the significance of touch in relationships – specifically in Christ's relationship with the hemorrhaging woman. In Luke 8:43–48, we read:

And a woman who had a flow of blood for twelve years and had spent all her living on physicians and could not be healed by any one, came up behind him, and touched the fringe of his garment; and immediately her flow of blood ceased. And Jesus said, "Who was it that touched me?" When all denied it, Peter said, "Master, the multitudes surround you and press upon you!" But Jesus said, "Some one touched me; for I perceive that power has gone forth from me." And when the woman saw that she was not hidden, she came trembling, and falling down before him declared in the presence of all the people why she had touched him, and how she had been immediately healed. And he said to her, "Daughter, your faith has made you well; go in peace.

2   Cardinal Ratzinger, in his book, *Introduction to Christianity,* Ignatius Press, San Francisco (1990), states that, "the confession of faith in God as a person necessarily includes the acknowledgement of God as relatedness, as communicability, as fruitfulness. The unrelated, unrelatable, absolutely one could not be person." (p.128) He goes on to explain that the Trinity "exist(s) on a different level, on that of relation, of the 'relative.'" (130)

In the one and indivisible God there exists the phenomenon of dialogue, the reciprocal exchange of word and love. This again signifies that the "three persons" who exist in God are the reality of word and love in their attachment to each other...St. Augustine once enshrined this idea in the following formula: "He is not called Father with reference to himself but only in relation to the Son; seen by himself he is simply God..." "Father" is purely a concept of relationship. Only in being-for-the-other is he Father; in his own being-in himself, he is simply God. Person is the pure relation of being related, nothing else. Relationship is not something extra added to the person, as it is with us; it only exists at all as relatedness."

In another work, "Retrieving the Tradition: Concerning the Notion of Person in Theology," *Communio* 17, Fall, 1990, Cardinal Ratzinger explains more fully the connection between God as relation and the human person as a relational being:

> In God, person means relation. Relation, being related, is not something superadded to the person, but it is the person itself. In its nature, the person exists only *as* relation...One could thus define the first person as self-donation in fruitful knowledge and love; it is not the one who gives himself, in whom the act of self-donation is found, but it is this self-donation, pure reality of act. (p.444)...[M]an does not posit the reservation of what is merely and properly his own, does not strive to form the substance of the closed self, but enters into pure relativity toward the other and toward God. It is in this way that he truly comes to himself and into the fullness of his own, because he enters into unity with the one to whom he is related. (445)

> Let us summarize: in God there are three persons – which implies...that persons are relations, pure relatedness. Although this is in the first place only a statement about the Trinity, it is at the same time the fundamental statement about what is at stake in the concept of person. It opens the concept of person into the human spirit and provides its foundation and origin. (p. 447)

> This is the meaning of Christology from its origin: what is disclosed in Christ, whom faith certainly presents as unique, is not only a speculative exception; what is disclosed in truth is what the riddle of the human person really intends...Christ is not the ontological exception...he is, on the contrary, the fulfillment of the entire human being...then the Christological concept of person is an indication for theology of how person is to be understood as such...(p.450)

> If the human person is all the more with itself, and is itself, the more it is able to reach beyond itself, the more it is with the other , then the person is all the more itself the more it is with the wholly other, with God. (450–1) In other words, the spirit comes to itself in the other, it becomes completely itself the more it is with the other, with God. ...relativity toward the other constitutes the human person. The human person is the event or being of relativity. The more the person's relativity aims totally and directly at its final goal, at transcendence, the more the person is itself. (451)

3   John Paul II, *Letter to Families* , no. 7 (1994)

4   Stack, D, "The Salience of Touch and Physical Contact During Infancy: Unraveling Some of the Mysteries of the Somesthetic Sense," *Blackwell Handbook of Infant Development* , ed by Gavin Bremner and Alan Fogel, Blackwell Publishers (2001), p.352

5   Weiss, S.J., "Parental Touching: Correlates of a Child's Body Concept and Body Sentiment," *Touch: The Foundation of Experience* , Kathryn E. Barnard and T. Berry Brazelton, eds., In durational University Press, Inc., Conn. (1990), p. 427

6   Weiss, p. 426

7   Weiss, p. 426

8   Stack, D., "The Salience of Touch and Physical Contact During Infancy:
     Unraveling Some of the Mysteries of the Somesthetic Sense," *Blackwell
     Handbook of Infant Development*, edited by Gavin Bremner and Alan
     Fogel, Blackwell Publishers (2001), p. 368

9   Stack, p. 369

10   Sptiz, R.A., "Hospitalism: An Inquiry into the Genesis of Psychiatric
     Conditions in Early Childhood," *Psychoanalytic Study of the Child*, Yale
     University Press, Vol. 1, (1945), p. 53

11   Spitz, p. 53

12   Spitz, p. 54

13   Spitz, p. 55

14   Spitz, p. 59

15   Spitz, p. 64

16   Spitz, p. 65

17   Spitz, p. 68

18   Sptiz, R.A., "Anaclitic Depression," *Psychoanalytic Study of the Child* ,
     Yale University Press_, vol. 2 (1946)

19   Spitz, Anaclitic, p. 330.

20   Goldfarb, W. "Psychological Privation in Infancy and Subsequent
     Adjustment", *American Jounal of Orthopsychiatry,* vol 15. (1945) p.19.

21   Goldfarb,W. "Psychological Privation in Infancy and Subsequent
     Adjustment," *American Journal of Orthopsychiatry* , vol .15 (1945), p. 252

22   Goldfarb, 253–254.

23   Stack, p. 352

24   Stack, p. 353

25   Stack, p. 354 and 364.

26   Korner,A.F., "The Many Faces of Touch", *Touch: The Foundation of
     Experience*, Kathryn E. Barnard & T. Berry Brazelton, eds., International
     University Press (1990), p. 281

27   Korner, p.281

28   Korner, p. 273

29   Korner, 291

30   Weiss, p. 428

31   Weiss, p. 428

32   Stack, p. 355

33   Stack, p. 356

34   Stack, p. 357

35   Weiss, 430–432

36   Weiss, p. 430

37   Stack, p. 362

38   Hertenstein, M. "Touch: Its Communicative Functions in Infancy," *Human
     Development*, vol. 45 (2002), p. 72

39   Hertenstein, p. 75–76

40   Weiss, p. 430

41   Hertenstein, p. 77

42   Hertenstein, p. 77
43   Hertenstein, p. 77
44   Hertenstein, p. 79
45   Stack, p. 363 In addition, if the mother is feeling more affectionate, she tends to express affection more frequently. Conversely, "Positive touch stimulation has been shown to enhance positive affect and attention in infants of depressed mothers." Stack, p. 364. Depressed moms touched their infants more but in "intrusive " and "overstimulatory" ways. Stack, p. 364
46   Hertenstein, p. 80
47   Weiss, p. 427–8
48   Weiss, p. 434. Weiss' study yielded interesting but preliminary results showing different effects of parental touch on boys and girls. Father-touch tended to be more instrumental, while mother-touch tended to be more nurturing. More research is needed in this area to study the effects of touch from each parent on the different sexes.
49   Weiss, p. 425 Weiss notes elsewhere that the experiences of pain and pleasure also shape the body image: Studies have shown "that painful tactile stimuli (discomfort sensations) distort the body image by preventing adequate functioning of the body's perceptual system. Additionally…[another researcher] indicates that pleasurable tactile interaction (the comfort quality of sensation) allows for maximal discrimination, providing vital information for development of a positive and stable cathexis of one's body as a worthwhile and valuable part of self." Weiss, p. 433–4.
50   Goldfarb,W., Effects of Psychological Deprivation in Infancy and Subsequent Stimulation , *American Journal of Psychiatry*, vol. 102 (1945), p. 18
51   Love occurs in the context of self-giving relationships, especially the family. In his encyclical *Fides et Ratio*, Sept. 14, 1998, John Paul II pointed out that man obtains knowledge about his world and about what is true through reason and experience, but also through trust and through our relationships with others (particularly family relationships). He emphasizes that

   Human beings are not made to live alone. They are born into a family and in a family they grow…From birth, therefore, they are immersed in traditions which give them not only a language and a cultural formation but also a range of truths in which they can believe almost instinctively…there are in the life of a human being many more truths which are simply believed than truths which are acquired by way of personal verification….This means that the human being – the one who seeks the truth – is also *the one who lives by belief.* [31] In believing, we entrust ourselves to the knowledge acquired by other people…belief is often humanly richer than mere evidence, because it involves an interpersonal relationship and brings into play not only a person's capacity to know but also the deeper capacity to entrust oneself to others, to enter into a relationship with them which is intimate and enduring. It should be stressed that the truths sought in this interpersonal relationship are not primarily empirical or philosophical. Rather what is sought is *the truth of the person* – what the person is and what the person reveals from deep within. Human perfection, then consists not simply in acquiring an abstract knowledge of the truth, but in a dynamic relationship of faithful self-giving with others. It is in this faithful self-giving that a person finds a fullness of certainty and security. [32]

52   John Paul II, *Letter to Women* , (June 29, 1995), no. 2.

Bodliness and Relationality in Philosophy and Psychology

E. CHRISTIAN BRUGGER

Introduction

This panel is a scholarly exercise illustrating a part of the larger intellectual project of the Institute for Psychological Sciences (IPS), which is to integrate into the subject matter of modern clinical psychology relevant truths on the nature and flourishing of the human person, derived both from divine revelation and philosophical reflection. This exercise (indeed the existence of the IPS itself), we think, is justified by the following two propositions:

> 1) That modern psychology can be corrected and developed (i.e., helped to do better what it does) by being brought into systematic, critical, and reciprocal dialogue with Catholic faith and philosophy; and
>
> 2) That anthropological truths, whether derived from divine revelation or philosophical reflection, whether formulated as descriptive ontological premises (e.g., human nature, and each man and woman, are made in the image God, human nature is rational, is bodily, is relational, is fallen, is redeemed, etc.); or as normative moral truths (e.g., it is never good to intend to kill the innocent), will have some corroborative correlate in empirical psychology.

We do not intend to argue here deductively for the truthfulness of these propositions, the first of which you might think rather obvious, the second perhaps more interesting. Rather, we hope to illustrate their truthfulness by reflecting on a common aspect of the human person from the three domains in which we are intellectually interested at the IPS, i.e., philosophy, theology, and clinical psychology.

Our aim, as has been said, is to consider an aspect of human personhood, first through the lenses of Catholic philosophy and theology, and then to show how certain important truths, affirmed philosophically and theologically, are underwritten by the data of clinical psychology. This aim is not ambitious. In time we hope for clinical data to help us develop, correct, and formulate more persuasively our philosophical and theological expositions and defense of the complex nature and eudaemonic needs of the human person.

What suggests that an exercise of this kind will be successful is the Christian doctrine of Creation, which posits the created universe as an orderly intelligible whole with the human person occupying a unique position which is at once material and non-material, with natural and supernatural significances. We know from revelation that faith and reason are complementary sources of knowledge about the human person. It follows that sound systematic reflection on human nature and its operations should encounter no fundamental discontinuities when moving from the perspective of faith to that of reason and vice versa. Whatever can be said about the human person that is true from the perspective of theological anthropology should, therefore, have some resonating correlate with truths arising from philosophical anthropological reflection, as well as truths arising from the psychological, biological, and physical sciences.

The aspect of human personhood that we intend as a panel to consider is the constitutive bodiliness of persons, and in particular, the necessity of bodiliness for human relationality. The philosophical propositions that I will defend as my part of the panel's exercise are: 1) bodiliness is a constitutive part of (i.e., defining feature of) full human personhood; and 2) there is no human relationality that, for the human person, is not always also bodily.

Bodiliness in Philosophy and Theology

Bodies are philosophically problematic. The complexities of consciousness, and the problem of articulating the precise relationship between it and its bodily counterpart, has given rise to two general theoretical positions on the nature of their relationship, two, that is, that start from the premise that bodiliness and consciousness (or mind) both exist, that they are a natural feature of human life on earth, and that neither can be reduced entirely to the other. The first is mind-body dualism, most influentially proposed by Plato. The second is the hylomorphism of Aristotle, systematized and developed by Aquinas. For purposes of this essay, I set aside accounts that reduce mind to body (e.g., as in materialist reductivist accounts, repeated most recently in modern psychology in the burgeoning field of cognitive neuroscience); and also accounts that consign body and matter in general to the condition of illusion (e.g., as in classical Hinduism, where believers are warned that materiality is *maya* – "a conjurers trick," expressed enduringly and most beautifully in the teaching of the Bagavad Gita).

Plato's Account: Plato's account, found in the *Phaedo* (the account of the final hours of the life of Socrates), teaches that bodies cannot be true substances because true substances exist only as eternal forms. A soul *is* a true substance because it is a pure form, invisible, glorious, and godlike.[1] Plato holds that the intellectual soul could not be united to its body as form to matter, for then it too would need to be matter since everything whose being is *in matter* must, he thought, itself be matter. The soul, therefore, must be related to body as some mover is related to the thing it moves: "The soul is in the body 'as a sailor in a ship.'"[2] Again: "Man is not a being composed of body and soul, but...the soul itself *using the body* is man; just as Peter is not a thing composed of man and clothes, but a man using clothes."[3] Material bodies are like shadows cast on a wall: "The soul is a helpless prisoner, chained hand and foot in the body, compelled to view reality not directly but only through its prison bars, and wallowing in utter ignorance."[4] Bodies are not intelligible in themselves but are made intelligible by the transcendent forms. Truth is a transcendent reality and bodies must be transcended in order to apprehend it. Philosophers learn this early on and struggle for the rest of their lives to extricate themselves from the obstacle of the body. The soul has a natural affinity to separate from the body, to free itself from the body's darkening and adulterating influence in the pursuit of wisdom:

> So long as we keep to the body and our soul is contaminated with this imperfection, there is no chance of our ever attaining satisfactorily to our object, which we assert to be truth. In the first place, the body provides us with innumerable distractions in the pursuit of our necessary substance, and any diseases which attack us hinder our quest for reality. Besides, the body fills us with loves and desires and fears and all sorts of fancies and a great deal of nonsense, with the result that we literally never get an opportunity to think at all about anything. Wars and revolutions and battles are due simply and solely to the body and its desires...Worst of all, if we do obtain any leisure from the body's claims and turn to some line of inquiry, the body intrudes once more into our investigations, interrupting, disturbing, distracting, and preventing us from getting a glimpse of the truth...The soul is most like that which is divine, immortal, intelligible, uniform, indissoluble, and ever self-consistent and invariable, whereas the body is most like that which is human, mortal, multiform, unintelligible, dissoluble, and never self-consistent.[5]

Aristotle's Account: Aristotle rejects Plato's idealism. Although like Plato he holds that a thing's form allows us to know what kind of thing it is, form for Aristotle is not an invisible immaterial reality in a transcendent realm. Form rather means a principle of actuation. Form exists in a hylomorphic relationship to matter (Gk: hulê – wood/matter, & morphê – form or shape). Matter and form exist together in an individuating, unified relationship. Aristotle posited two types of forms, accidental forms, qualities of some thing that do *not* make it what it is (e.g., whiteness); and substantial forms, that which makes something what it is. The latter is a thing's *whatness*, or essence. The substantial form of an axe is 'axe-ness' (i.e., 'being-an-axe'), an accidental form is that the axe is brown.

For a living being, Aristotle calls the substantial form *soul* (Gk: *psuchê*, Lt: *anima*). Aristotle assigns names to different types of souls according to the types of living things they animate, e.g., vegetative souls animate plant life, sensitive souls animate non-rational sentient animals, and intellectual souls animate human persons. In humans, the body gets its being as *this* kind of body – a *human* body – from the soul. We might say the soul is the cause or the source of the body *as living*, the source of its being alive. Aristotle calls soul an essence, that which is the cause of a thing's being: the soul is the essence of the living body. Another way of saying this is the soul is the whole body's actuality (*form* equals actuality in a thing). And so Aristotle writes: "The soul is the primary actuality of a physical body capable of life."[6] Capable here means it must have an active potency to be alive (as Aristotle says, "in a matter of its own appropriate to it"[7]); so a rock cannot have a soul; nor can a corpse. A thing can only be actualized as *some* thing if that thing is already potentially that thing.

It follows that Aristotle also rejects Plato's view that the essence of man is his soul, and that body is merely instrumental – that *I* am my soul, but my body is *not* me. Aristotle's hylomorphism says man is a unity of body and soul: a natural, sensible, individuated, complex substance constituted of body and soul. If *Plato* were correct, and *I* am soul and not body, then *I* am not a sensible and natural reality. Aristotle, and with him Aquinas, rejects this.[8] Their hylomorphism holds that in a living human body, there are not two complete substances, a material substance (the body), and an immaterial substance (the soul), but a *single*, composite substance composed of matter and form.[9]

Can we then say that the soul and the body are one? According to Aristotle, this question has already been answered in what's been said: "So we can dismiss the question...It is as though we were to ask whether the wax and its shape are one, or generally the matter of a thing and that of which it is the matter."[10] Unity in this sense simply means actuality, to actually be *something*; and to be something, matter has to be informed, since form actuates matter, i.e., makes it what it is. The soul actuates the body making it a human (i.e., living) body. Plato's dualism says the soul is united to body as a driver is to a machine. The body therefore is what it is apart from the soul (i.e., it does not owe to the soul what it is). It follows that at death, when the soul passes, the body remains a human body and its parts human body parts. Aquinas points out the error in this saying that when life departs a substantial change takes place; the thing is no longer, properly speaking, a human body, except in an equivocal sense. The eyes and flesh of a corpse are only equivocally referred to as human eyes and human flesh since neither possesses its proper operation qua human.[11]

Does this mean that the soul is nothing more than the actuation of the material body, and that the soul's operations are the actuations of the various body parts (e.g., digestion and nutrition, movement, sensation, and intellection); and, therefore, that the soul is inseparable from the body?[12] Aristotle, responds hesitantly saying, yes: the soul *is* inseparable from the body, "or at any rate...certain parts of [the soul] are [inseparable] (if it has parts) – for the actuality of some of them is the actuality of the parts themselves. Yet some may be separable because they are not the actualities of the body at all."[13]

Aquinas' Account: Aquinas is less hesitant. Reflecting on the body-soul problem from the revealed premises that 1) all will "stand before the judgement seat of God" after bodily death [Rom. 14:10, Heb. 9:27, cf. 2 Cor. 5:10]; and that 2) at the end of the age there will be a bodily resurrection of the dead, he was at once more sure of the separability of body and soul, *and* of the essential bodiliness of human personal existence.[14] And although in none of the over 400 questions and several thousand articles of the *Summa Theologiae* does he dedicate even one article to bodiliness per se, nevertheless, Aquinas's anthropological ideas do give us subject matter for a stronger conclusion than Aristotle about the body's centrality to full human being.[15] In particular, it will be instructive to look at Aquinas' ideas in light of a wider theological debate that took place in the high middle ages over the question of the blessedness of disembodied souls in heaven.

As we saw above, body and soul are not two independent substances, but a single composite substance.[16] And although souls, Aquinas affirms, are immortal and can exist without their bodies, because the soul and body are united, it is *contra naturam* for the two to be separated. Since souls are immortal, and nothing can exist perpetually in an unnatural state, it follows that soul and body *must* once again be reunited, which is what the Christian doctrine of the resurrection of the body teaches.[17] It follows, for Aquinas, that persons need their bodies to achieve complete fulfillment (happiness). Anyone in whom is lacking the realization of some capacity, the realization of which is defining of his or her complete fulfillment, is by definition, not completely fulfilled. In one in whom the soul is separated from body, there is lacking the realization of a natural capacity, namely, the capacity for the realization of the body-soul unity and the *full* actuation of bodily capacities. Therefore, the human person cannot be completely fulfilled unless his soul and body are united.[18] This is analogous to the way one who is missing a leg, or is blind, is not completely fulfilled. St. Bonaventure, commenting on the relationship between Our Lady's beatitude in heaven and her requisite bodiliness, says something similar: "The person is not the soul; [he] is a composite…Thus [Mary] must be [i.e., exist] as a composite [in heaven]; otherwise, she would not be there in perfect joy."[19]

This raises an interesting question for Christians: what if anything will the reunification of body and soul at the general resurrection *add* to the life enjoyed by the souls of the saints in the interim between death and resurrection? The question was contentiously debated in the first decades of the fourteenth century. In 1331, Pope John XXII preached two sermons in which he asserted that because the separated soul lacks the perfection of a body, it is incapable of enjoying the perfect joy of the *visio Dei*. The beatific vision – "face to face" vision – waits therefore to the general resurrection.[20] The pope received considerable opposition to his teaching at both a popular level, as well as from scholars at Paris and Oxford. In 1334, as he lay dying, he reformulated his teaching: he said that the "holy souls see God and the divine essence face to face and as clearly as their condition as souls separated from their bodies allows."[21] (Notice his continued insistence on the significance of the body.[22]) Two years later, his successor, Pope Benedict XII, published the constitution *Benedictus Deus* ("On the Beatific Vision of God"), forcefully correcting what he took to be his predecessor's error of 1331. Benedict's papal bull asserted that the blessed souls in heaven enjoy the vision of God:

> By this Constitution, which is to remain in force for ever, we, with apostolic authority, define the following:..the souls of all the saints…immediately (*mox*) after death and, in the case of those in need of purification, after the purification… already before they take up their bodies again and before the general judgment, have been, are and will be with Christ in heaven…these souls…see the divine essence with an intuitive vision and even face to face, without the mediation of any creature by way of object of vision.[23]

Benedict was careful not to state or imply that *nothing at all* is added to the vision of God enjoyed by the saints at the reunification of body and soul. But he did intend to deny the proposition that souls in the interim period do not possess the *visio Dei*. Theologically, Benedict taught nothing more than Aquinas argued for sixty or so years earlier. Aquinas holds that the happiness of the separated souls in heaven is full, but not complete: their "desire," he writes, "is entirely at rest, as regards the thing desired [namely, God]; since, to wit, it has that which suffices its appetite. But it is not wholly at rest, as regards the desirer, since it does not possess that good in every way that it would wish to possess it. Consequently, after the body has been resumed, happiness increases not in intensity, but in extent."[24] Elsewhere, quoting St. Gregory, Aquinas writes: "Surely it will be a gain to them (i.e., the souls of the saints) at the judgment, that whereas now they enjoy only the happiness of the soul, afterwards they will enjoy also that of the body, so as to rejoice also in the flesh wherein they bore sorrow and torments for the Lord." The same is to be said in reference to the damned."[25] In other words, the beatitude of the souls of the saints is as complete as their condition as souls separated from their bodies allows. But since *they* are not substantially complete as persons, the beatitude they enjoy, although it is as complete as a soul in this condition can enjoy, it is not the complete beatitude of a substantially complete human person in heaven. It is not, for example, the kind of beatitude enjoyed by Our Lady.

One might question whether such scholastic taciturnity lends itself readily to a full-bodied account of the importance of human bodiliness for human fulfillment. Dante apparently found in Aquinas' ideas adequate subject matter to poet-pen some of the most beautiful verse ever written on bodiliness and beatific fulfillment. In Canto fourteen of the *Paradiso*, published ten years before Benedict XII's *Benedictus Deus,* the Thomist poet wrote:

> When our flesh, then glorified and holy,
> Is put on us once more,
> Our persons will be
> In *greater perfection*
> As being *complete at last*:
> Because there will be
> An *increase of that light*
> Which is freely given us by the highest good,
> Light which enables us to see him;
> In this way the *vision [of God—visio Dei] must grow clearer,*
> And the *warmth produced by it must grow too,*
> As well as the rays which shine out of it (Lines 43–51).[26]

Dante's imagery, derived from Thomistic principles, enables us to formulate a more robust picture of the importance of bodiliness: to be human is to be bodily; a human without a body lacks a mode of intrinsic perfectability; the reunification of body and soul at the resurrection of the dead will thus make possible a human perfection that is impossible without it; at that time the human person will again be a single, composite body soul unity; his perfection will make us complete ("complete at last"), living a human life of "greater perfection"; we will enjoy an increase of God's "light," a "clearer" vision of God, and take delight in the "warmth" produced by that vision with greater intensity. Commenting on bodiliness and its relation to beatitude in Dante, Caroline Bynum writes: "So glorious and necessary is body to Dante, in all its fullness and complexity, that the aerial body (pre-resurrection heavenly form) is not enough. We "yearn" for the "luster" and "ripeness" of a resurrection that completes (us)…and we desire it not only in order to know but also *in order to love*."[27] This latter point on bodiliness and love is illustrated in the mystical writings of the thirteenth century German religious, Mechthild of Magdenburg (ca. 1282):

> When I think that my body will be lost in death and I shall no longer be able to suffer for Jesus or to praise him, this is so heavy to me that I long, if it were possible, to live until Judgment Day. My love forces me to this.[28]

Beneath these ecstatic reflections is a profound anthropological principle: since sensible desire is a part of love, and sensible desire is a bodily reality, separated souls cannot fully desire God, therefore they cannot fully love God. Aquinas would seem to agree. He locates human love in the concupiscible appetite, and divides it into sensitive love and intellectual (or rational) love.[29] Sensitive love is the joining together (*coaptatio*) of sensible desire (i.e., the sensitive appetite) with the sensibly desired object, which arises on account of our sensible apprehension of that object; rational love is the joining together of the will (rational appetite) with the intelligible good, which arises as a result of our rational apprehension of intelligible good. Both are human love and the former is unrealizable without a body. This is another way of saying, if without my body I am not a person, literally not my *self*, then without my body, I cannot fully love God, or others, nor for that matter fully receive God's love, or the love of others.

Bodiliness and Relationality:

Reflecting on the heavenly condition of disembodied souls has been a way of singling out the importance of bodiliness in human personhood.

The eschatological reality introduces the problem of the disembodied soul. But such a problem is not a natural temporal reality. The human temporal reality is always also a bodily reality. This makes Mechtild's insights regarding the bodily dependent nature of love all the more acute. Sensible love is a bodily reality; but it does not follow that rational love is a disembodied reality, as if reason has no bodily counterpart. It is easy for philosophical analysis to proceed with discussions about will and reason as if their natures and operations *in persons* constitute free-standing categories of their own without reference to body; both epistemological and moral theory have been guilty of this. Descartes' ghostly ego, Kant's purely autonomous will, and Hegel's world spirit realizing itself in history through human consciousness are shadowy abstractions. Will and mind exist only in embodied realities. They not only act upon the body but are also acted upon by the body. This psychosomatic interaction is no novel insight of contemporary psychology. Soul, Aquinas said 700 years ago, "suffers with a bodily passion through bodily hurt; for since the soul is the form of the body, soul and body have but one being; and hence, when the body is disturbed by any bodily passion, the soul, too, *must* be disturbed."[30] Contemporary brain science too affirms the interdependence of bodily and spiritual acts. One influential text states:

> The conclusion to be drawn from this growing fund of knowledge is that every event that happens to us or any action that we take can be associated with activity in one or more specific regions of the brain. This includes, necessarily, all religious and spiritual experiences.[31]

The authors do not deny an immanent non-material principle to the human person nor the existence of the Christian God. They simply assert that every mental event, including mystical and so-called out-of-body experiences, has an organic counterpart in the brain. They do not say that that counterpart sufficiently explains the mental event or experience. Indeed, their method is incapable of returning such a conclusion. Their research however does indicate that highly specified neural activity (i.e., *bodily* activity) accompanies the most sublime and seemingly spiritual human experiences. This underwrites my assertion that human activity is always also bodily activity.

If what I have said is correct, it follows that acts of consciousness, acts of will, acts of memory, and acts of imagination are also bodily acts, at least partially. Singling out consciousness and its operations to the exclusion of body in any human activity therefore is an error.

So here is the conclusion to which I have been progressing: all human activity is always also bodily; human relationality is a human activity; human relationality is always also a bodily activity. Actualized in a fuller way – say in the reciprocity of friendship – it also entails consciousness and will, but then its bodiliness is even more distinct. Friendship is an example of an intensely psychosomatic activity. And the unique procreative friendship we call marriage is paradigmatic of the psychosomatic reality of relationality (e.g., there is touch, sight, conversation, conjugal love, pregnancy, miscarriage, childbirth, diapers, breastfeeding, weaning, skinned knees, slammed doors, piano lessons, popsicles, bedtime stories, smearing on sunscreen, finger painting, family pictures, temper tantrums, soccer practice, scolding, praising, preening, praying, and many other psycho-somatic realities and jointly realized projects that arise from the commitment to enter into this kind of relationship.

Conclusion: Towards a Reply to Neo-Gnosticism

The conclusion that human relationality is intrinsically bodily follows from the premise that the human person in intrinsically bodily. This is consistent with Aristotle and Aquinas' hylomorphic reply to the body-soul question. It also seems consistent with the tradition of hylomorphism to argue, although I do not intend to argue it here, that to be a human person requires no more than to be a whole, living, self-organized human body, in Aristotelian language, to be a human body informed by a rational soul. This conclusion is an important reply to the Gnostic anthropology that characterizes much discussion, especially in bioethics, about ethical treatment of whole, living human bodily beings, such as human embryos, discussion that progresses on the often unstated assumption that body is instrumental of persons and possessive of human value only when consciousness is actualized or readily actualizable (e.g., by arousing someone who has fainted). On my account, to be a human person does not imply possessing an actualized or even necessarily an actualizable rationality (e.g., someone with severe and irremediable brain damage is still a person). But it does require possessing an actualized body. In other words, to be a human person is by nature to exist as an actualized bodily being (which characterizes an embryo). It follows that we (persons) are bodily long before we are conscious, and some times for a considerable time after we are conscious. As long as we are alive we are bodily. We can be alive, though, and not conscious. The preoccupation with the autonomous disembodied conscious self needs to be balanced with a fuller conception of humans *as* bodily and bodiliness as intrinsic to all things properly called human, and ultimately human flourishing.[32]

E. Christian Brugger is an Assistant Professor of Theology at the Institute for Psychological Sciences in Arlington, Virginia. He earned his Ph.D. in Christian Ethics from the University of Oxford in England. He also holds a Master's in moral theology from the Harvard Divinity School and another Master's in moral theology from Seton Hall University in South Orange, New Jersey. He is the author of *Capital Punishment and Roman Catholic Moral Tradition* (Notre Dame Press, 2003), and has published widely on topics in ethics and natural law in journals such as *The Thomist, National Catholic Bioethics Quarterly, Notre Dame Journal of Law, Josehpinum Journal of Theology,* and *Vera Lex.*

ENDNOTES

1   Plato, *Phaedo,* 80d2–3.
2   Aquinas, *Summa Contra Gentiles (SCG),* book II, q. 57, no. 2; the quote attributed to Plato IS taken from Aristotle, who appears to be quoting with doubtfulness the view of his teacher, see *De Anima,* bk. II, 413a8.
3   Aquinas, *SCG,* bk. II, q. 57, no. 4, emphasis added.
4   Plato, *Phaedo,* 82e1–4.
5   *Phaedo,* 66b3–d5, 80b1–3.
6   Aquinas, *Commentary on Aristotle's De Anima,* bk. II, lecture IV, par. 271.
7   *De Anima,* bk. II, 414a25.
8   *SCG,* bk. II, ch. 57, no. 5, p. 169.
9   For Aquinas on this see *SCG,* bk. II, ch. 69, no. 2, 207.
10 *De Anima* II, 412b5–7.
11 *SCG,* bk. II, ch. 57, no. 10, p. 171.
12 *SCG,* bk, II, ch.. 69, no. 5, 208.
13 *De Anima,* 413a4–7.
14 He asserts that, although most operations of the human soul are performed by means of the body, such that those operations are *acts* of a bodily thing, not every operation of the soul is effected by means of a bodily organ. In such case that operation will not be an act of the body, and in this sense is separate from the body. This is true of the intellect, which, Aquinas says, "has no operation in common with the body." *Ibid.,* no. 9, p. 209; see his defense of body-soul unity in chs. 49–51.
15 For an historical summary of philosophical and theological accounts of the mind body problem, see Fr. Benedict Ashley's lengthy book, *Theologies of the Body: Humanist and Christian* (Braintree, MA: The Pope John Center, 1985).
16 "The soul is part of human nature, and hence, although it can exist apart from the body, because it still retains the nature of a part which can be reunited [with the body], it cannot be called an individual substance which is a *hypostatis* or first substance; just as neither can a hand or any other part

of man; and thus neither the name nor the definition of person pertains to it." *ST*, I, q. 29, a. 1, ad 5.

17 *SCG*, bk. IV, ch.. 79, no. 10, p. 299

18 "Anyone to whom some perfection is wanting does not yet have perfect happiness, because his desire is not entirely at rest, for every imperfect thing naturally desires to achieve its perfection. But the soul separated from the body is in a way imperfect, as is every part existing outside of its whole, for the soul is naturally part of human nature. Therefore, man cannot achieve his ultimate happiness unless the soul be once again united to the body." *SCG*, bk. IV, ch. 79, no. 11, p. 299.

19 Bonaventure, *De Assumptione B. Virginis Mariae*, sermon 1, section 2, *S. Bonaventurae Opera Omnia*, ed. Collegium S. Bonaventurae, vol. 9 (Quarrachi, 1901), p. 690.

20 Caroline Walker Bynum reviews the visio Dei debates of the period in her fine text *The Resurrection of the Body in Western Christianity*, 200   1336 (New York: Columbia University Press, 1995), 279–317; See also Robert L. Wilken's fine review of Bynum's book in *First Things* 56 (October 1995), 62–67.

21 Decima Douie, "John XXII and the Beatific Vision," *Dominican Studies* 3, no. 2 (1950), 168; referenced in Bynum, op. cit., at p. 285.

22 Bynum, op. cit. at 285.

23 Benedict XII, Constitution *Benedictus Deus* (1336), in *The Christian Faith*, eds., J. Neuner and J. Dupuis, 6ᵗʰ ed. (New York: Alba House, 1996), no. 2305, pp. 942–43; the teaching is repeated by the General Council of Florence, Decree for the Greeks (1439): "(These blessed) souls are received immediately into heaven, and see clearly God himself, one and three, as he is" (*The Christian Faith*, no. 2309, pp. 944–45); Vatican II's *Lumen Gentium* repeats the teaching, quoting Florence's statement that the blessed souls will see "clearly God himself, one and three, as he is" (*The Christian Faith*, no. 2312, p. 948).

24 Aquinas, *Summa Theologiae (ST)*, I-II, q. 4, a. 5, ad 5; he treats the same issue in *Compendium of Theology*, c. 151 *De Potentia*, q. 5, a. 10c; *Summa Contra Gentiles* bk. IV, chs. 79, 91.

25 Aquinas, *ST*, Supplement, q. 69, a. 2, ad 4.

26 Dante, *The Divine Comedy*, tr. C.H. Sisson (Oxford: Oxford University Press, 1993), 410, emphases added.

27 Caroline Walker Bynum, *op. cit.* at p. 298, emphasis added.

28 Ibid., 340; Mechtild, writing well before the *visio Dei* debates of the 1330s apparently held to the 1331 view of Pope John XXII rejected in *Benedictus Deus*, i.e., that the disembodied souls of the saints do not enjoy the "face to face" vision of God; see 337–41.

29 *ST*, I-II, q. 26, a. 1c, emphasis added; Bynum notes the widespread assumption of the middle ages of the body-soul reality of the human person in Caroline Walker Bynum, *Fragmentation and Redemption: Essays on*

Gender and the Human Body in Medieval Religion (New York: Zone Books, 1991), p. 234–35.

30 *ST*, III, q. 15, a. 4c, emphasis added; Aquinas says elsewhere, the "mind (can) be weighed down so much, that even the limbs become motionless" *ST*, I-II, q. 35, a. 8c.

31 Andrew Newberg, Eugene D'Aquili, *Why God Won't Go Away: Brain Science and the Biology of Belief* (New York: Ballantine Books, 2001), 53.

32 I have chosen not to engage the very fruitful sources of theological and philosophical reflection on the human significance of bodiliness found in the 129 public addresses of John Paul II delivered between 1979–84, sometimes referred to as the "theology of the body." The addresses are conveniently compiled into a one volume book: John Paul II, *The Theology of the Body: Human Love in the Divine Plan* (Boston: Pauline Books and Media, 1997).

The Relational and the Embodied Self
Evidence from Psychology Supporting a Neo-Thomist Understanding of Person

Paul C. Vitz

Many postmodern theorists today claim that there is no human nature, that is, that there is nothing important that is intrinsic to the human person or self. Consistent with this general view, such theorists have also claimed that there is no self at all, or at least no natural or true self. What postmodernists mean by this is that the self is a socially constructed concept and therefore is essentially plastic and is capable of being constructed in whatever way you or society might dictate. There is, therefore, for each individual no self with enduring characteristics. Also, the more general idea of a human nature is seen as a socially constructed idea. Like most postmodernist theories the focus is on deconstructing common assumptions or accepted concepts of the modern world. In the present case it is the modern understanding of the self that is being deconstructed. (Examples of psychologists and social theorists that present such interpretations include Kenneth Gergen, 1991; Philip Cushman, 1990, 1995 and Robert Landy, 1993).

This paper challenges the preceding postmodern viewpoint. Specifically, evidence will be presented here which identifies *universal characteristics* of the human body, of human mental development, and of early interpersonal experiences that contribute to form a *genuine core of a continuing stable self*. The existence of these characteristics, I believe, makes untenable the postmodern position of an essentially arbitrary social or self-constructed self.

In addition, I believe this evidence gives substantial support to a major contemporary theological and philosophical understanding of the person. The terms "self" and "person" will be used here as equivalents even though there are significant differences. In general, the self is a part or subset of the person, since the person includes the body and all mental attributes of an individual, whether part of the self or not; and there is also the relation of the body and mind to God. I have particularly in mind the work of Norris Clarke, whose Neo-Thomist interpretation also uses personalist/ phenomenological concepts taken, for example, from Cardinal Ratzinger. Here I give some brief quotes from Clarke's 2004 article in *Communio* so as to provide a context for understanding the subsequent supporting psychological literature:

> 1. "Every existing being as active has a relational dimension to its being that is inseparable from its own full perfection. As Cardinal Ratzinger [1970, p.132] puts it powerfully: 'Relationality and substantiality are equally primordial dimensions of reality'" (p.442).
>
> 2. "This relationality, following upon self-communicating action, also implies that being itself, for its full unfolding, requires a basic duality of giving and receiving. For there can be no self-communicating action unless there is some receiver to whom the being is communicating, on whom it is acting. If no receiving, then no completed giving" (p.442).
>
> 3. "It follows from all this that the supreme perfection of being itself consists precisely in *persons-in-communication*, both in divine being itself and in our own highest created participation in this fullness of interpersonal love. This is indeed a profound trans-formation − and enrichment − of the meaning of being itself in Thomistic metaphysics; but I think it is in the last analysis only drawing out into explicit expression, under the stimulus of person-alist phenomenology, the deepest implications of Thomas' own deeply creative metaphysics of being as dynamic, self-communi-cating act of presence. One may call this contemporary integration a personalization of being; or a rooting of personal being in the deeper Thomistic metaphysics of being as existential act; or both. I prefer both" (p.445).

Finally, in this paper I am positing that the philosophical concept of substance is at the psychological level analogous to the human body. Likewise, what is meant by relation or relationality at the philosophical level corresponds to interpersonal relationships that we have at the psy-chological level.

The Sensory/Perceptual Self

We start by covering some of the evidence recently discussed by José Bermudez (1998) in which he notes the importance of early visual, auditory, and other sensory -perceptual experience in forming the self. Bermudez begins by summarizing a point made by the prominent psy-chologist of perception, J.J. Gibson (1979), who makes clear that the visual field specifies the existence of a self. For example, the visual field is bounded by the edges of what we can see in front of us at any particular moment, that is, the visual field comes with an edge all around it – and that edge continually identifies the boundary of the visual self. We also know that the visual field, in the direction of our gaze, is in front of us. And we know that behind us, the visual world exists but cannot be seen unless we turn around. As Bermudez puts it: "The boundedness of the field of vision is part of what is seen" (p. 105). What Gibson means by the powerful but indirect visual creation of the self is that the visual field is not only bounded but also that much of the visual world is hidden at any particular moment; and that as you move around in the visual environment you keep changing the boundaries of the visual field. And the "changer" – the source of all those changes – is your self, an invariant consciousness present during each of those views of the world. We also know that these visual fields contain within them the visual experience of parts of our body. For example, our nose in many respects, however dimly aware we are of it, constantly defines, as a minor mountain, the direction of our gaze and the presence of our face in the visual field. Other parts of our body are often visually present. Our hands and feet give us a distinctive bodily self-awareness of our presence in the visual world. We know that our hands and feet are not part of the outside visual environment but part of the self – that is, part of what is attached to us-to our experience of self as at the center of a constantly changing visual world. Furthermore, as we move in the visual environment we are especially aware, though often unconsciously, of our body parts moving in the field; our hand passes in front of our face, our feet precede us, etc. Gibson goes on to argue for still other perceptual information of a more complex kind that also specifies our self in the visual field, and hence helps to define a perceptually based self.

Certainly one other major aspect of the self, besides consciousness as it operates in the visual field, is the experience of *agency*. That is, we are aware that where we look in the visual field is subject to our intention. I look at what I want to look at. That is, my will, my motives, my desires determine much of what I see – let us use the word agency as a general term for this primarily conscious experience. As Bermudez (1998, p. 150) puts it: "It seems fair to say that the limits of the will mark the distinction between the self and the non self just as much as does the skin, although in a different way."

Still another major sensory experience that gives rise to the notion of one's self is proprioceptive feedback from the body, that is, internal experiences tell us the state and location of our body. These experiences give rise to what is called "the bodily self" (Bermudez, 131–162). These cues include: 1) information about pressure, temperature, and friction from receptors on the skin and beneath its surface; 2) information about the relation of body-segments from receptors in the joints; 3) information about balance and posture from the inner ear; 4) information about muscular fatigue from receptors in the muscles; and so on. In short, there is a vast array of internal proprioceptive information telling us about our bodily self. In addition, this kind of information is intimately coordinated with the visual information previously described.

Finally, another important source of information is what comes from hearing. We know much about the spatial world in which we move from the constantly changing auditory experience that identifies our awareness as at the center of an acoustic field.

These bodily based acoustic and visual fields are all in a general sense spatial, and they are closely coordinated so as to give rise to the idea and experience of a single multi-sensory space at the center of which is the perceptual self.

It is not just adults who know these things, or even children who have been around for a while, but even tiny infants have a rudimentary notion of this sensory space and of themselves as located in it. For example, a three-minute old infant when a click is sounded on one side or another of its head will reliably shift its eyes in the direction of the click (Wertheimer, 1961; see also Butterworth, 1981; Muir and Field, 1979; Clarkson, Swain, Clifton and Cohen, 1991). This capacity begins long before an infant can even move its own body. Infants of a month or two in age already pay much less attention to an object that is outside of their reach than an object that is reachable by it. Work by T.G.R. Bower (1972) suggests that this discrimination begins as early as 2 weeks. (See also Von Hosten, 1982; also Schmuckler and Tsang-Tong, 2002). Likewise, babies, when observing an object coming toward them, that is, looming, getting bigger as it comes nearer, will move their head away if the object is on a collision course but will just observe it if the object's course will miss them (See, e.g., Dunkeld & Bower, 1980; Nanez, 1988). As a summary of the very early infant sensory-perceptual-motoric capacities with respect to the self, consider the following quote from the well-known cognitive psychologist Ulric Neisser: "The information that specifies the ecological (i.e., the sensory-perceptual) self is omnipresent, and babies are not slow to pick it up. They respond to looming and optical flow from a very early age, discriminate among objects, and easily distinguish the immediate consequences of their own actions from events of other kinds. The old hypothesis that a young infant cannot tell the difference between itself and its environment, or between itself and its mother, can be decisively rejected. The ecological self is present from the first "(1988, 40). Indeed, a recent book edited by Neisser can be interpreted as a sustained scientific argument for the perceptual and interpersonal origin of a person's core self.

The Early Interpersonal Self

Human infants, long before they are capable of speaking, have normally developed a large number of interpersonal skills that demonstrate their awareness of a self in the context of interpersonal relations, most of which are with the mother or mother-figure. This interpersonal self begins with the sensory-perceptual self and develops along with it. For example, infants as young as three-days prefer their own mother's voice to that of another infant's mother (DeCasper and Fifer, 1980). There is evidence that by two weeks infants are more likely to stop crying on hearing their mother's voice than when hearing that of a female stranger (Bremner, 1988, 157). Some of this voice preference is probably the result of still earlier pre-natal experience but there is similar evidence with respect to infants' preference for faces. By an average age of 45 hours, infants reveal a clear preference for the face of their mother over that of a stranger (Field, Woodson, Greenberg and Cohen, 1982). It has long been known that infants respond to the crying of other infants by crying themselves. See Simner (1971) and also Martin and Clark (1982), who used infants averaging just 18.3 hours. Further, Martin and Clark observed that infants stopped crying or cried less when they heard a recording of themselves crying. That is, the researchers found reliable evidence that newborns recognize their own crying as distinct from that of others – an early case of self-perception (See Bermudez, 1998, 124–125). Other examples of very rudimentary interpersonal self- and other-recognition with infants include the following: one and two-month old infants showed distress when looking at their mothers while hearing their mother's voice displaced by 90 degrees to the right or left side. This certainly means that infants are integrating acoustic and visual information in the same space and in particular as it is related to the human face and to speech. Even more striking findings have been reported with respect to facial imitation in very young infants. Meltzoff and Moore (1977) found that infants 12–21 days in age could imitate successfully three distinct facial acts – lip protrusion, mouth opening, and tongue protrusion, as well as finger movement. Later, Meltzoff and Moore (1983) looked at the same capacities in newborns ranging from 42 minutes to 32 hours old. These infants imitated mouth opening and tongue protrusion. And T.M. Field, *et al.* (1982) found that 2-day-old infants could imitate adult smiles, frowns, and expressions of surprise. In short, socially coordinated behavior develops very quickly between the infant and others. By the time they are two-months old infants engage in extended coordinated "dialogues" or proto-conversations with their mother or mother figure. I will quote an insightful description of the psychologist Trevarthen (1993): " Babies six weeks or older focus on the mother's face and express concentrated interest by stilling of movement and a momentary pause in breathing. The infant's interest as a whole conscious being is indicated by the coordination and directedness of this behavior, which aims all modalities to gain information about the mother's presence and expressions. Hands and feet move and clasp the mother's body or her supporting hand, the head turns to face her, eyes fix on her eyes or mouth, and ears hold and track her voice. The next, and crucial, phase is signaled by the infant's making a 'statement of feeling' in the form of a movement of the body, a change in hand gesture away from clasping the mother, a smile or a pout, a pleasure sound or a fretful cry. The mother, if she is alert and attentive, reacts in a complimentary way. A positive, happy expression of smiling and cooing causes her to make a happy imitation, often complimenting or praising the baby in a laughing way, and then the two of them join in a synchronized display that leads the infant to perform a more serious utterance that has a remarkably precocious form. This infant utterance is the behavior, in that context of interpersonal coordination and sharing of feelings, which justifies the term proto-conversation. It looks and sounds as though the infant, in replying to the mother, is offering a message or statement about something it knows and wants to tell. Mothers respond and speak to these bursts of expression as if the infant were really saying something intelligible and propositional that merits a spoken acknowledgement" (130–132).

There is even an experimental paradigm supporting this persuasive case for describing this early interpersonal behavior as a form of conversation. Murray and Trevarthen (1985) used closed-circuit television to create remote interactions between six to eight week-old infants and their mothers. Each infant and each mother saw a life-sized face-image of the other. Although this environment was somewhat artificial, the mother and child established a fairly normal proto-conversation of the kind just described. The experimenters then broke the closed-circuit link and began replaying to the infants the video tapes of their mothers filmed earlier in a real-time interaction. The infants showed significant distress at this change even though the videotapes showed the same images of the mother that had recently given them pleasure. Of course, the missing element was the contingency between their mother's utterances and the expression of their own response. In short, the babies saw half a dialogue directed at them from their mother, but they had no sense of participation in the dialogue and they didn't like it! This kind of interactive conversation already present at two months continues to evolve in complexity as the months go by. By approximately nine months a new element enters into the infant's repertoire. Previous interactions had been dyadic, that is, the infant related to a person or to an object. At nine months triadic interaction becomes possible. That is, the infant can look at an object that the mother is looking at and then relate to the mother with respect to the object. The mother and infant can jointly attend to an object. What has been mastered, as Jerome Bruner (1977) puts it, "is a procedure for homing in on the attentional locus of another. It is a disclosure and discovery routine and not a naming procedure. It has, moreover, equipped the child with a technique for transcending egocentrism, for insofar as he can appreciate another's line of regard and decipher their marking intentions, he has plainly achieved a basis for what Piaget has called decentration, using a coordinate system for the world other than the one of which he is the center" (p. 276). In other words, the nine-month-old is capable of joint visual attention with its mother. Again we see, before the development of language per se, the beginning of social interaction involving the coordinated communication between two selves.

Early Language

It is very clear from the experimental literature that all humans are strongly pre-programed to learn language. Here I present a summary primarily taken from Coren, Ward, and Enns (1999, p 370). Infants are born with a remarkable ability to respond to human speech (Jusczyk, 1986; Kuhl, 1987). Recordings of the electrical activity of the brain have revealed that even premature infants of 30–35 weeks gestational age can discriminate among vowel sounds (Cheour-Luhtanen et al., 1996). At birth, infants move their limbs in synchrony with connected adult speech but not with other sounds, such as tapping sounds or disconnected vowel sounds (Condon & Sander, 1974). In addition, infants show much the same patterns of responses to spoken phonemes that adults do. For example, infants as young as 1 month of age discriminate speech stimuli better across phonemic boundaries than within phonemic categories, showing categorical perception in the way that adults do (Eimas, Siqueland, Jusczyk, & Vigorito, 1971). Because, at 1 month of age, infants have had only minimal exposure to speech sounds and their utterances consist only of cries, screams, and babbles, they clearly have not yet learned language. Their ability to make speech discriminations similar to those of adults has thus been taken as evidence of an innate mechanism for speech processing.

Other developmental evidence for an innate speech system comes from studies of children's babbling (Locke, 1983). By 7–10 months of age infants normally engage in vocalizations that are characterized as repetitive (e.g., saying "dada") and syllabic in structure (i.e. consonant-vowel clusters), without apparent reference or meaning, and that progress through a well-defined series of stages. Some critics have dismissed babbling as nothing more than evidence that motoric aspects of the vocal speech apparatus are developing. However, severely hearing-impaired infants raised by parents whose only linguistic communication was American Sign Language (ASL) produce "manual babbling" that, although made with hands and fingers, is indistinguishable in its time course, structure, and function from the vocal babbling of hearing infants (Petitto & Marentette, 1991). Thus, babbling seems to be related to the development of an a-modal language system. Interestingly, hand and finger movements of the hearing infants bear no resemblance to those of the young ASL "signers" in the study of manual babbling. Another very impressive demonstration of infants' speech perception ability is that infants can integrate auditory information and visual information about speech. For example, Aronson and Rosenbloom, 1971, showed that 1–2 month-old infants exhibited distress when hearing their mother's voice displaced in space from the mother's visual location. In one study, 4-month-old infants were presented with two video displays of the same person's face speaking two different vowel sounds (Kuhl and Meltzoff, 1982). At the same time, each infant was presented (from a loud-speaker midway between the faces) with the sound of the person's voice producing one or the other of the vowel sounds. The voice and the two faces were all in synchrony with each other, but the voice corresponded to only one of the face's articulatory movements. The infant spent about 73% of the time looking at the face that was articulating the vowel sound it was hearing. Thus, very young infants also demonstrate cross-modal integration of speech cues, just as adults do, even though they have had only limited experience with such cues and do not yet speak. Moreover, this ability is apparently a function of the left hemisphere of the brain in infants, just as speech production is a function of that hemisphere in adults (MacKain, Studdert-Kennedy, Spieker, & Stern, 1983).

In short, we find a linguistic structure rooted in our nervous system that gets elicited and specified through a universal form of experience, namely the learning of one's mother tongue. This foundational language for each individual creates a basic linguistic and interpersonal property of the self that will be completely resistant to any later attempts to remove or change it. And of course one of the first things – roughly around age one and a half – that every child learns is the notion of "me" and "mine." This, again, represents the child's linguistic description of the previous earlier perceptual awareness of self and other. Very quickly with early language a child also learns his or her name, "Momma," "Poppa," and the names of other family members. The child's name, although coming from the culture, becomes part of him or her on a permanent basis.

There are still other important sources of support for the early universal bodily and interpersonal foundation of each person or self. For example, there is the important work begun by John Bowlby (1953, 1958,1969,1973,1980) on early attachment between the child and its mother. The findings on the long lasting significance of early attachment patterns for adult personality are now well documented. (Some of this extensive literature is the following: Ainsworth, 1985, 1985; Bohlin, Hagekull, & Rydell, 2000; Collins & Reid, 1990; Feeney & Noller, 1991; Kilpatrick & Davis, 1994; Simpson, 1990).

Theorists in the neo-psychoanalytic tradition known as "object relations" theory have also clearly conceptualized the great importance for adult life of interpersonal relations as established in the first two years of life. (For summaries of this literature see Greenberg and Mitchell, 1983; Summers, 1994).

Recent research has also discovered the importance of such biological substances as oxytocin for establishing very early mother-child bonding. (An introduction to the social significance of this topic is the report: *Hardwired to Connect* 2003).

In conclusion, recall Ratzinger's (1970, p. 132) pithy summary with special reference to the concept of the human person: "Relationality and substantiality are equally primordial dimensions of reality."

The preceding psychological and neuro-psychological evidence *underwrites* or *resonates with* the concepts of substance and relationality at the higher levels of philosophy and theology. Also, psychology, after various false starts involving autonomous disembodied selves, is providing very strong support for both the importance our body and our personal relationships as essential to forming a core to the person or self that lasts a life-time.

Paul C. Vitz, Ph.D., is Professor of Psychology Emeritus at New York University, as well as Professor of Psychology and Senior Scholar at the Institute for Psychological Sciences in Arlington, Virginia. Professor Vitz is the author of numerous articles and several books. His most recent book is *Faith of the Fatherless: The Psychology of Atheism.* His current interests include the topics of fatherhood, the nature of the person, and the psychology of forgiveness.

REFERENCES

Aronson, E. and Rosenbloom, S. (1971). Space perception in early infancy: Perception within a common auditory-visual space, *Science, 172*, 1161–1163.

Ainsworth, M. (1985). Attachment across the life span, *Bulletin of the New York Academy of Medicine, 61*, 792–812.

Ainsworth, M. (1989). Attachment beyond infancy, *American Psychologist, 44*. 709–716.

Bermudez, (1998). *The paradox of self-consciousness.* Cambridge, MA: MIT Press.

Bohlin, G.,Hagekull,B.,and Rydell, A.M.(2000). Attachment and social functioning: A longitudinal study from infancy to middle school, *Social Development, 9,* 24–39.

Bowlby, J. (1953). *Child care and the growth of love.* Harmondsworth, UK: Penguin.

Bowlby, J. (1958). The nature of the child's tie to his mother, *International Journal of Psycho-Analysis, 39*, 350–373.

Bowlby, J. (1969). *Attachment.* New York: Basic Books.

Bowlby, J. (1973). *Separation.* New York: Basic Books.

Bowlby, J. (1980). *Loss.* New York: Basic Books.

Bower, T.G.R. (1972). Object perception in infants, *Perception 1*, 15–30.

Bremner, J.G. (1988). *Infancy.* Oxford: Basil Blackwell.

Bruner, J. (1977). Early social interaction and language acquisition, In Schaffer, H.R. (Ed.) *Studies in mother-infant interactions.* Proceedings of the Loch Lomond Symposium, Ross Priory, University of Strathclyde, September 1975. New York: Academic Press.

Butterworth, G. (1981). The origins of auditory-visual perception and visual proprioception in human development, In Walk, J.D. and Pick. H.L. (Eds.) *Intersensory perception and sensory integration.* New York: Plenum Press, p. 37–70.

Cheour-Luhtanen, M., Alho, K., Saino, L., Rinne, T., Reinikainen, K.,Pohjavouri, M., Renlund, M., Aaltonen, O., Eerola, O. and Näätänen,

R.(1996). The ontogenetically earliest discriminative response of the human brain, *Psychophysiology, 33*, 478–481.

Clarke, N. (2004) The integration of person and being in twentieth-century Thomism, *Communio, 31*, 435–446.

Clarkson, M.G., Swain, I.V., Clifton, R.K & Cohen, K. (1991). Newborns' hear orientation toward trains of brief sounds, *Journal of the Acoustical Society of America, 89*, 2411–2420.

Collins, N. and Read, A. (1990). Adult attachment, working models, and relationship quality in dating couples, *Journal of Personality and Social Psychology, 58*, 644–663.

Condon, W.S. and Sander, L.W. (1974). Neonate movement is synchronized with adult speech: Interactional participation and language acquisition, *Science, 183*, 99–101.

Coren, S., Ward, L.M. and Enns, J.T. (1999) *Sensation and perception,* 5th ed. Fort Worth, TX: Harcourt Brace.

Cushman, P. (1990). Why the self is empty: Toward a historically situated psychology, *American Psychologist, 45,* 599–611.

Cushman, P. (1995). *Constructing the self, constructing America: A cultural history of psychotherapy.* New York: Addison Wesley.

Davidson, R.J. and Hugdahl, K. (Eds.1995). *Brain asymmetry.* Cambridge, MA: MIT Press.

DeCasper, A.J. and Fifer, W. (1980). Of human bonding: Newborns prefer their mothers' voices, *Science, 208*, 1174–1176.

Dunkeld, J & Bower, T.G.R. (1980). Infant response to impending optical collision, *Perception, 9*, 599–554.

Eimas, P.D., Siqueland, E.R., Jusczyk, P. and Vigorito, J. (1971). Speech perception in infants, *Science, 171,* 303–306.

Feeney, J. and Noller, P. (1991) Attachment style and verbal descriptions of romantic partners, *Journal of Personal and Social Relationships, 8*, 87–215.

Field, T.M., Woodson, R., Greenburg, R. and Cohen, D. (1982). Discrimination and imitation of facial expression in neonates, *Science, 218,* 179–181.

Gergen, K. J. (1991). *The saturated self: Dilemmas of identity in modern life.* New York: Basic Books.

Gibson, J.J. (1979). *The Ecological approach to visual perception* Boston: Houghton Mifflin.

Greenberg, J. R. and Mitchell, S.A. (1983). *Object relations in psychoanalytic theory.* Cambridge, MA: Harvard University Press.

Hardwired to connect. Report to the nation from the commission on children at risk (2003). New York: Institute for American Values.

Jusczyk, P.W. (1986). Toward a model of the development of speech perception, In J.S. Perkell and D.H. Klatt (Eds.) *Invariance and variability in speech processes.* Hillsdale, NJ: Erlbaum, pp. 1–19.

Kilpatrick, L. and Davis, K. (1994). Attachment style, gender, and relationship stability: A longitudinal analysis, *Journal of Personality and Social Psychology, 66,* 502–512.

Kuhl, P.K. and Meltzoff, A.N. (1982). The bimodal perception of speech in infancy, *Science, 218,* 1138–1141.

Kuhl, P.K. (1987). Perception of speech and sound in early infancy, In P. Salapatek and I. Cohen (Eds.) *Handbook of infant perception, Vol. 2 From perception to cognition.* Orlando, FL: Academic Press, pp. 275–382.

Landy,R.J. (1993). *Persona and performance: The meaning of role in drama, therapy* and everyday life. New York: Guilford.

Locke, J.L. (1983). *Phonological acquisition and change,* New York: Academic Press MacKain, K., Studdert-Kennedy, M., Spieker, S. and Stern, D. (1983). Infant intermodal speech perception is a left hemisphere function, *Science, 219,* 3147–1349.

Martin, G.B. and Clark, R.D. (1982). Distress crying in neonates: species and peer specificity, *Developmental Psychology 18,* 39.

Meltzoff, A.N. and Moore, M.K. (1977). Imitation of facial and manual gestures by human neonates, *Science, 198,* 75–78.

Meltzoff, A.N. and Moore, M.K. (1983). Newborn infants imitate adult facial gestures, *Child Development, 54,* 702–709.

Muir, D. and Field, J. (1979). Newborn infants orient to sound, *Child Development 50,* 431–36.

Murray, L. and Trevarthen, C. (1985). Emotional regulation of interactions between two-month-olds and their mothers, In Field, T.M. and Fox, N.A. (Eds.) *Social perception in infancy,* Norwood, NJ: Ablex.

Nanez, J. (1988). Perception of impending collision in 3-to-6 week-old infants, *Infant Behavior and Development, 11,* 447–463.

Neisser, U. (1988). Five kinds of self-knowledge, *Philosophical Psychology, 1,* 35–59.

Neisser, U. (Ed. 1993). The perceived self: Ecological and interpersonal sources of self-knowledge. Cambridge, UK: Cambridge University Press.

Petitto, L.A. and Marentette, P.E. (1991). Babbling in the manual mode: Evidence for the ontogeny of language, *Science, 251,* 1493–1496.

Ratzinger, J. (1970). *Introduction to Christianity.* New York: Herder & Herder.

Schmuckler, M.A. & Tsang-Tong, H.Y. (2002). The role of visual and body movement information in infant search,. *Developmental Psychology, 36,* 499–510.

Simner, M.L. (1971). Newborn's response to the cry of another infant, *Developmental Psychology, 5,* 136–150.

Simpson, J. (1990). Influence of attachment styles on romantic relationships, *Journal of Personality and Social Psychology, 59,* 571–580.

Solomon, J. and George, C. (1999). *Attachment disorganization.* New York: Guilford.

Summers, F. (1994). *Object relations theories and psychopathology.* Hillsdale, NJ: Analytic Press.

Trevarthen, C. (1993). The self born in intersubjectivity. In Neisser, U. (Ed) *The perceived self.* Cambridge: Cambridge University Press, pp.121–175.

Von Hosten, C. (1982). Foundations for perceptual development, *Advances in infancy research, 2,* 241–261.

Wertheimer, M. (1961). Psychomotor coordination of auditory and visual space at birth, *Science, 134,* 1692.

Lumen Gentium
The Once and Future Constitution

REVEREND JOHN M. MCDERMOTT, S.J.

Something happened at Vatican II even if most people cannot agree on what happened. Conservatives see it as the beginning of the Church's decline, when the spirit of disobedience and subjectivism was introduced into the Church. Progressives interpret it as the providential opening of the Catholic Church to modernity, which a reactionary pope has tried ever since to stifle. Almost two centuries after the French Revolution, Pope John XXIII, that devout, traditional diplomat, opened the windows of the Church upon the world, and, as one wag put it, everyone began jumping out the windows. No wonder that conservatives are accused of desperately tying to close those windows: they are opposed in principle to suicide, spiritual as well as physical. Meanwhile, the progressives insist that the opening be maintained and even expanded, for the Holy Spirit who blows where He wills. They forget, however, that the Holy Spirit's role is to blow people into the Catholic Church, not out of it. For the Church is ultimately the Body of Christ and the Spirit is Christ's Spirit, uniting us to Christ through His Body, the ordinary way of salvation.[1]

According to historians of Vatican II, the great struggle and turning point in its development occurred over the two dogmatic constitutions, *Dei Verbum* and *Lumen Gentium*.[2] Looking back on these documents, especially in view of the *Nota previa explicativa* added by Paul VI at the Council in order to win the votes of resisting members of the minority, one hardly sees the reason for the excitement. No heresy was at stake. These two so-called "dogmatic constitutions" intended to propose no new dogma. All is good, traditional Catholic doctrine, which everyone here can affirm. Whence then did the post-conciliar convulsions arise that gave birth to the Fellowship of Catholic Scholars and other organizations committed to orthodoxy?

Presuppositions

To answer that question, we must recall that faith is a gift of God. Through faith we accept not only the self-revealing God but also "the mystery of His will" revealed in the "deeds and words" of Jesus Christ, "who is Himself the mediator and the sum total of revelation"(DV #2). In this *Dei Verbum* seems in perfect accord with Vatican I's Dogmatic Constitution *Dei Filius* which proclaimed that "it pleased God's wisdom and goodness to reveal Himself and the eternal decrees of His will to the human race in a supernatural way" different from the knowledge of Himself mediated by created things (DS 3004). By faith we believe what Christ, Scripture, and the Church teach. Yet there is a problem. Christ failed to write a theology textbook for the Church. He did not even compose a catechism. These "deficiencies" theologians have been trying to make good ever since. Fortunately or unfortunately, there is a difference between what is revealed and what theologians say about revelation. The carefully worded dogmatic statements of the great councils emerged only after a long process of debate, definition, and decision. The resultant dogmas were understood in reference to Scripture and Tradition. But the dogmas were not accompanied by a handbook of clear and clarifying definitions. They themselves had to be interpreted, and in that hermeneutical playground theologians frolicked with their exegesis, commentaries, and speculative systems.

We human beings seek a certain consistency in our thought as in our actions; our words and concepts have to fit into a larger whole, a metaphysical vision of reality which gives meaning to the individual parts of a synthetic *Weltanschauung*. In other words, we need a philosophy to understand our theology. Ultimately, all our theological problems are philosophical problems. God does not have difficulty revealing Himself and His will; we have difficulties in grasping and living His mysteries. The post-conciliar convulsions within the Church arose not from the documents themselves but from the underlying philosophical theologies which interpreted them. At the risk of egregious simplification, let me say that all our post-conciliar difficulties occurred because theologians changed the "metaphysical spectacles" through which they viewed revelation. They went from a philosophy based on a concept of being to a philosophy based on a judgment of being.[3]

At Vatican II almost all Catholic thinkers professed allegiance to St. Thomas Aquinas. How then did the earth-shaking philosophical revolution occur? Brilliant as is St. Thomas' synthesis of Platonic and Aristotelian traditions, it contains certain unresolved tensions. In the twentieth century those tensions emerged in the dispute whether being, i.e., all reality, is grasped in a concept or a judgment. Let me work out the implications of that difference by contrasting, in very broad outline, the Cajetanian interpretation with transcendental Thomism.[4]

Conceptualist Thomism

For the Cajetanian school, if a concept of being can be achieved, all of reality can be conceptualized. Thus truth, the conformity of the mind to reality, can be caught in concepts whose correspondence to reality is subsequently affirmed in judgment. Since the Christian faith involves the intellect's acceptance of a novel historical revelation, this revelation will be proposed in conceptually formulated propositions as dogmatic truths. But because the historical revelation goes beyond what man knows from nature, or creation, its truths must be supernatural. As such their truth value cannot be ascertained or judged by the natural powers of the human intellect. If they are believed as true, their acceptance must depend upon supernatural grace moving man's will and intellect in an act of faith. Yet, lest faith's acceptance of supernatural truths be irrational and contrary to man's rational nature – it is immoral to affirm as true what cannot be known as true – some reasons must be found to justify faith's acceptance. One believes on the word of a veridical witness, specifically Jesus Christ, the divine legate, whose trustworthiness is demonstrated through God's testimony. Because Jesus fulfilled prophecies and worked miracles, the resurrection being simultaneously the greatest miracle and prophetic fulfillment, God testified to Jesus' veracity. What Jesus revealed can therefore be accepted on divine authority. Moreover he instituted a hierarchical Church, founded on the apostles, to continue his preaching; and he endowed it with an infallible authority lest men be without guidance in the realm of supernatural truth.

A strong apologetics was then constructed to prove that the Catholic Church was Christ's true Church: one, holy, Catholic, and apostolic. With papal authority secure, governance is easy. The magisterium decides, theologians accept, and missionaries preach, while the people pray, pay, obey, and provide vocations. Protestants might accuse the Church of taking the place of God insofar as her decisions are binding for salvation, but Catholics point out that the Church is only the servant, albeit infallible, of God's revelation. Her task is to preserve and interpret the deposit of faith given by Christ to the apostles, not to invent anything new.

In this theological vision, the Church's role is pivotal. It completes the revelation, being its necessary interpreter, and supplies the foundation for all dogmatic theology. Whatever the magisterium decides, the theologians accept and seek to understand. If they do not understand, that is hardly surprising since supernatural truths are at issue, and they surpass human understanding. Essential is faith's acceptance of dogma, not its understanding; that is only secondary. Various theological systems can contradict each other's interpretations of dogma, but this conflict does not trouble the unity of faith. The cardinal issue is apologetics, especially where the Church confronts Protestantism and argues over the meaning of biblical revelation and the need for Tradition and true interpretation. In such a context, words matter since Scripture consists of words and their interpretation consists of further words. The dogmatic opposition between Catholic and Protestant is clear and only one Church can be correct.

In this theology the Church's role depends upon an understanding of revelation, which depends upon an understanding of human understanding. It all holds together. What happens when revelation consists not just of words but of "deeds and words"(DV #2)? Deeds are more concrete than words. They are particular, whereas words transmit universal, abstract concepts.[5] What happens when revelation is conceived not primarily as a communication of supernatural propositions, but as the self-revelation of God, whose infinity can never be exhausted by finite concepts? This change was encouraged by certain problems that affected ecclesiology deeply. For example, if the content of faith was given by Jesus Christ in supernatural propositions, and revelation ceased with the death of the last apostle, then the Church merely has to preserve the deposit of revelation and interpret it properly once it is attacked. But how can one interpret what is in principle unintelligible to natural reason? How did the bishops in council ever come to binding dogmas with such words as *homoousios, hypostasis,* and transubstantiation, which are not found in Scripture, or at least not in their later technical meaning? Another problem concerned the definition of Mary's corporeal assumption into heaven proclaimed by Pius XII in 1950, and accepted by all theologians on the Church's authority. Yet there was no written evidence of that teaching before the sixth century.[6] Furthermore, studies on the deposit of revelation concerning the Church showed that Scripture and the Fathers conceived the Church primarily not as a bureaucratic institution for the resolution of Scriptural difficulties, but as intimately united to the saving mystery of Christ. The Church is the Body and Bride of Christ.[7] Such studies received papal approval when Pius XII published his encyclical *Mystici Corporis* in June, 1943, just three months before *Divino Afflante Spiritu* opened the door to use of literary genres in

Scriptural exegesis. The pope made it clear that all the baptized(#17, ##22–24), not just the hierarchy, constitute the Body of Christ, even though he "maintained uncompromisingly" that "those who exercise sacred power in this Body are its first and chief members"(#17, ##70–74, ##78–83) and all owe obedience to the pope as the Church's supreme visible head (##38–42, #69).[8] Nonetheless, the presentation of this more organic view of the Church stood in a certain tension with typical pre-Vatican II texts on ecclesiology.

Historically, ecclesiology developed as a separate theological treatise rather late, in the fourteenth or even the fifteenth century. From its birth it was suckled on the milk of controversy in reaction against medieval spiritualist movements, Gallicanists, Conciliarists, and finally Protestants.[9] Two questions had to be answered: is the Church visible or invisible? What is its authority structure? In his *Controversies,* Bellarmine defined the Church for subsequent ecclesiologies: "The Church is an assembly of men as visible and tangible as is the assembly of the Roman people, or the kingdom of France, or the Venetian Republic." This was admittedly a limited view. Bellarmine continued: "One must take into account…that the Church is a living body, in which are soul and body, and indeed the soul is the internal gifts of the Holy Spirit: faith, hope, charity, etc. The body is the external profession of faith, and the communication in the sacraments…under the rule of pastors." While allowing that some believers may be only of the Church's soul, he deliberately restricted his definition to the minimum because he was refuting the Protestants who denied the essential visibility of Christ's Church.[10] He was concerned with her hierarchical structure and division of authority. As a result Catholic ecclesiology amalgamated apologetics and canon law. This amalgam occupied a central position, serving as the pivot on which theology moved from assuring itself of its foundations in apologetics to the actual specification and explication of dogma. Ecclesiology was apologetics and dogmatics in one. To touch it could have vast implications for the whole structure of theology. That became clear at Vatican II.

Changes at Vatican II

Vatican II's changes in ecclesiology occurred not in any dogma or doctrinal statement but in the order of presentation. Previous to the Council in the great conceptualist syntheses *De Ecclesia* usually continued apologetics, completing the section on Christian Revelation (with Christ as the divine legate), and preceding the methodological section on the sources of revelation, Scripture and Tradition.[11] Some considered revelation's sources just before the Church and immediately after the Christian religion.[12] Others placed *De Ecclesia* in a consideration of revelation's sources, seeing the Church as the infallible teacher of revelation.[13] Treatments of apologetics regularly included a treatise on the Church.[14] Even when ecclesiology was treated separately, the Church was studied primarily as a visible institution established by Christ, possessing an authoritative hierarchical structure, endowed with the four marks of the true Church, and counting its members according to public norms of confession and obedience.[15] Some early ecclesiologies treated the Church as Christ's Mystical Body, but the proportional amount of space dedicated to that topic was relatively small.[16] After *Mystici Corporis,* more attention was given to the topic but it was not well integrated into the institutional Church already presented.[17] The first draft of the Council's Constitution on the Church, *De Ecclesia*, which was offered to the Council Fathers in 1962, was a product of such a conceptualist tradition. It considered the Church from the top down in heavily juridical terminology.

De Ecclesia provides an enlightening contrast with what would finally emerge from the Council. The first chapter, dealing with the nature of the Church militant, recognizes her as the new Israel, a priestly people, but it primarily describes her as "a compact army...which, victorious against hell's gates and the devil's deceits, will continue perpetually until the end of the age in the unity of faith, sacramental communion, and apostolic governance"(2). Bestowing the means necessary for the attainment of her end, Christ founded her upon Peter and his successors. Hence when the Body of Christ is pronounced the principle "figure" of the Church (4), no separation of the hierarchical, juridical Church from "a charismatic Church of love" is possible (6). For "the Roman Catholic Church is the Body of Christ"; indeed, "only the Roman Catholic Church is rightly called a Church" (7). Consequently, the second chapter links salvation to those explicitly belonging to the Catholic Church by profession of faith and acknowledgement of her authority "in visible connection with her Head, viz., Christ, who rules her through His vicar." The schema also declares that grace is available to those sincerely seeking God's will; the Spirit works even in separated churches, which are joined to the Church "by a desire, even if unknown"(9f.). But the schema leaves unspecified how, when, and what types of graces are bestowed, only assuring non-Catholics that the Church prays for their entrance into full confession and access to numerous spiritual gifts which only actual members enjoy (10).

After defining the Church's nature from her full visibility, the schema in chapters 3–6 considers her internal structure in terms of powers of teaching, sanctifying, and ruling. The bishops possess those powers supremely; by superabundance they overflow upon priests, who act sacramentally *in persona Christi*. But just as priests receive jurisdiction from the pope or the competent bishop, so episcopal jurisdiction depends ultimately upon the pope who can amplify or curtail any bishop's exercise of it. For the pope exercises a universal immediate jurisdiction over all churches and over every pastor and believer (14). While the whole episcopal college together with its head, the pope, exists as "the one subject of full and supreme power over the universal Church," its power is exercised only extraordinarily and "in devoted subordination" to Christ's earthly vicar (16). For, as individual bishops ground the unity of their particular churches, the pope grounds the unity of the whole Church which exists from the particular churches (15). Within the Church, the state of evangelical perfection is recommended as the "less impeded and safer way to the realization of charity, the fullness of divine law." Religious are liberated from worldly cares in order to follow Christ obedient, poor, and virginal (17–19). The laity, joined to the Church by faith and charity, are entrusted with the task of bringing salvation to all under the rule of the pastors, with whom they cooperate (20). Hence they possess the "right" (*jus*) to participate in the Church's saving work and to receive from pastors the helps necessary for salvation, especially the sacraments (23). Besides testifying to the world and working in it to achieve its "immediate end, i.e., the temporal common good" (26), lay people may even accept a canonical mission to participate in the hierarchy's apostolate and exercise works of an explicitly religious nature (23f.). Yet the essential difference between the universal and the ministerial priesthoods is made crystal clear: properly speaking, priests are only the ordained who "with sacred authority" care for the people, offer the means of salvation, and administer religious worship, especially pronouncing the words of consecration *in persona Christi* (21).

The long seventh chapter dedicates particular attention to the Church's magisterium, which has been endowed with the charism of indefectibility to preach the gospel's truth to all nations. The magisterium's indefectibility grounds the whole Church's indefectibility as its "proximate principle and perpetual instrument." From the Spirit the Apostles' successors receive "the power to teach with authority"(28). Hence the magisterium listens to God, not to men, in order that it might teach the faithful and preserve the deposit of faith in Scripture and tradition "always in the same sense and meaning," while allowing further explication in time (29). This magisterium, "one and indivisible," is exercised in the first place by the pope on behalf of the whole Church. He teaches the faithful and confirms the faith of his brother bishops by defending and infallibly proposing salvific doctrine. Even when he does not teach *ex cathedra*, he is owed the "religious submission (*obsequium*) of will and intellect," excluding public disputation on the part of theologians (30). Thereafter, great emphasis is placed on obedience as well as conformity, cooperation, and caution in theological endeavors (31–35). The following paragraphs continue the same trajectory, considering the proper understanding of authority (power from God to oblige in conscience), its use for service, and the corresponding duty of obedience according to Christ's example (36–39).

The final three chapters deal with the Church's external relations: Church-state relations, the necessity incumbent upon her to evangelize the world, and ecumenism. Although the state's purpose, or goal, is subordinate to the Church's supernatural purpose, both societies are recognized as perfect in their own realm, with their own legislative, juridical, and executive powers (40). Nonetheless, since the separate realms concern the same persons, they should cooperate to achieve temporal happiness while promoting man's ultimate end, eternal salvation. Implicitly recognizing the changes effected by democracy, the schema holds that while true worship was established by Christ, civil society is not obliged to recognize the Church's special mission until Christ's revelation is accepted by the citizens whom the civil power represents; yet it should never impede the free preaching of the gospel and man's salvation (41–44). For Christ entrusted the gospel to the Church with the right of preaching and establishing Christian communities, over which she exercises the power of teaching, governing, and sanctifying. This evangelization is the concern of all Christians, especially the pope, who possesses the "supreme, absolute, and universal right" to send missionaries into the whole world (45–47).

Finally, while upholding the ecumenical movement's goal, the unity of Christians, the Church invites all individuals and communities to return to her unity in faith, sacraments, and governance, and to her plenitude of the means of salvation. In the meantime, cooperation with non-Catholics for the "good of the human family" and the conquest of mutual prejudice is approved, but only with great prudence and appropriate episcopal approval might common worship be accorded; it should not, however, anticipate full Eucharistic communion, the sign of perfected unity (54f.). Thus, *De Ecclesia* presents an ecclesiology from above in which clearly defined juridical rights and duties are oriented to the Church's Christ-given mission to lead all to salvation by preaching the truth and administering the sacraments in visible unity under papal authority.

How different in structure and content is the presentation of *Lumen Gentium*! It is the result of several important changes.[18] Grounded in the Trinity's design of salvation, which was fulfilled and revealed in Jesus Christ, the Church belongs to that salvific mystery. Indeed, the constitution's first chapter is entitled "The Mystery of the Church." The universal Church is described as "a people brought into unity from the unity of the Father, the Son, and the Holy Spirit"(LG #4). She is presented as "a type of sacrament, i.e., a sign and instrument of communion with God and of unity among all men." This notion of Church as sacrament is quite novel. Conceptualist theology reserved the term sacrament for the seven means of communicating grace established by Christ. In view of the long, confused debate about sacramental causality, the application of "sacrament" to the Church is most surprising. Even the Fathers of the Church, with their much broader understanding of sacrament, rarely used that designation for the Church.[19] The Council is not defining the Church in clear, juridical terminology. Indeed, *Lumen Gentium* then appeals to at least eleven biblical "images," or "symbols," before considering the main image, the Body of Christ.[20] The Body of Christ is understood not primarily as a visible institution, but in terms of the life uniting Christ, the head, to believers. "In that body the life of Christ is communicated to those who believe and who, through the sacraments, are united in a hidden and real way to Christ in His Passion and glorification" (LG #7).

Only in the following paragraph is this "community of faith, hope, and charity" clearly identified as a "visible organization" so that "the society structured with hierarchical organs and the mystical body of Christ" are seen to "form one complex reality which comes together from a human and a divine element." This "sole Church of Christ," confessed as one, holy, Catholic, and apostolic, is then said to "subsist in the Catholic Church." Rivers of ink have flowed over the meaning of *subsistit in*. Why did the Council not simply write: "This sole Church of Christ is the Catholic Church"? In this distinction many have seen the Council's notion of Christ's Church being drawn wider than the visible bounds of the Catholic Church.[21] Similarly, in paragraph 7, it is possible to interpret those who believe as a wider circle than those who receive the sacraments in the visible Church. Catholic theology recognized a salvific baptism of desire as well as valid sacraments outside her juridical bounds.

Whichever way the text is interpreted, certainly a change of theological emphasis has occurred. The Church's internal, invisible life enjoys a priority over the external, hierarchical structure; the sacrament precedes the juridical institution. This change is also manifested in the structure of the remaining document: before chapter 3 presents the Hierarchical Church, chapter 2 considers the People of God as a whole. The hierarchy is thereby seen as a means helping the whole people to attain their goal, salvation.[22] Since Israel was God's people wandering through the desert and history, that designation underlines the unity of Old and New Covenants and highlights a favorite conciliar theme of a pilgrim people (LG #6, #8, #9, #14, ##48–51). This stress on the Church's historicity allows room for the human component and its weaknesses, even while it is structured by God's will. It also opens a window to Protestant theology, whose stress on God's absolute transcendence, resists binding Him definitively to any human structure; all human beings wander on their pilgrimage. Prioritizing the Church's interior life allows two further shifts of emphasis. First, the equality of all believers is seen as more fundamental than hierarchical distinctions. All believers are priests and prophets, and all alike are called to holiness. Correspondingly, diversity among particular churches and believers is understood as a richness adorning the unity, not a fall from ideal uniformity. Second, though Christian fullness is predicated of the Catholic Church alone, non-Catholic Christians are "in some real way joined to us in the Holy Spirit," whereas non-Christians and non-believers are related to that fullness in varying degrees (LG ##14–16). The distinction between "true faith based on authority" and lack of faith is not employed. And it is said that even "those who, through no fault of their own, do not know the Gospel of Christ or His Church but who nevertheless seek God with a sincere heart, and, moved by grace, try in their actions to do His will as they know it through the dictates of their conscience – those too may achieve eternal salvation" (LG #16).[23]

Chapter 3 considers the hierarchical Church instituted by Christ. Bishops are recognized as successors of the apostles responsible for sanctifying, teaching, and ruling, collectively for the universal Church and individually for the local diocese assigned to each (LG #20f., #26f.). As a collegial body, they possess "supreme and full authority over the universal Church," though this authority can never be exercised apart from the pope. In unanimity, especially in ecumenical councils, the bishops can speak infallibly on questions of faith and morals, coextensively with the deposit of revelation.

The gift of infallibility also belongs to the pope as head of the college and as the Church's supreme pastor and teacher (LG #25). There are novel emphases here. Conceptualist treatises stressed the monarchial structure of the Church as necessary for unity and often rejected the notion that an episcopal synod or group would have supreme authority in the Church.[24] In question of jurisdictional authority, they agreed with the councils of Florence and Vatican I that the pope possesses a universal, immediate jurisdiction over all churches, bishops, and faithful (DS 1307, 3059–3064).[25] At Trent a fierce dispute had arisen whether bishops received their jurisdiction immediately by divine institution or mediately through the pope. Recognizing the dispute, conceptualist theologians preferred the opinion that while the bishop was granted his power of orders immediately by God, jurisdiction was mediated by the pope since the pope possessed the fullness of jurisdiction and the bishop's authority could not be exercised contrary to papal authority.[26]

De Ecclesia moderated that view, yet now more clearly the bishops' authority is recognized as "proper, ordinary, and immediate, although its exercise is ultimately controlled by the supreme authority of the Church and can be confined within certain limits should the usefulness of the Church and the faithful require that." Hence "they are not to be regarded as vicars of the Roman Pontiff; for they exercise the power which they possess in their own right" (LG #27). Moreover, episcopal infallibility is not directly deduced from papal infallibility. Bishops in union with Peter's successor can proclaim infallibly the doctrine of Christ on matters of faith and morals when "they are in agreement that a particular teaching is to be held definitively and absolutely," especially when they are assembled in an ecumenical council (LG #25).

Yet even before episcopal infallibility was mentioned, the infallibility of the whole Church had been affirmed in chapter 2: "The whole body of the faithful cannot err in matters of belief....The people unfailingly adheres to this faith, penetrates it more deeply with right judgment, and applies it more fully in daily life"(LG #12). Conceptualist theology distinguished between the passive infallibility of the believing or learning Church, and the active infallibility of the teaching Church, identified with the hierarchy.[27] But here no such distinction is made; indeed, the whole People of God is considered infallible precisely as prophetic. The hierarchical constituents have been inverted. Whereas *De Ecclesia* had the people listening to the magisterium which listens to God, now the whole Church is infallible while the bishops' and the pope's infallibility is comprised within the Church's infallibility.

Clearly Vatican II preferred to see the Church as a whole, laity, clergy, and pope, before considering her various constituent, hierarchical elements. This emphasis on the personal and universal over the structural and particular is found also regarding the Church's sanctity. Whereas conceptualist ecclesiologies saw the Church as holy because of the sacraments, which communicate sanctifying grace, and of the many saints produced by that grace, especially as witnessed in religious life according to the evangelical counsels, the new emphasis on the people constituting the Church allowed the Council to write: "The Church, clasping sinners to her bosom, at once holy and always in need of purification, follows constantly the path of penance and renewal"(LH #8).

In chapter 4 on the laity the broad approach to the Church as People of God stresses the common task, dignity, and activity of all the baptized (LG ##30–38); the principal difference between clerics and lay people seems to consist in this: the laity fulfill their mission mainly in the temporal affairs with their own initiatives, whereas the clergy are ordained for sacred ministry (LG #31, #35, #37). Indeed, before the Council Fathers treated the religious state in chapter 6, they propounded the universal call to holiness in chapter 5: "All Christians in any state or walk of life are called to the fullness of Christian life and to the perfection of love"(LG #40). "The forms and tasks of life are many but holiness is one"(LG #41).

After a short chapter on religious life, which accentuates the submission of religious to bishops, the seventh chapter on the Pilgrim Church highlights the transitoriness and imperfection marking a pilgrim people. "The Church...will receive her perfection only in the glory of heaven." Though the final age of the world has begun and the Church's sanctity is real, it is still imperfect (LG #48). This is a far cry from the apologetic ecclesiology in which the Church was presented as offering the full, visible realization of the unity, holiness, catholicity, and apostolicity intended by Christ for His Church. Then the final chapter considers the Blessed Virgin Mary as the Church's preeminent member and model in faith and charity, Mother of God and of men.

Reasons for the Changes

Certainly nothing that Vatican II said contradicted previous councils. But there has been a change of emphasis in its presentation of Catholic truth. Why did these changes occur? Here speculation must advance hesitantly. Certainly climates of opinion had changed. Direct attacks on the Church by secular governments had greatly abated. In the capitalistic democracies of Europe and North America the Church was enjoying an era of good feeling because of her service in both World Wars and against Communism. In post-war European democracies, many leaders were strong, practicing Catholics. The lines of confession-al divisions had weakened. Protestants were somewhat confused in their own theologies, were striving for unity through the ecumenical movement, and were interested in Catholic participation. The expansion of material well-being, especially in the United States, led to a pragmatic, egalitarian tolerance of religious differences and the championing of religious freedom. The desire to emerge from the "Catholic ghetto" into the cultural mainstream also played a role, even if the Church was the biggest ghetto in a pluralistic world. Philosophy's reaction against totalitarian ideologies led to existentialism's emphasis on individual experience instead of a priori answers to reality. But changes were occurring within Catholic theology itself.

In the intellectual realm, historical studies made it clear that the monarchical view of the papacy developed only over time.[28] However clearly baroque Scholasticism had drawn out the lines of demarcation between Catholic and Protestant positions in ecclesiology, history did not quite conform to that sketch. Since conceptualist theology was bound to a revelation of timeless valid truths, and the early Church was not explicitly aware of all the dogmas about herself which later Councils elaborated, a different approach was necessary. Moreover, historical studies indicated that baroque Scholasticism did not simply expand upon St. Thomas' clear view. Thomas' doctrine had been adapted to the needs and presuppositions of later ages and changed in the process. Neither Cajetan nor John of St. Thomas was completely faithful to the mind of the *Doctor Angelicus*. Other interpretations of Thomas' doctrine were being evolved.[29] The view that came to dominate after the Council was dubbed "transcendental Thomism." It was championed by such thinkers as Pierre Rousselot, Pierre Teilhard de Chardin, Henri de Lubac, Karl Rahner, and Bernard Lonergan. Despite many differences, they agreed in emphasizing the neo-Platonic strand of Thomas' synthesis and locating truth in the judgment. Our brief sketch shall concentrate on a simplified version of Rahner's thought since the disciples of this German theologian had great influence upon post-conciliar theology in the United States.[30]

Transcendental Thomism

Judgment involves an activity of the mind synthesizing not only the form and matter, which abstraction had divorced, but also the subject and the predicate of the sentence, essence and existence. If truth is found in judgment, the concept does not attain reality of itself. Indeed it is only over subjectivity, the mind's movement, that objectivity is reached. The mind's natural movement carries it beyond the abstract concept to reality, beyond essence to existence. Since all concepts are transcended by the mind's movement, no concept, indeed nothing finite can satisfy the mind's quest for truth. Once a limit is recognized, the mind already intellectually surpasses it. "You have made us for yourself, O Lord, and we cannot rest until we rest in you." (Augustine, *Confessions*, I, 1). The mind is oriented to the infinite God as its fulfilling goal. The infinite God is to be known, therefore, not in a concept, but in Himself. Since the direct, intellectual vision of God is the beatific vision, a supernatural endowment, Rahner and other transcendental Thomists speak of the paradoxical natural desire for the supernatural.[31] Thus inherent in man's intellectual nature is an exigency for a completion in grace.

Such a "paradox" has many repercussions. For one, it prevents rationalists from claiming that since the natural order makes sense of itself, man has, in the strict sense, no need of grace to attain his fulfillment in felicity. For another, it leads easily to Protestantism: insofar as the natural order cannot supply its own fulfillment, grace is required to overcome its inherent insufficiency; hence the natural order does not make sense of itself; it is fallen and the fall can be overcome only by grace. For a third, since human nature manifests an inherent openness to grace and God wishes all men to be saved, grace can be given to every soul immediately. Faith is understood primarily not as the acceptance of supernatural truths proposed by an external authority but as the realization of a "personal" relationship with God: one entrusts oneself to God.

Since this human response is caused by grace and grace is understood primarily as uncreated grace, i.e., God offering Himself to the soul, Rahner understands sanctifying grace as the created, supernatural effect of the divine presence in the soul. Hence it is possible to have saving grace and faith without recourse to the explicit message of Christ and the Church.[32] Thus "anonymous Christianity" is born, and dogmas are understood in terms of a gradual explication of what is implicit in the original faith experience. This allows for great flexibility in the development of dogma, a great advance over conceptualist Thomism. Indeed, since the highest self-communication of God occurs in the Incarnation, Jesus Christ can be understood as the culmination of the historical process of God's self-revelation. All of history points to him as its fulfillment. He is the supreme real symbol of God in time. His humanity manifests the unity in diversity of God and man; this symbol does not just point to something different from itself. Rather, since a "real symbol" involves "the self-realization of one being in another, which is constitutive of its essence," God "becomes the other" even while remaining immutable in himself.[33]

Because Jesus possessed a non-conceptual, human awareness of God, the intuitive vision of the divinity, only gradually did he come to explicit consciousness of his own deepest identity and mission; just like all other human beings, he grew in explicit knowledge and grace. Because his awareness is deeper than words, all that Jesus did, as well as all that he said, is considered revelation. But on account of the gap between his deepest, unthematic knowledge of God and himself, on the one hand, and his explicit knowledge, on the other, he is said to suffer an identity crisis and to "err" insofar as his expectation of the kingdom's immanent arrival was the translation into temporal terms of his experience of God's proximity.

The Church likewise is understood from the experience of grace. Since the soul, as form of the body, comes to expression in the body, and since human nature is social, grace finds a corporeal, social expression, the Body of Christ. The Church is understood as the primordial sacrament, the expression of grace which is the foundation and goal of all the other sacraments. Although grace is everywhere given, there should be continuity in time between the full expression of grace in Jesus and the present-day Church. Hence men are oriented to external history as well as to the interior experience of grace.

The Immediate Post-Conciliar Period

Such an ecclesiology from below, i.e., from the lived experience of grace, explains well many aspects of *Lumen Gentium*: organic, vital union among all the members of Christ's Body previous to juridical structure; basic equality in the experience of grace and the importance of the laity; the Church as sacrament of unity for all mankind; the notion of doctrinal development and the ability to adapt the Church's message and structure to surrounding cultures. Instead of apologetical arguments, there is the invitation to dialogue on the basis of revelation and faith outside the Church's visible boundaries. Did Rahnerian theology conquer the Council? By no means. The Council Fathers did not adopt any one theology. It is hard to imagine a group of responsible elder statesmen, many of whom had suffered or were still suffering for fidelity to the faith, suddenly throwing out the theology learned in their seminaries to proclaim that "the faith of Teilhard – or the faith of Rahner – is the faith of the Church." Indeed, they explicitly rejected the Rahner notion of conversion as the leading to explicit confession of what was interiorly, antecedently believed.[34] Nonetheless, they did indicate their desire for a more pastorally intelligible and effective theology which would help the Church to communicate Christ's message to the modern world; they thought that the need for a defensive stance vis-à-vis the world no longer existed. Moreover, they doubtless favored a theology that stressed the importance of the local churches as more than bureaucratic outposts of a Roman central office. The theological *periti* at the Council also made them aware of certain theoretical difficulties that had to be accommodated. Therefore they were ready to amalgamate various elements of the new theology and historical research within the traditional conceptualist Thomism. Renovation, not revolution was their intent.

What the Council Fathers decreed then met a strange fate when it was transposed from Rome. The media had been playing up the novelty of the Council, portraying a conflict between the good progressive forces and the bad reactionaries. Moreover, when the Council's decrees had to be transmitted to seminarians and others, the teachers realized that the wineskins of the old theology had split. A new theological *Weltanschauung* had to be discovered to carry the Council's doctrine. Transcendental Thomism offered itself, was accepted by the publishing houses and theologians, and conquered. Its victory was all the speedier because it fit in so well with various cultural trends. In the United States and Europe, the late 1960s witnessed a strong anti-institutional, anti-authoritarian movement which preferred individual experience to traditional wisdom. John Kennedy's New Frontier, Martin Luther King's dream, and Lyndon Johnson's Great Society were projecting futuristic Utopias even for those not already spaced out on pot. The age's expanding materialism, demanding instant gratification from the cornucopia of consumer goods – "Utopia now"! – also played a role in urging the demolition of limiting structures and the reconstruction of reality. Prosperity seemed endless and future shock set in.

The Enlightenment and German Idealism, which had taken two centuries to develop, were now being concentrated into simplified slogans and injected into the institution that had most fervently resisted their claims. All this "renewal" occurred within a five year period. So the returning bishops met the restless progressives back home and wondered what a cauldron of confusion they had mixed and stirred in Rome.

Post-Conciliar Exaggerations

Not the conciliar documents but the theological structure used to interpret them was at fault. It did not take long for the theologians to draw the consequences of the new theology. If concepts are only abstractions and are surpassed by the judgment, all abstractions dealing with natures are relativized. They need not have universal validity. Apply that to morals and you have the rejection of *Humanae Vitae* and the accept-

ance of *Human Sexuality*, the study commissioned by the Catholic
Theological Society of America which refused to consider any sexual
eccentricity, even bestiality, wrong in itself, but opened the door to artificial birth control, masturbation, premarital and extramarital sex,
homosexuality, and so on.[35] Dogmatic theologians were not to be caught
napping in the effort to make theological progress. Once it is recognized
that all dogmatic formulations derive from an ineffable encounter with
the infinite God, which no language can exhaust, to insist on the permanence of any dogmatic formulation was to declare oneself an antiquarian, if not a reactionary spirit.[36] To insist on papal infallibility was sense-
less if no theological proposition exhausted truth, which is open to so
many different, even contradictory interpretations.[37]

Theologians then felt challenged to rethink and reformulate all dogmas, adapting faith to the needs and tastes of modern man, open to creative praxis and the future whence meaning comes.[38] Transubstantiation
was transformed into transignification and transfinalization.[39] Jesus,
fully human, became a human person, a believer just like the rest of us.[40]
Of course the Church was composed of sinners, still on the way to the
kingdom of God. The hierarchy was instituted to serve, persuade, and
encourage, not to squash dialogue; and the Petrine ministry was well
suited to be a communications center.[41] Ecclesial structures had to be
adapted to the age, especially to our democratic age, if the message was
to get through. Every church was to be judged faithful or not, depending
upon its effective service of the kingdom, and every church, if unfaith-
ful to its mission, could cease to be an effective, sacramental mediator
of grace.[42] Given the basic equality of all believers, there was no need of
a permanent priestly caste, and greater openness to the Spirit was
required instead of formal, juridical conformity to law. Why could
priests not be married? Why could women not be ordained? If sacraments are signs of grace already received, why cannot nuns and other
women assemble to celebrate their own Eucharist? Why cannot anything
happen in a church that lives from the future? Why be narrow-minded?
If God wished all men to be saved and if Jesus' humanity is only one
finite symbol of God's self-communication in grace, why not recognize
that grace has been received by many men throughout the ages and they
too serve as mediators of grace and salvation alongside Jesus?[43]

Such was the "spirit" of Vatican II which washed over the Catholic
Church in the decades following the Council. Fortunately Karol Wojtyla
participated actively at the Council, engaging in its debates and helping
composite the documents. He knew the text as well as the spirit of the
Council, and he was intelligent enough to stand up to the theological

pressure of the experts in academe. If he had the fortitude to resist Nazis and Communists, what was a gaggle of academics by comparison? The progressive wave that battered the Church after Council is ebbing quickly. Since Joseph Ratzinger served as a *peritus* at the Council and was dismayed by the subsequent deconstruction which contradicted the Council's intent,[44] it is most likely that he will remain true to the text and the intent of the Council. The Spirit was at work in the Council, and he is a Spirit of peace, not of disorder (I Cor 14:33).

Toward the Future

How then is the Council to be interpreted? As with every text, the Council's documents have to be read first literally, then placed in their proper context, which is that of the bishops present and of the whole Catholic tradition, to which the bishops intended to be faithful; finally they are to be interpreted under the guidance of the living magisterium, which recognizes necessary adaptations. But how does the magisterium interpret those texts in their context? Let me make this suggestion. At the Council two principal interpretations of St. Thomas met and compromised. The conceptualist tradition stressed the inner-worldly intelligibility of finite realities and structures. Transcendentalist theologians showed how all finite realities are relative to the pure infinity of God, who is always more than this world. The first interpretation is tempted to absolutize finite intelligibility and structures, the second tends to relativize the finite before the infinite God, dissolving all finite intelligibility in incomprehensible mystery. Neither extreme alone is valid; both are only partial interpretations of St. Thomas, who in his own speculative synthesis employed Aristotelian and neo-Platonic elements according to need. Ultimately his vision of reality was formed by Jesus Christ, present to him in the sacramental structure of the Church. In Jesus finite human nature is preserved "without confusion or change, without division or separation," in unity with His divine nature, as Chalcedon proclaimed (DS 301). Concepts preserve distinctions while the synthetic movement of judgment surpasses, even while presupposing, those distinctions. When Thomas needed distinctions, he appealed to concepts; when he needed unity, he appealed to judgment. Reality contains both static and dynamic moments, being and becoming.

The best thinkers in both conceptualist and transcendental schools recognized the need to keep the sane balance between form and matter, essence and existence, nature and grace, etc. The Christian *Weltanschauung* transcends all reductionist rationalisms; it insists on the Catholic "both...and" which corresponds to so many aspects of reality.

This polar thinking is best recognized in the Catholic response to the Lutheran "only faith, only Scripture, only grace": faith and reason, scripture and tradition, grace and freedom. But the principle extends much further, since reality is profoundly bi-polar: Jesus is both God and man, the Church both divine and human, sacraments both sign and reality; moreover, freedom involves both intellect and will, reality comprises universal and particular, form and matter, necessity and freedom.[45] Indeed the vital tension between universal and particular, form and matter, is essential to freedom.

Human beings must have a reason for their choice, yet reason cannot determine the choice. Concepts help define a field of activity, offering possibilities for choice, but the actual choice is particular, escaping the necessity of abstract universal laws. The philosophical notion of matter, that paradoxical existing "non-being," safeguards the element of mystery in man's composition and opens him to God's invention in grace and the Incarnation. For human freedom is actualized when it encounters the demand for absolute commitment in the concrete. Such is love which demands total commitment in the here and now. Such is Jesus Christ who in an individual human nature offered Himself to us and demanded our response in freedom. Indeed the structure of freedom and revelation is sacramental: i.e., in and through a finite figure the infinite God makes Himself present, calling for the total commitment of love, and upon man's response depends his eternal salvation or damnation. The whole structure of Catholic theology is sacramental, joining the infinite God to a finite sign in such a way that man's response to God's gift of infinite love, of Himself, is summoned and produced.[46]

From that perspective the contributions to Vatican II of both conceptualist and transcendental Thomisms can be evaluated and appreciated. Conceptualist theologians rightly insisted upon finite intelligibility while transcendental thinkers reminded them that all finite intelligibility is grounded ultimately in the infinite mystery of God. Both were able to compromise in the production of the conciliar documents since both accepted as normative the Church's faith and tradition, both realized the need to maintain the tension between concept and judgment, and both confessed themselves disciples of the *Doctor Communis*. Like Thomas himself, they were nourished by the Church's wider tradition which was mediated to them through their historical studies as well as the Church's lived worship, and the best of them knew the limitations of their own systematic thought. Were all the bishops, the Fathers of Vatican II, aware of this theological balancing act? Probably not. Though many were well educated, even former seminary and university professors, most were acting principally as pastors, trying to bring Christ to the world. Yet they knew what they were doing. For by their life in the Church they possessed a lived awareness of Christ and the structure of His revelation which is deeper than words.[47] This the late John Kobler correctly recognized as he showed how *Lumen Gentium* reflects the structure of Christ in relation to the Church.[48] For Christ impressed His structure upon the Church, His Body and Bride, and all her sacraments and offices pulse with the life of grace that is God's love.

How then is the Council to be interpreted? In the Catholic tradition. This is not the mere repetition of previous dogmatic statements but involves the effort of rethinking the tradition in depth. It should not escape the notice of theologians that both conceptualist and transcendental Thomists base their philosophies on natures, those principles of motion and rest which develop according to their inherent laws. Conceptualists think that the human mind can grasp a "nature" in an objective universal concept; transcendentalists think that human nature comprises an individual spiritual dynamism oriented to God. Both develop a philosophy of natures and then employ that philosophy to structure and explain theological truths. Though the best thinkers in both camps recognize the limits of their reconstructions of reality and make allowances for them by introducing various distinctions, they both start with natures whose internal structure corresponds to the laws of the mind. Any metaphysician starting with natures presupposes necessary laws of development and thought. Thereafter room has to be made for freedom. But is not freedom the unique distinction of man and the place where he knows himself to be most himself? Why not start with freedom? Indeed the point of union between human and divine in Jesus Christ is not natural, but personal: the hypostatic union. Is not the person a self-conscious spiritual individual who exercises freedom? That is the basic insight of Pope John Paul II: the person acts. For him man *qua* person is the image of God. Natures provide the presuppositions of free action, but do not determine it. Freedom is ultimately located not in the natural will but in the person who actualizes the will's choice.

Freedom of choice is the necessary condition of possibility for the authentic freedom actualized in the choice of love: we are called to become who we are, the image of God in the Image who is Jesus Christ, the incarnate Son of God. Thus John Paul II not only resisted the dissolution of dogma and morals in the Church, he also pointed out the way for speculative theology's further development. Then, I suspect, when one understands how central personal freedom is to his message and the message of Vatican II,[49] *Lumen Gentium* will be read as a foundational document for the preservation and growth of Christ's Church in the third millennium. Its time is still to come.

Reverend John M. McDermott, S.J., S.T.D., is a native of New York City and a member since 1961 of the New York Province of the Society of Jesus. Father McDermott is currently a Professor of Theology at the Pontifical College Josephinum in Columbus, Ohio, and since 2004 a member of the International Theological Commission. Formerly (1987–1999) he taught theology at the Gregorian University in Rome (where he also received his doctorate in 1976) and before that he taught at Fordham University in New York (1976–1987). He is a member of the editorial boards of the *Josephinum Journal of Theology* as well as of *Sapientia*, and he also served on the Historical-Theological Committee for the Preparation for the Jubilee Year. Since 1990 he has been the organizer with Terrence Prendergast, S.J., archbishop of Halifax, of the bi-annual Jesuit Conference on the Thought of Pope John Paul II. Father McDermott is the author of more than 100 articles on philosophy, dogmatic theology, Scripture, moral theology, history, and pastoral and spiritual theology. He is also the author of a book, *The Bible on Human Suffering* (1990), and the editor of the volume, *The Thought of Pope John Paul II* (1993). He has written around 80 book reviews.

ENDNOTES

1   A good summary of "progressive" criticisms and demands is found is *Modern Catholicism: Vatican II and After*, ed. A. Hastings (London: SPCK, 1991). Cf. our "Reflections on *Modern Catholicism*," Div. 37 (1994), 46–68. R. McBrien, *Do We Need the Church*? (New York: Harper & Row, 1969), is among those who thinks that Vatican II did not go far enough (8): the Church is not the ordinary means of salvation nor are all called to it (15, 64, 76, 98, 113, 151, 156, 165, 173, 198), and there is no absolute certitude about faith (170, 200). McBrien considers the theologian C. Davis, who publicly left the Catholic Church, to be "in good faith," one who has simply altered his place within the Body of Christ, and McBrien is not sure that he has departed at all (176–179). Yet since there is no advantage to being a member of the Church in terms of ultimate salvation, the Church should have the courage to "promote actively" the "disaffiliation" of its members (207–209).

2   G. Philips, *L'Église et son mystère au IIe Concile du Vatican* (Paris: Desclée, 1967), I, p. 5, considers *Lumen Gentium* (LG) "the cornerstone" by which all the published decrees "are supported directly or indirectly." Describing the attitude of the Council Fathers to LG, he writes in "Dogmatic Constitution on the Church: History of the Constitution," *Commentary on the Documents of Vatican II*, ed. H. Vorgrimler, tr. L.

Adolphus et alii (New York: Herder and Herder, 1967–68), 107: "On one point there was general agreement. All looked on the Constitution on the Church as the centre and climax of the Council." J. Medina Estevez, "The Constitution on the Church: *Lumen Gentium,*" in *Vatican II: An Interfaith Appraisal,* ed. J. Miller (Notre Dame: U. of Notre Dame, 1966), 101: LG is "the most important document promulgated by Vatican Council II." J. Ratzinger, "Dogmatic Constitution on Divine Revelation: Origin and Background," *ibid.*, III, 155, sees the history of *Dei Verbum* (DV) as indicative of the Council's vicissitudes, indeed "fused with the history of this Council into a kind of unity." For the history of the debates cf. Medina Estevez, 101–122; G. Ruggieri, "The First Doctrinal Clash," in *History of Vatican II*, ed., G. Alberigo, Eng. ed. J. Komonchak, tr. M. O'Connell (Maryknoll: Orbis, 1995-), II, 233–261 (on DV); – , "Beyond an Ecclesiology of Polemics: the Debate on the Church," *ibid.*, 281–347 (on LG), 347–357 (on DV); J. Grootaers, "The Drama Continues between the Acts: The 'Second Preparation' and Its Opponents," *ibid.*, 383–391 (on DV), 391–412, 450–455 (on LG); A. Meloni, "The Beginning of the Second Period: The Great Debate on the Church," *ibid.*, III, 40–50, 58–115 (on LG); E. Vilanova, "The Intersession (1962–1964)," *ibid.*, 363–372 (on LG), 372–377 (on DV); X. Rynne, *Vatican Council II* (New York: Farrar, Straus and Giroux, 1968), pp. 76–92, 305–313, 536–544 (on DV), 109–120, 128f., 155–215, 294f., 313–317, 405–415 (on LG). Although these last two books are somewhat tendentious, clearly favoring the "progressive" forces, they are useful.

3   We prescind for the moment from sociological and cultural influences as well as the catalytic encyclical *Humanae Vitae*. Two fine articles marking the philosophical change are: H. John, S.N.D., "The Emergence of the Act of Existing in Recent Thomism," *IPQ* 2 (1962), 595–620, and N. Lobkowicz, "What Happened to Thomism? From *Aeterni Patris* to *Vaticanum Secundum,*" *ACPQ* 69 (1995), 397–423. We would disagree with John on placing de Finance in the Maréchal school; though de Finance is interested in intentionality, he stayed closer to the Gilsonian balance between essence and existence. Indeed, though Hayen claimed inspiration from Maréchal, Maréchal did not recognize him as a disciple: cf. D. Moretto, *Il Dinamismo intellettuale davantil al Mistero* (Milan: Glossa, 2001), p. 9, n. 9; Moretto's most interesting study, using unpublished notes and meticulously studying changes in successive editions of Maréchal's works, has demonstrated that Maréchal never intended to prove God's existence from the subjective intellectual dynamism; or, to put it paradoxically, Maréchal was not a Maréchalian. Actually, there were many interpretations of Thomism and variety within schools. For example, some transcendental Thomists, like Lonergan, also recognize a decisive intuition or insight into the phantasm which precedes the concept's formation. Our presentation is necessarily simplistic to trace a path through the jungle of divergent views and provide some overall intelligibility behind the changes at Vatican II.

4   Our own interpretation of Thomas' balance of existential and essential orders is found in "The Analogy of Human Knowing in the *Prima Pars*," *Gr* 77 (1996), 261–286, 501–525. The two following paragraphs are summaries of our "Faith and Critical Intelligence in Theology," in *Excellence in Seminary Education*, ed. S. Minkiel, R. Lawler, and F. Lescoe (Erie: Gannon U. Press, 1988), 71–75, and "The Methodological Shift in Twentieth Century Thomism," *Seminarium* 31 (1991), 245–253.

5   The importance of the change was noted at Vatican II: cf. Vilanova, 376; Rynne, pp. 307f.

6   B. Altaner, "Zur Frage der Definibilität der Assumption B.V.M.," *Theologische Revue* 44 (1948), 129–140; M. Schmaus, *Katholische Dogmatik*, V (Munich: Hueber, 1955), pp. 232–236.

7   Cf.., e.g., E. Mersch, S.J., *The Whole Christ*, trans. J. Kelly (Milwaukee: Bruce, 1938); -, *The Theology of the Mystical Body*, trans. C. Vollert (St. Louis: Herder, 1951); S. Tromp, S.J., *De Spiritu Sancto Anima Corporis Mystici* (Roma: Gregoriana, 1931); -, *Corpus Christi Quod Est Ecclesia* (Rome: Gregoriana, 1937); J. Anger, *La Doctrine du Corps Mystique de Jesus Christ*, 5th ed. (Paris: Beauchesne, 1934); P. Galtier, S.J., *L'Habitation en nous des trois personnes* (Paris: Beauchesne, 1927); -, *De SS. Trinitate in se et in nobis* (Paris: Beauchesne, 1933). O. Semmelroth, S.J., "La Chiesa, nuovo popolo di Dio," *La Chiesa del Vaticano II*, ed. G. Baraúna, 3rd ed. (Florence: Vallecchi, 1967), 444, pointed out, however, that the notion of the ecclesial Body of Christ dominated the first schema *De Ecclesia* at Vatican I as composed by Kleutgen and was also central to Schrader's ecclesiology.

8   The paragraph numbers follow the translation in the NCWC translation in the *Papal Encyclicals 1939–1958*, ed. C. Carlem (Raleigh: McGrath, 1981), since the Latin original, published in *AAS*, did not include paragraph numbers.

9   Cf. Y. Congar, O.P., "Historical Considerations on the Schism of the Sixteenth Century in Relation to the Catholic Realization of Unity," *Dialogue Between Christians: Catholic Contributions to Ecumenism*, tr. P. Loretz (Westminster, Newman, 1966), 333–357; – , *Lay People in the Church: A Study for a Theology of the Laity*, tr. D. Attwater (Westminster: Newman, 2957), pp. 22–44.

10   R. Bellarmine, S.J., *De Controversiis Christianae Fidei Adversus Haereticos*, 4 vols. (Rome: Bonae Artes, 1832–40), II, iii, 3, 2 , p. 90.

11   So J. Hervé, *Manuale Theologiae Dogmaticae*, I, 19th ed. (Westminster: Newman, 1943); pp. J. Perrone, S.J., *Praelectiones Theologicae* (Ratisborn: Manz, 1854); L. Lercher, S.J., *Institutiones Theologiae Dogmaticae*, I, 2nd ed.(Innsbruck: Rauch, 1934); C. Pesch, S.J., *Praelectiones Dogmaticae*, 5th ed. (Freiburg: Herder, 1915); A. Tanquerey, *Synopsis Theologiae Dogmaticae*, 24th ed., ed. J. Bord (New York: Benziger, 1937).

12   H. Hurter, S.J., *Theologiae Dogmaticae Compendium* (Innsbruck: Wagner, 1909).

13 J. Heinrich, *Dogmatische Theologie* (Mainz: Kirchheim, 1872–1901).

14 C. Mazzella, S.J., *De Vera Religione*, 4th ed. (Rome: Forzani, 1892).

15 L. Billot, S.J., *De Ecclesia Christi*, 5th ed. (Rome: Gregoriana, 1927); E. Dublancy, "?glise," *DTC* IV, 2108–2224.

16 E.g., Mazzella, pp. 342–349; Franzelin, pp. 293–311; Pesch, I, pp. 284f.; Hurter, pp. 242–248; Hervé, I, pp. 427–448; Lercher, pp. 400–403; Tanquerey, pp. 571–577.

17 T. Zapelena, S.J., *De Ecclesia Christi*, II, 2nd ed. (Rome: Gregoriana, 1954), pp. 331–579; C. Journet, *L'Église du Verbe incarné* (Bruges: Desclée de Brouwer, 1962) dedicated the first volume to the Church's institutional structure before considering the Body of Christ; yet the ample treatment attempted a synthesis of internal grace with external structure. M. Schmaus, *Katholische Dogmatik*, III/1 (München: Hueber, 1958) is notable for presenting a non-apologetic ecclesiology; starting with the Church's grounding in God's salvific will as it involves all of history, he integrates the Mystical Body into a dogmatic ecclesiology. Yet Schmaus also developed at length the jurisdictional aspects of the Church and her four notes, or marks. Franzelin was also exceptional insofar as he presented the Church historically as the fulfillment of Old Testament's economy and the postpaschal result of Jesus' preaching of the Kingdom; but almost three-quarters of his treatise dealt with jurisdictional questions. Most ecclesiology manuals before 1943 ignored the Body of Christ. Two other exceptions are Lercher, pp. 386–404, who uses "Body of Christ" to demonstrate the Church's supernatural end and dignity, and Hervé, pp. 423–448, who places "Mystical Body of Christ" immediately after the apologetical part to introduce the section on the Church's members with their obligations and jurisdictional rights. (The preface, p. x, states that the section was added already in 1935 to the twelfth edition).

18 Y. Congar, O.P., showed an early awareness of the implications of the change: cf. his *Report from Rome II: On the Second Session of the Vatican Council*, tr. L. Sheppard (London: Chapman, 1964), pp. 68–70, 85–88 (developed in "The People of God," 197–200); Grootaers, 411: "The restructuring meant a fundamental reordering of ecclesiology that would put an end to the pyramidal vision of the Church"; C. Moeller, "History of *Lumen Gentium's* Structure and Ideas," in *Vatican II*, 127f.: "The shifting of one part of former chapter three (on "The People of God and in Particular on the Laymen") to second place, before the hierarchy, was a stroke of genius; this produced the first of the Copernican revolutions which marked the elaboration of the Constitution." Such was their reaction to the first major change in the Constitution; many further changes in order of presentation would occur: cf. Medina Estevez, 109–120; Philips, "Dogmatic Constitution," 110–137. K. Wojtyla in *Acta Synodalia Sacrosancti Concilii Oecumenici Vaticani II* (Vatican: Vaticana, 1970–1978), I/4, 154–156, strongly suggested that the chapter on the hierarchy follow that on the people of God since the hierarchy is intended to serve the people.

19   Admitted by P. Smulders, S.J., "La Chiesa sacramento della salvezza," *La Chiesa del Vaticano II*, 364; this article, 363–377, gives a good overview of the development of the application of "sacrament" to the Church.

20   When Melloni, p. 50, writes abut the Council abandoning "the dominance of the image of the mystical body," he must be referring to its juridical interpretation as in the preparatory schema. *Periti* consider the image still very significant: Congar, "'*Lumen Gentium*' n° 7, 'L'?glise, Corps mystique du Christ', vu au terme de huit siècles d'histoire de la théologie du Corps mystique," *Le Concile de Vatican II* (Paris: Beauchesne, 1984), 159–161; – , "D'une 'ecclésiologie en gestation' à *Lumen Gentium* chap. I et II," *ibid.*, 133f.; Moeller, 126f. LG 7, entirely dedicated to the Body of Christ image, is longer than LG 6 which contains all the other Scriptural images. The *Relatio* of the Theological Committee for *Lumen Gentium* in *Acta Synodalia*, III/1, 173, explains that because the Theological Committee agreed with many Fathers that the Mystical Body "is more than an image and leads more deeply into the mystery of the Church," its paragraph was placed after the consideration of other Scriptural images. This corresponds to the wishes of, among others, the Polish bishops, whose spokesman, K. Wojtyla, *ibid.*, II/3, maintained that "the mystical Body of Christ…is more than an image; for it determines the very nature of the Church under a Christological aspect and simultaneously under the aspect of the mysteries of the Incarnation and the Redemption."

21   For various interpretations of *subsistit in* cf. F. Sullivan, S.J., "The Significance of the Vatican II Declaration that the Church of Christ 'Subsists in' the Roman Catholic Church," in *Vatican II: Assessment and Perspectives*, ed. R. Latourelle (New York: Paulist, 1989), II, 274–276. Sullivan's own interpretation "of the universal Church as a communion, at various levels of fullness, of bodies that are more or less fully churches" does not do justice to the whole sentence which he is interpreting. The text speaks of the unique "one, holy, Catholic, (i.e., universal) and apostolic" Church entrusted to Peter and the other Apostles to extend and rule and continues: "This Church, in this world as a constituted and ordered society, subsists in the Catholic Church, governed by Peter's successor and the bishops in communion with him." Sullivan's universal Church is hardly an ordered society in this world. It is also difficult to agree with Sullivan that "a non-Catholic community, perhaps lacking much in the order of sacrament, can achieve the *res*, the communion of the life of Christ in faith, hope, and love, more perfectly than many a Catholic community." (278f). Confusion is introduced when Sullivan compares "a Catholic community" with "a non-Catholic community," whereas *Lumen Gentium* speaks of the Catholic Church in comparison with non-Catholic "ecclesial communities" (as well as Eastern Churches not in communion with Rome). While none can deny that God is not bound to the sacraments (cf. St. Thomas, *S.T.*, III, 64, 7c; 66, 6c), but can give grace where and when He wills, it is another question whether a community *qua* community can mediate or effect more

faith, hope, and charity than a Catholic local church in communion with Peter. Sullivan, 281f., is concerned with the role of ecclesiastic communities *qua* communities. Were that true, the sacramental economy of the Catholic Church would be relativized, and there would be no strict need for the Catholic Church in God's plan of salvation. It is hard to see how any ecclesial community, imperfect at least insofar as it lacks the full unity desired by Christ, can mediate more faith, hope, and love to Christ than the Catholic Church in which resides, as Sullivan admits, 278, the full institutional integrity of the means of salvation. *Unitatis Reintegratio* 3f. also relates all other Churches and ecclesial communities to the concrete fullness of means of salvation that is to be found in the one Catholic Church entrusted to the apostolic college with Peter at its head. Admittedly *LG* 8 substituted *subsistit in* for an earlier "is" (*est*) that simply identified the Church of Christ with the Catholic Church. Certainly the notion of "subsistence" in Catholic theology, already before this usage, was very unclear, sometimes signifying "existence," sometimes "person," sometimes "standing under" as the equivalent of *substantia* or *suppositum*. Actually the Council's text, composed in committee and resulting from theological compromises, leaves a penumbra of uncertainty. If "this Church" is recognized as the Catholic Church, which the previous sentence confessed, what does it mean to say that "the Catholic Church subsists in the Catholic Church"? If anything more than a tautology is intended, a very analogous use of language must be in play, and the Council did not intend to define doctrine. But what other Church would be governed by Peter and his successor than the one entrusted to them by Christ? In fact the *Relatio*, 180, insists, "The mystery of the Church is not an idealistic nor unreal construction (*figmentum*) but exists in this concrete catholic society under the leadership of Peter's successor and the bishops in communion with him." Maybe the Fathers and theologians, avoiding two extremes, were leaving the door open to a new and more comprehensive ecclesiology. (Cf. Congar, "'*Lumen Gentium*,'" 160f.; A. Grillmeier, S.J., "The Mystery of the Church," in *Commentary on the Documents of Vatican II*, I, 139f). Although *subsistit* may not be so intellectually stimulating as Chalcedon's *persona*, the Council's new terminology points the way for future theological endeavors. That the imprecision of meaning is deliberate may be gathered from Philips, *Église,* p. 119: "It is to be presumed that the Latin expression *subsistit in* will cause oceans of ink to flow." He was the author of the schema (including the rejected *est*) adopted as the basis of *Lumen Gentium* and was very involved in the Constitution's composition. If he cannot give a precise meaning, who can? His attempted translation is: "It is there that we find Christ's Church in its entire fullness and force." The *Relatio*, 177, merely states, "in the place of 'is' the expression 'subsists in' is used in order that it might better harmonize with the affirmation about the ecclesial elements that *are present* elsewhere." Truly the text is treating a mystery "with very weak human words" (*ibid.*, 180). Cf. Moeller, Congar, T. Stransky, and C.

Butler in "Session IV Discussion," *Vatican II*, 178–180; G. Philips, "The Church: Mystery and Sacrament," *ibid.*, 191f., 194f.; Congregation for the Doctrine of the Faith, *Mysterium Ecclesiae, AAS* 65 (1973), 396–398; "Notificatio de scripto P. Leonardi Boff, OFM, 'Chiesa: Carisma et Potere,'" *AAS* 77 (1985), 758f.; and A. von Teuffenbach, *Die Bedeutung des "Subsistit in" (LG 8)* (Munich: Utz, 2002).

22   Cf. *Relatio*, 209f.

23   Congar, "People of God," 200–206; – , "The Church: The People of God," *The Church and Mankind (Concilium* vol 1) (New York: Paulist, 1965), 11–37; Semmelroth, 446–452; A. Dulles, S.J., *Models of the Church* (Garden City: Doubleday, 1974), pp. 48–51. It is worthy of note that LG 3 does not say that the whole people is "kingly," even though one would expect that characteristic by their participation in Christ and their "sharing in the priestly, prophetic, and kingly office of Christ" (31). Instead they are said to be citizens of a universal kingdom (13). The "ministerial priest...forms and rules the priestly people" (10). On the question of salvation outside the visible bounds of the Church, LG 16 only speaks of its possibility for those outside the Church, without determining how and when that possibility may be realized, as, e.g., by actual entry into the Church (despite Rahner's frequent affirmations of the contrary). Cf. the Final Report of the Synod of Bishops of 1985, D, 5: "The Council also affirms that God does not deny the *possibility* of salvation to all men of good will" (Cf. LG 16; my italics); also J. McDermott, S.J., "A Response to Cardinal Dulles," in *Creed and Culture*, ed. J. Koterski and J. Conley (Philadelphia: St. Joseph's University Press, 2004), 26–29. (On rereading, even *Redemptoris Missio* 10 does not affirm the actual salvation of people outside the Church; it holds the tension of the mystery between "the real possibility of salvation in Christ for all mankind and the necessity of the Church for salvation": 9, 14, 18, 20, 28f., 44f., 55). G. Philips, *L'?glise*, I, pp. 207–215, remains, like the Council, very balanced between the "ordaining" of all to the Church and the need of conversion from the Evil One.

24   Mazzella, pp. 560–562, 570f., 602, 613f., 687–689; Perrone, pp. 321–334; D. Palmieri, S.J., *De Romano Pontifice cum Prolegomeno de Ecclesia*, 2nd ed (Prati: Giachetti, 1892), pp. 201, 359–364, 387–391, 513–520, 609–659; 670–691; Hurter, pp. 362–367; Hervé, pp. 374–403. 25 Mazzella, pp. 751–753; Franzelin, pp. 144–147; Pesch, pp. 262f., 266–268; Hurter, pp. 430–436; Hervé, pp. 463–467; Tanquerey, pp. 649–651; Lercher, pp. 476–479.

26   Mazzella, pp. 785–789; Pesch, pp. 268f.; Lercher, pp. 480–484; Hervé, pp. 468–470; Tanquerey, pp. 662–664.

27   E.g., Mazzella, pp. 599–601; Hervé, p. 471.

28   Schmaus, pp. 486–542, well reflects the growing awareness of historical development; cf. his extended bibliography, pp. 860–868, on this topic. Worthy of special notice are Y. Congar, O.P., *Sainte ?glise* (Paris: Cerf, 1962); – (ed.), *La Collegialité episcopale* (Paris: Cerf, 1965); J. Ratzinger,

Volk und Haus Gottes in Augustins Lehre von der Kirche (München: Zink, 1954); B. Tierney, *Foundations of the Conciliar Theory* (Cambridge: University Press, 1955). H. Küng, *Structures of the Church*, tr. S. Athanasio (New York: Nelson, 1964) had great influence in its day, though it is tendentious, presenting hypotheses for fact. For a modern historical presentation of the relation pope-council cf. H. Sieben, S.J., "Historische Dimensionen der Konzilsidee," *Studien zur Gestalt und Überlieferung der Konzilien* (Paderborn: Schöningh, 2005), 15–34; – , "Zum Verhältnis zwischen Konzil und Papst bis zur Mitte des 5. Jahrhunderts," ibid., 35–42.

29   Besides the overriding problem of the development of dogma, it should also be mentioned that there were many internal difficulties and disputes within the conceptualist theologies: e.g., the extrinsic relation of revelation, grace, freedom, and reason in the act of faith; the differing notions of person in Trinitarian theology and Christology; the reconciliation of divine omnipotence and human freedom in grace; the causality of sacraments; the theory of redemption and the Mass as a sacrifice. The "new theology" promised to resolve some of them.

30   We have given a brief summary of Rahner's thought in "Karl Rahner," in *Storia della Teologia: III Da Vitus Pichler a Henre de Lubac*, ed. R. Fisichella (Rome: Dehoniane, 1996), 735–749; more detailed are our "The Christologies of Karl Rahner," *Gr* 67 (1986), 87–123, 297–327; "Dialectical Analogy: The Oscillating Center of Rahner's thought," *ibid.*, 75 (1994), 675–703; "The Analogy of Knowing in Karl Rahner," *IPQ* 26 (1996), 21–216, and "Karl Rahner in Tradition: The One and the Many," to appear in *Fides Quaerens Intellectum*. P. Burke, *Reinterpreting Rahner* (New York: Fordham, 2002) for an excellent presentation of Rahner's thought. Cf. also McDermott, "Faithful and Critical Reason," 75–83; – , "Methodological Shift," 253–266.

31   The paradox is affirmed by Maréchal, Lonergan, Alfaro, de Lubac, von Balthasar, Mouroux, and Rahner: cf. our "The Theology of John Paul II; A Response," in *The Thought of John Paul II*, ed. J. McDermott (Rome: Gregorian, 1993), 63f., n. 36, for references.

32   Since a judgment is a reflexive act, there is an original self-consciousness in knowing. "Being is self-consciousness" for Rahner. Hence the presence of God in the soul must be perceived by the self-conscious soul. Thus grace is also revelation. This gives rise to the theoretical problem how the beatific vision is different from the experience of grace on earth insofar as both are intuitive, not mediated by concepts.

33   K. Rahner, "Zur Theologie des Symbols," *Schriften zur Theologie*, IV (Einsiedeln: Benziger, 1960), 278, 290, 303; – , "Zur Theologie der Menschwerdung," ibid., 146–150 and n. 3.

34   Y. Congar, O.P., "Dekret über die Missionstätigkeit der Kirche: Theologische Grundlegung (Nr. 2–9)," in *Mission nach dem Konzil*, ed. J. Schütte (Mainz: Grünewald, 1967), 163. Cf. K. Rahner, S.J., "Faith: Way to Faith," *Sacramentum Mundi*, ed. K. Rahner and A. Darlap, II (New York:

Herder and Herder, 1968), 310f. Cf. C. Moeller in "Section IV Discussion," in *Vatican II: An Interfaith Appraisal*, 177: "A council never adopts, as such, a theological theory or interpretation." Though Moeller was specifically responding a question about *Ursakrament* at Vatican II, his answer has wider import.

35   A. Kosnik et alii, *Human Sexuality: New Directions in American Catholic Thought* (New York: Paulist, 1977); this volume, pp. 90–98, facilitated its conclusions by arbitrarily redefining the purpose of sexual activity as "creative and integrative" instead of the traditional "procreative and unitive"; for other extreme views cf. J. McDermott, S.J., "The Context of *Veritatis Splendor*," in *Prophecy and Diplomacy: The Moral Doctrine of John Paul II*, ed. J. Conley and J. Koterski (New York: Fordham, 1999), 141–166 (although the publisher's imposition of "inclusive language" – without permission of the editors or knowledge of the author – distorts the meaning in places, at least the difficulties of the transcendental morality are clear). The Congregation for the Doctrine of the Faith (CDF) dedicated a specific condemnation to *Human Sexuality* on July 13, 1979: "The Book *Human Sexuality*," in *Vatican Council II*, ed. A. Flannery, II (Boston: St. Paul, 1982), 505–509, after a more general condemnation of such errors in *Personae Humanae* on Dec. 29, 1975, ibid., 486–499.

36   McBrien, pp. 192–195; in more detail L. Dewart, *The Future of Belief* (London: Burns & Oates), pp. 90–118.

37   McBrien, pp. 183, 187f.; H. Küng, *Unfehlbar?* (Zurich: Benziger, 1971), pp. 128–132, 137f., 143–157. K. Rahner, S.J., "Kritik an Hans Kung," *Stimmen der Zeit* 186 (1970), esp. 368–376, originally attacked this position but, as Burke, pp. 204–222, has shown, ultimately came around to its equivalent. Cf. also the CDF's decree *Mysterium Ecclesiae*, issued on June 24, 1973, in *Vatican II* (Flannery), II, 428–440.

38   McBrien, pp. 192–195, 221f.; J. Nolte, *Dogma in Geschichte* (Freiburg: Herder, 1971), pp. 148–268; R. Haight, S.J., *Dynamics of Theology* (New York: Paulist, 1990), esp. pp. 169–188.

39   P. Schoonenberg, S.J., "Presence and the Eucharistic Presence," *Cross Currents* 16 (1967), 39–54; E. Schillebeeckx, O.P., *The Eucharist*, tr. N. Smith (New York: Sheed and Ward, 1968), pp. 117–121. In response cf. Paul VI, *Mysterium Fidei* (Sept. 3, 1965).

40   P. Schoonenberg, S.J., *Ein Gott der Menschen*, tr. H. Mertens (Köln: Benziger, 1969) pp. 74–96; L. Boff, O.F.M., *Jesus Christ Liberator*, tr. P. Hughes (Maryknoll: Orbis, 1978), pp. 181, 193–198; E. Schillebeeckx, O.P., *Jesus: An Experiment in Christology*, tr. H. Hoskins (New York: Seabury, 1979), pp. 94, 569, 655f.; R. Haight, S.J., *Jesus Symbol of God* (Maryknoll: Orbis, 1999), pp. 205, 242, 380, 441f.; W. Dych, S.J., *Thy Kingdom Come: Jesus and the Reign of God* (New York: Herder & Herder, 1999), pp. 16–18, 37, 45, 55. The CDF already warned about such tendencies in *Mysterium Filii Dei*, on Feb. 21, 1972 in *Vatican II* (Flannery), II, 423–427.

41 H. Hoefnagels, *Demokratisierung der kirchlichen Autorität* (Freiburg: Herder, 1969), pp. 93–116; H. Häring, "Can a Petrine Office Be Meaningful in the Church?" *Papal Ministry in the Church*, ed. H. Küng (*Concilium* 64) (New York: Herder and Herder, 1971); G. Baum, *The Credibility of the Church Today* (New York: Herder and Herder, 1968), pp. 205–210; L. Swidler, "Demo-kratia or Consensus Fidelium," in *Authority in the Church*, ed. P. Franzen (Leuven: University, 1983), 236–243; H. Fries, "Is There a Magisterium of the Faithful?" *The Teaching Authority of the Believers*, ed. J. Metz and E. Schillebeeckx (*Concilium* 180) (New York: Paulist, 1985), 89f.;

42 McBrien, pp. 124, 147; R. Haight, S.J., "Mission: Symbol for Understanding the Church Today," *TS* 37 (1976), 620f.

43 P. Knitter, *No Other Name?* (Maryknoll: Orbis, 1985), pp. 166f.; 182f.; 186–204; Haight, *Jesus*, pp. 415, 422. For a good criticism cf. G. Rota, "L'Unicità di Gesù nel dibattito teologico sulle religioni," in *Fede cristiana e diversità religiosa* (Bergamo: Litostampa Istituto Grafico, 2003), 53–90. Cf. also Paul VI, *Evangelii Nuntiandi* (Dec. 8, 1975, and John Paul II, *Redemptoris Missio* (Dec. 7, 1990). On priestly celibacy cf. *Sacerdotalis Caelibatus* (June 24, 1969). On women's admission to the priesthood cf. CDF, *Interlinsigniores* (Oct. 15, 1976), in *Vatican II* (Flannery), II, 331–345, and John Paul II, *Ordinatio Sacerdotalis* (May 22, 1994).

44 Cf. J. Ratzinger with V. Messori, *The Ratzinger Report*, tr. S. Attanasio and G. Harrison (San Francisco: Ignatius, 1985), pp. 27–44 *et passim*.

45 G. Philips, "Deux tendances dans la théolgie contemporaine," *NRT* 85 (1963), 225–238, esp.234, 238, early recognized the two opposed theologies and explicitly saw the need of balance on the basis of the Catholic "et…et." He was the secretary responsible for the drafting of LG. His irenic seeking of balance comes through his commentaries on the Council. What Ratzinger, "Dogmatic Constitution," 164, writes of DV can also be applied, *mutatis mutandis*, to LG: "The fundamental compromise which pervades it is more than a compromise, it is a synthesis of great importance." For other theologians aware of the need for balance between concept and judgment cf. J. McDermott, S.J., "Sheehan, Rousselot, and Theological Method," *Gr* 69 (1987), 714–716, for a references to a list of theologians aware of the proper balance: Gardeil, Sertillanges, Maritain, Gilson, Przywara, Rousselot, Maréchal, Rahner, Lonergan, de Lubac, von Balthasar, Kasper. Many of my writings aimed at showing the balance in these and similar thinkers.

46 Cf. J. McDermott, S.J., "Faith, Reason, and Freedom," *ITQ* 67 (2002), 307–332, and "La struttura sacramentale della realtá," *La Scuola Cattolica* 128 (2000), 273–299, for a grounding and development of this sacramental structure.

47 Responses to this presentation at the Fellowship of Catholic Scholars convention, especially that of the Rev. M. Lamb, rightly emphasized that the Vatican II reflects the whole sapiential tradition of the Church, which goes

back beyond the two principal theologies sketched above. Hence one should be careful about judging the adequacy of any theological system from a single part of it. Every system in one way or another seeks to reflect the full life of the Church. So, when a respondent asked whether the juridical ecclesiology, lacking the notion of the

The Millennial *Ressourcement* for Vatican II's Renewal
A Response to Father John M. McDermott, S.J. on *Lumen Gentium*

REVEREND MATTHEW L. LAMB

Father McDermott's lecture, by its very title, indicates a problem regarding Vatican II, and, specifically, *Lumen Gentium*: "The Once and Future Constitution." What is at stake is the reception of the Council with its constitutions, decrees, and declarations. As he correctly observes, the reception of *Lumen Gentium* by the Church is one with the general reception of the Council itself. I wish to indicate a much larger panorama for understanding the significance of Vatican II and *Lumen Gentium* than the two contrasting "Thomisms" analyzed by Fr. McDermott.

Beginning where he concluded, I wish to bring out the millennial contexts in which John Paul II and Benedict XVI place the Council and the challenges the Council poses to the Church. Indeed, the sober realism of the documents of Vatican II, as well as the papal and synodal exposition of the conciliar documents, indicate that, whatever the frolic of theological interpretations, all concepts and judgments of the papal and conciliar magisterium communicate a knowledge of the divinely revealed realities. We are called to worship the Triune God and follow faithfully Jesus Christ as the Word Incarnate – not our concepts or propositions per se.[1] The millennial context of the Council was clearly articulated by Pope Benedict XVI in his first statement as Pope:

> Pope John Paul II indicated the [Second Vatican] Council precisely as a "compass" with which to orient oneself in the vast ocean of the third millennium (cf. apostolic letter "Novo Millennio Ineunte," Nos. 57–58). In his spiritual testament he noted: "I am convinced that the new generations will still be able to draw for a long time from the riches that this council of the 20th century has

lavished on us"(17.III.2000). Therefore, in preparing myself also for the service that is proper to the Successor of Peter, I wish to affirm strongly my determination to continue the commitment to implement the Second Vatican Council, in the footsteps of my Predecessors and in faithful continuity with the two millennial tradition of the Church.[2]

What does it mean to implement Vatican II "in faithful continuity with the two millennial tradition of the Church," being thereby a "compass" guiding us at the dawn of the third millennium? This broad panorama of the millennia involves the Church in a vast *ressourcement*, or return to the sources, if the Church is to renew and orient an *aggiornamento*, or updating, that measures up to the tasks of our times. Let me all too briefly outline the *ressourcement* that is needed to appreciate Vatican II.

The first millennium of Catholicism could be characterized as a patristic-monastic millennium, in which the fidelity to the truth of revelation set up the dioceses, cathedral schools, monasteries, and convents that emphasized the importance of a dedication to wisdom and holiness. Theological problems, Fr. McDermott reminds us, are often traceable to philosophical ones. In the evangelization of the Greek and Roman cultures the Church fathers could demonstrate how the true Word of God revealed the redemptive wisdom of the Word Incarnate in his life, suffering, death, and resurrection. The greatest philosophers of Greece and Rome had taught the need for intellectual and moral excellence, of living a virtuous life according to right reason. They could not, however, account for the pervasive evil and injustice that eventually led, as the Apologists and Augustine showed, the intellectually excellent to decline into skepticism, and the morally excellent to either withdraw into Stoicism or degenerate into Epicureanism. The good and just life of intellectual and moral excellence began to flourish again, however, thanks to the preaching, teaching, sanctifying Church whose sacramental governance both taught and infused the theological virtues of faith, hope, and charity. The revealed wisdom of the Gospel and of faith did not extinguish or blind, but rather healed and strengthened the quest for human theoretical and practical wisdom.

As the great Roman culture was collapsing from the weight of its own vices, Augustine wryly remarked that it would have been better had they built temples in honor of Socrates or Plato rather than the gods and goddesses that were projections of their own disordered and irrational desires. So the Church's first millennium saw its eventual triumph throughout Europe as its intellectual and ecclesial apostolates flourished

in those parish, convent, cathedral, and monastic communities dedicated to the quests for wisdom and holiness. What derailed the philosophical life of reason, as the Fathers and Benedict saw so well, was the root
sin of pride with its accompanying "*acedia*" as the flight from God as
friend.

Where the first millennium was a patristic, cathedral, and monastic
millennium, the second millennium witnessed the emergence of a new
form of the intellectual apostolate as universities emerged in Catholic
Europe. Theology would be pursued in communities committed to the
quest for science and scholarship. The differentiation of science and
scholarship from the quest for wisdom and holiness was always in danger, as Bernard warned Abelard, of becoming a separation and opposition because of pride. Despite the efforts of the mendicant theologians
such as Aquinas, Bonaventure, or Cajetan, the spread of nominalism and
voluntarism eroded the notion of wisdom as a serious contemplative-the-
oretical attunement to the whole. With the loss of wisdom traditions,
modern enlightenment cultures cultivated empirical sciences of the particular. There is no heuristic attention to the intelligibility and pattern of
the whole; instead there is attention only to the individual things, and
any efforts to pattern or order them are taken to be conventional and
arbitrary.[3]

A major fault in post-Enlightenment cultures rejecting wisdom is
the lowering of expectations and standards. These are not only privatized
but are also identified as resulting from force and fraud. In the face of
these cultural challenges, it is important to emphasize how the holiness
of the Church is brought about by the infinite holiness and goodness of
Jesus Christ and his saints. The hierarchy is not one of force or fraud, but
one with the mystery of Christ's redemptive mission from the Father in
the Holy Spirit. Charles Taylor has analyzed how the post-Enlightenment
evaluations of everyday life developed from a Protestant rejection of the
Roman Catholic notion of an ecclesial and hierarchical mediation of the
sacred.[4] In these cultures there is no notion of the Church in the full
Catholic sense of sacramentally carrying forward the missions of the
Son and Spirit. Each Christian is alone before God and alone responsible for his or her personal commitment to Christ. If individual Catholics
are passengers "in the ecclesial ship on its journey to God," for
Protestants "...there can be no passengers. This is because there is no
ship in the Catholic sense, no common movement carrying humans to
salvation. Each believer rows his or her own boat."[5] Indeed, the bark of
Peter was rather roundly denounced by Spinoza, who was followed by
Herder and Voltaire, Hobbes, Hume, and Locke, as little more than a

clerically dominative "Leviathan" seducing the credulous and superstitious by fraudulent force.[6]

Without wisdom and holiness attuning the minds and hearts of theologians and scholars to the revealed realities, the development of doctrine is lost. It is misunderstood as arbitrary decisions on propositions
whose truth is not recognized as the revelation of the infinite wisdom
and love of the Triune God. Sacred doctrine loses its very soul. Spinoza
set forth the presuppositions of this denigration of revealed truth in his
Theologico-Political Treatise. Like nature, the Bible can no longer be
treated as a whole; it must be broken up into fragmented parts. These
isolated texts must then be interpreted only by other texts. Because the
wise attunement to the whole was lost, Spinoza remarks that one must
never raise the truth question, only the meaning question to be answered
only with reference to other fragmented texts. The development of doctrine within the Bible from Old to New Testament, and within the ongoing mission of the Church is rendered impossible. Wisdom is replaced
with arbitrary power.[7]

Precisely because of this pervasive anti-wisdom and anti-Catholic –
kaq olon, or according to the whole – character of contemporary cultures, *Lumen Gentium* begins with the mystery of the Church: a call to
revealed wisdom and sacramental holiness. The foundation of the episcopacy is the very Mystery of the Trinity, for each bishop is commissioned by the sacrament of his ordination to carry forward with the
whole Church the visible and invisible missions of the Son and the Holy
Spirit. As Christ is the primordial icon of the Father and the manifestation of his merciful presence among men and women, so the ministry to
the people of God requires the bishop and his priests and religious to be
living signs of the Lord Jesus among the people. The anointing of the
Holy Spirit incorporates the faithful into the Body of Christ, and the
anointing of the same Holy Spirit at his ordination configures the bishop and priest to Christ, enabling them to be a living continuation of the
mystery of Christ for the Church.[8]

Therefore, I suggest that Fr. McDermott's appeal to John Paul II as
providing the context for understanding the foundational significance of
Lumen Gentium is an important directive. For the late pope, along with
Benedict XVI, sees the task confronting the Church at the dawn of her
third millennium as one of finding ways to integrate the first millennial
quest for wisdom and holiness with the second millennial quest for science, technology, and scholarship. Without human and divine wisdom
and holiness, science and technology only further empower the nihilism
at the dark heart of the culture of death.

Why is this millennial *ressourcement* for Vatican II so little under-stood or appreciated in Catholic theological and scholarly circles today? It is a commonplace today to contrast the Catholic Church "before and after" the Council. Usually the Council itself and/or its documents and decisions are either praised or blamed. There is, however, something unique about Vatican II that should not be overlooked. No other Council in the two millennial history of the Catholic Church had such extensive and all-pervasive mass media coverage. Philosophical and theological differences have always been with us, but never before was there the technologies of mass communication to broadcast those differences, not with scholarly subtlety but with mass superficiality. Indeed, as Archbishop Agostino Marchetto has indicated in his most recent and important critique of the historiography of Vatican II, too often theolo-gians and historians have surrendered sound scholarly judgment to the superficial paradigm of "conservatives versus liberals," or "restora-tionists versus progressives," as imposed by the mass media on the Council.[9]

What Archbishop Marchetto's devastating reviews of Professor Alberigo and his collaborators multivolume history of Vatican II shows is the depth to which historical and theological scholarship on the Council has been derailed by the ideological categories of conservative and liberal. When the "spirit" or the "style" of Vatican II is invoked, it is not the Holy Spirit but the *Zeitgeist* that blew through mass media cor-ridors blessing all things labeled "liberal" or "progressive." As the then Cardinal Ratzinger so clearly analyzed, there was a tendency to distort the Council and its teachings through the use of such ideological blind-ers.[10] By the second session, the "conservative versus liberal" paradigm was being universally applied. Those *periti* and theologians who adopt-ed it were the ones most often quoted in the media. Archbishop Marchetto gives detailed evidence of historians and theologians compro-mising objectivity and truth by distorting their work to fit biased cate-gories. For the Institute of Religious Studies at Bologna under the direc-torship of Prof. Alberigo, what is important is the "event" of the Council; the texts are inserted into an event that is described in variations on the conservative versus liberal paradigm. So often those texts showing the continuity with previous councils such as Trent or Vatican I, or previous popes or church fathers, can be taken as concessions to the conserva-tives. The fact that the liberals or progressives "won" the "battle" of the council is portrayed as a rupture or a "new beginning" discontinuous with a Tridentine past of the Church.[11]

The specifically theological import of the conciliar documents, especially their continuity with the two millennial traditions of the Church, were also neglected because of the woeful lack of adequate theological formation as fewer and fewer graduate theological programs formed their graduates in the linguistic skills and philosophical and theological habits of mind and scholarly judgment needed to appropriate the primary patristic, monastic, scholastic, and counter-reformation sources.[12]

Such a millennial perspective on Vatican II and *Lumen Gentium* also bears upon Father McDermott's discussion of the conceptualist and transcendentalist Thomists. The neglect of metaphysical wisdom and the replacement of the theoretical-speculative-contemplative way of living with a Cartesian and Kantian epistemology of an isolated monadic thinker (*res cogitans*) confronting bodies (*res extensa*) complicates enormously the ability of moderns and post-moderns to understand the realism of an Augustine or an Aquinas or a Cajetan. Indeed, it was Cajetan in the 16th century who realized the importance for the Dominicans of beginning after three centuries to teach their theologians with Aquinas's *Summa Theologiae* rather than the Sentence commentaries they used till then – contrary to St. Thomas's own admonition.[13] Only by undergoing what Augustine narrates in Books V through VII of his *Confessions* as the intellectual conversion can one understand the importance of the revelation of the "*imago Dei*" both for him and later, as Father Merriell has profoundly shown, for Aquinas's own development.[14]

Of America Alex de Tocqueville wrote that in no other country are "the precepts of Descartes least studied and best followed."[15] The metaphysical and cognitive realism of Aquinas's "*sensibile in actu est sensus in actu*" and "*intelligibile in actu est intellectus in actu*" as enabling the act of judgment to know the real is foundational for both reason and faith. We know being and not only a concept of being. The act of faith does not end at the propositions of the creed but through them at the divine realities revealed.[16] What is at stake in sacred doctrine and the magisterial teachings of the Church are divinely revealed realities.

The great bishops and theologians of the first millennium emphasized that the Triune God redeems the good creation disoriented by the prideful sins of intelligent creatures. At the end of the second millennium the loss of metaphysical wisdom has led to a loss of any notion of nature as both spiritual and material. The new evangelization in this regard is more demanding than that done by the Greek and Latin fathers. Vatican II and modern popes indicate that contemporary cultures lack adequate notions of the finality of natural realities, especially in such areas as human sexuality, ecology, and natural law.[17]

This loss of nature, and the vanishing practices of even the natural virtue of religion, led Christopher Dawson to complain that in this sense modern cultures were not in the mould of the old "pagan" cultures, with their natural if distorted religions. Often Dawson called attention to what he termed "the new Leviathan" of a materialist and consumerist culture that subordinates everything to the pursuit of wealth and material satisfaction without regard to the limits of either nature or the guidance of wisdom. He once remarked that "a secular society that has no end beyond its own satisfaction is a monstrosity – a cancerous growth which will ultimately destroy itself."[18] The new evangelization must itself draw upon not only a theology, but also a philosophy that can disclose the "natural things" which contemporary cultures ignore to their peril – such things as wisdom, friendship, the excellence of virtues, and nature.[19] We can only pray and work so that, as Fr. McDermott indicates at the end of his reflections, *Lumen Gentium* will increasingly be read "as the foundational document for the preservation and growth of Christ's Church in the third millennium. Its time is still to come."

The next time you read *Lumen Gentium* – and the other conciliar documents – notice the references to the need for human and divine wisdom and holiness, integrating these with science, scholarship, technology, and art as we embark on the "vast ocean of the third millennium." Vatican II is indeed a compass. By way of conclusion, here is an example – one of many – from *Lumen Gentium*:

> The Lord Jesus, the divine Teacher and Model of all perfection, preached holiness of life to each and everyone of His disciples of every condition. He Himself stands as the author and consummator of this holiness of life (LG # 40)...it remains for each [of the laity] to cooperate in the external spread and the dynamic growth of the Kingdom of Christ in the world.
>
> Therefore, let the laity devotedly strive to acquire a more profound grasp of revealed truth, and let them insistently beg of God the gift of wisdom (LG #35).
>
> Therefore, by their competence in secular training and by their activity, elevated from within by the grace of Christ, let them vigorously contribute their effort, so that created goods may be perfected by human labor, technical skill and civic culture for the benefit of all men according to the design of the Creator and the light of His Word (LG #36).

Reverend Matthew L. Lamb began his graduate studies in the Trappist monastery of the Holy Spirit in Conyers, Georgia, which he entered when he was fourteen years old. He plans on returning to a contemplative monastery life after teaching. He received his S.T.L. in theology, *Magna cum Laude*, from the Pontifical Gregorian University in Rome, and, in 1974, his doctorate (Dr.Theo), S*umma cum Laude*, from the Westfälische Wilhelms Universität in Münster, Germany. In 2002 he received an honorary doctorate from the Franciscan University of Steubenville. He was ordained to the priesthood in the archdiocese of Milwaukee.

Currently he is a Professor of Theology and chairman of the Theology Department at Ave Maria University in Naples, Florida. He previously taught theology at both Marquette University and Boston College. He has authored some 130 articles and several books, and at present he is editing at book, *Vatican II: Renewal within Tradition*, and completing the writing of a book, *Eternity, Time, and the Life of Wisdom*.

ENDNOTES

1   See St. Thomas Aquinas, *Summa Theologiae* II-II, 2 ad 2: "*actus autem credentis non terminatur ad enuntiabile, sed ad rem: non enim formamus enuntiabilia nisi ut per ea de rebus cognitionem habeamus, sicut in scientia, ita et in fide.*"

2   First Statement of Pope Benedict XVI after the Mass with the Cardinals, April 20, 2005: #3: Iustissima quidem de causa Pontifex Ioannes Paulus Secundus Ecclesiae in Concilio illo demonstravit indicem seu ut dicitur quasi "nauticam pyxidem," qua in vasto mari tertii millennii dirigeretur (cfr Litt. Ap. *Novo millennio ineunte*, 57–58). In suo spiritali quoque Testamento scripsit: "Persuasum mihi habeo advenientes homines diutius etiam quaedam sumpturos ex divitiis illis quas hoc Concilium saeculi vicesimi nobis est elargitum" (17.III.200). Nos quoque propterea munus ingredientes quod est proprium Successoris Petri, firmam certamque voluntatem declarare volumus Concilii Vaticani Secundi continuandi exsecutionem, Praegredientibus Decessoribus Nostris, atque in fideli perpetuitate duorum milium annorum Ecclesiae traditionis.

3   Alasdair MacIntyre's *Three Rival Traditions of Moral Inquiry* has chartered how contemporary universities and cultures take their bearings from two Enlightenment traditions: the encyclopedists and the genealogists. The encyclopedists attend carefully to the endless particularities open to human study, but lack any internal intelligent ordering of the whole. The alphabet provides the scholars, as it does also the administrative bureaucrats, with their impoverished substitute for order: the filing system. God is filed under "G" along with "gold" and "gorillas." The genealogists then come along to claim that any language is only a dialect with an army and a navy, so that all orders are only conventions imposed by dominative power. All order and pattern are merely conventional, so whatever pattern is operative is due to those in power deciding it is so. Truth becomes just another name for power.

4   Charles Taylor, *The Sources of the Self: The Making of Modern Identity* (Cambridge: Harvard University Press, 1989) pp. 215 ff.

5   *Ibid.* p. 217.

6   See Jonathan Israel, *The Radical Enlightenment: Philosophy and the Making of Modernity 1650–1750* (Oxford University Press, 2001) p. 218–229.

7   See Jonathan Israel, *Op. Cit.* pp. 157–274, 445–476; and Spinoza, *A Theologico-Political Treatise* (New York: Dover, 2004) pp. 98–119, esp. p. 101.

8   *Lumen Gentium,* Chapters 2 and 3; then Chapter 4 is on laity and Chapter 5 on the universal call to holiness. See also John Paul II, *Pastores Gregis* # 7.

9   Agostino Marchetto, *Il Concilio Ecumenico Vaticano II: Contrappunto per la sua storia* (Liberia Editrice Vaticana, 2005) pp. 84 ff. and 358 ff.

10 Joseph Ratzinger, *The Ratzinger Report* (San Francisco: Ignatius Press, 1985).

11 Marchetto, *op.cit.* pp. 93–174; note also the treatment of "tradition" in the Alberigo volumes, as well as the accounts that draw upon press coverage with little critical objectivity, Giuseppe Alberigo & Joseph Komonchak , eds., *History of Vatican II* (Maryknoll: Orbis, 1996–2004).

12 See Matthew Lamb "Will There Be Catholic Theology in the United States?" in *America*, vol. 162, May 26, 1990, pp. 523–34. Also "The Catholic Theological Society of America: Theologians Unbound" in *Crisis: Politics, Culture, and the Church* December 1997 pp. 36–37; and "The Catholic Theological Society of America: A Preliminary Profile", in *The Fellowship of Catholic Scholars Quarterly,* vol. 21, no. 2 (Spring, 1998) pp. 8–10; see also responses to Fr. Hollenbach in *Crisis: Politics, Culture & The Church* vol. 16, no. 2 (February 1998) pp. 3 & 14; and Sr. Farley in *The Fellowship of Catholic Scholars Quarterly,* vol. 21, no. 4, (Fall 1998) pp. 2–5. Over the past three decades prior to 1997, 75% of doctoral dissertations in theology done by CTSA members had been on 20th century thinkers; 10% done on 19th century thinkers. Of the remaining 15% most were in biblical studies. Research on specifically Catholic theological traditions – patristic, monastic, scholastic, counter-reformation – is woefully meager. See also Walter Principe's plaintiff presidential address to the CTSA in 1991 and the response "History and Systematics: A Response" in *The Proceedings of the Catholic Theological Society of America* (Atlanta: 1991), pp. 98–107.

13 See M. Michèle Mulchahey, *"First the Bow is Bent in Study:" Dominican Education before 1350* (Toronto: Pontifical Institute of Medieval Studies, 1998), pp. 161–167.

14 D. Juvenal Merriell *To the Image of the Trinity: A Study in the Development of Aquinas' Teaching* (Toronto: Pontifical Institute of Medieval Studies, 1990).

15 Alexis de Tocqueville, *Democracy in America* (New York: Doubleday, 1969) p. 429.

16 *Summa Theologiae II-II*, 1, where Aquinas analyzes the object of faith. Regarding the inadequacies of Karl Rahner's transcendentalist construal of judgment, the analysis of Patrick Burke of Rahner's *Schwebe* (dynamic oscillation between the opposites of object and subject, of concrete particular and universal) draws upon the earlier work of Fr. McDermott. Rahner through Heidegger owes more of his position to a Kantian and Hegelian *Begrifflichkeit* than to Aquinas. See Patrick Burke, *Reinterpreting Rahner: A Critical Study of His Major Themes* (New York: Fordham University Press, 2002). Bernard Lonergan has been too casually lumped together with the "movement or school" of Transcendental Thomism. R. J. Henle's study of the movement indicates that Lonergan is not in that school; see Henle's *The American Thomistic Revival* (St. Louis: St. Louis University Press, 1999) pp. 348 ff.; also Matthew Lamb's "Lonergan's Transposition of Augustine and Aquinas" in the forthcoming *Festschrift* for Michael Vertin with the University of Toronto Press.

17 See Russell Hittinger, *The First Grace: Rediscovering the Natural Law in a Post-Christian World* (Wilmington, Delaware: ISI Books, 2003).

18 Christopher Dawson, "What is a Christian Civilization?", in *Christianity and European Culture* edited by Gerald J. Russello (Washington DC: Catholic University of America Press, 1998), p. 32; on the new Leviathan, see Dawson's *Enquiries into Religion and Culture* (London: Sheed & Ward, 1937) pp. 3–19.

19 *Gaudium et Spes* #89: "Since in virtue of her mission received from God, the Church preaches the Gospel to all men and dispenses the treasures of grace, she contributes to the ensuring of peace everywhere on earth and to the placing of the fraternal exchange between men on solid ground by imparting knowledge of the divine and natural law. Therefore, to encourage and stimulate cooperation among men, the Church must be clearly present in the midst of the community of nations both through her official channels and through the full and sincere collaboration of all Christians – a collaboration motivated solely by the desire to be of service to all."

Dei Verbum
Sacred Scripture Since Vatican II

REVEREND WILLIAM S. KURZ, S.J.

Introduction

A dominant stimulus for transition in Catholic approaches to biblical exegesis and interpretation has been Vatican II's Dogmatic Constitution on Divine Revelation, *Dei Verbum* (promulgated by Pope Paul VI on November 18, 1965). This document removed most remaining official hesitations and solidified and greatly accelerated the Catholic Church's embrace of historical-critical approaches to the Bible. It reaffirmed Pius XII's encyclical, *Divino Afflante Spiritu*, from about twenty-two years earlier (September 30, 1943), when Catholic magisterial suspicion of and resistance to these critical methods began to give way instead to their acceptance. The way for their reception was further and more immediately prepared by the Pontifical Biblical Commission's Instruction on the Historical Truth of the Gospels, *Sancta Mater Ecclesia*," dated April 21, 1964.[1]

This paper will first argue that, although Vatican II mandated a double charge to Catholic exegetes and biblical scholars, in the forty years since *Dei Verbum* was promulgated, Catholic scholars have admirably implemented only their first charge. At least until recently, many of them have to a great extent neglected or even avoided their second mandated task. Second, this paper will recommend some lessons from patristic writers that offer assistance for satisfying this second mandate, i.e., how to read the Bible more theologically and how to discover the revelational intent of the divine author.

Dei Verbum's Double Mandate

Dei Verbum charged the biblical interpreter as follows: "However, since God speaks in Sacred Scripture through men in human fashion, the interpreter of Sacred Scripture, in order to see clearly what God wanted to communicate to us, *should carefully investigate what meaning the sacred writers really intended,* and *what God wanted to manifest by means of their words*"(DV #12).[2] Catholic exegetes have enthusiastically and with admirable success fulfilled this first mandate, namely, that they "should carefully investigate what meaning the sacred writers really intended." However, they have been neither as enthusiastic nor as successful in fulfilling *Dei Verbum's* second charge, namely, that they investigate "what God wanted to manifest by means of their words"(DV #12).[3]

Among the possible explanations for this discrepancy in observing the double directive of *Dei Verbum*, there are both methodological considerations and reasons that related more to metaphysics and faith. Methodologically, contemporary critical approaches to Scripture are directed primarily if not exclusively toward understanding the Bible on the human level. Because of this focus on only the human level, not enough attention has been given to a more basic root problem at the level of faith and of metaphysical presuppositions about the nature of the Bible. Since the Enlightenment, both modernistic and now post-modernistic underpinnings of critical approaches to Scripture have been averse to beliefs and to metaphysical presuppositions that the Bible is in actual reality the Word of God written in human words.

The premise for Vatican II's directives for interpreting Scripture is the Council Fathers' endorsement of traditional Catholic belief in the two-fold nature of the Bible. The origin of this view goes back to the pre-modern pre-Enlightenment period. Vatican II's Dogmatic Constitution on Divine Revelation, *Dei Verbum*, re-affirms the traditional view that Scripture has a two-fold nature as God's Word expressed in human words. "In Sacred Scripture, therefore, while the truth and holiness of God always remains intact, the marvelous 'condescension' of eternal wisdom is clearly shown, 'that we may learn the gentle kindness of God, which words cannot express, and how far He has gone in adapting His language with thoughtful concern for our weak human nature.'"[4]

The Council bishops even compared the divine and human nature of the Word of God in Scripture with the divine and human nature of the Word or Son of God made flesh in the Incarnation. "For the words of God, expressed in human language, have been made like human discourse, just as the Word of the eternal Father, when He took to Himself the flesh of human weakness, was in every way made like men"(DV #13).[5] In both of these references, *Dei Verbum* accentuates how the divine-human nature of both the Incarnate Word, Jesus, and of the word of Scripture, facilitates the communication between God and humans.

It is this belief in the two-fold divine and human nature of Scripture that is the primary foundation for the double mandate given to Catholic biblical exegetes. Because of the Catholic belief that the biblical Word has both human and divine aspects, exegetes must interpret both the human level of the historical writers and the divine level of God as ultimate author of all of Scripture. This is the ultimate reason why Vatican II requires that interpreters investigate not only the meaning of the human writers, but also "what God wanted to manifest by means of their words"(DV #12).

There is potential for conflict between the professed belief of Catholic biblical scholars that Scripture is the Word of God in human words, and their methodological training and practice, which is quite unrelated to such a belief in the two-fold nature of Scripture. The disparity in accomplishments regarding the two goals proposed to Catholic scholars seems logically related to the fact that only the goal of interpreting the meaning intended by the human authors is immediately accessible to historical and other academic forms of criticism. Contemporary Catholic scholars have been trained in historical criticism, which for decades has been regarded not only as the governing paradigm for interpreting Scripture, but also as the exclusively "technical" and academically respectable model for doing so.

Because the first commission to Catholic Scripture scholars is more suited to their training and scholarly interaction, following its ideals flows almost connaturally for them. "The interpreter must investigate what meaning the sacred writer intended to express and actually expressed in particular circumstances by using contemporary literary forms in accordance with the situation of his own time and culture. For the correct understanding of what the sacred author wanted to assert, due attention must be paid to the customary and characteristic styles of feeling, speaking and narrating which prevailed at the time of the sacred writer, and to the patterns men normally employed at that period in their everyday dealings with one another"(DV #12).[6]

On the other hand, most contemporary Catholic scholars have received little or no formal training in methods or ways of achieving Vatican II's second goal of investigating what *God* wanted to manifest through the human writers. Most scholars find themselves unsure about how to pursue the Council's goal of reading Scripture in the sacred spirit in which it was written (or in some translations, the same Spirit by whom it was written).[7] I prefer a more literal translation of the (slightly ambiguous) Latin: "Sacred Scripture is to be also read and interpreted in the same Spirit in which it is written (or less grammatically, 'by whom' it is written)."

Concerns Raised about This Discrepancy

For some time after Vatican II, a minority of Catholic exegetes called attention to this mandate. Ignace de la Potterie, Hans Urs von Balthasar, and Dennis Farkasfalvy were among the forerunners of the current resurgence of concern about interpreting Scripture by the Spirit by whom it was written.[8] More recently, among both Catholic exegetes and those of other Christian denominations, there has been a developing awareness of the biblical guild's deficiency in addressing Scripture as the word and revelation of God.

One of the first books to confront this deficiency was co-authored by Luke Timothy Johnson and me. It challenged the exclusiveness of contemporary claims of historical criticism as the only rational approach to Scripture, while acknowledging the good historical-critical work of current and previous generations of Catholic biblical scholars.[9] In response to common "either/or" dichotomizing approaches in historical criticism among various sources, levels, theologies, and biblical authors – and between Scripture and tradition – we called for a renewed appreciation of characteristically Catholic interpretive principles such as a "both/and" inclusiveness that consults both Scripture and Catholic tradition in determining the messages of the Bible.[10]

Other Recent Writings with Parallel Concerns

Already in 1993, the Pontifical Biblical Commission had briefly summarized and evaluated the many developing approaches to bibical interpretation beyond the classical methods of historical criticism. Although the Commission acknowledged many other approaches and was generally accepting of most of them, it nevertheless underscored historical-critical methods as indispensable for attaining the primary literal sense of Scripture. Not a few scholars were somewhat surprised to see so little PBC criticism of more radical approaches, such as some liberationist, feminist, and deconstructionist exegesis – which at least in their more radical forms appear quite alien to Catholic tradition and teachings.

In contrast to its general openness toward virtually all contemporary academic approaches to Scripture, though, the PBC exercised significant rhetorical force in condemning fundamentalist exegesis. This, at least, might hint at a possible preoccupation by the members with defending historical and other scholarly approaches from certain alien pietistic forms of fundamentalist interpretation. The document seems to show less urgency for restoring theological and spiritual interpretation of Scripture as God's inspired word and revelation.[11]

Some very recent ecumenical publications have shown increasing emphasis on recovering the values of pre-modern theological and spiritual interpretations. They have much to offer contemporary Catholic concern about interpreting in Scripture the message of its divine author. Two collections contain very helpful chapters: Stephen Fowl's *The Theological Interpretation of Scripture* includes especially useful essays by de Lubac on spiritual understanding, by Steinmetz on pre-critical exegesis, and by Yeago on recovering theological exegesis. The 2003 collection by Davis and Hays, *The Art of Reading Scripture*, summarizes and promulgates the work of Princeton's ecumenical and interdisciplinary Scripture Project. Especially relevant to Catholic concerns about reading Scripture more theologically is the synopsis of the Scripture Project's main findings: "Nine Theses on the Interpretation of Scripture, *The Scripture Project*."[12] I have found particularly helpful the essays by Steinmetz comparing Christian reading of both Testaments with the experience of re-reading a mystery novel, by Bauckham on reading Scripture as a coherent story, by Daley on usability of patristic exegesis, by Howell on how saints' lives help interpret Scripture, and by Hays on reading Scripture in light of the resurrection.[13]

Some of the recent movement among New Testament exegetes toward reading Scripture more spiritually is the result of greater interdisciplinary cooperation with specialists in patristics and hermeneutics. David Williams compares classic pre-modern and modern authors and argues for an expanded meaning for the literal sense of Scripture, one that accounts for the authorial intention of the divine author.[14] Increasingly, exegetes have begun turning to scholars like Henri de Lubac, Frances M. Young, and Paul Quay for insights on how patristic and medieval authors read Scripture theologically.[15] A 2005 work by John J. O'Keefe & R.R. Reno and an introduction by Christopher Seitz have captured the essentials of patristic exegetical approaches in very understandable form and in ways that can be replicated in the twenty-first century.[16]

Questions remain about how one can live in a scriptural universe in the twenty-first century. I continue to look to pre-modern exegesis in the hopes that it can reintroduce some approaches and principles that would be viable today. One productive patristic paradigm is the importance of combining both philosophical and purely rational approaches with living within a biblical world view.[17]

The objective of my 2004–5 sabbatical was to discover ways to ascertain and articulate the intentions of the divine author of Scripture and, consequently, the spiritual senses of what God was communicating in Scripture. To be useful in scholarship and teaching, findings about the divine author's intentions and communications cannot remain purely subjective and individual, such as some insights gained in prayer. These conclusions have to be able to be observed, taught, internalized, and furthered by other competent believing scholars.

Three Interpretive Principles in Dei Verbum

The Constitution on Divine Revelation does not fail to provide some methodological suggestions for how to interpret Scripture in or by the Holy Spirit. It recommends three approaches or principles or evidence for discovering the divine spirit in which or by whom it was written, which have been repeated and summarized by the *Catechism of the Catholic Church* (*CCC*). These three principles are: 1) the content and unity of all of Scripture; 2) the living tradition of the Church, and 3) the harmony that exists between the elements of the faith.

The first approach for getting beyond restrictive historical methods that pay no attention to divine intent of biblical passages is the admonition to scholars that "no less serious attention" be given "to the content and unity of the whole of Scripture if the meaning of the sacred texts is to be correctly worked out"(DV #12). This statement plainly implies that exclusively historical methods which focus only on their original meanings and settings do not provide sufficiently correct meaning of individual biblical texts. Their meaning is only correctly determined if the texts are studied in the context of the entire biblical story and message.

The unity of Scripture has been persistently attacked, denied, or disregarded in historical-critical training and practice, in which the Bible is regularly treated as a collection of books from different authors, times, and places, with differing, even disagreeing theologies and perspectives. Although it is true that on the human level the Bible is a collection, belief that Sacred Scripture is God's revealing Word and message to humanity postulates in addition a single divine author ultimately responsible for the entire canonical Bible. Ever since the New Testament, Christian faith has believed that the (Old Testament) "Writings" are God's revealed message of salvation, with a unity based on this message's single author, God, and on its unified saving character, despite all the differences that the Bible incorporates.

The unity of Scripture is a judgment based more on faith than on empirical observation. Indeed the unity of Scripture is one of the foundations of Catholic and Christian faith. Because of their faith, the patristic authors insisted that Old and New Testaments together reveal an overarching biblical narrative and worldview that differs significantly, though not entirely, from all other competing worldviews. This biblical worldview remains today as alien from most contemporary secular and scientific worldviews as it was from the worldviews of the ancient gnostics, other heretics, and non-religious populace of that day.

Patristic authors, who were pastors and/or teachers or catechists as well as scholars, read individual books and passages of Scripture in the context of the overarching story of the Bible. They almost universally agreed that Scripture's teachings and revelation are fundamentally grounded in a unifying and overarching story of God's saving providence. This story of God's providence proceeded from creation through the fall and divine attempts to rescue and reconcile God's people to himself.

God's saving works and Scripture itself, in Old and New Testaments combined, come to a climax in the Incarnation of the Word, the Second Person in the Trinity, and in his continued presence through his body, the Church, until the final judgment and fulfillment at the end of time, as promised in Revelation. For example, in his book, *On the Incarnation*, St. Athanasius mentioned the following as key points of divine intervention into the world: "creation, fall, inspiration, incarnation, eschaton."[18] In the two-testament Scripture, patristic authors like Irenaeus also discerned recapitulation of human history and salvation in Christ.[19]

This worldview, to which Luke Timothy Johnson refers in a somewhat post-modern fashion as "imagining the world as the Scripture imagines it," insists that there is only one God, who created both the universe and human beings – good but free. In our freedom, we humans from the very beginning have rejected God's gifts as limitations on our autonomy and have so found ourselves alienated from God and from one another. After the original sin and fall from grace, sin became rampant, as narrated in the Old Testament.

A prominent context for observing, experiencing, teaching, internalizing, and developing this biblical worldview is the liturgy. According to the liturgical dictum, "God did not abandon us to the power of death," God promised to rescue us and reconcile us to himself. God formed a people through Abraham which was to prepare for the Incarnation of the Son of God. By this God-man and unique mediator, we are being reconciled to God, and, at the end of time, he will come in glory for a final public judgment.

The unity of Scripture in the eyes of Christian faith is thus centered on the salvation of humans by the God-man Christ. Christian faith views the Old Testament as preparing for this salvation, and the New Testament as explaining it. Christian interpretation of Scripture – both Old and New Testaments – is therefore unapologetically Christological.

Already in the New Testament, authors like St. Paul saw persons and figures in the Old Testament as types of the antitype Christ. Thus Paul contrasts the first Adam to the second (and eschatological) Adam in Romans, Corinthians, and Philippians. The comparison between the first and last man and their respective effects on humanity is explicit in Romans 5:12–19.[20] In Corinthians, Paul contrasts the first Adam with Christ the last Adam by name.[21] Philippians implicitly contrasts the behaviors of the first Adam, who tried to be as God, and thus brought death to all humans, and Christ, who let go equality with God and emptied himself unto death so that humans could live.[22]

One reason for the contemporary unpopularity of the notion of the unity of the two-Testament Scripture is that such unity clearly implies that the meaning of Old Testament texts for Christians is only adequately clarified if these texts are somehow located within God's entire biblical plan for saving humans, and in its New Testament culmination in the incarnation, death, and resurrection of God's Son. In other words, the bishops at Vatican II at least implicitly maintained a similar perspective concerning the Christological unity of Scripture centered around the Incarnate Son of God, as was virtually universal among patristic and medieval authors. The contrast between faith in the unity of Scripture and the contemporary methodological rejection of biblical unity to emphasize biblical multiplicity and diversity in critical exegesis can be a source of significant discomfort for Christian exegetes. Another and related cause of discomfort is the contemporary desire to avoid exaggeration of some forms of patristic and medieval supersessionism and anti-Judaism, and more generally not to seem to devalue the intrinsic worth of the Hebrew Scriptures and Judaism.[23]

Equally alien to contemporary academic approaches to Scripture are the Council's next two principles for interpreting the Bible as God's Word. "The living tradition of the whole Church must be taken into account along with the harmony which exists between elements of the faith"(DV #12). Academic methods have been frequently adverse to acknowledging any clear-cut role of tradition in ascertaining the meaning of Scripture. In fact, critical methods initially were welcomed during the Enlightenment as rejections of traditional and doctrinal accretions to Scripture and as substitutions for them.[24]

Nevertheless, *Dei Verbum* from Vatican II insists that to understand

Scripture, Catholics must read it in the light of Catholic tradition. This tradition includes patristic and medieval Catholic interpretive traditions. It encompasses liturgical and ecclesial worship, living, preaching, catechesis, moral guidance, and government from the first to the twenty-first centuries.[25] Pre-modern exegesis showed a striking consensus about the need for reading Scripture in the light of church tradition, especially with the help of the Church's rule of faith.[26]

Even denominations that deny a prominent role to tradition in interpreting Scripture, including those that emphasize a *sola Scriptura* approach to biblical interpretation, nevertheless evidence a substantial influence from their respective ecclesial traditions of interpretation on how they interpret the Bible. For example, although Lutherans, Baptists, Presbyterians, and Pentecostals all profess *sola Scriptura* approaches to exegeting Scripture, their respective interpretations quite evidently differ from each other along traditional denominational lines.[27]

The council also expects Catholic interpreters to consult recent Catholic magisterial instructions for interpretation. It presumes that Catholic exegetes will be guided by the contemporary magisterium of pope and bishops regarding Scripture, doctrine, and morality. Reluctance by academics, not excluding academic exegetes, to acknowledge such a guiding influence from Catholic or other religious authority is certainly a well-known and a not very surprising phenomenon.

Finally, *Dei Verbum*'s exhortation to consider the harmony that exists between elements of the faith, although referring historically and primarily to objective relationships among the truths of the faith, might seem to some to introduce a further expectation that interpreters compare the matters treated in biblical texts with their own related personal or communal religious experience. This might appear to inject into exegesis and interpretation an unacademic element of "subjectivity." To do this could possibly also necessitate an uncomfortable self-revelation by the scholar regarding his or her personally held beliefs and religious experiences.

Yet for some of us, it was precisely a subjective nuance of harmony between elements of the faith as our personal experience, especially in charismatic settings, that "innoculated" us as graduate students from the reductionism of much of our training and biblical scholarship, which was routinely denying or downplaying acknowledgement of the miraculous, even of the bodily resurrection of Jesus. Personal experience of powerful communal worship of Jesus as alive, present and divine, as well as witnessing healings through prayer, provided us an antidote to reductionist exegetical theories. Personal experience of extraordinary events that were analogous to those mentioned in the Scriptures trumped theoretical denials by even learned professors that miracles can happen.

Assistance from Patristic Writers

Therefore, in our book, *The Future of Catholic Biblical Scholarship: A Constructive Conversation*, Luke Timothy Johnson and I tried not only to reaffirm the importance of historical criticism as Vatican II acknowledges it, but also to challenge any exclusive focus on historical and other forms of academic criticism. Our challenge was one way of heeding Vatican II's call for spiritual or theological exegesis and interpretation in addition to historical and critical interpretation. As helps to understanding spiritual interpretation, Luke Timothy Johnson recommended renewing our conversation with the early patristic authors. He exemplified this conversation with chapters that sought to learn from the Greek father, Origen, and from the Latin father, Augustine.

I have focused my sabbatical research on investigating from the patristic authors what spiritual interpretation means, and how we might interpret Scripture spiritually in the twenty-first century. A few basic insights gleaned from patristic writers indicate their fundamental similarity to the interpretive principles of *Dei Verbum* #12. This similarity should not be surprising, since the bishops of Vatican II were greatly influenced by the patristic exegetes, by patristic and medieval *ressourcement*, as well as by later Catholic biblical interpreters.[28]

Whereas *Dei Verbum* laid out in the abstract three ways to read Scripture according to the Spirit in which it was written or to the mind of the divine author, patristic interpreters illustrated these and other approaches in their actual practice of exegesis and interpretation of Scripture. My first question to the Fathers was therefore "what is spiritual or theological interpretation of Scripture? What does it mean, and how does one read Scripture not merely as an ancient document from a vastly different time and culture, but also as the Word of God in which God is addressing believing readers and communities today?

Most studies of patristic interpretation have emphasized the four senses of Scripture. The initial guide for my 2004–5 sabbatical research on the four senses of Scripture was Henri de Lubac. For my limited sabbatical temporal window, however, I found the four senses too complex for me to be able both to digest their foundational insights, and also to find ways in which the four senses might be adapted and utilized in our quite dissimilar postmodern and religiously pluralistic interpretive setting. In my reading I was relieved to discover a more elementary point of entrance into the patristic approach to Scripture.

To take any "road less traveled" in research or methodological approaches to Scripture, my decided preference is for the simplest possible approach. Despite recognition of four senses of Scripture by biblical exegetes, they are not in fact commonly utilized by them. In my judgment, this simpler approach promises to be more productive and appealing for New Testament exegetes. Somewhat to my surprise, my favorites among possible initial patristic guides to this simpler point of entry into patristic interpretation turned out to be Irenaeus of Lyons and Athanasius of Alexandria.

The patristic authors, who were pastors and/or teachers or catechists as well as scholars, read individual books and passages of Scripture in the context of the overarching story of the Bible. As previously noted, the Fathers almost universally agreed that the teachings and revelation of Scripture are fundamentally grounded in a unifying and overarching story of God's saving providence. This story of God's providence proceeded from creation through the fall and divine attempts to rescue and reconcile his people to himself. God's saving works and Scripture itself, in Old and New Testaments combined, come to a climax in the Incarnation of the Word, the Second Person in the Trinity, and in his continued presence through his body the Church, until the final judgment and fulfillment at the end of time.

This overarching biblical narrative provided the early Fathers the unifying key to all the disparate events, strands, and theologies in the many books of the Bible. Because this narrative is centered on God's salvation through his incarnate Son, the Fathers understood the books of both Old and New Testaments according to a basically Christological interpretation. This helps explain the importance and popularity of the notion of the Christological unity of Scripture.

Christopher Seitz demonstrates that this kind of overall biblical narrative approach developed by the patristic authors has a grounding in the New Testament itself. Using especially Lukan examples, he illustrates how the expression "according to the Scriptures" situates the identity and mission of Jesus in the context of God's saving plan and actions recounted in the Old Testament. The Gospels and Fathers from the 2nd and 3rd centuries portrayed Jesus by situating him in God's saving plan as revealed in their Scripture (= OT), combined with the apostolic witness to Jesus (before the completed "canonized" NT).[29] Seitz also relates the patristic use of the rule of faith to this use of the Old Testament narrative of God's saving plan. Because for Christians the Son and Father are one, both Old and New Testaments provide a unified witness to them via the Holy Spirit.[30]

J.D. Ernest reviews the way Athanasius in his exegesis utilizes the "scope of Scripture," a summary narrative of the Word from his pre-incarnate existence with the Father as Word and Son, through his incarnation and mission, to his present coexistence with Father as Lord.[31] This becomes both his criterion and result of correct interpretation of Scripture. It amounts to placing oneself within the biblical story (with the help of summaries of the plot such as the rule of faith, or *regula fidei*, and the creeds).[32]

Thomas F. Torrance provides a more comprehensive treatment of the scope of Scripture in Athanasius as part of his chapter on Athanasius's hermeneutics. "The interpreter therefore operates on two levels: (a) that of the Scriptures in which he keeps to *the scope of biblical usage*; and (b) that of the objective reality in which he keeps to *the scope of faith or doctrine*."[33] "Athanasius thus refuses to isolate the understanding of the Scriptures from the continuity of faith and life in the Church, for since the Christian way of life is itself the product of the *kerygma* which has been handed down it furnishes a guide to the correct understanding of the biblical message."[34]

As a shorthand guide to keep the reader from getting lost in the maze of diverging, sometimes apparently even misleading, strands within the many Old and New Testament books and authors, the fathers used a rule of faith, or a basic hypothesis or story line of Scripture. They gleaned this rule of faith from scriptural narratives, teachings, and evidence. But the rule in turn helped to keep readers' bearings focused on the core of the overall biblical story and message so as not to get lost in myriad biblical details, stories, and theologies.

St. Irenaeus emphasized this "rule of faith" as an indispensable key to reading Scripture, especially to counteract the dramatically alien Gnostic interpretations of Scripture. Irenaeus commented on how Gnostics took biblical details completely out of their biblical context and significance, and created their own eccentric unbiblical doctrines by using biblical vocabulary in unbiblical ways. He likened their interpretations to taking apart a beautiful mosaic image of a king into its constituent pieces, and then rearranging those pieces into a new mosaic image of a dog.[35] To counter such chaotic and arbitrary "proof-texting" of biblical elements in ways completely alien to their biblical contexts and meanings, the fathers emphasized that the Scriptures needed to be read according to their basic message, which they summed up in "the rule of faith" or *regula fidei*.

In *On the Incarnation*, St. Athanasius conveys the primary dogmatic insights of the Council of Nicaea and its Nicene Creed. Through the course of his writings he came to consider one word as the pivotal and most important key to interpreting all of the Bible, both Old and New Testaments. This word was not even in the Bible, but for Athanasius and for the bishops at Nicaea, it summarizes the heart of the revelation that God makes of himself in both testaments of Scripture.[36]

For Athanasius, the Greek philosophical technical term, *homoousios*, became the key that unlocks the core meaning of both Testaments. Although this term *homoousios* comes not from Scripture itself but from Greek philosophy, Athanasius and others were convinced that it extracts the essential synopsis of what the Bible reveals about God in its many different stories, as well as in the revealing hindsight into Old Testament texts provided by the life of Jesus, his resurrection from the dead, and by the worship and life of the Church.[37] The term *homoousios* emphasizes that the Son shares the essence of the Father, that they are one and the same essence or being. This expresses the foundational insight that Jesus is the Son of God, not a creature of God, "begotten not made." Jesus is of the same nature, being and essence as the Father who sent him into this world.

If Jesus, the Son of God, is of the same being and essence as the Father, then, contrary to the Arians, the Son cannot be a creature made by God. The Son must be uncreated and therefore divine as much as the Father is divine. It also follows that the Son could never have begun to come into existence. He must exist eternally. As eternally existing but not a second God, the Son must always be I AM, the name that the Father revealed about himself to Moses in Exodus 3, and that Jesus claimed for himself to the Jews in John 8.

If the Son eternally exists as the same being, nature, and essence as the Father, then the patristic interpreters concluded that the God who revealed himself in the Old Testament as the creator of the entire universe is and must always have been the Father of the eternal Son. This remains true, even though the co-existence of the Son with the Father would not be explicitly revealed until millenia after the creation itself. The Church's still later explicit insight and acknowledgement that the Holy Spirit was also *homoousios*, or of the same being, essence, and nature as the Father and the Son, implied that the Holy Spirit is also eternally present and active from "the beginning," from before Creation until and beyond the End of Time.

If the Church later correctly realized that the sole eternal God is actually triune, then it necessarily follows that this only true God, whose words and deeds are revealed and narrated throughout the Old Testament, must in fact be eternally a triune God, a Trinity of three persons, Father, Son and Holy Spirit. This triune nature would not be revealed until the New Testament. It would not be explicitly clarified and pronounced to be a binding dogma of Christian faith until even centuries later. For it took time before the Church was able to articulate the fundamental dogmatic implications of what the New Testament writings and early Christian experience and tradition had revealed about God the Father, Jesus the Son, and the Holy Spirit who was sent by them both to the Church.

Unquestionably, the early Israelites who first read accounts that later were canonized in the Bible did not know that God was a Trinity. For the earliest revelation of God took place in contradistinction to the Israelites' pagan environments, in which neighboring nations were prone to the polytheistic worship of many gods. Therefore the first truth that God had to reveal to humans is that there is only one God, not many gods as most humans then believed.

However, the early Christian readers of Scripture were not the original Israelites. When they read their Scriptures (now the Old Testament) they maintained their monotheistic belief that there is only one God. But they also believed that the God of the Old Testament was the Father of Jesus, and that not only the Father himself but Jesus also was God.

Already in the New Testament, when Christians read about God, and about what God did and said in the Old Testament, they began to realize, at least implicitly, that this one and only God, who revealed himself to Israel as I AM, was actually Father, Son and Holy Spirit. Paul's letters were already using quasi-trinitarian blessings (e.g., II Cor 13:14: "The grace of the Lord Jesus Christ and the love of God and the fellowship of the Holy Spirit be with you all."). Matthew's Gospel commanded Christians to baptize "in the name [singular, not plural] of the Father and of the Son and of the Holy Spirit" (Mt 28:19). Eventually Christians realized that the single name that is shared by Father, Son and Spirit was a singular divine name because it reflected the reality of only one God. The fact that three persons, Father, Son and Holy Spirit, were named in baptism as a single divine name eventually contributed to the Christian conclusion about the triune nature of the God of the Bible as three persons in one God, a Trinity. This also illustrates how "*lex orandi, lex credendi*," and how liturgy contributes to a disciplined objective approach to spiritual exegesis.

Most patristic writers were trained in Greco-Roman rhetoric. In their book, *Sanctified Vision: An Introduction to Early Christian Interpretation of the Bible*, John J. O'Keefe and R. R. Reno describe how

Irenaeus borrows from classical rhetoric three key terms, *hypothesis*, *economy*, and *recapitulation*. Rhetorical teaching and theory called "the gist of a literary work" its hypothesis.[38] It follows that the hypothesis of an argument is the basic outline of that argument, whereas the hypothesis of a narrative is the basic story line of that narrative. According to Irenaeus, the main problem with heretical interpretation of Scripture was that it ignored the primary "hypothesis" of the Bible. While focusing on details and symbols, it failed to show how "the beginning, middle, and end hang together."[39]

Thus for Irenaeus, the hypothesis of Scripture is that Jesus fulfills all things. Jesus came in accordance with God's economy, and recapitulated everything in himself.[40] For Irenaeus the economy is the "outline or table of contents of Scripture."[41] Later generations were to prefer the expression "salvation history" to the patristic word "economy." The recapitulation (in Greek, *anakephalaiosis*) is a work's final summing up, repetition, drawing to a conclusion. In rhetoric it refers to the summary at the end of a speech that drives home the point of its strongest arguments. For Irenaeus, Jesus is the Father's summary statement, the Word or Logos, the purpose for the biblical economy as incarnating the purpose of God's economy.[42]

Contrary to some misconceptions, patristic interpreters did not simply impose an extrinsic hypothesis or plot outline on Scripture to give it an artificial order it did not have.[43] That illegitimate process was precisely what Irenaeus accused the Gnostics of doing with Scripture. Rather, we have seen that the Fathers distilled the basic plot line from their Christian reading of the story of God's saving plan and providence communicated in the books of the Old and New Testaments and in the light of the Church's experience.

In their very close and perceptive reading of the text, at least the Greek Fathers had another advantage over us contemporary exegetes – the Greek of Scripture was very close to their native tongue. Thus they were more easily able than most twenty-first century interpreters to catch the nuances of biblical words, grammar, idioms, and linguistic contexts in their intensive reading of the texts of their Greek Old and New Testaments. This connatural linguistic advantage provided another control against an *a priori* eisegesis when they applied the hypothesis of Scripture to guide their close textual readings and to keep their interpretations within an interlocking biblical whole.[44]

The Analogy of a Mystery Novel.

David Steinmetz of Duke has a very helpful analogy and comparison between reading the Christian Bible (Old and New Testaments) and reading a mystery novel. His analogy can help contemporary readers appreciate the patristic writers' approach to both Old and New Testaments of Scripture. He draws an analogy to the plot of a detective mystery or "Who-done-it."[45] As readers progress through mystery story narratives, they are often distracted or confused by evidence that turns out to be either misleading or irrelevant. Finally, in the last chapter of the mystery narrative, the detective hero summarizes what really happened in the murder and reveals who the murderer was. The detective ignores all the false leads in order to trace out the relevant plot lines that point to the actual killer and circumstances.

Once one knows "what really happened," one cannot re-read the original mystery novel the same way a second time. The final summarizing second narrative of "what really happened" and "who really did it" has made clear which among the many plot lines and pieces of evidence and information were most relevant to solving the mystery. Some events will be known in retrospect to be the heart of the matter, others the proverbial "red herrings" of mystery novels.

Similarly, once the New Testament's second narrative explains what was really going on in God's plan and in the story of salvation in the Old Testament, Christian readers will no longer be able to re-read the Old Testament the way the original Hebrew readers read it. By hindsight, Christians can distinguish which threads of salvation history were less pertinent, and which were core components in God's saving plan. For example, New Testament hindsight makes clear that some plot lines were not, as widely expected, at the center of God's plan. Contrary to many expectations, God's design did not feature restored Davidic kings liberating God's people from oppressive empires like Rome by physical warfare. Instead, seemingly minor plots and themes, such as the "suffering servant" motifs in Isaiah or the "persecuted righteous man" in Wisdom, took on far greater importance than would have been noticed by earlier readers of the Old Testament books and proved to be at the heart of God's plan.[46]

Amidst the reciprocal action and reaction of sinfulness and heroic virtue in the many Old Testament books, amidst the true and false theologies and teachings propounded by saints or sinners, God's people or pagan neighbors, a central line of thought and action becomes discernible after the incarnation, death, resurrection, and vindication of the Son of God as Savior. He is revealed to be a Savior not through conquest, as expected, but through sacrificing himself and submitting to the most painful rejection, torture and death to which his human brothers and sisters could subject him.

Conclusion

As I have mentioned, what the fathers referred to as the "overarching story," which is related to the rule of faith, is similar to what, in our book, *The Future of Catholic Biblical Scholarship: A Constructive Conversation*, I call "the biblical worldview," and to what Johnson refers under the more post-modern expression of "imagining the world that the Scripture imagines." The way that the patristic authors typify about how to read and interpret the Bible, scripturally and theologically, as God's Word and not merely as an ancient human document, is to insert oneself as reader into the overarching story, into the basic storyline. However, this insertion is done not after the post-modern manner of the autonomous reader making of the text whatever he or she wills, but as one's personally fundamental and willed act of faith.

As a way of fulfilling the second mandate of *Dei Verbum*, therefore, as a believing reader I choose to approach the text with a hermeneutic of faith and trust. Because I believe that the biblical text is God's Word, I submit my own life and thoughts to the judgment of Scripture. This is in direct contrast to some exaggerated forms of post-modern hermeneutics of suspicion, by which one mistrusts, doubts, and judges the biblical text as a limited time- or culture-bound product of an obsolete perspective, which is somehow ethically unworthy of our more enlightened consciousness today.[47]

With adjustments appropriate for our changed twenty-first-century circumstances and insights, I believe that Catholic exegetes as well as historians and theologians can learn much from patristic writers about how to read the Bible as God's Word, according to the intent of the divine author and attuned to spiritual senses of Scripture interpreted within a unified overarching narrative of God's saving plan. Like the ancient Church Fathers, contemporary Catholic exegetes and theologians can find ways to insert themselves in an act of faith into the overarching narrative of Scripture.

Reverend William S. Kurz, S.J., received his Ph.D. in biblical studies in 1976 from Yale University. He has been teaching Scripture at Marquette University in Milwaukee since 1975, where he is currently a Professor of New Testament. He has published over 40 professional articles and a number of books: *The Acts of the Apostles; Following Jesus: A Biblical Narrative; Farewell Addresses in the New Testament; Reading Luke-Acts: Dynamics of Biblical Narrative*. In 2002, he co-authored with Luke Timothy Johnson *The Future of Biblical Scholarship: A Constructive Conversation*, about which the journal *Nova et Vetera* dedicated a special issue consisting of a symposium in which various notable biblical scholars contributed open-ended "responses" to the issues raised in the book, to which the two co-authors then replied. The latest book by Father Kurz, *What Does the Bible Say about the End Times? A Catholic View*, was published by St. Anthony/Servant in 2004.

ENDNOTES

1   For all these texts and other related ones, see *The Scripture Documents: An Anthology of Official Catholic Teachings*, ed. & trans. Dean P. Bechard; foreword by Joseph A. Fitzmyer (Collegeville, Minn.: Liturgical Press, 2002).

2   Emphasis added. The Latin reads, "interpres Sacrae Scripturae, ut perspiciat, quid Ipse nobiscum communicare voluerit, attente investigare debet, *quid hagiographi reapse significare intenderint* et *eorum verbis manifestare Deo placuerit.*"

3   Among classic commentaries on *Dei Verbum*, including this paragraph 12, see esp. *Commentary on the Documents of Vatican II, Volume III* (New York: Herder and Herder, 1969 [German original 1967]), "Dogmatic Constitution on Divine Revelation," with commentaries on different chapters by Joseph Ratzinger, Alois Grillmeier, and Béda Rigaux. Bernard-Dominique Dupuy, ed., *La Révélation Divine. Constitution dogmatique "Dei Verbum," texte latin, et traduction française* par J.-P. Torrell, *Commentaires* par B.-D. Dupuy, J. Feiner, H. de Lubac, Ch. Moeller, P. Grelot, L. Alonso-Schoekel, X. Léon-Dufour, A. Grillmeier, R. Schutz, M. Thurian, J. L. Leuba, E. Schlink, K. Barth, A. Scrima, A. Kniazeff; 2 Vols. (Unam Sanctam 70A/B; Paris: Cerf, 1968); René Latourelle, S.J., *Theology of Revelation: Including a Commentary on the Constitution "Dei Verbum" of Vatican II* (Staten Island, N.Y.: Alba House, 1966); and Latourelle's two articles, "La Révélation et sa transmission selon la Constitution "Dei Verbum," *Gregorianum* 47 (1966) 5–40; and "Le Christ Signe de la révélation selon la constitution, "Dei Verbum," *Gregorianum* 47 (1966) 685–709; Gerald O'Collins, *Retrieving Fundamental Theology. The Three Styles of Contemporary Theology* (New York: Paulist, 1993), 48–78 (notes pp. 159–64), 136–49 (notes pp. 170–3); G. G. Blum (RESUME GETFULL), *Offenbarung und Überlieferung. Die dogmatische Konstitution 'Dei Verbum' des II. Vaticanums im Lichte altkirchlicher und moderner Theologie* (Forschungen zur zystematischen und ökumenischen Theologie, 28 (Gottingen: GETFULL, 1971); M.A. Molina Palma, *La interpretación de la Escritura en el Espiritu. Estudio histórico y teológico de un principio hermeneútico de la Constitución 'Dei Verbum'* 12 (Burgos, GETFULL, 1987). Regarding the need for more emphasis on the divine author's intent, see esp. Peter S. Williamson, *Catholic Principles for Interpreting Scripture: A Study of the Pontifical Biblical Commission's* The Interpretation of the Bible in the Church (Subsidia Biblica; Rome: Editrice Pontificio Istituto Biblico, 2001).

4   *Dei Verbum* #13, citing St. John Chrysostom, "On Genesis," 3, 8 (Homily 17, 1); *PG* 03,134; "Attemperatio," in Greek "*synkatabasis*."

5   A similar comparison between the Incarnate divine-human Word or Son, and the divine-human natures of Scripture in the PBC's *Interpretation of the Bible in the Church*, was sharply criticized from a post-modern perspective by Lewis Ayres and Stephen E. Fowl, "(Mis)Reading the Face of God: *The Interpretation of the Bible in the Church*," *Theological Studies* 60 (1999) 513–528. Especially telling is their refutation of the PBC's use of *Dei Verbum*'s analogy between Scripture and the Incarnation to argue the necessity of historical critical methods to ascertain the literal sense of Scripture (pp. 521–3), and how the PBC's notion of literal sense differs significantly from that of the patristic authors and Aquinas (pp. 518–21).

6   *Dei Verbum* #12 adds the intriguing qualifying phrase "and actually expressed" to its mention of intention of the sacred writer. Perhaps this modification of the notion of authorial intent is meant to address post-modern uneasiness over the extent to which it is even possible to determine an author's intention, since generally the only evidence for authorial intention is what the author actually wrote. What one actually writes may or may not conform fully to what one intended to communicate. See the critical and bibliographic note 2 in Gerard O'Collins, *Retrieving Fundamental Theology*, 170–2.

7   The translation, "in the sacred spirit in which it was written," is from the Vatican web site (accessed June 13, 2005): http://www.vatican.va/archive/hist_councils/ii_vatican_council/documents/vat-ii_const_19651118_dei-verbum_en.html. The translation, "by the same Spirit by whom it was written" is from the 1966 translation supervised by Walter M. Abbott, S.J. The Latin is ambiguous and provides only limited support for either translation. It reads "Sed, cum Sacra Scriptura eodem Spiritu quo scripta est etiam legenda et interpretanda sit," *Dei Verbum* §12; cf. Benedictus XV, Litt. Encycl. *Spiritus Paraclitus*, 15 sept. 1920: EB 469; Hieronymus, *In Gal.* 5, 19–21: PL 26, 417. The translation by A. Flannery is rather loosely related to the Latin, and "weakens considerably the advice the Second Vatican Council drew from St. Jerome...about reading and interpreting the Sriptures with the same Spirit through which they were written" (O'Collins, *Retrieving Fundamental Theology*, 139). It reads: "But since sacred Scripture must be read and interpreted *with its divine authorship in mind*" (emphasis added); Austin Flannery, O.P., gen. ed., *Vatican Council II: The Conciliar and Post Conciliar Documents*, Vol. 1 (Northport, N.Y.: Costello Publishing Company, 1975), 758. The translation in the Tanner edition more accurately reads, "Further, holy scripture requires to be read and interpreted *in the light of the same Spirit through whom it was written*" (emphasis added); Norman P. Tanner, S.J., ed., *Decrees of the Ecumenical Councils. Volume Two: Trent to Vatican II* (Washington, D.C.: Georgetown University Press, 1990), 976. This is similar to the standard French translation in the Latin-French edition of *Dei Verbum* in *Les Conciles Oecuméniques*, Tome II-2, *Les Décrets Trente à Vatican II*, eds., G. Alberigo

et al (Paris: Cerf, 1994): "Mais puisque la sainte Écriture doit aussi être lue et interprétée *à la lumière due même Esprit que celui qui la fit rédiger.*" Cf. also the earlier translation reprinted in *Nouvelle Revue Théologique*: "Cependant, puisque la sainte Écriture doit être lue et interprétée *à la lumière du même Esprit qui la fit rédiger...*" (*NRT* 88 (1966): 170–188, p. 179).

8   For a convenient gathering of articles, see especially the special issue of Communio 13/4 (Winter 1986) 280–377, "On the Reading of Scripture," with articles by von Balthasar, de la Potterie, Farkasfalvy, Quinn, Kereszty, and Lectio divina by Roose: see especially Denis Farkasfalvy, "In search of a 'post-critical' method of biblical interpretation," 288–307; and Ignace de la Potterie, "Reading Holy Scripture 'in the Spirit': Is the patristic way of reading the Bible still possible today?" 308–325. See also the classic twenty-fifth year assessment of Vatican II, *Vatican II: Assessment and Perspectives: Twenty-Five Years After (1962–1987)*, Vol. I, ed. René Latourelle (New York: Paulist, 1988). Note esp. Ignace de la Potterie, S.J., "Interpretation of Holy Scripture in the Spirit in Which It Was Written (*Dei Verbum* #12)," 220–66. At 25 years, he complained that these recommendations of the Council have received scarcely any attention since the Council and have "not yet been truly 'received' into contemporary Catholic exegesis.'" (p. 220). Editor David L. Schindler dedicated a significant portion of the 2001 *Communio* volume to updating and bringing out contemporary applications of the theme of the "Word of God": *Communio: International Catholic Review* 28 (1 Spring) 3–111.

9   Luke Timothy Johnson and William S. Kurz, *The Future of Catholic Biblical Scholarship: A Constructive Conversation* (Grand Rapids, Mich.: W.B. Eerdmans Pub. Co., 2002). In 2005, the journal *Nova et Vetera* is dedicating a special forthcoming interdisciplinary and interdenominational symposium issue to responses to our book. Frank Matera of CUA in NT, Stephen Ryan, O.P., in OT, and Olivier-Thomas Venard, O.P., of the École Biblique, and Protestants David Yeago and Richard Hays wrote assessments, to which Johnson and I as authors responded.

10 Recovering pre-modern (in this case, patristic) exegesis is a major goal of the ecumenical series, "Ancient Christian Commentary on Scripture." Its first volumes began appearing in 1998: *Mark*, ed. Thomas C. Oden & Christopher A. Hall (Downers Grove, Ill.: InterVarsity Press, 1998) and *Romans*, ed. Gerald Bray (Downers Grove, Ill.: InterVarsity Press, 1998). At the time of this writing, about 17 of the projected 28 volumes of Old and New Testament have appeared.

11 Pontifical Biblical Commission, *The Interpretation of the Bible in the Church* (Boston: St. Paul Books & Media, 1993). Cf. Avery Dulles, "the Interpretation of the Bible in the Church: A Theological Appraisal," in W. Geerlings and Max Seckler, eds., *Kirche sein. Nachkonziliare Theologie im Dienst der Kirchenreform: Für Josef Pottmeyer* (Freiberg: Herder, 1994) 29–37; Terence J. Forestell, "The Interpretation of the Bible in the Church,"

Canadian Catholic Review 13 (1995) 11–21; Christoph Dohmen, "Was Gott sagen wollte: der 'sensus plenior' im Dokument der Päpstlichen Bibelkommission," *Bibel und Liturgie* 69 (1996) 251–54; James Leslie Houlden, ed., *The Interpretation of the Bible in the Church: A Document from the PBC* (London: SCM, 1995).

The priority of historical criticism is quite evident in the commentary by commission member Joseph Fitzmyer, S.J., *The Biblical Commission's document "The Interpretation of the Bible in the Church": Text and Commentary* (Roma: Editrice Pontificio Istituto Biblico, 1995). The document's predilection for historical methods and comparatively less enthusiastic emphasis on spiritual or theological interpretation is explicitly queried by Peter S. Williamson, *Catholic Principles for Interpreting Scripture: A Study of the Pontifical Biblical Commission's* The Interpretation of the Bible in the Church (Subsidia Biblica; Rome: Editrice Pontificio Istituto Biblico, 2001). Cf. also Peter Williamson, "Catholicism and the Bible: An Interview with Albert Vanhoye," *First Things* 74 (June/July 1997) 35–40.

12   The nine theses are as follows: 1. Scripture truthfully tells the story of God's action of creating, judging, and saving the world; 2. Scripture is rightly understood in light of the church's rule of faith as a coherent dramatic structure; 3. Faithful interpretation of Scripture requires an engagement with the entire narrative: the New Testament cannot be rightly understood apart from the Old, nor can the Old be rightly understood apart from the New; 4. Texts of Scripture do not have a single meaning limited to the intent of the original author. In accord with Jewish and Christian traditions, we affirm that Scripture has multiple complex senses given by God, the author of the whole drama; 5. The four canonical Gospels narrate the truth about Jesus; 6. Faithful interpretation of Scripture invites and presupposes participation in the community brought into being by God's redemptive action – the church; 7. The saints of the church provide guidance in how to interpret and perform Scripture; 8. Christians need to read the Bible in dialogue with diverse others outside the church; 9. We live in the tension between the "already" and the "not yet" of the kingdom of God; consequently, Scripture calls the church to ongoing discernment, to continually fresh rereadings of the text in the light of the Holy Spirit's ongoing work in the world. (Ellen F. Davis and Richard B. Hays, eds. *The Art of Reading Scripture* (Grand Rapids, Mich.: Eerdmans, 2003), "Nine Theses on the Interpretation of Scripture," 1–5).

13   Fowl, Stephen E., ed. *The Theological Interpretation of Scripture: Classic and Contemporary Readings* (Malden, Mass.: Blackwell Publishers Ltd, 1997). I especially recommend the following essays: Henri de Lubac, "Spiritual Understanding," 3–25; David C. Steinmetz, "The Superiority of Pre-Critical Exegesis," 26–38; David S. Yeago, "The New Testament and the Nicene Dogma: A Contribution to the Recovery of Theological Exegesis," 87–100. Davis and Hays, *Art of Reading Scripture.* See esp. "Nine Theses on the Interpretation of Scripture," 1–5; David C. Steinmetz,

"Uncovering a Second Narrative: Detective Fiction and the Construction of Historical Method," 54–65; Brian E. Daley, S.J., "Is Patristic Exegesis Still Usable? Some Reflections on Early Christian Interpretation of the Psalms," 69–88; Richard Bauckham, "Reading Scripture as a Coherent Story," 38–53; James C. Howell, "Christ Was like St. Francis," 89–108; Richard B. Hays, "Reading Scripture in Light of the Resurrection," 216–38.

14 David M. Williams, *Receiving the Bible in Faith: Historical and Theological Exegesis* (Washington, D.C.: Catholic University of America Press, 2004).

15 Henri de Lubac, *Scripture in the Tradition*, trans. Luke O'Neill (Milestones in Catholic Theology; New York: Crossroad, 2000), has excerpts from his classic four volume work on medieval exegesis and his seminal study of Origen. Frances M. Young, *Biblical Exegesis and the Formation of Christian Culture* (Peabody, Mass.: Hendrickson, 2002; orig. Cambridge Univ. Press, 1997) is quite helpful for exegetes, as are her other writings. Paul M. Quay, *The Mystery Hidden for Ages in God* (American University Studies; New York: P. Lang, 1995) draws theological inspiration especially from Irenaeus's theory of recapitulation in Christ.

16 John J. O'Keefe, and R. R. Reno, *Sanctified Vision: An Introduction to Early Christian Interpretation of the Bible* (Baltimore: Johns Hopkins University Press, 2005); Christopher R. Seitz, *Figured Out: Typology and Providence in Christian Scripture* (Louisville [Ky.]: Westminster John Knox Press, 2001). See also Christopher A. Hall, *Reading Scripture with the Church Fathers* (Downers Grove, Ill.: InterVarsity Press, 1998).

17 Especially helpful is the treatment of how rhetoric, philosophy, culture and the biblical vision mutually influence each other in patristic interpretation in Frances Young, *Biblical Exegesis and the Formation of Christian Culture*.

18 Cited from Telford Work, *Living and Active: Scripture in the Economy of Salvation* (Grand Rapids, Mich.: Eerdmans, 2002) 36. See *St. Athanasius on the Incarnation: The Treatise* De Incarnatione Verbi Dei (Crestwood, N.Y.: St. Vladimir's Orthodox Theological Seminary, reprinted 1982 [orig. 1944, rev. 1953]).

19 Cf. Paul M. Quay, *The Mystery Hidden for Ages in God* (American University Studies; New York: P. Lang, 1995).

20 "Therefore as sin came into the world through one man and death through sin, and so death spread to all men because all men sinned (Rom 5:12 RSV)...Then as one man's trespass led to condemnation for all men, so one man's act of righteousness leads to acquittal and life for all men. For as by one man's disobedience many were made sinners, so by one man's obedience many will be made righteous" (Rom 5:18–19).

21 "For as in Adam all die, so also in Christ shall all be made alive (I Cor 15:22 RSV)...Thus it is written, 'The first man Adam became a living being'; the last Adam became a life-giving spirit. But it is not the spiritual which is first but the physical, and then the spiritual. The first man was from the earth, a

man of dust; the second man is from heaven. As was the man of dust, so are those who are of the dust; and as is the man of heaven, so are those who are of heaven. Just as we have borne the image of the man of dust, we shall also bear the image of the man of heaven" (I Cor 15:45–49).

22   "Have this mind among yourselves, which is yours in Christ Jesus, who, though he was in the form of God, did not count equality with God a thing to be grasped, but emptied himself, taking the form of a servant, being born in the likeness of men. And being found in human form he humbled himself and became obedient unto death, even death on a cross. Therefore God has highly exalted him and bestowed on him the name which is above every name ..." (Phil 2:5–9 RSV). The comparison with Adam and presence or absence of preexistence in Philippians 2 have been debated in recent historical criticism of the hymn, but most early fathers presumed both the comparison of first and second Adam and also preexistence in their interpretation of Philippians 2 as part of the biblical canon. See William S. Kurz, "Kenotic Imitation of Paul and of Christ in Philippians 2 and 3," *Discipleship in the New Testament* (Fernando F. Segovia, ed. with introd.; Philadelphia: Fortress, 1985) 103–126.

23   See esp. Pontifical Biblical Commission, *The Jewish People and Their Sacred Scriptures in the Christian Bible* (Vatican Press/Libreria Editrice Vaticana, 2001), also accessed July 2005 at: http://www.vatican.va/ roman_curia/congregations/cfaith/pcb_documents/rc_con_cfaith_doc_200 20212_popolo-ebraico_en.html. For a balanced monograph on the issue, see Roy H. Schoeman, *"Salvation Is from the Jews" (John 4:22): The Role of Judaism in Salvation History from Abraham to the Second Coming* (San Francisco: Ignatius, 2003).

24   For historical context, see the brief overview of the Enlightenment critique of theology, scriptural interpretation, Christology, and religious beliefs in revelation and miracles in Alister E. McGrath, *Historical Theology: An Introduction to the History of Christian Thought* (Malden, Mass.: Blackwell Publishers, 1998), 219–225.

25   See *Dei Verbum* #8. This whole section is relevant, but note in particular: "The expression 'what has been handed down from the apostles' includes everything that helps the people of God to live a holy life and to grow in faith. In this way, the Church, in its teaching, life, and worship, perpetuates and hands on to every generation all that it is and all that it believes." (Tanner, *Decrees of the Ecumencial Councils*, Vol. 2, p. 974).

26   For example, see the account of how Irenaeus, Augustine, and Clement of Alexandria, exemplified the common patristic view of the role and relationship of the church's rule of faith in interpreting Scripture in *Sanctified Vision* by O'Keefe and Reno, pp. 119–28.

27   Cf. my claim in the Baptist Professors of Religion *Festschrift* for Charles Talbert: "The second criterion (within tradition) is more explicit in Catholic interpretation than in most denominations, but in fact all Christian churches have at least implicit traditions of interpretation and practice. Even

though Baptists, Lutherans, Pentecostals and others all emphasize *sola Scriptura*, they nevertheless self-evidently differ among themselves in their ecclesial and interpretative traditions and uses of the Bible" (William S. Kurz, S.J., "The Johannine Word as Revealing the Father: A Christian Credal Actualization," *Perspectives in Religious Studies* 28.1 (Spring 2001): 67–84, p. 82. Similarly, Richard Hays argues for the necessity also of extra-biblical sources of authority, *tradition, reason,* and *experience,* since even *sola Scriptura* Protestants cannot interpret Scripture in a vacuum (Richard B. Hays, *The Moral Vision of the New Testament: Community, Cross, New Creation; A Contemporary Introduction to New Testament Ethics* (New York, N.Y.: HarperCollins Publishers, HarperSanFrancisco, 1996), 208–10.

28   The insights from the patristic authors also are quite similar to many of the "nine theses" of the Princeton Scripture project cited above, probably because they influenced the formulation of those theses.

29   Christopher R. Seitz, *Figured Out: Typology and Providence in Christian Scripture* (Louisville [Ky.]: Westminster John Knox Press, 2001), 104.

30   *Ibid,* 6. Cf. Luke 16:31, "He said to him, – If they do not hear Moses and the prophets, neither will they be convinced if some one should rise from the dead.'" Cf. also Luke 24:27, "And beginning with Moses and all the prophets, he interpreted to them in all the scriptures the things concerning himself." Cf. also Luke 24:44–49, "Then he said to them, 'These are my words which I spoke to you, while I was still with you, that everything written about me in the law of Moses and the prophets and the psalms must be fulfilled.' Then he opened their minds to understand the scriptures, and said to them, 'Thus it is written, that the Christ should suffer and on the third day rise from the dead, and that repentance and forgiveness of sins should be preached in his name to all nations, beginning from Jerusalem. You are witnesses of these things. And behold, I send the promise of my Father upon you; but stay in the city, until you are clothed with power from on high'" (RSV).

31   J. D. Ernest, "Athanasius of Alexandria: The Scope of Scripture in Polemical and Pastoral Context," *Vigiliae Christianae* 47 (1993): 341–362, pp. 343–344.

32   Cf. Craig G. Bartholomew and Michael W. Goheen, *The Drama of Scripture: Finding Our Place in the Biblical Story* (Grand Rapids: Baker Academic, 2004).

33   Thomas F. Torrance, *Divine Meaning: Studies in Patristic Hermeneutics* (Edinburgh: T & T Clark, 1995), chap. 8, "The Hermeneutics of Athanasius": 229–88; part 1, "The scope of Divine Scripture,": 235–44, p. 237.

34   *Ibid.,* 244.

35   *Irenaeus Against Heresies,* Book I, Chap. VIII: How the Valentinians pervert the Scriptures to support their own pious opinions: "Their manner of acting is just as if one, when a beautiful image of a king has been construct-

ed by some skilful artist out of precious jewels, should then take this likeness of the man all to pieces, should rearrange the gems, and so fit them
together as to make them into the form of a dog or of a fox, and even that
but poorly executed; and should then maintain and declare that this was the
beautiful image of the king which the skilful artist constructed, pointing to
the jewels which had been admirably fitted together by the first artist to
form the image of the king, but have been with bad effect transferred by the
latter one to the shape of a dog, and by thus exhibiting the jewels, should
deceive the ignorant who had no conception what a king's form was like,
and persuade them that that miserable likeness of the fox was, in fact, the
beautiful image of the king. In like manner do these persons patch together old wives' fables, and then endeavour, by violently drawing away from
their proper connection, words, expressions, and parables whenever found,
to adapt the oracles of God to their baseless fictions." (*The Ante-Nicene
Fathers: Translations of the Fathers down to A.D. 325*, ed. Alexander
Roberts and James Donaldson, rev. A. Cleveland Coxe; Vol. 1, *The
Apostolic Fathers with Justin Martyr and Irenaeus* [American reprint of
Edinburgh ed.; Grand Rapids, Mich.: Eerdmans, 1969], 326.)

36   Many of Athanasius's fullest arguments against the Arians that Father and
Son shared the same essence or being, which focused on the meaning of
controverted biblical passages, can be found in St. Athanasius, *Ad Afros
Epistola Synodica*, in *Four Discourses against the Arians* (the fourth seems
pseudonymous, possibly also the third), and in his *De Synodis*. Concerning
his admission that his technical term is not in Scripture, see *De Sententia
Dionysii* (On the Opinion of Dionysius) #18: "For even if I argue that I have
not found this word (*homoou'sion*) nor read it anywhere in the Holy
Scriptures, yet my subsequent reasonings, which they have suppressed, do
not discord with its meaning," (in *Nicene and Post-Nicene Fathers*, Series
II, Vol. IV, ed. Henry Wace, 1891). Perhaps surprisingly, St. Athanasius, *On
the Incarnation of the Word*, focuses less on questions of essence and more
on the overarching biblical narrative of why and how the Son became incarnate. Thus it begins with this initial overview (from the same volume IV of
the Nicene Fathers edition): "1. Introductory – The subject of this treatise:
the humiliation and incarnation of the Word. Presupposes the doctrine of
Creation, and that by the Word. The Father has saved the world by Him
through Whom He first made it."

37   Cf. Torrance, *Divine Meaning*, 253: "The *homoousion* is thus a supreme
example of a strict theological statement arising out of the examination of
biblical statements, derived by following through the ostensive reference of
biblical images, and giving compressed expression, in exact and equivalent
language, not so much to the biblical words themselves but to the meaning
or reality they were designed to point out or convey. Once established it
served as a further guide to the Scriptures, although of course it continued
to be subordinate to the inspired teaching of the Apostles and to what the
Church learned from the Scriptures which mediated it." Cf. also T. F.

Torrance, *Theology in Reconstruction* (Grand Rapids: Eerdmans reprint of SCM Press Ltd, 1965), 35–40, esp. p. 40: "We must now return to the fact that the *homoousion* was gained through hard exegetical activity. It is not itself a biblical term, but it is by no means a speculative construction, an interpretation put upon the facts by the fathers of Nicaea; rather is it a truth that was forced upon the understanding of the Church as it allowed the biblical witness to imprint its own patterns upon its mind."

38   John J. O'Keefe and R. R. Reno, *Sanctified Vision: An Introduction to Early Christian Interpretation of the Bible* (Baltimore: Johns Hopkins University Press, 2005), 34.

39   *Ibid.*, 35.

40   *Ibid.*, 37.

41   *Ibid.*, 38.

42   *Ibid.*, 39.

43   Torrance, *Theology in Reconstruction*, 40.

44   *Ibid.*, 45.

45   David C. Steinmetz, "Uncovering a Second Narrative: Detective Fiction and the Construction of Historical Method," pp. 54–65 in Ellen F. Davis and Richard B. Hays (eds.), The *Art of Reading Scripture* (Grand Rapids/Cambridge: Eerdmans, 2003).

46   Nevertheless, there remains a value in trying to re-read the Old Testament through the eyes of the original readers. Even though Christians may know "the ending of the story," they can get a deeper appreciation of the richness of God's providential plan by attending to its intricate windings from its early stages with "fresh eyes." Therefore, at least in educational settings, there remains a place for a focus on "Hebrew Scriptures" for their own theological insights, without flattening out their distinctiveness from later Christian re-readings.

47   However, with common-sense moderation, some hermeneutic of suspicion is necessary and useful against abuses in applications of Scripture, just as secularism provided a needed historical antidote to the evils of the wars of religion.

Dei Verbum
The Literal and Theological Senses of Mark 1:1–3

Stephen F. Miletic

The beginning of the Gospel of Jesus Christ, the Son of God. As it is written in Isaiah the prophet, "Behold, I send my messenger before thy face, who shall prepare thy way; the voice of one crying in the wilderness: prepare the way of the Lord – "(Mk 1:1–3).

Introduction

It is an honor to respond to the presentation of the Reverend William S. Kurz, S.J. Father Kurz was my first teacher of exegesis and one of the readers for my doctoral dissertation at Marquette University now almost a quarter of a century ago. Over the years his offer of friendship has not ceased, for which I am grateful. His impact on my professional and personal life has been significant. Let me offer just one example.

One of my first doctoral courses at Marquette was an introduction to New Testament exegesis. On the academic side, the course was so well organized, and Father Kurz was so thoroughly well prepared, that I wanted to model my own future teaching on his evident depth of knowledge and level of preparation. He also integrated a living faith into the academic enterprise. Of the many elements of faith, one very small instance stands out in memory and engendered a positive effect on me. In that course he required us to learn by heart the Our Father in Greek so that we could recite it together with New Testaments closed before each class. Prior to that time my experience of memorizing New Testament texts was limited to vocabulary and grammatical constructions in order to past tests and read the New Testament. My experience of memorizing the Our Father in Greek in order to pray it impacted my development as a believer. It opened up to me a new dimension of *Lectio Divina* that assisted me in engaging the text on its own terms.

I still pray this text in Greek, every day in private and during the liturgy. His witness as kind teacher and a vigorous and courageous scholar is exceeded only by his witness as a genuine Christian gentleman, priest, and an authentic son of Ignatius of Loyola. Given these attributions, I shall courageously resist the temptation to blame-cast my former teacher for the many flaws which no doubt remain in this presentation. And finally, I hope that this presentation does not provoke Father Kurz either to remorse or regret for having attempted to teach me.

Without rehearsing all the details of his presentation, we might summarize Father Kurz's double thesis as follows: First, the Dogmatic Constitution on Divine Revelation, *Dei Verbum* (DV)[1] promulgates a double mandate for Catholic exegetes. They must ascertain both the human *and* the divine intent of Scripture. Second, following the lead of Athanasius of Alexandria and Irenaeus of Lyons, Father Kurz proposes that contemporary Catholic exegesis should interpret biblical texts in the light of the overarching, unified story or plot line found in Scripture (both the Old and New Testaments). In particular, he continues, the examples of these two great patristic figures would greatly assist contemporary exegetes in discovering and ascertaining the theological meanings found in Scripture.

If it is correct to describe Father Kurz's presentation as a reflection on current exegetical theory and method in the light of the teaching of *Dei Verbum* and patristic principles of interpretation, then this presentation should be taken as an attempt to concretely apply some of those principles to a specific text. Below I offer two kinds of reflections on the Gospel of Mark, one historical-literary, the other catechetical-critical. These two types of reflections will assist us in accomplishing a number of goals. First, I will demonstrate that responsible historical-literary exegesis can support and sustain authentic and responsible catechesis. Second, we shall see that these two approaches are ordered towards different goals and so represent distinct disciplinary approaches with their own first principles. The implication is that neither should domesticate nor capture the other but rather the one (exegesis) should support the other (catechesis). Third, the divine origins of Scripture (i.e., it is, first of all, the Word of God[2] in human language, not the reverse) requires significant methodological adjustments corresponding to identifying the referents of such language.

What this means is that, if Scripture is essentially "God speak" in the form of human language, then it first mediates that which is transcendent; its origins are ultimately in God not in the human mind. In effect, "human speak" mediates "God speak," it does not invent it. Such "speak," regardless of the human author's theological or religious sophistication, does not represent *only* the thoughts of the human author.

The ultimate referent of "God speak" is God, but God is mediated through human language and therefore human sociology and history. We might call this sense of Scripture the "spiritual sense" of the literal in that such language evidences genuine contact with a, or better, THE transcendent being, God.[3] And so, the integration of both the historical-literary and catechetical approaches is but one way of discerning the many possible literal senses of a text.[4] Given the above, it will be useful to point out briefly what distinguishes the historical-literary approach from that of the catechetical.

First, the historical-literary and catechetical approaches to Scripture represent two distinct hermeneutical systems, each with their own internal first principles. The goal of the historical-literary approach is to determine the intended meaning of the human author. If the human author intends a claim about spiritual or supernatural realities, the historical-literary approach would attempt to ascertain the nature of the claim (language) in order to better understand how that claim refers to the realities signaled. Generally speaking, this approach need not accept nor reject the realities signified.

Therefore, the first principle is that the interpreter must take into account the historical, cultural, sociological, political, and economic forces exerted upon the author's immediate setting in life. In addition, the "corpus" of material examined includes any kind of information from the period of the author which can shed light on a text under scrutiny. We might characterize this approach as *horizontally* focused even if it recognizes and understands the nature of a spiritual or theological reality.[5] This is a first, necessary step for Catholic exegesis.[6]

The catechetical approach takes a completely different line of view to the biblical text. This approach could be characterized as *vertically* focused – it is ordered towards the supernatural and so draws from the historical-literary approach, but only as it seeks to unfold the great mysteries of God and his plan of salvation. This approach is required because the catechetical approach understands Scripture as the Word of God mediated through human language. That is, the starting point for catechesis is the ontological nature of biblical language as divine language. Therefore, it must read the words of men in order to understand the thoughts of God. A second foundation principle concerns the understanding that catechesis is in its essence an ecclesial act. Catechesis is the Church's second great missionary act following its first great act – to proclaim the Gospel of salvation to the world. That is, the act of catechesis follows the Church's act of proclaiming the Good News.

Thus, catechesis is necessarily ordered towards a supernatural end, the *divine Author* and what He has revealed. That *divine Author's* "corpus of texts" is much broader than one gospel, the four-fold gospel, or even the entire New Testament! It includes all of Sacred Tradition as well as the prophetic voice known as the living, teaching office of the Church's Magisterium. Reconstructing meaning from this kind of "corpus" requires and assumes exegesis, but *only as one part of a larger interpretive project*. Such an interpretive project is an unfolding, a drawing out of that which is deeper from that which is obvious. Catechesis, then, first proclaims and then unfolds the deepest mysteries, and so must take a line of vision which is comprehensive and articulated in concise language, much like the early rules of faith, creeds, etc.

Finally, the catechetical line of vision towards God admits to asking two essential questions of the text, namely, what does this text tell us about God and God's will? Questions such as these lead the reader to the realization that the literal sense has referents beyond history but referents nonetheless manifested in and through it. With the above distinctions in mind, we may now begin our exegetical observations.

These exegetical reflections will establish that the literal senses of the text include historical and "spiritual" *referents* for Mark 1:1–3, while the catechetical reflections build on that foundation in order to determine the spiritual *meanings* contained within the literal and spiritual senses.

I have chosen Mark 1:1–3 because of its many interesting exegetical conundrums, and because it contains, so I would argue, deep theological and spiritual meanings. My overall argument is that the function of the three Old Testament texts cited at Mark 1:2–3 (Ex 23:20; Mal 3:1; Is 40:3) is as follows. First, the presence of the three texts directs the reader backwards in salvation history to God's redemptive acts on behalf of ancient Israel, establishing those three narrative contexts as the first referents for the narrative about to unfold. Then, when these three OT texts are modified so as to be applied to John the Baptist and to Jesus Christ, the Son of God, at Mark 1:2–3 they uncover or present the reader with aspects of the eternal life of God, their theological and spiritual meanings. In effect, Mark intends to begin his narrative[7] with ancient Israel's story of salvation history and so indicate that his story begins in the past as it resumes that older story. The specific changes of the references of the three texts as applied to John the Baptist and Jesus forces the reader to now understand what these texts mean for these two gospel figures. The questions provoked by directing the reader to the past and then modifying the texts to describe John and Jesus are the means of understanding what Mark is constructing. The questions for Mark 1:1–3 are: Who is speaking, who is listening, and where does this conversation take place?

As I shall argue, answers to these three questions direct the reader to "see" that while the conversations once took place in ancient Israel's history, and now do take place in Mark's Gospel, there is a new a new frame of reference for us to understand the eternal context for this conversation, namely, the eternal life of God the Father, Son, and Holy Spirit. Thus, there are two literal senses of Mark 1:2–3 (OT and imminent Trinity) as seen through the texts' theological and spiritual meanings at Mark 1:2–3.

Exegetical Observations

Mark 1:1–3

1.1 Ἀρχὴ τοῦ εὐαγγελίου Ἰησοῦ Χριστοῦ [υἱοῦ Θεοῦ].

1.1 [The] beginning of the Gospel of Jesus Christ, [the] Son of God.

1.2 Καθὼς γέγραπται ἐν τῷ Ἠσαΐᾳ τῷ προφήτῃ· ἰδοὺ ἀποστέλλω τὸν ἄγγελόν μου πρὸ προσώπου σου, ὅς κατασκευάσει τὴν ὁδόν σου·

1.2 Just as it is written in Isaiah the prophet, "Behold, I send my messenger before thy face, who shall prepare thy way;

1.3 φωνὴ βοῶντος ἐν τῇ ἐρήμῳ· ἑτοιμάσατε τὴν ὁδὸν κυρίου, εὐθείας ποιεῖτε τὰς τρίβους αὐτοῦ·

1.3 the voice of one crying in the wilderness: Prepare the way of the Lord, make his paths straight — "[8]

A number of scholars understand Mark 1:1–3 in terms of the ancient rhetorical category of prologue.[9] According to ancient Greek rhetorical practices, prologues function to introduce the major thematic *focii* of an ensuing narrative. This means that Mark 1:1–3 articulates the thematic keys unlocking the remainder of the narrative. As an aside, we might note that this prologue functions much like the prologue of John 1:1–18, which (i) also begins just outside of time (Jn 1:1; Gen 1:1: "In the beginning;" Ἐν ἀρχῃ),[10] and which (ii) presents the divine intent "from all of eternity," and (iii) also introduces the dominant themes of that narrative in synopsis form.[11]

Mark 1:2–3 is a distinct unit within the prologue because these two verses are bound together under their ascription to the prophet Isaiah at verse 2. To date, exegetes offer only a few points of consensus concerning the many problems presented by these verses.[12] First, Mark 1:2–3 is a compilation of Exodus 23:20, Malachi 3:1, and Isaiah 40:3.,and together the verses refer to and introduce the ministry of John the Baptist as God's messenger who prepares the way for the expected Messiah. Second, the immediate contexts of the OT texts cited in Mark 1:2–3 echo the rich biblical themes of the return of the figure Elijah in the last days, the anticipated Messiah, the wilderness journey, the forgiveness of sins, and the redemptive presence of God.[13] Third, taken together, these themes are the first proclamation about the identity and mission of Jesus Christ.

I would like to focus on one exegetical issue, namely, the Markan literal sense(s) of Mark 1:2–3. Our historical-literary question is: How do these verses introduce the ministry of John the Baptist and the identity and mission of Jesus Christ? To anticipate the answer, Mark uses three OT texts to create a theological context for understanding how John the Baptist and Jesus Christ represent a continuation and completion of ancient Israel's story of salvation. And, once we ask the question about the setting of verses 2–3, the theological and spiritual meanings of the text emerge.

The Literal Sense(s)

Mark 1:2–3 is ascribed to the prophet Isaiah at verse 2 ("just as it is written in the prophet Isaiah"; Καθὼς γέγραπται ἐν τῷ Ἡσαΐα τῷ προφήτῃ·). Between the ascription at verse 2 and the actual citation from Isaiah 40:3 (LXX) at verse 3 we find portions of Exodus 23:20 and Malachi 3:1 (at Mark 1:2). A comparison of the contexts of these three OT texts with their use in Mark indicates that their modifications completely change their direct referents and so change their meaning. Those modifications are the keys to understanding their literal and other senses. Below is a rough English translation of these texts drawn from the Septuagint (LXX) and the Greek text of Mark (GNT).[14]

Exodus 23:2015 & Mark 1:2

Mark 1:2	Exodus 23.20 (LXX)
Behold I am sending an angel before you, who will **_prepare_** your **_way_**.	**_Behold I am sending an angel before you_**, so that he may guard you in the way so that he might bring you to the land I have **_prepared_** for **_you_**.
ἰδοὺ ἀποστέλλω τὸν ἄγγελόν μου πρὸ προσώπου σου, ὅς κατασκευάσει τὴν **ὁδόν σου**·	ἰδοὺ ἐγὼ ἀποστέλλω τὸν ἄγγελόν μου πρὸ προσώπου σου ἵνα φυλάξῃ σε ἐν τῇ **ὁδῷ** ὅπως εἰσαγάγῃ σε εἰς τὴν γῆν ἥν ἡτοίμασά σοι

The text of Mark 1:2 thus closely follows the first portion of Exodus. 23:20 (LXX)[16] and slightly modifies the end. Both passages share the opening phrase "Behold I am sending an angel before you" (ἰδοὺ ἀποστέλλω τὸν ἄγγελόν μου πρὸ προσώπου σου), and share a variation of "your way" (Mk 1:2: ὁδόν σου; Ex. 23.20: τῇ ὁδῷ). Mark modifies the end of Exodus 23:20 by using the third person, future active indicative verb, "he will prepare" (κατασκευάσει) instead of the first person, aorist active indicative verb, "I have prepared" (Ex 23:20: ἡτοίμασα). This last change is significant for the reader who has followed Mark's reference to this OT narrative. The reader immediately sees that instead of God preparing the land for ancient Israel, God still sends a messenger who is given "God's job" to prepare "your way" (Mk 1:2). The immediate questions a reader might raise are: Is the "messenger" of Exodus the same as the one in Mark? To whom does the possessive pronoun "your" refer? A third question might even be: Why is the messenger of Mark assuming what was a divine task in Exodus? The text is silent. We need to read on.

Malachi 3:1 ff. represents the next piece of the theological mosaic. The text does not reveal the identity of either the messenger or the individual referred to by the masculine genitive singular "you." However, the modification of Malachi 3:1 provides some clues about the *new* theological meaning of the messenger and the individual referred to as "you."

Malachi 3.1[17] & Mark 1.2

Mark 1.2	Malachi 3.1 (LXX)
Behold I am sending an angel before you, who will *prepare* your *way.*	*Behold I am sending an angel* and he will *prepare* [lit. "will look out with care"] a *way before* me.
ἰδοὺ ἀποστέλλω τὸν ἄγγελόν μου πρὸ προσώπου σου. ὅς κατασκευάσει τὴν ὁδόν σου·	**ἰδοὺ ἐγὼ ἐξαποστέλλω τὸν ἄγγελόν μου καὶ ἐπιβλέψεται ὁδὸν πρὸ προσώπου** μου[18]

The literary overlap between Mark 1:2 and the first phrase of Malachi 3:1 ("behold I am sending an angel"; ἰδοὺ ἐγὼ εξαποστέλλω τὸν ἄγγελόν μου) indicates that Mark intends to allude to the second OT text. Mark modifies Malachi 3:1 by keeping the noun "way" (ὁδόν) and changing the phrase "before me" of Mal. 3:1 (πρὸ προσώπου μου) to "you" (μου) at Mark 1:2. The addition of Malachi 3:1 at Mark 1:2 does not modify the divine act of sending a messenger, but does assist us in identifying the nature of the individual referred to by the masculine possessive pronoun "your."

The new clue is found in a very small linguistic change which represents a significant referential shift. As noted above, Mark changes the phrase "before me" (πρὸ προσώπου μου) of Malachi 3:1 to "you" (σου) at Mk. 1.2. The referent for "me" in Malachi 3:1 is God but the referent for "you" in Mark is unspecified.[19] The reader must infer that it refers to someone who now (in Mark) will represent or is the divine presence. The reader may conclude that the reference is to Jesus Christ based on the following grounds. First, the second person singular pronoun "you" cannot refer to John the Baptist since, according to Mk.1:3, 4–8, his identity as the "messenger" crying out in the wilderness is quite clear. Second, given that Jesus Christ (a) is identified as "the Son of God" (Mk 1:1), (b) is the only other character thus far introduced in the narrative, and (c) is the chief protagonist of the narrative according to Mark 1:1, by the principle of subtraction, Jesus is the only suitable choice for understanding the referent for both "you" and "Lord" (Mk 1:3). Unlike Exodus 23:20, in which God sends a messenger before Israel, and unlike Malachi 3:1 ff., in which God sends a messenger for His own anticipated presence, Mark 1:2 shifts the focus away from God to Jesus, now associated with the divine presence, and at Mark 1:3 now identified as "Lord." That is, the new clue is that there is a shift from a singular "Theocentric" to a collaborative "Theocentric-Christocentric" focus. We shall call this shift Christocentric since, even though the Theocentric focus is not lost, the new accent or emphasis is on the Son of God. In short, Mark's development of the OT texts introduces an entirely new, unexpected figure, "the Son of God" (Mk 1:1).

Given the above, we may now probe the use of Isaiah 40.3 at Mark 1.3 and see what this text at adds to Mark's mosaic.

Isaiah 40:3[20] & Mark 1:3

Mark 1:3	Isaiah 40:3 (LXX)
[The] voice of one crying in the wilderness, "prepare the way of the Lord, make his paths straight—"	A *voice crying in the wilderness prepare the way of the Lord,* next *make* the *path* of our God.

φωνὴ βοῶντος ἐν τῇ ἐρήμῳ· ἐτοιμάσατε τὴν ὁδὸν κυρίου, εὐθείας ποιεῖτε τὰς τρίβους αὐτοῦ.

φωνὴ βοῶντος ἐν τῇ ἐρήμῳ ἐτοιμάσατε τὴν ὁδὸν κυρίου εὐθείας ποιεῖτε τὰς τρίβους του θεου ημων.

There can be no doubt about the presence of some version of the Greek text of Isaiah 40:3 at Mark 1:3.[21] Mark modifies the text of Isaiah

40:3 by replacing the final phrase "of our God" ($\tau o\hat{v}$ $\theta \varepsilon o\hat{v}$ $\dot{\eta}\mu\hat{\omega}\nu$) with the genitive masculine singular pronoun "his" ($a\dot{v}\tau o\hat{v}$). In Isaiah 40:3, the phrase "of our God" refers to YHWH, which Mark changes to "his," leading the reader to identify Jesus as "Lord" (Mk 1:3). In effect, the change to the singular possessive pronoun shifts the attention from God to a new character, Jesus. Now Jesus appears to be identified with God (implied claim of divinity), which also suggests a new expression of the divine presence. What God was about to do in ancient Israel according to Isaiah will now be resumed by a new messenger and by the divine Messiah, the Lord.

The Markan modifications of the original context of Isaiah 40:3 (within the broader context of chapters 40–48) now in Mark 1:3 suggest the following: When Mark uses the noun "Lord" he substitutes YHWH (the original referent of Isaiah 40:3) with Jesus Christ, suggesting that Jesus now stands in the stead of YWHW. Second, the literal sense of both texts continues to share the same Theocentric focus in relation to the messenger. God sends both the messenger of Isaiah 40:3 and John the Baptist. What God was about to begin with ancient Israel as Israel left Egypt and journeyed in the wilderness will now (in Mark) be resumed. In both contexts the messenger is associated with the forgiveness of sins and the divine presence (Ex 40–48; Mk 1:4, 8).

We must now address the role of the ascription to the "prophet Isaiah." What did Mark intend by ascribing Exodus 23:20, Malachi 3:1, and Isaiah 40:3 all under the rubric of the prophet Isaiah[22] at Mark 1:2? The first fact to note is that while there are many quotes, allusions and references to OT texts throughout the narrative, Mark 1:2 is the only place containing a reference to an OT book by name.[23] Whatever else Mark could intend by this ascription, it is reasonable to propose the following, namely, that Mark wants the reader to understand Exodus 23:20, Malachi 3.1, and Isaiah 40:3 in the light of Isaiah's :prophetic words. Mark may even have the broader context of Isaiah 40–48 in mind. If so, then Mark's prologue should be read in light of God's intent to forgive, the promise of redemption and deliverance from the Babylonian exile.[24]

Given the above, the literal senses and plot line of Mark 1:1–3[25] may be understood as follows. Mark 1:1 opens the narrative with a proclamation, namely, "Here begins[26] the Gospel of Jesus Christ, [the Son of God]."[27] Then, Mark opens with a "prophecy" from Isaiah which recalls and promises a messenger who from the desert will prepare the way of the Lord. The prophecy recalls three specific aspects of ancient Israel's story of salvation. The changes in referents signals that the new messenger will be preparing for God's presence which will bring the forgiveness of sins. One recognizes that the prophecy of Mark 1:3 is realized when the Baptist "happened" (verse 4: ἐγένετο) in the desert (Mk 1.4–8).

The referential changes of the OT texts applied in Mark 1:2–3 suggest several things. First, there is a continuation of the "OT story of salvation" with what is about to unfold in the Gospel – same story, but different agents. The new messenger maintains the OT texts' literal sense or referent – God sent and sends a messenger as a preparatory step. The addition to the OT story line is seen in the change from an exclusive Theocentric focus (God will be present) to a Theocentric-Christocentric view (God prepares the way for the Jesus Christ His Son, the Lord). Mark intends the reader to understand John the Baptist's ministry and the mission and identity of Jesus Christ in the light of these key OT themes: a new Exodus, a journey into the wilderness, the divine forgiveness of sins, and, finally, the imminent and redemptive presence of God.

Clearly, there is more than one literal sense for Mark 1:1–3. While the primary referents of the OT texts in Mark are John the Baptist and Jesus Christ, their theological spiritual senses are yet to be explored. The above exegetical reflections set the stage for a catechetical reading of Mark's first three verses.

Catechetical Reflections

Consistent with the Church's missionary identity, catechesis is the second phase of the Church's initial dominical mandate to proclaim Jesus Christ to all nations. Therefore, all catechesis begins with proclamation[28] followed by unfolding what was proclaimed – that is, catechists first announce and then unfold the deepest mysteries of the invisible Triune God![29] The final goal of all catechesis is to "gaze on the face of God," to be *more* deeply converted to Him, *more* deeply inserted into the mystery of the person of Christ.[30] The divine origins of these mysteries exist first in eternity and then in human language. Thus, the biblical text is the primary power of evangelization and catechesis.

Given that catechesis has a different goal than exegesis, it is important to distinguish it clearly from exegesis. As currently practiced, the historical-literary approach seeks to describe and explain carefully the human author's intent. To use an analogy, one makes very careful observations of the details and interconnections of an immense, powerful and life-giving tree. One determines its first principles of organization and overall purpose. One studies every aspect and learns how the parts fit together into a natural whole.

Catechesis also scrutinizes the great, life-giving tree, but seeks its powerful roots, invisible to the naked eye, but nevertheless present, giving life to the great tree. In this sense catechesis seeks knowledge and an encounter with the "invisible roots," the Living Person of God, the Word of God mediated through the human language of Scripture. The catechetical critical reading of Scripture is ordered towards the supernatural, the theological, the spiritual.

There is a special telescopic or hermeneutical lens which can greatly assist in discerning these supernatural, theological, and spiritual roots. A basic summary of this lens consists of is well stated in #236 of the *Catechism of the Catholic Church*. The text reads as follows.

> The Fathers of the Church distinguish between theology (*theologia*) and economy (*oikonomia*). "Theology" refers to the mystery of God's inmost life within the Blessed Trinity and "economy" to all the works by which God reveals himself and communicates his life. Through the *oikonomia* the *theologia* is revealed to us; but conversely, the *theologia* illuminates the whole *oikonomia*. God's works reveal who he is in himself; the mystery of his inmost being enlightens our understanding of all his works. So it is, analogously, among human persons. A person discloses himself in his actions, and the better we know a person, the better we understand his actions.[31]

This text is a masterful methodological summary of how the Greek and Latin patristic authors discovered the mosaic of the imminent Trinity within Scripture. As one follows each event within salvation history (*oikonomia*), one always finds new answers to the question, "Who is God?" The *oikonomia* is the locus of God's self-disclosure. As one reads Scripture in this way, following the three stages of the divine pedagogy of salvation history (OT, NT, the life of the Church), one builds up an ever deepening understanding of both the economic and imminent Trinity. One finally arrives at the meaning of the whole story with the narrative about Jesus Christ and then one rereads the texts with the newly revealed "end of the story" in mind.

This approach to Scripture is the backbone not only of catechesis but also of how post-NT doctrines and post-NT liturgical texts were developed. Patristic exegetes called this approach the *hypothesis, scopos* or plot-line of Scripture, that continuous story line of the great deeds of salvation that God initiated on our behalf, the great divine plan of salvation.[32] As Fr. Kurz has pointed out, this plot line[33] is analogous to what some patristic authors call *regula fidei* ("rule of faith").[34] In short, revelation occurs in history, in the *oikonomia,* and reveals something about

God's eternal life, the *theologia*. This special telescopic lens helps the believer's eye penetrate the great tree down to its hidden but very real roots.

A Catechetical Rereading of Mark 1:1–3

Let us now reread Mark 1:1–3 from within a catechetical approach, looking for what the text reveals about God and the divine will.

The gospel of Mark begins with a proclamation about Jesus as the Messiah and the Son of God. Then follows three texts from the OT bound together under the name of the prophet Isaiah. There will be a messenger sent to prepare the way of the Lord. This much is part of the core proclamation of the prologue (Mk 1:1–23). We must then move on to the unfolding of the mystery.

How does Mark 1:1–3 answer the questions, "Who is God and What does God want?" An excellent way to answer our questions is to pose three more basic questions directly to the text, questions equally appropriate for children as for adults, namely:Who is speaking? Who hears that speaking? Where does this speaking take place?

Who is speaking? On the surface level, our exegesis indicates that Mark is speaking, perhaps on behalf of Peter[35] and certainly for the authors of Exodus, Malachi, and Isaiah. We can see that there are many voices speaking in one message. And yet, we could also say that in an ultimate sense there is only one voice speaking, namely, God. How so?

Here we should recall that Mark opens his gospel with prophetic language.[36] Ancient rabbinic, then early Church, and then patristic authors all understood prophecy as divine speech, as God's Word, God's very own thoughts. Prophets were accepted as such precisely because they spoke not from their own understanding, but from what God wanted them to say. Such divine language could not be changed nor be modified because it originated from beyond heaven and earth, from God's eternal life in eternity.[37]

Therefore, the language of Mark 1:1–3, although drawn from four different narratives of salvation history (e.g., Exodus, Isaiah, Malachi, and Peter), actually originates in eternity. Like the prologue in the Gospel of John, these prophetic texts represent, so to speak, a great metaphysical telescope which brings the reader's line of vision beyond creation, reaching the invisible, eternal life of the imminent Trinity. In short, it is God who speaks at the beginning of Mark's gospel.

Who hears this divine speech? To whom is God speaking, and where? Who hears? Beginning with the *oikonomia*, we can state that Mark, Peter, and the authors of Exodus, Malachi, and Isaiah all spoke to the intended hearers. And yet, the text of Mark 1:2–3 does not have the original hearers in mind since it is applied to the Jesus Christ and John the Baptist. Approaching the same reality from the *theologia*, we may rephrase our question: Who originally hears the divine speech? If God speaks from eternity, is there someone listening "there?" Here I wish to posit that the eternal Father speaks his eternal words to the eternal Son.[38]

As noted above, Mark makes two significant modifications with respect to Malachi 3:1 and Isaiah 40:3. He changes the phrase "before me," which in Malachi 3:1 refers to YHWH, to the second person singular pronoun "you," and the phrase "of our God," which in Isaiah 40:3 refers to YHWH, to the third person singular pronoun "his." Recall that these changes in language represented a shift from a Theocentric to a Theocentric-Christocentric referent – that is, it is no longer God speaking to ancient Israel through prophetic utterances, but rather God the Father speaking to His Beloved Son "within" eternity.

The literal sense in Mark 1:1–3, then, contains a spiritual meaning in that prophetic language has been used to unveil or reveal what we may call a "divine colloquy" in which the eternal Father speaks to the Eternal and Beloved Son, promising to prepare his way. What is spoken in eternity (e.g., the *theologia*) is immediately realized within the *oikonomia* in verse 4, when John the Baptist "appeared" in the desert. The abrupt shift from eternity to history between verse 3 and verse 4 seems to suggest that what the Father promised to the Son was immediately realized, from the reader's point of view, with the appearance of John the Baptist.

To synthesize the answers to our questions: Mark begins his Gospel by unveiling God the Father speaking to His Beloved Son beyond the heavenly places in eternity. The Father promises to prepare the way for His Son, called beloved further on in the narrative. He begins his narrative with a vision of the *theologia*, the eternal life of God. Does God stop preparing the way for the Son after the handing over of John the Baptist. It seems not. It is God who sends the Spirit at Jesus' baptism (Mk 1.10), and it is the Spirit who leads Jesus into the time of testing the desert (Mk 1.12). It is God who prepares the way for the Son throughout the narrative, so that he might die on the Cross for the forgiveness of sins. God the Father is in charge of Jesus' earthly ministry. Perhaps the whole of Mark's narrative may be read as one continuous act of the Father preparing the way for His Son so that the Son might offer Himself back to the Father on the Cross.

Mark the evangelist proclaims: "Here begins the good news about Jesus Christ, the Son of God." Mark the catechist then begins his story by immediately pointing his readers to the *theologia*, beyond the heavenly places, to where God lives in eternity. He opens up to us that which existed before the creation of the world, opening up to all the new truth about God and His mighty plan of salvation – He will send a messenger who will prepare the way for the Beloved Son. This is Mark's catechesis of how the Father relates to the Son either eternally or imminently and economically. And, this is really Good News for us all!

Stephen F. Miletic has Ph.D. from Marquette University in Milwaukee. He is currently a Professor of Scripture and Catechetics in the Department of Theology of the Franciscan University of Steubenville in Ohio. He has taught both Scripture and catechetics at both the graduate and undergraduate levels in both the United States and Canada. He served as Director of the National Office of Religious Education for the Canadian Conference of Catholic Bishops. He was Provost and Academic Dean at the Notre Dame Institute in Northern Virginia (which later became the Notre Dame Graduate School of Christendom College). He served for five years as Dean of the Faculty at the Franciscan University of Steubenville. He lectures widely on both biblical and catechetical topics. His writings include various articles and a book, *One Flesh: Marriage and the New Creation* (Rome: Pontifical Biblical Institute Press, 1985). He is married to Joyce and they have four children and two grandchildren.

ENDNOTES

1   *Dei Verbum: Dogmatic Constitution on Divine Revelation of Vatican Council II*, trans. Commentary and translation by George H. Tavard (Glen Rock, N.J.: Paulist Press, 1966).

2   See, for example, *Ibid.*, §§1, 9, 10, 12, 14, 21, 22, 24, 26. The reformulation of this point at §102 makes it all the more emphatic, see *Catechism of the Catholic Church*, 2nd ed. (Vatican City/Washington, D.C.: Libreria Editrice Vaticana; [distributed by United States Catholic Conference], 2000).

3   Louis Bouyer offers useful distinctions about the interior, religious, and spiritual lives. The interior life is that capacity to imagine, to "see" what is real but not material (e.g., the imagination of an artist or a mathematician or a poet, etc.). The religious life is the person in search of God by means of the interior life (*homo religiosus* in search of the ultimate transcendent). The spiritual life is the interior life, religiously aware, but which experiences genuine contact with God as evidenced by a transformed life. See Louis Bouyer, *Introduction to Spirituality,* trans. Mary Perkins Ryan, Paperback ed. (Collegeville, MN: The Liturgical Press, 1961), esp., "The Spiritual Life according to Catholic Tradition," 1–4.

4   One need only think of comic narratives with double *entendres* in order to understand how the literal sense can intend two referents.

5   Here I would include any method of exegesis which focuses itself exclusively on the human author's intent without any consideration of the divine intent. The "referential fallacy" (unintended, excess meaning of the author found in the text) is a logical possibility which impacts on one's interpretation of any given text. This essay also admits the possibility that, in fact, there is some connection between what was written and what was intended.

6   *DV*, ##11–12, 13.

7   For the purposes of this presentation, the term "Mark" refers to that person responsible for the final, canonical shape of the entire Gospel. The noun "Gospel" refers to the final, canonical Greek narrative of Mark's narrative as we now have it.

8   This translation is a modified version of the Revised Standard Version.

9   William L. Lane, *The Gospel According to Mark; the English Text with Introduction, Exposition, and Notes, The New International Commentary on the New Testament*. (Grand Rapids: Eerdmans, 1993 [1974]), 29.

10   Whether or not John's text is a direct allusion to Genesis 1:1 or to texts which mediate John 1:1 is not relevant to the basic point that in some way there is an allusion to Genesis 1:1.

11   Space limitations do not permit us to pursue further comparisons.

12   E.g., Is the first verse ("The beginning of the Gospel of Jesus Christ, Son of God") a part of the superscript KATA MARKON, or an integral part of the narrative, or both? Does the term "Gospel" reflect both the oral, apostolic teaching, or the inauguration of a specifically Christian form of literary narrative under that name, or both? Is the title "Son of God" (υἱοῦ θεου) at Mark 1:1 original or a later scribal insertion? Does the different use of Isaiah 40:3 in the four Gospels suggest a pre-Gospel tradition common to all but modified by each author? The ascription to Isaiah could appear as incorrect given the presence of parts of Exodus 23:20 and Malachi 3:1? This type of surface confusion could have prompted scribes or copyists to correct what is likely the original reading by substituting "in the prophets" (τοις προωηταις) for "in Isaiah the prophet" (ἐν τῷ Ἡσαΐα τῷ προφήτῃ). See the critical apparatus for Mark 1:1–3 in Barbara Aland, Kurt Aland, and *et. al.*, *Novum Testamentum Graece*, 27 ed. (Stuttgart: Deutsche Bibelgesellschaft, 1993 [1981]). For an excellent and readable summary of some of these issues, see Virgil Howard and David B. Peabody, "Mark," in *The International Bible Commentary: A Catholic and Ecumenical Commentary for the Twenty-First Century*, ed. William Reuben Farmer, *et al.* (Collegeville, Minn: Liturgical Press, 1998), 1331–1335.

13   For example, see Morna Dorothy Hooker, *The Gospel According to Saint Mark* (Peabody, Mass.: Hendrickson, 1991), 34–35. Lane, *Mark*, 45.

14   The reading of the Hebrew texts (MT) are in the notes below.

15   ***Behold I am sending an angel before you***, to *guard you* on the ***way*** and to *bring you to the place I have* ***prepared***. בדרך ולהביאך אל־המקום אשר הכנתי
הנה אנכי שלח מלאך לפניך לשמרך

16   *Contra* Rev. Ezra P. Gould, *A Critical and Exegetical Commentary on the*

    Gospel According to St. Mark, Icc (Edinburgh: T & T Clark, 1983 [1896]), 4–5. He argues that all of Mark 1:2 is from Malachi 3:1.

17   **Behold I am sending an angel before me**, to **clear** the **way** before me. לִפְנֵי

         הִנְנִי שֹׁלֵחַ מַלְאָכִי וּפִנָּה־דָרֶךְ

18   Some argue that the text of Malachi 3:1 is not from the LXX but rather a post-LXX and pre-Gospel, Christian tradition based on the fact that the form quoted at Mark 1.2 is the same in Matthew 11:10 and Luke 7:27. If Mark was written first, then Matthew and Luke could easily have adopted Mark's modification of the LXX text. This problem cannot be addressed here. It is plausible to propose that there is a pre-Christian formulation shared by the synoptic Gospels if one not does not accept Markan priority.

19   We shall return to this in the catechetical reflections.

20   Notice the differences between the MT and LXX, at least in this English translation. "<u>A **voice cries**: In the **wilderness prepare** the **way for the LORD**, [YHWH] **make straight** in the **desert** </u>a highway for our <u>God</u>." קוֹל קוֹרֵא בַּמִּדְבָּר פַּנּוּ דֶּרֶךְ יְהוָה יַשְּׁרוּ בָּעֲרָבָה מְסִלָּה לֵאלֹהֵינוּ

21   Scholars do not agree as to whether Isaiah 40:3 is directly from the Septuagint, or some development of it, or another Greek translation.

22   The use of one biblical text to interpret another was a common practice in antiquity. For pre-Christian Jewish examples see 4QFlorilegium and 4QTestimonia in André Dupont-Sommer, *The Essene Writings from Qumran*, trans. G. Vermes, *Meridian Books; Mg44* (Cleveland: World Pub. Co, 1962), 310–317. For convenient references to other examples see also Lane, *Mark*, 46. For a dated but still valuable summary of the kinds of hermeneutical rules governing this type of interpretation by pre-Christian rabbis but preserved in post-Christian traditions collected in the Talmud, see Hermann L. Strack, *Introduction to the Talmud and Midrash* (New York: Atheneum, 1969 [1931]), 93–98.

23   There are many references to OT texts by means of reference to the writings or "what was written." For γραφή (reference to a written document, scripture) see Mark 12.10, 24; 14.49. For γράφω (reference to write, engrave, inscribe, record) see Mark 1.2; 7.6; 9.12–13; 10.4–5; 11.17; 12.19; 14.21, 27. None of the references, excepting Mark 1:2, identify an OT book by name.

24   A number of scholars propose a variation of this theory. A detailed argument along these lines can be found in Rikki E. Watts, *Isaiah's New Exodus and Mark*, vol. 88 (Series 2), *Wissenschaftliche Untersuchungen Zum Neuen Testament* (Tubingen: Mohr Siebeck, 1997).

25   Mark1:3 seems to end abruptly. There may be an explanation from the grammar of the text. An implied comparison between Mark 1:2 and 4 may be in mind. At verse 2 the subordinating conjunction Καθὼς ("just as") may be subordinated to the verb ἐγένετο at verse 4 ("it happened"). According to this understanding the text could be read as follows: "*just as* (Καθὼς) x, y and z was prophesied (Mark 1:2–3), [*so now*] *it happens that* or *it happened that* (ἐγένετο) John the Baptist ..." (verse 4).

26   The anarthrous Ἀρχη could permit us to translate 1:1. as "The Gospel
       about/of Jesus Christ, the Son of God begins here," with "here" meaning
       the whole of the narrative and not just the materials which immediately fol-
       low (e.g., Mark 1:1–13). A noun without the definite article usually refers
       to something general, to the whole of something rather than to this or that
       particular aspect of it. Within the context of the whole gospel, the noun
       would then refer to the whole narrative and not simply what follows imme-
       diately in 1:2–13. See Max Zerwick, and Joseph Smith, *Biblical Greek:
       Illustrated by Examples*, English ed. (Rome: 1963), §171.

27   Many scholars accept "Son of Man" as original to the text which is also
       reflected in numerous contemporary translations.

28   John Paul II, *Catechesi Tradendae:* Apostolic Exhortation of His Holiness,
       Pope John Paul II, to the Episcopate, the Clergy and the Faithful of the
       Entire Catholic Church on Catechesis in Our Time (Washington, D.C.:
       United States Catholic Conference, 1979), #18.

29   Granted the magisterial reiterations of this two-fold missionary act, it is
       nonetheless quite ancient. For example, Augustine advises Deogratias to
       first proclaim and then unfold the key points of the story of salvation found
       in Scripture, see Augustine, *The First Catechetical Instruction [De
       Catechizandis Rudibus]*, trans. The Rev. Joseph P. Christopher Ph.D., vol.
       No. 2, *Ancient Christian Writers* (New York: Newman Press, 1946), ##4–9.

30   To quote again the *Magna Carta* for catechesis since Vatican II: "The pri-
       mary and essential object of catechesis is, to use an expression dear to Saint
       Paul   and   also   to   contemporary   theology,   'the   mystery   of
       Christ'…Accordingly, the definitive aim of catechesis is to put people not
       only in touch but in communion, in intimacy, with Jesus Christ: only he can
       lead us to the love of the Father in the Spirit and make us share in the life
       of the Holy Trinity." See II, *Catechesi Tradendae*, #5.

31   Emphasis in original.

32   In this essay, "divine economy" is synonymous with "salvation history,"
       "economy of salvation," or just "economy." One finds these terms inter-
       changeable within the writings of the Greek and Latin fathers.

33   Father Kurz's contribution to this volume, "*Dei Verbum:* Sacred Scripture
       Since Vatican II," outlines this in much greater detail, see his section, "2.
       Assistance from Patristic Writers." He is following the work of Craig G.
       Bartholomew and Michael W. Goheen, *The Drama of Scripture: Finding
       Our Place in the Biblical Story* (Grand Rapids, MI: Baker Academic, 2004).

34   In addition to the comments and notes in Father Kurz's paper see also
       Frances M. Young, *Biblical Exegesis and the Formation of Christian
       Culture* (Peabody, Mass.: Hendrickson, 2002), 21–27 and "The Mind of
       Scripture," 29–45.

35   According to tradition, Mark was Peter's "translator" and wrote this gospel
       in Rome.

36   The book of Exodus is prophetic in that it is attributed to Moses, Israel's
       greatest prophet.

37   See Augustine's comments quoted in *CCC* #102: "You recall that one and
the same Word of God extends throughout Scripture, that it is one and the
same Utterance that resounds in the mouths of all the sacred writers, since
he who was in the beginning God with God has no need of separate sylla-
bles; for he is not subject to time" (St. Augustine, *En. in Ps.*103, 4,1: PL 37,
1378.
38   I am stating this by way of analogy. Even so, the link between the *oikonomia* and *theologia* is inseperable given the ontological simplicity of God's
existence.

BIBLIOGRAPHY

Aland, Barbara, Kurt Aland, and *et. al. Novum Testamentum Graece*. 27 ed.
Stuttgart: Deutsche Bibelgesellschaft, 1993 [1981].

Augustine. *The First Catechetical Instruction [De Catechizandis Rudibus]*.
Translated by The Rev. Joseph P. Christopher Ph.D. Vol. No. 2, Ancient
Christian Writers. New York: Newman Press, 1946.

Bartholomew, Craig G., and Michael W. Goheen. *The Drama of Scripture:
Finding Our Place in the Biblical Story*. Grand Rapids, MI: Baker
Academic, 2004.

Bouyer, Louis. *Introduction to Spirituality*. Translated by Mary Perkins Ryan.
Paperback ed. Collegeville, Minn: Liturgical Press, 1961.

Catechism of the Catholic Church. 2nd ed. Vatican City/Washington, D.C.:
Libreria Editrice Vaticana; [distributed by United States Catholic
Conference], 2000.

Dei Verbum: Dogmatic Constitution on Divine Revelation of Vatican Council
II. Translated by Commentary and translation by George H. Tavard. Glen
Rock, N.J.: Paulist Press, 1966.

Dupont-Sommer, André. *The Essene Writings from Qumran*. Translated by G.
Vermes, Meridian Books; Mg44. Cleveland: World Pub. Co, 1962.

Gould, Rev. Ezra P. *A Critical and Exegetical Commentary on the Gospel
According to St. Mark*, Icc. Edinburgh: T & T Clark, 1983 [1896].

Hooker, Morna Dorothy. *The Gospel According to Saint Mark*. Peabody, Mass.:
Hendrickson, 1991.

Howard, Virgil, and David B. Peabody. "Mark." In *The International Bible
Commentary: A Catholic and Ecumenical Commentary for the Twenty-
First Century*, edited by William Reuben Farmer, Sean E. McEvenue,
Armando J. Levoratti and David L. Dungan, 1331–1367. Collegeville,
Minn: Liturgical Press, 1998.

Pope John Paul II *Catechesi Tradendae:* Apostolic Exhortation of His
Holiness, Pope John Paul II, to the Episcopate, the Clergy and the Faithful
of the Entire Catholic Church on Catechesis in Our Time. Washington,
D.C.: United States Catholic Conference, 1979.

Lane, William L. *The Gospel According to Mark; the English Text with Introduction, Exposition, and Notes,* The New International Commentary on the New Testament. Grand Rapids: Eerdmans, 1993 [1974].

Strack, Hermann L. *Introduction to the Talmud and Midrash.* New York: Atheneum, 1969 [1931].

Watts, Rikki E. *Isaiah's New Exodus and Mark.* Vol. 88 (Series 2), Wissenschaftliche Untersuchungen Zum Neuen Testament. Tubingen: Mohr Siebeck, 1997.

Young, Frances M. *Biblical Exegesis and the Formation of Christian Culture.* Peabody, Mass.: Hendrickson, 2002.

Zerwick, Max, and Joseph Smith. *Biblical Greek: Illustrated by Examples.* English ed. Rome, 1963.

Dei Verbum
Inerrancy and the Council

Joseph C. Atkinson

The uniqueness of *Dei Verbum* lies in the fact that its life is coextensive with that of the second Vatican Council. The history of this document – and the numerous stages in its evolution – reflect the many tensions which existed within the council itself. As Cardinal Ratzinger noted: "The history of the draft of the Constitution on divine revelation has fused with the history of this Council into a kind of unity."[1] During the Council, there were great struggles over the thematic contents and the precise wording of this document on revelation; these struggles foreshadowed the larger theological conflicts that would emerge in the postconciliar era. The single most important issue following the Council was the question of who would determine the authentic interpretation of the Council. Who would provide the hermeneutic by which the various conciliar texts would be understood? The outcome of this struggle would determine the fate of the Church in the modern world to a large extent as well as the authenticity of its salvific message.

This interpretative process was critical to the understanding of *Dei Verbum* precisely because it is *the* document on divine revelation (its nature, its transmission, and its interpretation). Given that Scripture is foundational for all theology, the proper interpretation of *Dei Verbum* is absolutely essential. The crisis (which had been raging for over a century, and continues to do so) concerns the nature of the biblical text, itself. Is Scripture truly God's Word given to us in such a manner that it can be trusted and requires obedience, or is it so culturally conditioned that, while humanly inspiring, it must be adapted and *corrected* according to modern realities and constructs if any relevant truth is to emerge? This, of course, is fundamentally an epistemological question which concerns both the nature of the medium of truth and our capacity to grasp it. These questions were at the heart of the conciliar debate over the text and became the dominant forces which gave final shape to the definite text of *Dei Verbum*.[2]

Criteria for Interpretation

The question facing us now is how to discover the legitimate way to understand what DV is teaching. The authentic interpretation of this dogmatic constitution cannot be found in resorting to some supposed "spirit" of the Council. That merely ends up in a subjective morass of conflicting opinion in which virtually any interpretation of the *Dei Verbum* is possible. Instead, the *only* authentic approach has to be four-fold:

1) It must be rooted in the final definitive text of *Dei Verbum*.

2) It must be cognizant of the history of the text and the numerous stages in its evolution, particularly the contentious debates over the inclusion of specific concepts, words, and phrases.[3]

3) It must be grounded and controlled by the official determinations given by the Council's theological commission, which provided official explanations of disputed concepts and words used in the text, and which persuaded certain fathers to vote for the text.

4) It must not be separated from the organic, continuous teaching of the Church – as if novel and contradictory propositions were valued as parts of the deposit of faith – but must firmly take its place in authentic continuity with the truth that the Church has always proclaimed.

Thus, an authentic interpretation of the text must respect and incorporate textual definitiveness, historical consciousness, official hermeneutical determinations, and organicity with the *fidei depositum*. Only in this way can both the diachronic and synchronic dimensions of the conciliar text be held in proper balance.

Given both the record of the Vatican II debates and certain official determinations, it is possible to know with some precision what the mind of the Council was regarding the meaning of the text. Paying attention to the above criteria prevents certain perversions of the DV from taking root and directs us instead towards a rich understanding both of the authentic nature of the Biblical text itself and its central salvific role in the Body of Christ. As will be shown, the teaching of DV is at once root-

ed in, and affirming of the Tradition of the Church while also incorporating the in-depth perspectives which the modern context affords.
Concisely put, the *actual* history of *Dei Verbum*, the *actual* text, itself,
and its specific *Christocentric* emphasis provide the principles by which
the modern Biblical crisis can be properly addressed. In fact, DV shows
the way forward towards a proper resolution of the many difficulties
which have beset Biblical studies over the last century.

Hermeneutical Struggles

Unfortunately, definitive texts and even definitive interpretations do
not theological trends make. In the main, the "hermeneutical road signs"
afforded by *Dei Verbum* have not always been recognized and consequently the struggle over the nature of the Scriptures and their authentic
interpretation has not abated. This is clearly evidenced by (then)
Cardinal Ratzinger's Erasmus Lecture of 1988 in New York, 25 years
after the Council ended; it was published under the challenging title
"Biblical Interpretation in Crisis: The Ratzinger Conference on Bible
and Church." Tellingly, he began his now-famous lecture with
Solowjew's story of how the Antichrist earned a doctorate at Tübingen
and became "a famous exegete."[4] The separation between faith and interpretation could not be greater! In his lecture, Ratzinger offered an analysis of the then current exegetical situation and the philosophical principles which informed it.[5] At the heart of his lecture, the cardinal challenged some of the faulty philosophical presuppositions of critical
orthodoxy which had become iron-clad dogma in the modern exegetical
schools. His call ultimately was for a reasoned analysis of modern
methodological approaches regardless of how sacrosanct they had
become; it was necessary to sift out the good from the problematic:

> The time seems to have arrived for a new and thorough reflec-
> tion on exegetical method...What we *do* need is a critical look at
> the exegetical landscape we now have, so that we may return to the
> text and distinguish between those hypotheses which are helpful
> and those which are not.[6]

However, this type of "evaluation" cannot be carried out in a vacuum but must be guided by sound principles. Only such principles will
enable us to perceive the genuine nature of different proposed methodologies and to determine whether they in fact encounter and explain the
biblical text or end up distorting it. But from where do such principles
emanate? It is precisely here that we can turn to DV and find within it
sound principles by which authentic exegesis can be carried out.

History of a Document

Dei Verbum was promulgated as a dogmatic constitution in 1965, towards the end of Vatican II,[7] with the stated purpose of setting forth "authentic doctrine on divine revelation, and how it is handed on" (DV #1). As a dogmatic constitution, it is concerned with the Church's fundamental teachings and understanding of Scripture and revelation. In keeping with the nature of the Council, DV's aim was not to proclaim any *new* doctrines *per se* but rather to enunciate authentic Catholic teaching on the nature and interpretation of Scripture and revelation with a view to orienting it, taking account of the modern situation.[8] This desire to acknowledge modernity, however, did not entail a rejection of the past, as is sometimes intimated. To confirm the organic link with the past, the document *begins* by stating that it is "following in the footsteps of the Council of Trent and of the First Vatican Council" (DV #1). Negatively, this affirmation states that there is no break with the developing tradition of the Church. Positively, it links the conciliar constitution organically to that tradition. This hardly argues for a radical re-definition of the Church's understanding of Scripture. Within that framework, DV attempted to engage the problems associated with revelation and to articulate them in such a way as to make them accessible to the modern world. Given the modern state of biblical studies, this proved to be a complex and controversial task which explains why it took so long for the formal text to be finalized.

While there are numerous themes in the conciliar text which are of critical importance, none is as foundational or has such profound ramifications as its teaching on inspiration which is central to any discussion of the Scriptures. The conciliar treatment of this theme has had significant impact on modern Catholic approaches to Scripture – although this has at times been observed in its breach rather than in its observance.[9]

Just as DV became a reflection of the whole Council, it can also be understood to be prophetic vis-à-vis the future in many ways. First, the troubled textual evolution of the document prophetically foreshadowed the crisis and controversy in biblical exegesis that would emerge in the ensuing years. Secondly, as with biblical prophecy, the way forward out of the crisis would be contained within the text itself. Like ancient prophecy, DV, by its very thematic structure and its specific Christocentric emphasis points the way forward towards resolution in this troubled area of exegesis. Finally, DV concludes with what almost amounts to a prophetic announcement which we will explore at the end of this paper. But first let us turn to the task at hand.

The Understanding of Inspiration and Its Direct Effect

While avoiding a technical discussion, the earlier parts of DV present the fundamental nature of sacred Scripture. By way of preface, DV #6, teaches that the purpose of the revelation is to enable religious truth to be known "with no trace of error." This is followed by the affirmative declaration in DV #9 which states that "sacred Scripture is the Word of God," which is further specified by its causality: "Inasmuch as it is consigned to writing under the inspiration of the divine Spirit"(DV #9). This reaffirms the Church's constant teaching, which is derived directly from the Scriptures themselves. Any survey of magisterial teaching conclusively comes to this same conclusion.[10]

However, serious problems began to emerge in the Council when the topic of inspiration and its direct effects was raised. This was predictable given the turbulent climate of biblical studies in the decades prior to the Council. The struggle, in essence, was over to what degree the presuppositions of modernity and its categories of thought were to form the Church's approach to revelation. As Ratzinger comments, with the introduction of the first draft, which was traditional (in the narrow sense of the word), "the inevitable storm broke."[11] Some seeking greater ecumenical openness, while others seeking to challenge the church's tradition in this area, fought against the acceptance of this traditional sounding text. The atmosphere was so tense that seven days later, Paul VI removed the text from the Council and set up a Mixed Commission to reformulate it.[12] It became clear that the bishops as a whole were very divided as to what the Church should teach on this issue. It was evident that for some, the document on revelation was not merely to be an exercise in "updating." The contentious issues involved were the material completeness/sufficiency of Scripture, the role of modern exegetical endeavors, tradition, the inerrancy of Scripture and the historicity of the Gospels.[13] These often led to heated debates and even to a direct intervention by Pope Paul VI asking for clarification of the last three issues, including inerrancy.[14] A tense struggle ensued which was only resolved when the theological commission gave a definitive interpretation concerning inerrancy and *a change in the wording of the text was made to prevent inspiration from being limited.*

The Question of Inspiration

In Chapter 3 (DV ##11–13), the question of inspiration and interpretation was directly addressed; in fact the original title was "The Interpretation of Inerrancy."[15] On the one hand, there was the desire to present the Church's teaching in positive terms. Thus, a change was made from the term *inerrancy* (a negative concept) to the idea of the *truths of salvation* (a positive construct). On the other hand, there were those who wished to challenge the constant teaching of the Church (which can easily be traced from the Scriptures and the Fathers, all the way up to and including Pope Pius XII's *Divino Afflante Spiritu*), and to "admit" that Scripture, rather than being without error, actually speaks in a way that is *deficere a veritate*.[16] This, as is shown from the examples used by Cardinal König, is premised on a belief that the Scripture contains material errors. While Cardinal König attempted to have this position canonized during the Council (and while it has become the working presupposition of a number of modern exegetes of differing persuasions), this view was challenged and fought against by others in the Council who saw that this novelty stood in complete opposition to all magisterial teaching on the subject.[17] The position was ultimately not endorsed, as the history of the wording of the text and the required interventions of the Theological Commission show. The contention on König's part was that the Scriptures were in fact erroneous in certain parts but truthful in others. This position (illogically) maintains that such error does not affect the integral witness of the other parts of Scripture. To prove his point, Cardinal König rose during the debates and cited three standard exegetical problems:[18]

1. Mark 2:26 states that David went into the house of the Lord while Abiathar was the high priest and ate the ritual bread there but this appears to be in conflict with 1 Samuel 21:1ff which states it was during the high priesthood of Abimilech.

2. In Matthew 27:9–10, the prophecy concerning Judas' death is attributed to Jeremiah but it appears that the citation is from Zecheriah 11:12–13.

3. In Daniel 1:1, the chronology of the Babylonian king appears to be wrong.

All three of these issues could have been addressed by scholars using specific Semitic or biblical constructs. Solutions to these difficulties could have been constructed and preferred to the Council based on such things as a) the Jewish practice of citing persons who held office , b) an understanding of inter-textual referencing, i.e., a knowledge of how Scriptural authors make citations when two or more texts or prophets are involved; b) and through a comparison between Babylonian chronology which counts beginning dates differently from Roman calculations.[19] The problems become insoluble however when one reads the Biblical text, isolated from both the Semitic traditions and other scriptural texts, and without allowing for common biblical literary techniques or for the differences in cultural methodological approaches (such as in chronological reckoning). (This is similar to the faulty Protestant exegesis of the "brothers of Jesus," which only see this text through a modern Western perspective and thus interprets "brothers" through the lens of the nuclear family.)

But as the reader acquires a broader biblical mindset,[20] (rather than reading texts in isolation, or limiting oneself to *only* modern historical or linguist constructs), he views data from an increasing intra-Biblical worldview. Again, the logical basis and the historical reality of the text emerges which is not at variance with reality but indeed communicates it. This is not to say that there are not difficulties within the text. It is clear there are (particularly given the time spans) and have been noticed from the earliest periods in the Church. The Church never claimed that all the Scriptures were easy to understand. That they *can* be understood, and that they *are* reliable and without error, on the other hand, is a constant of Church teaching. What this calls for is an ever most assiduous study of ancient cultures, literary methodologies, types, and above all Semitic categories of thought.

From the debates over the text of DV, it became clear that there were some who were proposing, as official doctrine, a dichotomy between inspiration and the received biblical text which now, in their opinion, was an admixture of errors and truth. Their proposal was that only *truths of salvation* were inerrant; other truths, facts, or assertions were not so protected. It was clear that the stakes were high in this debate.[21]

There should be no doubt as to what the Church's mind on this issue is. The original draft of the document on revelation – which, it should be remembered, was only a presentation in traditional terms of what the Church had always believed – had spoken in the unambiguous language of previous dogmatic statements and described the Scriptures explicitly as being "without any error."[22] This was clearly not a novelty nor the invention of the tradition-minded preparatory committee. But in the redaction process, the Council thought it best to turn this into a positive construct, denoted by the phrase "truths of salvation." While this has the advantage of being positive, it has the serious disadvantage of being ambiguous. The phrase could be interpreted (especially if one wanted to distance oneself from the Tradition and previous magisterial statements on this issue) as establishing a dichotomy between different types of assertions within the Scriptures – some with, and some without, error.

The logical consequences of this would be that the Church would have to define *formally* what parts of Scripture (which were somehow all inspired by God) were actually truth-filled and to be relied upon, and what parts were erroneous yet still 'inspired' by God. If this process of distinction did not formally take place, then how could one know which texts to trust, which texts could be used to establish theological truths, etc. It is clear that the Church has never done this in her history.

When the new formulation was introduced, some within the Council immediately saw the implications of this position, and how it ultimately undermined the primary authorship of God for all of Scripture, since it is "impossible that God Himself, the supreme Truth, can utter that which is not true."[23] Strenuous objections were raised in unambiguous terms. In particular, Archbishop Paul Philippe refused to divorce the conciliar debates from the organic continuity of Church teaching or from the definitive conclusions that had already been promulgated by the Church in the past 100 years. As he stated:

If it says the holy books "teach the saving truth …without error, it would seem that inerrancy is restricted to matters of faith and morals, for that reason or even to a greater extent because as acknowledged by the Relator this formula was chosen in order that the demands of the (Council) Fathers be satisfied who were requesting that the effects of inspiration be expressed positively and that the object of inerrancy be clearly circumscribed. The Relator explained the mind of the Commission saying that in the word "saving" were understood the deeds which in Scripture are brought together with the history of salvation. And furthermore, with this explanation it is not possible to limit the object of inerrancy. I think therefore that this formulation cannot be harmonized with the constant doctrine of the magisterium of the Church. In fact, inerrancy is the effect of divine inspiration and extends itself to all the sacred books and all the parts of them without any distinction or discrimination (Benedictus XV, Spiritus Paraclitus, EB 455)… Therefore, the Holy Scripture cannot be said 'to teach' the saving truth without error because it then insinuates distinctions amongst the assertions of the Scriptures, as if they taught some truths which pertained to salvation without error, and then others do not have such content and hence are not under inerrancy in the same degree. But the Holy Scriptures are said to express the divine truth or the very Word of God truthfully to the highest degree. Finally, I request the phrase of the prior text "without any error" be restored as the documents of the Magisterium (indicated above) always express themselves, so that they (these words) thoroughly exclude every sort of error from Sacred Scripture.[24]

Of course, this debate cannot be isolated from the preceding century of conflict over the nature of Scripture which the Church engaged in with deliberation and decisiveness. Archbishop's Philippe's comments were an accurate portrayal of the positions which the Church had staked out in this debate and felt bound to defend magisterially in order to preserve the truth about Scripture and the revelation it contained. The twentieth century had seen ferocious attacks on the supernatural order of revelation and the divine nature of Scripture. In an authoritative response, Leo XIII issued *Providentissimus Deus* which clearly defined the nature and extent of inspiration and the logical reasoning on which this was based:

> It is absolutely wrong and forbidden, either to narrow inspiration to certain parts only of Holy Scripture, or to admit that the sacred writer has erred...For all the books which the Church receives as sacred and canonical, are written wholly and entirely, with all their parts, at the dictation of the Holy Ghost; and so far is it from being possible that any error can co-exist with inspiration, that inspiration not only is essentially incompatible with error, but excludes and rejects it as absolutely and necessarily as it is impossible that God Himself, the supreme Truth, can utter that which is not true(#20).[25]

Pius XII in *Divino Afflante Spiritu*, commenting on this passage, concludes by stating "this is the ancient and constant faith of the Church"(#3).

It was this doctrine which was being challenged once again at Vatican II. The concept of a "truth of salvation" cut at the heart of the doctrine of inerrancy. It was clear from the vote on September 22, 1965, that "the fathers feared this false interpretation" of this new phrase.[26] It was suggested that the term *salutaris* be deleted so that *truths* would not be restricted. Paul VI sent a letter to the president of the Theological Commission suggesting that they consider the advantage of dropping the phrase *veritas salutaris*.[27] It is clear from this exchange that the pope and the Council were very aware of the dangers of this understanding and how it could dissolve the unity between the inspiration and inerrancy of the texts. This was no figment of the imagination on the part of only a small party.

In the end, after much struggle, the term *veritas salutaris* was indeed dropped, and another phrase substituted for it. It now became "veritatem, quam Deus nostrae salutis causa litteris sacris consignari voluit"; "truth, which God wanted put into sacred writing for our salvation." Furthermore, to arrive at a precise understanding of this phrase, one must also take into account a further move which was taken to safeguard the proper interpretation of the phrase. The Theological Commission gave a definitive explanation of this term: "The expression *salutaris* should in no way imply that Scripture is not, in its totality, inspired and the Word of God."[28]

Finally, to further protect the traditional understanding of inspiration and inerrancy, and to ensure that no false limiting of inspiration was intended, *Providentissiums Deus* and *Divino Afflante Spiritu*, which give magisterial definitions of inerrancy, and which extend it to the whole of Scripture are referenced in this disputed portion of the text here.[29]

In summary, the very evolution of the text clearly showed that there were significant tensions and, indeed, diametrically opposed opinions, at the Council as to the meaning and extent of inspiration and inerrancy. The debates show that any sense of limiting inspiration or inerrancy was considered a grave error by a number of the Council Fathers and entailed a rejection of the Tradition.[30] The wording of the final text was changed precisely to alleviate this concern. Further, the Theological Commission gave a definitive interpretation which underlined precisely the plenary inspiration of Scripture. The final document clearly affirms the constant teaching of the Church in this area and *Dei Verbum* can only be seen as an organic growth of *Providentissiums* and *Divino Afflante* which are given as a hermeneutical lens through which to interpret DV. Far from being renounced, these earlier definitions were actually used to clarify and define the statements of the final text of DV.

However, the years following Vatican II saw an increasing questioning of this teaching in the academic world and also a concomitant questioning of many central truths of the faith. Some Catholic Biblical exegetes (perhaps unwittingly) ended up promoting a dichotomy between faith and Scripture. From their newly liberated academic perspective, Scripture did not affirm certain specific truths of the faith and indeed might militate against some, but because the Church teaches these truths, they are to be believed. This is a poor appeal to fideism, and is in fact self-contradictory. In essence, it can only be described as a problematic approach which neglects the intrinsic relationship between the truth of faith and the Word of God which is the "soul of theology."[31] It is impossible to appeal to the Church as if she could be in conflict with the Word of God because she teaches the indispensability of Scriptures for the understanding of theological truth.[32]

That there is still a crisis in biblical exegesis is not to be gainsaid. One of the great values of *Dei Verbum* is that it shows us how to resolve the modern exegetical crisis (alluded to by Ratzinger) not only through its clear theological definitions but also through its very thematic structure. Both the Council, itself, and DV had a decided Christological emphasis which acted as a hermeneutical control. Constantly throughout DV there are numerous references to Christ as the Word. Finally, in DV #13 there is a parallel made between the incarnation and the Scripture: "For the words of God have been made like human discourse, just as the word of the eternal Father was in every way made like men"(DV #13).

This relationship of the Scripture and the Incarnation is developed by John Paul II in his address to the pontifical Biblical Commission, where he states that: "It is true that putting God's words into writing, though the charism of scriptural inspiration, was the first step toward the incarnation of the Word of God."[33]

This Christological dimension of the Word must always be accounted for in any exegetical encounter with the Word. In fact, it becomes the clue to unravel the modern exegetical crisis. In the first centuries of the Church's life, she had to unravel the "exegetical" crisis of the *Word-Enfleshed*. What was the true nature of Jesus of Nazareth? Faithful to the written Word and guided by the Holy Spirit, the Church was able to articulate what she had always experienced: Jesus is truly God and truly man *yet without sin*. In the same way, the exegetical crisis over the nature of the *Word-Written* can also be resolved in a similar manner. This is eminently valid because the *enfleshed* Word and the *written* Word are intrinsically linked. Because the Word became flesh, then it can be posited that what one says of the *Word-Written*, can also be said of Christ. The Scriptures therefore are truly human and truly divine, yet without error.

Conclusion

Many shudder when they hear the phrase "properly understood" attached to a concept. Inevitably, one feels that one is about to enter Wonderland with Alice where the norm is: "I can make a word mean what ever I want." This principle seems to be rife in all pursuits of life. Given the difficulties of the text, the variety of approaches, and the acknowledged (and sometimes unacknowledged) presuppositions operative within the exegetical endeavor, it is not particularly surprising to find some evidence of such approaches in the exegetical field which we all must be careful to avoid. Ratzinger wisely showed that our approaches need to be properly evaluated and not merely accepted. It is this type of honest evaluation which will help us all to understand more deeply the Word of God.

There must be limits to which one can push the interpretation of a text, whether it be the Scriptures or the conciliar documents themselves. To go beyond these limits is no longer to be working with the text or to be bound by it, but rather it is to be controlled by one's own agenda, whatever that may be. There must also be, within reason, and indeed dictated by reason, a congruence between interpretation and the *markers* of objective reality, i.e., history, true literary forms, authoritative traditional understanding, and the coherence of the Scriptures as a whole. Otherwise we are caught in a Derridian world of de-constructionism, left with only a disintegrated text, rudderless, and wandering about in a sea of subjective surmisings. It is only as we seek the objectivity of truth that we are drawn up into reality which frees us from all false images and which allows us to enter into true communion with our fellow man, with our true selves, and finally with God. But to do that, we must first encounter Scripture as the Word of God, breathed by Him into His creation to communicate truth to us. This encounter with the living Word is ultimately the fruitful task of the faithful exegete.

As we encounter ever more deeply the reality of Christ in His Word, as we come to know the true nature of this written Word which has become incarnate amongst us, then the fulfillment of the "prophecy" given at the end of *Dei Verbum* hopefully may come to be realized: "Just as the life of the Church is strengthened through more frequent celebration of the Eucharistic mystery, similarly we may hope for a new stimulus for the life of the Spirit from a growing reverence for the word of God, which 'lasts forever'" (DV #26).

Like Benedict of old who brought the transforming Word to Europe, may the new Benedict help bring alive this Word of God to our generation.

Joseph Atkinson, Ph.D., is an Assistant Professor of Sacred Scripture at the John Paul II Institute for Studies on Marriage and the Family. His work includes foundational research in developing the biblical and theological bases of the "domestic Church" and his critical article "Family As Domestic Church: Developmental Trajectory, Legitimacy and Problems of Appropriation" appeared in Theology Studies (66/ 2005) His 13 part series of the Biblical Vision of the Family will soon be aired on EWTN. Others articles include "Nuptiality as a Paradigmatic Structure of Biblical Revelation," "Paternity in Crisis: Biblical and Philosophical Roots of Fatherhood." and, "Person as Substantive Relation and Reproductive Technologies: Biblical and Philosophical Foundations" (co-authorezsd).

ENDNOTES

1   Here Joseph Ratzinger is quoting Archbishop Florit's relation given on Sept 30, 1964. J Ratzinger, "Dogmatic Constitution on Divine Relation: Origin and Background" in *Commentary On the Documents of Vatican II*, Vol. III, ed. H. Vorgrimler (New York: Herder and Herder, 1969) 155. (Hereafter: Commentary.)

2   Hereafter DV.

3   See also Ratzinger, *Commentary*, 209: "In accordance with the legitimate method of the interpretation of conciliar documents in general, here also the whole discussion in the Council and the Theological Commission must be used as sources for a better understanding."

4   Joseph, Cardinal Ratzinger, *Biblical Interpretation in Crisis: The Ratzinger Conference on Bible and Church* (Grand Rapids, MI: Eerdmans Publishing Co., 1989) 1. (Hereafter, *Interpretation in Crisis*.)

5   The following two points which Ratzinger makes illustrate his incisive analysis: "First and foremost, one must challenge that basic notion dependent upon a simplistic transferal of science's evolutionary model to spiritual history" (p. 10). "The [historical critical] methodology itself seems to require such a radical approach...It must try to remove all the irrational residue and clarify everything. Faith itself is not a component of this method, nor is God a factor to be dealt with in historical events" (Ratzinger, *Interpretation in Crisis*, 2).

6   Ratzinger, *Interpretation in Crisis*, 21–22.

7   A dogmatic constitution is a *positive* presentation of the Church's teachings. This is in contrast with "canons that formally condemn contrary teaching" (*Modern Catholic Dictionary*, John A. Hardon, New York: Doubleday, 1966, 128).

8   It is interesting to note that the text for DV developed throughout the whole life of the Council. The first draft was presented in 1962. This was rejected and a Mixed Commission was set up to draw up another draft. This then went through several revisions and debate over precise meanings until it was finally passed towards the end of the Council in 1965.

9   One can never adequately address the nature of Scripture, its importance, or its interpretation apart from the question of inspiration. Given this, it is puzzling why the Pontifical Biblical Commission's document, *The Interpretation of the Bible in the Church*, states that it "does not aim to adopt a position on...the theology of inspiration" (p. 34). (Boston: Pauline Books & Media, 1993).

10   These are a few of the critical texts that apply:

     a) The grass is dry, the flower droops, but the word of our God stands forever. (Is 40:8).

     b) "All Scripture is God-breathed (*theopneustos*)" (II Timothy 3:16). The word *theopneustos* is often translated as "inspired"; however the Greek of the New Testament is much more graphic in its portrayal of the intimate and intrinsic relationship between God and the Scriptures. Literally, this word means "God-breathed" and it is this text, significantly referred to in the original Greek which underscores this relationship, and which is quoted in the text of DV #11.

c) "All the books both of the Old and of the New Testament-seeing that one God is the author of both…" (Council of Trent, 1546, #1).

d) "These books the Church holds to be sacred and canonical not because she subsequently approved them by her authority after they had been composed by unaided human skill, nor simply because they contain revelation without error, but because, being written under the inspiration of the Holy Spirit, they have God as their Author, and were as such committed to the Church" (First Vatican Council 1869–70, On Revelation).

e) "All the Fathers and Doctors agreed that the divine writings, as left by the hagiographers, are free from all error…for they were unanimous in laying it down, that those writings, in their entirety and in all their parts were equally from the afflatus of Almighty God, and that God, speaking by the sacred writers, could not set down anything but what was true" (Leo XIII, *Providentissimus Deus*, 1898, #21).

f) "But it is absolutely wrong and forbidden, either to narrow inspiration to certain parts only of Holy Scripture, or to admit that the sacred writer has erred…For all the books which the Church receives as sacred and canonical, are written wholly and entirely, with all their parts, at the dictation of the Holy Ghost; and so far is it from being possible that any error can co-exist with inspiration, that inspiration not only is essentially incompatible with error, but excludes and rejects it as absolutely and necessarily as it is impossible that God Himself, the supreme Truth, can utter that which is not true. *This is the ancient and unchanging faith of the Church*, solemnly defined in the Councils of Florence and of Trent, and finally confirmed and more expressly formulated by the Council of the Vatican "(Leo XIII, *Providentissimus Deus* i898, #20; empahsis added).

g) "When, subsequently, some Catholic writers, in spite of this solemn definition of Catholic doctrine, by which such divine authority is claimed for the "entire books with all their parts" as to secure freedom from any error whatsoever, ventured to restrict the truth of Sacred Scripture solely to matters of faith and morals, and to regard other matters, whether in the domain of physical science or history, as "*obiter dicta*" and – as they contended – in no wise connected with faith. Our Predecessor of immortal memory, Leo XIII, in the Encyclical Letter *Providentissimus Deus* …justly and rightly condemned these errors " (Pius XII, *Divino Afflante Spiritu* 1943, #1).

h.) In *Divino Afflante Spiritu,* Pius XII comments that *Providentissimus Deu*s "is considered the supreme guide in Biblical studies" (#2) and explicitly states that he is "ratifying and inculcating all that was wisely laid down by Our Predecessor" (#2).

11   Ratzinger, *Commentary*, 160.

12   Ratzinger, *Commentary*, 161.

13   Ratzinger, *Commentary*, 155–166.

14   Ratzinger, *Commentary*, 164.

15   This clearly shows that this was the accepted understanding of the nature of Scripture prior to the Council. The themes in the preparation documents were not theological novelties but basic presentations of the traditional faith.

16   See Alois Grillmeier, "The Divine Inspiration and the Interpretation of Sacred Scripture" in *Commentary On The Documents of Vatican II*, Vol. III, ed. H. Vorgrimler (New York: Herder and Herder, 1969) 206. (Hereafter, *Divine Inspiration*).

17   This position was developed in an attempt (amongst others) to give a place to the human element in Scripture which surely must be accounted for. But care must be taken in this regard (as Ratzinger has reminded us in general about our need to be properly critical in the current state of affairs) . It must be remember that as Christ is the Word made Flesh, then one can only properly interpret the nature of Scripture through the lens of the Incarnation. This is precisely what a number of the popes have done. While Grillmeier properly warned of a "'monophysite' doctrine of inerrancy" (Grillmeier, *Divine Inspiration*, 201) in which the human element is simply absorbed by the divine, an authentic approach sees the Scriptures as "fully human" and "fully divine" in which, just as Christ is truly human "yet without sin," so the Scriptures are truly human 'yet without error.' John Paul II, in his preface to the Pontifical Biblical Commission's 1993 report, stated that: "Just as the substantial Word of God became like men in every respect except sin, so too the words of God, expressed in human languages, became like human language in every respect except error" (p.16).

18   Acta *Synodalia Sacrosancti Oecumenici Vaticani II*, Vol 3, Pas III, p. 275–276.

19   These approaches allow for other influences to affect how a truth is presented. In order to determine what is actually being asserted in a text these constructs (cultural, grammatical, etc.) have to be taken into account. For example, the concept of first-born can have several meaning besides being the first of a number. In Judaism, it was a legal status which involved inheritance rights. Mary bringing forth her firstborn does not therefore unequivocally mean the first of a number of children ..

20   Jean de Fraine stated: "In order to understand the content of the concept under study, it will be necessary to divest oneself of the ordinary philosophical categories and create a new Semitic or biblical mentality" (de Fraine, *Adam and the Family of Man*, trans. D. Raible, New York: Alba House, 1965, 11).

21   *Providentissimus Deus* dealt with this issue directly: "It follows that those who maintain that an error is possible in any genuine passage of the sacred writings, either pervert the Catholic notion of inspiration, or make God the author of such error. And so emphatically were all the Fathers and Doctors

agreed that the divine writings, as left by the hagiographers, are free from all error, that they labored earnestly, with no less skill than reverence, to reconcile with each other those numerous passages which seem at variance – the very passages which in great measure have been taken up by the "higher criticism;" for they were unanimous in laying it down, that those writings, in their entirety and in all their parts were equally from the afflatus of Almighty God, and that God, speaking by the sacred writers, could not set down anything but what was true" (*Providentissiumus Deu,* #21) See also Most, *Free From All Error,* chapter 7.

22 Grillmeier, *Divine Inspiration,* 199–200: "The text…presented to the Council Fathers in the first session was…Chapter II, "De Scripturae Inspiratione, Inerrantia et Compositione litteraria"…Thus the 'absolute inerrancy' of Scripture is stated here in very strong terms."

23 *Providentissium Deus* :20.

24 *Acta Synodalia,* IV pars II, p. 979–980. "Si dicatur libros sacros "veritatem salutarem …sine errore docere" , videtur inerrantia restringi ad res fidei et morum, eo vel magis quod, fatente Relatore…haec formula electa est ut postulatis satisfieret Patrum qui petebant ut effectus inspirationis positive exprimereture atque obiectum inerrantiae clare circumscriberetur. Relator Commissionis mentem explicat dicendo quod verbo "salutarem" cointelliguntur facta quae in Scriptura cum historia salutis iunguntur. At, etiam cum illa explicatione, talis circumscripto obeicti inerrantiae admitti non potest. Censeo enim haec dicta cum firma doctrine magisterii Ecclesiae componi non posse. Inerrantia enim effectus est divinae inspirationis, quae quidem ad omnes libros sacros onmnesque eorum partes, "sine ullo delectu ac discrimine" sese extendit. (Benedictus XV, *Spiritus Paraclitus,* EB 455)… Igitur, non est dicendum Libros sacros veritatem salutarem sine errore "docere", quia tunc discrimen insinuatur inter ipsas Scriptureae assertiones, quasi aliae vertitates ad salutem pertinentes sine errore docerent, dum aliae tale contentum non haberent ac proinde inerrantiae non subessent. Sed dicatur Libros sacros *exprimere veritatem divinam,* seu ipsum verbum Dei summe veracis. Denique, peto ut reassumatur verbum "sine ullo errore" prioris textus, cum documenta Magisterii supra indicata semper ita se exprimant, ut omnimodum errorem a Scripturis sacris penitus excludant."

25 Note also the important formulation in #24. "For the Sacred Scriptures contain the word of God and since they are inspired really are the word of God." This formulation prevents any dichotomy from occurring. There are not two realities: Scripture and then a subsection of that which only is the Word of God. Scripture itself really is the Word of God.

26 Grillmeier, *Divine Inspiration,* 211. Grillmeier goes on to assess the situation and states the matter clearly: "In its reply…the Theological Commission had to go into the main difficulty: 'the truth of salvation' (*veritas salutaris*) restricts inerrancy to statements on faith and morals (*res fides et morum*) and is thus contrary to the documents of the teaching office."

27 Grillmeier, *Divine Inspiration*, 213.

28 Grillmeier, *Divine Inspiration*, 213.

29 Leo XIII, encyclical *"Providentissimus Deus,"* Nov. 18, 1893: Denzinger 1952 (3293); EB 125. cf. St. Augustine, "Gen. ad Litt." 2, 9, 20:PL 34, 270–271; Epistle 82, 3: PL 33, 277: CSEL 34, 2, p. 354. St. Thomas, "On Truth," Q. 12, A. 2, C.Council of Trent, session IV, Scriptural Canons: Denzinger 783 (1501). Leo XIII, encyclical *"Providentissimus Deus:"* EB 121, 124, 126–127. Pius XII, encyclical *"Divino Afflante Spiritu:"* EB 539.

30 See Augustin Cardinal Bea's article which details the evolution of this section of DV. "Vatican II and the Truth of Sacred Scripture" in *Letter and Spirit*, 1 (2005) 173–178.

31 DV:24

32 See *Providentissiums Deus* par.17: "The divine and infallible magisterium of the Church rests also on the authority of Holy Scripture."

33 The Interpretation of the Bible in the Church, p. 16.

Dignitatis Humanae and Religious Freedom in American Foreign Policy
A Practitioner's Perspective

Thomas F. Farr

It is generally acknowledged that the great Vatican II Declaration on Religious Liberty, *Dignitatis Humanae* (DH), was influenced by the American experience. Filtered through the work of the Jesuit theologian John Courtney Murray, the American understanding of religious liberty and its place in the nation's democratic experiment helped to inform the Council Fathers in developing the Church's doctrine of human freedom and its view of the proper role of government in addressing the religious dimension of individual and social life.[1]

It is, to say the least, ironic that the Founders' concept of religious freedom which influenced Father Murray's work, and through him *Dignitatis Humanae* has largely been abandoned by the American political class. What now pervades U.S. academic, judicial, and policy discourse is a thin and fragile view of religious liberty as mere personal preference, a privatized right with little legitimate connection to democratic public policy. The consequences of this understanding for our nation's moral and political well-being have been the subject of extensive commentary, including by members of this Fellowship.[2] What is perhaps less well known is that contemporary liberal notions of religious liberty have had a parallel and, I would argue, a crippling effect on American foreign policy.

In 1998 Congress passed the International Religious Freedom Act, which mandated that the United States advocate religious liberty worldwide. To guide that effort, the law established a State Department office in which I was privileged to serve for several years. As part of my job I negotiated issues of religious freedom with governments such as China and Vietnam, Egypt, Jordan, and Saudi Arabia. I also met with victims of religious persecution from all over the world.

That experience, combined with events since my departure from the

State Department, have led me to conclude that the U.S. experiment in promoting religious freedom is on the one hand quite important, but on the other hand needlessly and tragically faltering – needlessly because of the nation's own traditional understanding of the connection between religious liberty and democracy, and tragically because of the implications of failure, both for American national security and for world peace.

I propose to explore this issue from a Catholic perspective. Let me begin by posing three questions: First, can the United States, a nation whose concept of religious liberty has influenced the Roman Catholic Church in the development of its own doctrine of human freedom, regain the capacity to influence other nations to value religious liberty, both as an aspect of human rights and as a means of promoting justice, stability and peace within and among nations?

Second, can the deficiencies of U.S. international religious freedom policy usefully be addressed by a kind of reverse pollination from DH? Does DH provide principles that might improve our ability to promote religious freedom worldwide? Third, can DH assist both U.S. diplomacy and a major object of its attentions, Islam, in understanding how a truth-proclaiming religion, i.e., one which believes itself to have at stake the care of men's souls and their eternal salvation, might articulate and defend human freedom, particularly amid the reality of religious and moral pluralism?

Each of these questions can be answered in the affirmative, and I propose to explore the reasons why. First, a caveat is in order. *Dignitatis Humanae*, despite its American connections, was not written as a menu for American policy makers. One should tread carefully, as Russell Hittinger has wisely cautioned, in attempting to make the document do work it was not intended to do.[3] To this warning I can only plead an intent to remain faithful to the Declaration's purpose, which, as I understand it, is to articulate a development of Catholic doctrine on religious freedom as an immunity from coercion in civil society, while leaving in place the distinctive religious truth claims and moral requirements of the Catholic Church.

I want to explore these three questions by making three overlapping arguments. First, the United States has embarked on a project to facilitate the growth of democratic institutions in much of the Muslim world, an effort which cannot possibly succeed if it ignores, or misapplies, the factor of religious freedom. Second, American foreign policy is failing to incorporate religious freedom successfully because the foreign affairs community is for the most part suspicious of the religious impulses of mankind, believes religion a danger to democracy, and thinks "religious freedom" means the privatization of religion in order to protect democracy.

Third, *Dignitatis Humanae* sets out principles that can help inform American religious freedom policy in the Muslim world and elsewhere, not least in the practical application of what we might call "religious realism" – a more accurate and productive understanding of the legitimate role of religion in the actions of people and governments we seek to influence.

Religious Freedom as Keystone of Islamic Democracy

Concerning the centrality of religious freedom to the American democracy project in the Muslim world, President George W. Bush has argued that opposing tyranny and promoting democracy in the greater Middle East is the best long-term strategy for America's security. My own view is that, while it is fraught with risks, succeeding in this strategy is vital for the well being of the United States and the rest of the world, especially nations dominated by Islam.

For decades U.S. foreign policy sought "stability" in the Muslim world by cooperating with tyrants who abused their own citizens but, it was reasoned, would keep the lid on Islamist extremism. It took 9/11 to dislodge this "realist" assumption and force a major rethinking of American policy. Today that policy is not only to disable or kill the terrorists in the Global War on Terror, but to remove their *raison d'être* over the long-term by implanting political institutions of ordered liberty. Freedom, it is thought, is not only the lubricant of democracy, but the antidote to extremism.

Such a project stands little chance of success unless it incorporates a "realistic" understanding of religious freedom in a democracy, which means securing the rights of persons and communities to worship privately and to engage publicly on the basis of their beliefs, bounded by culturally-accepted limits that include a rightful measure of autonomy for the secular sphere. Democratic religious liberty ought to be, in other words, anti-theocratic and anti-extremist, but not anti-religion. It must include a negotiated set of boundaries between the overlapping authorities of government and religion.

Paying close attention to religious freedom is vital for American policy in part because most Muslim societies, despite the appearance of religious homogeneity, are in fact cauldrons of religious pluralism. The dispute in Iraq over the place of Islam in the constitution stems not only from the concerns of Christian minorities but is also a result of the Shiite-Sunni divide. This is a major conflict with theological, as well as political and ethnic roots. It exists almost everywhere in the Muslim world.

Part of the answer in places like Iraq is to let the political process work on parallel lines with religious belief and practice. Given the fears expressed by some that Iraqi "democracy" would lead inevitably to theocracy, it has been encouraging to see the way that Iraqi religious pluralism, from traditional clerics to Muslim women's movements, has yielded compromises in the constitutional process. The constitution certainly has flaws and it is unclear how its attempts to balance Islam and individual rights will evolve. But it is a mistake to believe that any constitution can alone change the habits and opinions of the religious groups that dominate Muslim societies, rendering them democrats overnight.

In fact, history demonstrates that successful transitions to democracy in societies where religious communities play a significant role in public life, such as 18th century Protestant America, or 20th century Hindu India, must be preceded and accompanied by a sustained debate *within* the dominant religious communities. This debate is typically less about separation or secularism than the compatibility of religious doctrine with political reform. In other words, the groundwork for durable democracy is often laid by doctrinal development, and an accommodation between religion and political order.[4] Indeed, as George Weigel, Samuel Huntington, and others have argued, it was Vatican II in general and *Dignitatis Humanae* in particular that provided Catholics with doctrinal reasons to support democratic reform in the "third wave" of democratization that occurred in the 1970s and 1980s.[5]

Although many wish to deny it, there is in fact a significant doctrinal barrier to democracy in many Islamic traditions. Modern Islamism, with some important exceptions, admits no legitimate distinction between the sacred and the secular. It is at base a monism that understands the ideal political order as one governed root and branch by divine (or Shari'a) law. Consequently, there is no durable moral or political concept of human freedom, and every reason for the state to employ coercion against the apostate and the infidel, and – depending on one's reading of Shari'a – to view women as less than equal persons under the law.

The democratic experiment now underway in Iraq, we can all hope, will provide a practical model of history and theology evolving together. But the greatest challenge will doubtless be Saudi Arabia, which is the birthplace of Islam and the exporter of Wahhabism – the most virulent form of Sunni extremism. My own experience with the Saudis suggests that there is more religious ferment, even within the Sunni majority, than meets the eye. But this is still a culture in which religious sanction is employed for acts of stunning cruelty. For example, Human

Rights Watch reported that in 2002 Saudi schoolgirls were prevented from fleeing a burning building because they were not properly covered. Several burned to death.[6]

Or there is the tragic case of Pat Rousch and her two girls, who had been raised as Christians in the United States. Roush's Saudi ex-husband kidnapped the girls and took them to Saudi Arabia where they remain today, despite her frantic efforts over 20 years to retrieve then. The problem here is two premises derived from Saudi Shari'a law: first, any issue of a Saudi man is by definition a Muslim, irrespective of contrary fact; second, a Saudi girl, even after reaching adulthood, has few rights that do not derive from her father, her husband or her closest male relative. The barrier to human dignity and ordered freedom implicit in such putatively divine authority is significant, and constitutions alone will not remove it.[7]

But it would be a mistake to conclude that Islam is fatally flawed as a religion. As Americans, we should recall that 17th century Quakers were branded like cattle and hanged like horse thieves by Congregationalists on Boston square. A century later, different Christian sensibilities were elevated into the religion clauses of the First Amendment.

As Catholics, we should recall the case of Edgardo Mortara, an Italian Jewish child who in the 1860s was thought to be dying. Unbeknownst to Edgardo's parents, a teenage Catholic friend baptized the young boy, thinking to win him for Christ before his death. But Edgardo did not die. Learning of his baptism, Catholic civil and religious authorities forcibly removed the child from the arms of his frantic mother and father, and had him raised as a Catholic, ignoring their lifelong attempts to retrieve him. A century later *Dignitatis Humanae* signaled a development in Catholic teaching on human freedom which rendered such an intervention unthinkable.[8] As Americans and Catholics, can we conclude that Muslims are incapable of doctrinal development?[9]

Fortunately there are Muslim reformers today struggling to develop a democratic public theology that acknowledges the legitimate autonomy of a secular civil order and posits a distinctly Muslim argument for universal human rights. Some of these reformers are Americans, and we should earnestly hope for a Muslim John Courtney Murray who might influence the development of a doctrine of religious liberty in the Islamic world.[10] But for the present, reform, if it comes, must come from places like Iran, Iraq, Pakistan, Egypt or Saudi Arabia.

U.S. policy must begin to engage with these and other religious communities, directly and indirectly, in order to facilitate their understanding of the compatibility of democracy with Islam. To accomplish

such a task, American diplomats must improve their ability to understand the stakeholders in Muslim societies as they understand themselves: agents of a theological imperative in which politics is a means,
not an end. U.S. policy must overcome the widespread suspicion in the
Muslim world that democracy is inherently anti-Islamic and requires the
banishment of religious conviction to the private margins of society and
politics.

Foggy Bottom and the Privatization Premise

The second argument is that U.S. religious freedom policy is not
being employed effectively as an instrument of broader American interests abroad. Instead of engaging with those communities whose religion-
based moral and political views drive their respective understandings of
democracy, American policy makers refuse to encounter them as religious communities at all.

Two brief examples should drive this point home. The United States
has greatly expanded its democracy promotion programs in the countries
of the Middle East as a means of expanding freedom and countering ter-
rorism. A perusal of U.S. funded democracy programs reveals scores of
millions of dollars being granted to non-governmental organizations that
are training Muslim individuals and communities on the conduct of elec-
tions, building political parties, drafting constitutions, training journal-
ists, developing women's and labor movements, and growing various
aspects of "civil society" – the intermediary associations that can limit
the powers of government, build democratic virtues, and increase social
cohesion.

These programs are good and necessary, but they do not focus on
the most important aspect of civil society in Muslim nations: *communities as bodies of religious thought and action*. With some grudging
exceptions, the United States is not spending money on grants to NGOs,
Muslim or non-Muslim, that seek to engage the mullahs on religion and
politics, the curricula of the *madrassas*, or the development of a democratic public theology. This hesitancy is terribly shortsighted. It virtually ignores the fervent debates over Islam and democracy taking place
within the Muslim world. It also misses an opportunity to address the
widespread Muslim suspicion that democracy requires the abandonment
of Islam to the private margins of life and is therefore inherently
Godless. There are within the U.S. bureaucracy voices calling for this to
change, but thus far they are not carrying the argument.

Perhaps the most telling indication of the ineffectiveness with which
America's international religious freedom policy is employed is precise-

ly the way the State Department has implemented the International Religious Freedom Act of 1998. Some believed this law would require attention to the relationship between religion and politics in nations vital to U.S. interests.[11] Ultimately, however, the new policy has *not* been seen as a means to address the larger implications of religion's growing importance, and has in effect been pigeonholed at State. Few senior U.S. officials believe advancing religious freedom could or should used to encourage stable relationships between political and religious authorities in countries of concern to the United States. Despite the ongoing efforts of some at State, "promoting religious freedom" generally means humanitarian activism: denouncing persecuting governments and engineering prisoner releases.

An irony of this narrow approach is that the IRF Act provides the means to address both persecution and the religio-political problem in a comprehensive and effective way. It established a high-level position, an Ambassador at Large, to head the office of international religious freedom within the Department of State, and designated the Ambassador as "advisor to the President and Secretary of State." On paper the new official and his office are given considerable authority to "advance religious freedom worldwide" and a variety of tools to do it.

But neither the Ambassador's title nor his legal authority has altered the official resistance to addressing religion systematically in American foreign policy. From the beginning, the IRF Ambassador and his office were placed under the Bureau of Democracy, Human Rights, and Labor (DRL). Staffed by talented and dedicated people, DRL carries little policy influence at State and is generally shunned by Foreign Service Officers as "out of the mainstream" of foreign policy. Few FSOs oppose human rights advocacy, but they tend to see it as a compartmentalized issue that has little connection to the diplomacy practiced in the powerhouse offices at State – the regional bureaus and desks that control American embassies and consulates abroad.

For its part, DRL has in recent years adopted an aggressively secular approach to the subject of human rights, shunning religious liberty as relatively unimportant – or even dangerous – in the larger scheme of priorities. The Clinton administration's human rights officials tended to view population control as a high human rights priority, and were doubtless aware that too much freedom for religious communities (e.g., the Catholic Church, Evangelical Christians, and Muslims) could frustrate that goal.[12] While Bush administration appointees have not carried that ideological baggage with them, they have done little to elevate religious freedom within the foreign policy bureaucracy.

The bureaucratic and functional quarantine of international religious freedom policy has been no secret in Washington. Among other things, the problem was publicly revealed in a 2003 report of the State Department's Inspector General, which was sent to Congress and has been reported in the media.[13] But neither Congress nor the coalition that sought the IRF Act has seen fit to address the issue. A separate IRF Commission, established by the Act as a watchdog agency, has made a number of excellent policy recommendations.[14] But it has largely ignored the State Department's bureaucratic isolation of IRF policy and its circumvention of the Ambassador and office of international religious freedom.

What are the reasons for this shortsightedness in American foreign policy? One is the State Department's well-developed ability to ignore unwanted Congressional mandates, but that is not always a bad thing. The underlying foundation for much of the problem is, in my view, a crippling assumption by foreign policy elites that religious freedom entails the privatization of religion, and the strict separation of religion from public life. Religion, according to this view is not only *not* a constituent of democracy, but the very nature of religion – irrational and unpredictable – places democracy at risk. Far from being what natural law philosophers would label a human good, religion is at best a private choice that, like consensual sex and stock car racing, merits some legal protection.

The "privatization" assumption has been absorbed like mother's milk by almost the entire range of those groups composing the foreign policy establishment, including the so-called foreign policy "realists," the liberal internationalists, and even the neoconservatives, who are thought to run contemporary American foreign and defense policy. Even many who are calling for more emphasis on "soft power" in American strategy – i.e., the power of persuasion rather than the power of military or economic might – give short shrift to the factor of religion.[15] Interestingly, the obstacle is heightened because some on the so-called Christian right who vigorously oppose the privatization of religion in domestic politics are content to see it dominate our democracy promotion programs in Muslim countries. For some in this group, "engaging Islam" is a metaphor for military action and little else.

In short, because our diplomatic establishment sees "religious freedom" as simply one of many privacy rights, without any special claim on the human person or his behavior, U.S. religious freedom policy lacks the vocabulary or the will to engage foreign religious communities, especially non-Western religious communities, on how their traditions might accommodate or be accommodated by democracy.

Dignitatis Humanae and the Way We Really Are

Now to my third and final argument: the Catholic Church's "Declaration on Religious Freedom," *Dignitatis Humanae* can help American foreign policy out of its self-defeating privatization premise. DH teaches that the natural religious dimension of the human person is intimately tied to human dignity and flourishing, and requires protection in the civil order precisely for that reason, not because it is one among many private human choices on offer. The drive to know the truth about God and man is natural and good to individuals and societies, and consequently the proper role of government is to *favor* religious life, within the just limits of public order.

If DH is correct about human nature and the government's responsibility, it provides reasonable grounds for abandoning the thin privatization approach to religious liberty and integrating religion into our policy assumptions about human behavior and how to influence it. If the drive to discover religious truth is as universal and productive as the drive to political power and economic gain, then no policy maker could reasonably ignore its implications for political order. Religious freedom would then necessarily take its place as a key factor in any strategy to facilitate democratic institutions, and to tie the religious impulses of men to public purposes in a democratic society.

The thin view of religious liberty as understood by our foreign affairs establishment, as well as its implicit anthropology, has long been buttressed by the so-called secularization theory. Born (as Tocqueville reminds us) in the 18th century French Enlightenment, that theory survives among Western academics, political, media and entertainment elites to this day.[16] It holds that religion will inevitably decline and ultimately disappear with the advance of reason, science and modernity. Implicit in the secularization theory is the belief that religious observance is not only unnatural and unconnected to human flourishing, but comprises little more than a superstitious grasping for meaning that cannot and ought not survive the maturing of human knowledge. Those who persist in maintaining that the superstition should be tolerated in a democratic system should be permitted no more influence on public policy than alchemists and sorcerers.

Now in 1965, the Council Fathers were asserting precisely the opposite theory of religion's place in the human makeup. Far from some leap into the dark, said DH, the religious yearning reflects men's "dignity as persons – that is, beings endowed with reason and free will and therefore privileged to bear individual responsibility...(DH #2)."[17] The search for truth must be carried out "in a manner proper to the dignity of the human person and his social nature. The inquiry is to be free, carried on with the aid of teaching or instruction, communication and dialogue, in the course of which men explain to one another the truth they have discovered, or think they have discovered, in order thus to assist one another in the search for truth"(DH #3).

If the religious enterprise is natural, necessary, and at the core of human dignity, then DH reasons that all persons, individually and as parts of religious communities, have a natural right not to be coerced by any human agency in matters of religion. This right is to be manifested in politics and society by means of a twofold constitutional immunity: 1) the right not to be forced to believe something contrary to conscience, and 2) the right not to be restricted from manifesting one's belief in public, except in cases where the government has the responsibility to protect what DH calls "the just demands of public order"(DH ##2, 4).

According to the Council, this right to religious freedom does not derive from "the subjective disposition of the person"(DH #2), including the quality of his religious opinions or commitments. The Church is here saying that the right to religious freedom as an immunity from coercion does not increase or decrease with the proximity to religious truth achieved by an individual or community. *Everyone* must be immune from coercion in the civil order because that immunity is required by the very nature of man. "In consequence, the right to this immunity continues to exist even in those who do not live up to their obligation of seeking the truth and adhering to it"(DH #2).

Is there any contemporary evidence that this argument about the religious nature of man, however appealing in theory, is true? The answer is a qualified "yes." We are today faced with overwhelming data that religious observance is spreading and deepening internationally. Sociologists of religion have in the last three decades begun to revise or abandon the secularization theory.[18] But the spread of religion per se, while it may indicate its natural occurrence, does not prove that the religious enterprise is connected to human dignity and flourishing.

For whatever reason, there is today growing scholarly attention to religion, society and politics. Max Weber, of course, examined the connections between the Protestant ethic and capitalism over a century ago, and scholars such as Michael Novak have worked in this field for years.[19] But there is now a growing body of scholarship suggesting that religious truth claims acting within democratic norms are productive of political harmony and economic prosperity. Much of this work focuses on Christianity, but there is also interesting work being done on Judaism, Hinduism, Confucianism, and Islam as it is evolving in Turkey.[20]

How is religious devotion, individually and collectively, best accommodated within the social and political order? If the United States intends to facilitate democracy in nations dominated by religious communities, how should it think about the role of those communities in civil society? What is their proper relationship to a democratic government? DH acknowledges both the inevitability and the appropriateness of religious communities: "the social nature of man requires...that he should give external expression to his internal acts of religion; that he should share with others in matters religious; that he should profess his religion in community"(DH #3). Accordingly, the constitutional immunity from coercion demanded for individuals must also extend to associations of like-minded religious adherents.

Part of the Council's interest in religious communities was, of course, intended to reaffirm the freedom of the Church itself, a freedom which DH grounds not only in natural law but also in revelation.[21] And yet, notwithstanding their reaffirmation of the Church's centrality in the life of men, the Council Fathers were not reasserting the Church's right to a privileged position in the civil order. Indeed, to the extent that position lingered as an acceptable one within the Church, they were abandoning it altogether and affirming the right of other religious communities to civil equality. DH demanded for all religious groups a host of rights, including the right publicly to demonstrate "the special value of their doctrine in what concerns the organization of society and the inspiration of the whole of human activity"(DH #4).

Here we arrive at the apex of the Declaration's logic, and its defense of truth-claiming religion in the democratic public square. The search for religious truth is innate and necessary to human dignity and flourishing, hence it must be protected by societies and governments. Because it is accomplished in community with others, the religious quest requires protection for communities, whose essence is the public proclamation of what they believe. The good of men and of societies mandates that governments not only protect the right to pursue these matters, but also, as DH puts it, government must "help create conditions favorable to the fostering of religious life." Such a role for government ensures that people might "exercise their religious rights and...fulfill their religious duties, and...that society itself may profit from the moral qualities of justice and peace which have their origin in men's faithfulness to God..."(DH #6).

Conclusion

In conclusion, my argument is that DH provides a rich menu of principles that might usefully be consulted by anyone designing a foreign policy whose purpose is to facilitate the development of liberal democratic institutions in Muslim societies, or, for that matter, in any country where religious communities abide and seek to influence the political arrangements and policies under which they live.

Those principles include an anthropology that posits and values the religious nature of man; an understanding of healthy societies as those that nurture and protect the social contributions of religious communities, and the positive role of government in favoring the religious life, both of individuals and communities. Finally, DH speaks of these principles to the modern world from the heart of its own claim that Jesus Christ is Lord, and that within the Catholic Church resides the fullest expression of the truth about God and man. It is from this claim that the Church teaches the modern world that tyranny is no friend of truth.

On this 40th anniversary of the Declaration on Religious Freedom, America's political leadership should take notice. We, of all peoples, should be more open to – and realistic about – the authentic religious wellsprings of human behavior. After all, the great development of Catholic doctrine found in *Dignitatis Humanae* drew much of its inspiration from the American experience.

Thomas F. Farr, who holds a Ph.D. in history from the University of North Carolina, is an author and a former American diplomat who served in the U.S. Foreign Service for 21 years. Between 1999 and 2003 he served as the Department of State's first Director of the Office of International Religious Freedom. He also served 7 years with the U.S. Army – as Adjutant General of the Army Transportation Command in Germany and as an Assistant Professor of History at the U.S. Military Academy at West Point, New York. After joining the U.S. Foreign Service in 1982, he focused on strategic arms control policy, political military affairs, and Europe. He served in such positions as Adviser to the U.S. Delegation on U.S.-Soviet Defense and Space talks in Geneva and in Washington, D.C., as desk officer for NATO and then for Cyprus and as a senior analyst in the Bureau of Intelligence and Research.

During his diplomatic career Dr. Farr also taught international relations, American government, and the politics of the American judiciary at the Air Force Academy in Colorado Springs, Colorado. He currently serves on the board of directors of Christian Solidarity Worldwide – U.S.A., an NGO that lobbies governments against persecution and in favor of religious freedom.

ENDNOTES

1   Murray's classic statement on American democracy and religious freedom is contained in *We Hold These Truths: Catholic Reflections on the American Proposition* (New York: Image Books, 1964). See especially chapter 2.

Otherwise, Murray mainly wrote articles and essays, many of which have been compiled and edited by L. Leon Hooper. S.J. See his *John Courtney Murray—Religious Liberty: Catholic Struggles with Pluralism* (John Knox Press, 1993); and also *Bridging the Sacred and the Secular: Selected Writings of John Courtney Murray, S.J.* (Georgetown University Press, 1994).

2   See, for example, James Hitchcock, *The Supreme Court and Religion in American Life*, 2 vols. (Princeton: Princeton University Press, 2004); Gerard V. Bradley, *Church-State Relationships in America* (New York, 1987); Robert P. George and William L. Saunders, "Religious Values and Politics,: in George, *The Clash of Orthodoxies: Law, Religion and Morality in Crisis* (Wilmington: ISI Books, 2001), 231-258; Mary Ann Glendon, "Religious Liberty and the Original Understanding of the Universal Declaration of Human Rights," a paper presented at the August 2000 Becket Fund Conference in Prague.

3   Russell Hittinger, "How to Read *Dignitatis Humanae* on Establishment of Religion," *Catholic Dossier*, March-April 2000, 15. See also Hittinger, *The First Grace* (ISI, 2003), chapter 9.

4   Alfred Stepan, "Religion, Democracy and the Twin Tolerations," in Larry Diamond, ed., *World Religions and Democracy*, (Johns Hopkins, 2005), 8-9, 11.

5   See Samuel Huntington, *The Third Wave, Democratization in the Late Twentieth Century* (University of Oklahoma, 1991), 77; George Weigel, *Freedom and Its Discontents: Catholicism Confronts Modernity* (Ethics and Public Policy Center, 1991), chapters 1 and 2.

6   See the report from March 15, 2002, at www.hrw.org. Also see Khaled Abou El Fadl's useful discussion of the incident in *The Great Theft: Wrestling Islam from the Extremists* (Harper, 2005), 250-55.

7   On the Roush case, see www.patroush.com

8   On the Mortara case see Edgardo Mortara's own account at the Zenit News Agency. Also see Bertram Wallace Korn, *The American Reaction to the Mortara Case: 1858-1859* (American Jewish Archives, 1957). A more recent work, although marred by rhetorical excess, is David I. Kertzer, *The Kidnapping of Edgardo Morara* ((Knopf, 1997). During its meeting of May, 2001, the International Catholic Jewish Liaison Committee, established after Vatican II, affirmed that the Mortara case "exemplifies the historical problem which *Nostra Aetate* and subsequent statements of the Holy See have solved 'in our time.'" See Vatican.va/roman_curia/pontifical_councils/chrstuni/relations-jews-doc.

9   See Michael Novak, *The Universal Hunger for Liberty: Why the Clash of Civilizations Is Not Inevitable* (Basic Books, 2004), xv, 191-218.

10   See for example Khaled Abou El Fadl, *The Great Theft,* as well as *Islam and the Challenge of Democracy*, (Princeton, 2004); Seyyed Hossein Nasr, *The Heart of Islam* (HarperSan Francisco, 2002); Abdullahi Ahmed An-Na'im, *Toward an Islamic Reformation* (Syracuse, 1990); Akbar S. Ahmed, *Islam Under Seige* (Blackwell, 2003).

11 The best treatment of the debate over the law is Allen D. Hertzke, *Freeing God's Children: The Unlikely Alliance for Global Human Rights* (Rowman and Littlefield, 2004).

12 The Department's efforts on population control took center stage during the 1994 international conference on population in Cairo. In a February 1, 1995, press briefing on the Department's Human Rights Report, Under Secretary for Global Affairs Timothy Wirth emphasized State's emphasis on "the new non-traditional issues" such as population. He argued elsewhere that "population...is the central switching issue that relates to everything else." See www.hwy9.com/psp/twirth.htm.

13 See Senator Rick Santorum, "Rattle the Cages for Religious Freedom, *Crisis Magazine*, November 4, 2003.

14 See, for example, the Commission's September 30, 2005, recommendations for State Department action in Saudi Arabia, available on its website www.uscirf.gov. The Commission has also consistently urged that the State Department do *a better job of reporting* how it is using foreign aid and program funding to promote religious freedom. That State has little to report because it is in fact doing very little in these areas seems to be less of a concern. The Commission has done a much better job of reporting and recommending than it has of identifying and solving the bureaucratic and functional obstacles in the Department of State.

15 See the most recent work of the preeminent advocate of "soft power," Joseph S. Nye, Jr., *Soft Power: the Means to Success in World Politics* (Public Affairs, 2004), 17, 59, 94. Nye recognizes religion and religious communities as purveyors of soft power, but does not integrate this insight into his analysis of what U.S. foreign policy should be doing in the world.

16 Gertrude Himmelfarb, *The Roads to Modernity* (Knopf, 2004), 205.

17 Parenthetical citations indicate numbered sections from the "Declaration on Religious Freedom," Walter M. Abbott, ed., *The Documents of Vatican II* (New Century Publishers, 1966), 675-696.

18 See, for example, the essays in Peter L. Berger, ed., *The Desecularization of the World: Resurgent Religion and World Politics* (Ethics and Public Policy Center, 1999). For an influential analysis of the "deprivatization of religion" outside the West, see Jose Casanova, *Public Religions in the Modern World* (University of Chicago, 1994). For a recent restatement by a pioneer of secularization theory, see David Martin, *On Secularization: Towards a Revised General Theory* (Ashgate, 2005).

19 See, for example, Michael Novak's "Max Weber Goes Global," *First Things*, April 2005, 26-29.

20 See the excellent volume of essays on this subject compiled by editors of the *Journal of Democracy*: Larry Diamond, *et al*, eds,, *World Religions and Democracy* (Johns Hopkins, 2005).

21 See footnote # 9 of DH, authored by John Courtney Murray, in Abbot, *The Documents of Vatican II*, p. 682.

Unitatis Redintegratio
Providential Turn or Historic Mistake?

KENNETH D. WHITEHEAD

I.

Most Catholics are very aware today that we live in an age of ecumenism. We are actively encouraged by the Church to show respect for and maintain good relations with non-Catholic Christians, work cooperatively with them on common tasks in society at large, and, on appropriate occasions, even pray with them. Visits back and forth by the leaders of various Churches and communions are the order of the day (with the pope being especially active in this regard). Joint statements and agreements by Church leaders are similarly quite frequent (with the pope again being quite prominently involved). Christian reunion may not have been achieved as yet, but this has seemingly not been on account of any lack of positive words and expressions of good will on all sides, especially on the part of many Christian leaders.

Those of us who go back awhile, though, remember when the atmosphere was very different. Christians outside the visible boundaries of the Catholic Church were known as "separated brethren," and were not cultivated. Catholics were not encouraged to be involved with them and were even forbidden to participate in their worship. They were considered to be sadly mistaken in their religious commitments, if they were not actually perverse. Separation from them was regarded as a more or less fixed and permanent feature of the Christian scene – unless and until by some miracle they should come to see the light and be reconciled with the true Church of Christ. Meanwhile, such feelings were widely reciprocated by most non-Catholic Christians – to the point where Catholics were sometimes considered not even to *be* Christians.

Yet Jesus Christ had prayed that his followers might "all be one": "I pray," he said, "for those who believe in me...that they may all be one; even as thou, Father, art in me and I in thee, that they may also be in us, that the world may believe that thou hast sent me (Jn 17:20-21). Already in the New Testament, however, there were reports (cf. I Jn 2:19) of

Christians separating themselves from what was already understood to be Christ's "body, the Church" (Col 1:18; 1:24). What the Second Vatican Council would characterize as "the sin of separation" (*Unitatis Redintegratio* #3) became only too common in the history of the Church thereafter.

There was the major break connected with the Arian heresy which followed the Church's first general council, the Council of Nicaea in 325 A.D., and which endured for centuries. Similar major defections followed the great Councils of Ephesus in 430 A.D., and Chalcedon some twenty years later, which resulted in organized Churches or Christian bodies consisting of "separated brethren," some of which have lasted up to our own day in the Ancient Churches of the East, numbering as many as ten million Christians not in communion either with either the Eastern Orthodox or with the Catholic Church.

Even during the first millennium of what we somewhat wishfully today characterize as "the undivided Church," there were several breaks between the East and the West before the rupture in 1054 A.D. which came to be considered *the* great breach of Christian unity – which itself has now lasted for nearly a millennium. Although the mutual excommunications of pope and patriarch made back in those distant days have now been lifted, there is still no restored unity between the Churches of the East and the West. Then, there was the other major break, the one which followed the Protestant Reformation of the sixteenth century, and which resulted in the splitting of Western Christendom into a number of mutually exclusive Christian bodies, all claiming to embody the true way that Christ had indicated.

Whatever the reasons for this splintering of the body of Christ, and however we might assign responsibility or even blame for it in various cases as we look back upon the first two millennia of Christianity, one thing can be asserted without fear of contradiction on any side, and that is that Christ's prayer "that they all may be one" has certainly not been very well heeded by Christ's professed followers.

Blessed Pope John XXIII was scandalized by this situation. His service as a papal diplomat in Eastern Orthodox territories had convinced him that the time had come to seek a remedy for Christian disunity. After he became pope in 1958 and decided to call the Second Vatican Council, he quite pointedly made the search for Christian unity one of his three main reasons for convoking the Council. The other two, it will be recalled from his famous Opening Address to the Council, were: the renewal and more effective dissemination of the Church's faith (and he considered the Church's faith to be solidly and unalterably established and beyond dispute; little did he anticipate the era of doctrinal dissent and disloyalty that was to come after the Council). Finally, the third of his reasons for calling the Council was the adaptation or up-dating (*aggiornamento)* of the Church's discipline and practices in order better to meet the needs of the present day.

But the quest for Christian unity was indisputably one of John XXIII's main reasons for summoning the Council. If we have now moved into a full-scale era of ecumenism, this is largely because of the decisions the Catholic Church made at the Council. These decisions subsequently became major Church priorities, as exemplified in such postconciliar documents as Pope John Paul II's 1995 encyclical on the Church's commitment to ecumenism, *Ut Unum Sint* ("That They May Be One"), in which the pontiff made the unprecedented invitation to the leaders of other Christian Churches to dialogue with the papacy concerning the exercise of the Catholic Church's claim of a Petrine primacy.

At the time of the Council, though, John XXIII's general practice was to leave the organization and outcomes of this solemn gathering of the Catholic bishops of the world to the good offices of the Holy Spirit – for the most part, he did not insist on running a very tight ship. Where the quest for Christian unity was concerned, he was both prudent and far-seeing, and he was not prepared to leave anything to chance. Even before the Council, in 1960, he had established a Secretariat for Christian Unity, and placed it under the direction of the noted German biblical scholar and ecumenist, Father Augustin Bea, S.J. This Christian unity Secretariat, which has survived as a Pontifical Council today, played a major role at the Second Vatican Council, and was basically responsible not only for developing the Council's Decree on Ecumenism, *Unitatis Redintegratio* ("Restoration of Unity"), but also for developing the Council's epochal Declarations on Religious Liberty, *Dignitatis Humanae*, and on the Relation of the Church to Non-Christian Religions, *Nostra Aetate.*

To say that the development of all these three topics at the Second Vatican Council represented the plowing of some new ground by the Catholic Church would be an understatement. Where ecumenism was concerned, it is no exaggeration to say that the Church fundamentally modified the stance that she had been consistently maintaining for the previous several centuries towards those professing Christians outside her visible boundaries. Especially following the solemn definitions of the First Vatican Council in 1870 concerning the primacy and infallibility of the pope, the Catholic Church's stance towards Christians outside her visible boundaries was quite simple; it was that they needed to *return* to the fullness of Christ's truth and grace believed to be present in the Catholic Church.

Pope Leo XIII expressed this attitude clearly in his 1894 *Praeclara Gratulationis* when he declared that "the yearning desire of Our heart bids Us conceive the hope that the day is not far distant, when the Eastern Churches, so illustrious in their ancient faith and glorious past, will return to the fold they have abandoned." Pope Pius XI articulated this same seemingly decided and settled position of the Catholic Church on ecumenism in his encyclical on Religious Unity, *Mortalium Animos*, issued on January 26, 1928. This encyclical represented the Catholic Church's answer to the organized modern ecumenical movement which had begun under Protestant auspices around 1910 and had succeeded in drawing an impressive number of Churches and denominations into its ranks, including many Eastern Orthodox. At the time, there had been some discussion about whether the Catholic Church too might take part in the ecumenical movement.

To this question Pope Pius XI responded in *Mortalium Animos* with a resounding: *No!* "The disciples of Christ must be united principally by the bond of *one faith*," Pius XI declared (MA #9; emphasis added). "Shall we suffer what would indeed be iniquitous, the truth, and truth divinely revealed, to be made a subject for compromise"? (MA #8). Describing Christian ecumenists, however sincere, as "pan-Christians," Pius XI saw the ecumenical movement as merely a "federation" of Churches, or an "assembly" of those calling themselves Christians, while not being in agreement with each other on what constituted Christianity. He concluded that "it should be clear why the Apostolic See has never allowed its subjects to take part in the[se] assemblies of non-Catholics: for the union of Christians can only be promoted by promoting the return to the one true Church of Christ of those who are separated from it, for in the past they have unhappily left it" (MA #10).

This was the fixed and firm attitude and stance of the Catholic Church up until Vatican Council II. Even Blessed Pope John XXIII, in his first encyclical, *Ad Petri Cathedram*, issued on June 29, 1959, although he spoke more lovingly of separated Christians than had been the custom, nevertheless passed in review all the established reasons why true Christian unity was only to be found within the bosom of the Catholic Church, and from that standpoint addressed himself to non-Catholic Christians by asking: "May we, in fond anticipation, address you as sons and brethren? May we hope with a father's love for your *return*"? (APC #79; emphasis added). "Return" was the established *Leitmotiv* for the achievement of Christian unity, as far as the Catholic Church was concerned.

The only problem was that few, if any, of the non-Catholic Christians to whom Blessed John XXIII was addressing himself seemed disposed to undertake anything resembling the "return" which the pontiff envisaged. There were always individual converts, of course – always had been, always would be (but not necessarily in only one direction!). But except for the relatively small number of individual converts, it did not seem that many or even any non-Catholic Churches or communions were in any way contemplating, or would contemplate, any "return" to the Catholic Church. For most of them the idea of a return was almost meaningless in any case, since they did not regard themselves as in any way having "left" or "abandoned" or become "separated from" the Catholic Church to begin with. Their ancestors, or the Churches and communions they belonged to, may well have done so at some point in the past; most of them did do so; but contemporary non-Catholic Christians themselves had never been "in" the Catholic Church in the first place so that they could have become "separated" from her.

At the time of the Council, then, the very idea of any return by non-Catholic Christians in a body to the Catholic Church was not only not a very active prospect; virtually nobody even thought about it any longer. The quest for Christian unity for which John XXIII so ardently yearned was pretty much at a standstill. Moreover, on the Catholic side too, most Catholics then, and perhaps not a few today, could not see how the Catholic Church, for her part, considering what she claims to be, could be involved in any ecumenical movement which did not involve the return of erring separated brethren to the true fold of Christ. For if it is true that the Catholic Church alone teaches Christ's truths in their most complete and developed form, at the same time as she offers the most complete sacramental means for our sanctification and salvation – as Vatican II itself would reiterate in several places, notably in the Dogmatic Constitution on the Church, *Lumen Gentium*, which describes the Catholic Church as "the *sole* Church of Christ which in the Creed we profess to be one, holy, Catholic, and apostolic" (LG #8; emphasis added) – then for the Church to enter into dialogue or discussion with other Churches and Christian bodies which, by definition, did *not* possess and offer all these same truths and means of grace in their fullness, almost inevitably appeared to weaken and even compromise the Church's own firm teaching, witness, and example.

How could the Catholic Church possibly enter into a *debate* about the truths and means of grace that she holds were confided to the apostles by Christ and transmitted down to us by means of the apostolic succession of bishops in communion with the bishop of Rome, the successor of Peter? To enter into a debate about such questions would surely be to admit that there could be more than one point of view about them. At the very least, it would open the question of whether the Catholic Church herself was perhaps *not*, after all, everything that she claimed to be. It would suggest that the Church herself was perhaps *not* totally confident about what human beings must believe and do in order to achieve their sanctification and salvation in Jesus Christ. Others might claim to know of equally valid ways, as, indeed, many did and do so claim in their characteristic ways, whether they are Evangelicals, Eastern Orthodox, or others. By entering into dialogue with them, the Catholic Church inevitably had to accord to them a large measure of legitimacy just as they were, namely, as separated from her.

Such was and is the logic which has not ceased to prompt questions, even today, about how the Catholic Church could possibly become just another "partner" in the ecumenical "dialogue," without prior reference to the truth or falsity of her claims, or those of her dialogue partners. Pope Pius XI surely did have a point. Truth can surely *not* just be prescinded from when matters of faith are at stake. In the meantime, though, the unity for which Christ prayed surely could not simply be set aside or disregarded as of no particular importance either.

II.

Blessed Pope John XXIII was determined to try to change whatever there might be standing in the way of Christian reunion that could be changed – to remove any obstacles to Christian unity that could be removed. As it happened, the Fathers of the Second Vatican Council eventually turned out to be in substantial agreement with the saintly pontiff about this. The same thing was true, it very soon also became clear, of the leaders of most non-Catholic Christian bodies, who quite happily sent observers to follow developments at Vatican II, and then, after the Council, engaged with some alacrity in the new ecumenical dialogue called for and promoted by the Council. The fact that the Catholic Church was now suddenly willing to engage in such dialogue gave new impetus to the ecumenical movement.

It was not a foregone conclusion, however, that the Council would necessarily follow the lead of John XXIII on the new ecumenism. Initially, many of the Council Fathers had serious reservations. There was no little anxiety on the part of many of them that getting into the ecumenical movement could weaken faith and even promote religious indifferentism. Debate about this was serious and prolonged. But attitudes had been changing, it turned out, and many Council Fathers saw that the Catholic Church did need to look with new eyes at the Christians outside her visible boundaries. The question of how to do this, given established positions and attitudes, was the question.

What the Council decided to do with regard to ecumenism was to look at the whole question in a different way and try to approach it from a new angle – to change the terms of the discussion, as it were. The basic idea was to inaugurate a new start in the quest for Christian unity by stepping around some of the past obstacles and trying to leave some past quarrels behind. The Church's *attitude* and her *policies* towards Christians outside her visible boundaries were not in any case established Church *teachings* in which the integrity of the Church's magisterium was engaged. The Church's stance towards the ecumenical movement was a Church policy, not a Church teaching. It could be changed. In the course of debating all this, however, it became clear that there could be no compromise concerning Catholic truth, including the truth that the Catholic Church was "the *sole* Church of Christ" (as we have just quoted Vatican II as affirming). But no longer would the Church simply wait around passively for an already long awaited but always continually delayed – if not emphatically *rejected* – "return." Instead the Church would actively seek out separated Christians.

Vatican II thus clearly recognized that a whole new approach to non-Catholic Christians needed to be tried. Centuries of separation had amounted to just that: separation. There was virtually no movement in inter-Christian relations; there was only stalemate; there was only stagnation. In laying out a new approach to the ecumenical question, the Council Fathers made use of the basic idea they had already adopted in *Lumen Gentium*, namely, that while Christians separated from the Catholic Church lacked the *fullness* of the faith and of the means of salvation in Christ, in their various Churches and communions, and in varying degrees, there were nevertheless also to be found among them "many elements of sanctification and truth" (LG #8). Separated Christians were thus not simply "in error," as they had so largely been regarded as being up to that point. Rather, they possessed at least some *elements* of Christian truth and of the sacramental means of grace. Simple experience confirmed, for example, that some Bible Christians believed in Jesus even more fervently than many Catholics; and most Christians possessed at least some of the sacramental means of sanctification and salvation, if only baptism. For the Council Fathers, therefore, the question became one of trying to look at the non-Catholic glass not as half empty, but as one quarter, one half, or perhaps even in some cases three quarters *full*.

The new Vatican II approach thus entailed that the Catholic Church herself, like the Good Shepherd in the parable, had to go out henceforth in search of the lost sheep (cf. Mt 18:12). This was the basic idea that was to inform what became the Council's Decree on Ecumenism. The whole question and its possible ramifications were vigorously and thoroughly debated in the *aula* of St. Peter's during the Council. All the doubts and questions about how the Church could so drastically revise what had been her negative position on ecumenism up to then were thoroughly aired. In the end, though, the final vote on the draft *schema*, which took place on November 21, 1964, registered 2,137 votes in favor and only 11 opposed. This certainly amounted to moral unanimity. Pope Paul VI promulgated this Decree on Ecumenism, *Unitatis Redintegratio,* the same day – one year before the end of the Council.

Although the approach was new, we should not imagine that it was all that "untraditional" in Catholic terms. The "tradition" of passively waiting for the "return" of erring and separated brethren was actually quite recent in the perspective of the long history of the Church. A Father of the Church such as St. Augustine, for example, had many centuries before articulated the idea of the *charity* that Catholics ought to have towards all Christians including those not in unity with them:

> We entreat you, brothers, as earnestly as we are able, to have charity, not only for one another, but also for those who are outside the Church. Of those some are still pagans, who have not yet made an act of faith in Christ. Others are separated insofar as they are joined with us in professing faith in Christ, our head, but are yet divided from the unity of his body. My friends, we must grieve over these as over our brothers. Whether they like it or not, they are our brothers; and they will only cease to be so when they no longer say *Our Father*…(*Discourse on the Psalms*).

A negative stance towards non-Catholic Christians may nevertheless have been only too understandable, however, especially considering the hardening of positions that took place on both sides following the breach of Church unity brought about by the Protestant Reformation. But it was hardly the only approach the Catholic Church had ever taken towards those Christians who had become separated from her. The historical record shows that the Church has more than once tried to reopen the dialogue with separated Christians in order to mend breaks which had occurred. This has been notably true in the case of the Eastern Orthodox after the schism of 1054. We should recall the Second Council of Lyons in 1274, for example, as well as the Council of Florence which wound up around 1445. In both of these approaches, the Holy See showed itself prepared to compromise on certain non-essentials in order to achieve reunion, for example, on the status of the See of Constantinople and on the Eastern patriarchates. It is true that these councils were ultimately rejected in the East, but it wasn't for lack of trying on the part of the Catholic Church.

Similarly, in the case of the Protestants, the Catholic Church on a number of occasions tried to make new approaches to them – the Council of Trent itself was intended to be that. Of course the Church also made some crucial mistakes in a situation that was unprecedented for the churchmen involved, as in retrospect the excommunications of Queen Elizabeth I and even of Martin Luther have been argued to have been. But as the decades and then the centuries followed upon the original splits, positions on both sides probably inevitably hardened. Soon there was no possibility of any real dialogue at all, except perhaps a dialogue of the deaf.

When Blessed Pope Pius IX wrote to all of the Eastern Orthodox bishops prior to the First Vatican Council inviting them to attend the upcoming general council *as* bishops, he did not even get the courtesy of a reply from any of them, in part, it seems, because his letter to them was for some reason made public before it had actually been received by them. Also, the terms in which his letter was couched were evidently considered both condescending and offensive. It can too often not be claimed, in fact, that effectiveness in public relations is one of the marks of the true Church! (Nor should it be.) Nevertheless, it is unfortunate that in not a few cases, the Holy See has apparently been unable to make what appeared to be perfectly reasonable cases *seem* reasonable. Similarly, Pius IX wrote to various Protestant communions inviting them to "return," and, again, there was no response.

A new approach to the whole question of possible Christian unity was not only required; it was long overdue. The question should have been reopened long since. Viewed in retrospect, it is amazing that anybody ever imagined that non-Catholic Christians were just going to return to the Catholic Church at some point. It bespoke an ignorance of how the non-Catholic Christians in question viewed the matter. It was thus Vatican II's express intention to reopen the question, which had been closed for so long.

III.

What kind of document is the Decree on Ecumenism which was finally approved by the Council? One of the distinguished Protestant observers at the Council, the Swiss theologian Dr. Oscar Cullmann – who was not always automatically favorable to the Council's work, indeed, he was quite critical of it at several points – described the Decree as "more than the opening of a door; new ground has been broken. No Catholic document has ever spoken of non-Catholic Christians in this way." If the Council truly intended to plow new ground on the subject of ecumenism, it certainly succeeded in opinion of this Protestant observer.

The very first sentence in the Introduction to the text declares that "the restoration of unity among Christians is one of the principal concerns of the Second Vatican Council." The second sentence is no less definite in stating that "Christ the Lord founded one Church and one Church only." Yet the text immediately points to the fact of division among Christians and mentions "the many Christian communions" all presenting themselves "as true inheritors of Jesus Christ."

"Such division," the text goes on to say, and quite emphatically, "openly contradicts the will of Christ, scandalizes the world, and damages that most holy cause, the preaching of the Gospel to every creature" (UR #1). The document makes clear that the ecumenism it is speaking of is an affair between and among Christians, whom it defines as all those "who invoke the Triune God and confess Jesus as Lord and Savior" (UR #1).

The Decree itself consists of an Introduction and three chapters. The first chapter is entitled "Catholic Principles on Ecumenism." The second chapter covers "The Practice of Ecumenism," while the third chapter discusses "Churches and Ecclesial Communities Separated from the Roman Apostolic See." The document is not a lengthy one; nevertheless, it concisely and economically treats the essential points. (In terms of the number of post-Vatican-II follow-up documents inspired by it or produced in its wake, this Decree, perhaps surprisingly, comes in second among all the documents of Vatican II after only the Constitution on the Sacred Liturgy, *Sacrosanctum Concilum.*)

No doubt because of the misgivings of many Council Fathers that an uncritical, unprincipled, or overly enthusiastic type of ecumenism could lead to religious indifferentism and the downgrading of essential truths of the faith, at least in some minds, the text very quickly proceeds to make clear that the Catholic Church, while fervently desiring the unity of all Christians, has nevertheless in no way relinquished her traditional claim to be "the one Church and the one Church only" founded by Jesus Christ.

After a brief, Scripture-based account of the foundation of the Church upon Peter and the other apostles – including references to the three famous Petrine passages in Matthew 16, Luke 22, and John 21 – the text proceeds in various ways to underline the essential oneness of

Christ's Church, referring to her as "God's only flock" (UR #2), and as the "one and only Church of God" (UR #3). It is in the following statement, however, that the Catholic Church's continuing claim to be the one, true Church of Christ is expressed more clearly and eloquently than anywhere else in the documents of Vatican II. The statement reads:

> For it is through Christ's Catholic Church alone, which is the universal help towards salvation, that the fullness of the means of salvation can be obtained. It was to the apostolic college alone, of which Peter is the head, that we believe that Our Lord entrusted all the blessings of the New Covenant, in order to establish on earth the one Body of Christ into which all those should be fully incorporated who belong in any way to the people of God (UR #3).

It is perhaps more than a little ironic that Vatican II's strongest and most insistent reiteration of the Church's traditional claim to be the one, true Church founded by Jesus Christ should have come, in all places, in the Council's Decree on Ecumenism. Yet the very same text goes on to speak further of "the unity of the one and only Church," about which, echoing *Lumen Gentium*, the text specifies that "we believe *subsists in* the Catholic Church as something she can never lose" (UR #4; emphasis added).

Thus, there can be no question but that the Second Vatican Council plainly and definitely reiterated the teaching of the Catholic Church to the effect that she herself is the one, true Church of Christ. If some, nevertheless, in the years after the Council, did, nevertheless, as a result of an uncritical, unprincipled, or overly enthusiastic type of ecumenism, allow their faith to be weakened in this regard, or even fell into the kind of religious indifferentism that some of the Council Fathers feared, this cannot be attributed to the teaching of *Unitatis Redintegratio* as such. On the contrary, the Decree plainly and unmistakably reiterated the traditional teaching.

Simple honesty, however, requires us to recognize that the fears of many of the Council Fathers that Catholic involvement in ecumenism and the ecumenical movement could lead to religious indifferentism and to the downgrading of some of the essential teachings of the faith were in some ways only too well founded. Some Catholics *did* lose their balance and depart from strict orthodoxy in their zeal for Christian reunion. We have seen this in such post-conciliar phenomena as widespread toleration of dissent, watered down catechetics, and what we have to hope is only a temporary curtailment of the Church's missionary impulse. Such phenomena arguably do stem from or are reinforced by the widespread modern idea, even within the Catholic Church, that one "faith" is as good as another, so why evangelize?

Since the subject of the Decree is ecumenism, that is, the relations between and among professing Christians, the text of the Decree goes on to point out how Christians and Christian communities outside the visible communion of the Catholic Church do not enjoy the "fullness" of the truths and of the sacramental means of salvation that the Catholic Church alone fully enjoys. Indeed, the "differences that exist...whether in doctrine or sometimes in discipline – or concerning the structure of the Church – do indeed create many obstacles, sometimes serious ones, to full ecclesiastical communion" (UR #4).

Still, the tone of the document remains positive, and affirms that "all who have been justified by faith in baptism" are held to have been "incorporated into Christ," at least in some measure. Moreover, in an extremely important psychological concession by the Catholic Church – if there ever is to be any real ecumenical progress in the practical order – the text plainly states that: "One cannot charge with the sin of separation those who at present are born into [separate] communities and in them are brought up in the faith of Christ...The Catholic Church accepts them with respect and affection as brothers...Often enough," the text goes on to say, "men *on both sides* were to blame" (*Ibid*; emphasis added).

The text elaborates on *Lumen Gentium* in listing some of the ecclesial "elements and endowments which...which can and do exist outside the visible boundaries of the Catholic Church: the written Word of God; the life of grace; faith, hope, and charity, with the other interior gifts of the Holy Spirit; as well as visible elements – all of which "come from Christ and lead back to him, [and] belong by right to the Church of Christ" (UR #4). Nevertheless, the text goes on with honesty to say that, whatever truths and means of grace separated Christians might possess, "our separated brethren, whether considered as individuals, or as communities and Churches, are not blessed with that unity which Jesus Christ wished to bestow on all those to whom he has given new birth into one body" (*Ibid.*).

In other words, it is Christ who desires Christian unity; it is Christ who prayed that "they may all be one" (Jn 17:20). In view of this the Council thought that the Catholic Church had a special responsibility to redouble her efforts to help create the conditions that might again make Christian unity possible. In order to do this, the text of the Decree identifies several actions to which it holds that Christians on all sides of the question should be dedicated:

> 1. Every effort should be made "to avoid expressions, judgments, and actions which do not represent the condition of our separated brethren with truth and fairness."

2. Dialogue should be carried on "between competent experts from different Churches and communities...[in which] each explains the teaching of his communion in greater depth and brings out clearly its distinctive features."

3. All Christians should cooperate more diligently in carrying out works "for the common good of humanity which are demanded by the Christian conscience."

4. All Christians should more often "come together for common prayer where this is permitted."

5. All Christians should "examine their own faithfulness to Christ's will for the Church and, wherever necessary, undertake with vigor the task of renewal and reform" (UR #4).

These, then, are the ecumenical principles which the Catholic Church has attempted to follow since Vatican Council II. That they in no way compromise any Church teaching should be evident. Nor is the Catholic Church in any way diminished by adopting and attempting to pursue them, in response to a prayer of Jesus Christ, even when her attempts to do so turn out to be unsuccessful or are actually rebuffed. That pursuit of these principles has not yet resulted in any notable examples of actual Christian reunion, however, should perhaps not surprise us. The Council, after all, did not establish either any timetable or provide any guaranteed method of proceeding – which, in the nature of the case, it could not have done. Christian unity is ultimately something that only God can bring about, as the Council fully appreciated; all any Christians can do, to risk a tautology, is what they can and should do: namely, refrain from blame, engage in sincere dialogue, cooperate in common works, "pray always and not lose heart" (Lk 18:1). These surely *are* the correct principles which the Church should be following with regard to ecumenism. From a strictly human standpoint, no reunion is likely to come about until separated Christians come to see *each other* differently than has been the case over the centuries.

In the meantime, much more could be said about the Decree on Ecumenism *Unitatis Redintegratio* itself. It bears rereading and study. In the brief space remaining, however, we can only glance very briefly and cursorily at some of the broad results of Vatican II's historic shift in the Catholic Church's approach to ecumenism.

IV.

Once Vatican Council II adopted the new ecumenism as the official Catholic Church policy towards Christians outside her visible boundaries, it was probably inevitable that the Church, owing not merely to her sheer size and numbers, but also to her new and formidable determination, directed from the Holy See, to seek unity with all Christians, would very soon become the dominant party in the whole ecumenical movement. This, in fact, happened very quickly. It is only necessary to consult the section entitled "Ecumenism and Interreligious Dialogue" in the latest *Catholic Almanac* to verify the degree to which much or most of today's Christian ecumenical activity stems from Catholic initiatives.

To go very extensively into the many ecumenical developments of the post-conciliar years would require a separate paper even longer than the present one. The same thing would be true simply of those developments following the issuance of Pope John Paul II's 1995 encyclical *Ut Unum Sint,* in which, as we have noted, the pontiff called upon the leaders and adherents of other Christian Churches and communions to enter into a serious dialogue concerning how the primacy of Peter claimed by the Catholic Church might possibly be *exercised* in a way more acceptable to separated Christians. To conclude here, however, we can only indicate very briefly how, following the Vatican II Decree on Ecumenism, the Catholic Church provided new impetus to the ecumenical movement by setting up theological commissions, organizing ecumenical dialogue and other ecumenical activities, and, in general, carrying through with such dialogue and discussion on a sustained basis in a way that continues up to the present day.

During the post-conciliar era, theological commissions, under that name or some variant name such as "colloquium," "conversation," or "dialogue," were set up, notably by the Pontifical Council for Promoting Christian Unity (which succeeded Cardinal Bea's "Secretariat" set up just before Vatican II), but also by many bishops' conferences. Today there are such commissions continuing to carry on consultations and dialogue between Catholics and: Anglicans, the Assyrian Church of the East, Baptists, Disciples of Christ, Evangelicals, Lutherans, Orthodox in both the Greek and Slavic traditions, Pentecostals, and Reformed. There have similarly been operating commissions (recently combined into one) with some of the Ancient Churches of the East: the Armenian, Coptic, Eritrean, Ethiopian, Malankaran, and Syro-Malankaran ("Jacobite") Orthodox Churches.

Some of these theological commissions have made greater progress than others. In some cases, major and indeed unprecedented agreed statements have been produced, such as the 1999 Joint Declaration on Justification concluded between the Catholic Church and the Lutheran World Federation in which both parties agreed that "by grace alone, in faith in Christ's saving work, and not because of any merit on our part, we are accepted by God and receive the Holy Spirit, who renews our hearts while equipping and calling us to good works." This agreement transcended one of the most disputed doctrines of the Reformation period, and both parties now agree that each party's understanding of the doctrine merits no condemnation by the other, as unhappily occurred during the Reformation.

Christological agreed statements between the Holy See and the Ancient Churches of the East have been notable and have even led some to believe that actual reunion with these small but vital communions, some of which go back to the beginning of Christianity, could come about sooner than most people imagine, perhaps even very soon.

Dialogue with the Anglican Communion, which initially seemed quite promising – Pope Paul VI, perhaps naïvely, seems to have believed that reunion with the Anglican Communion was not only possible but perhaps even imminent in his day – has recently seen such hopes dashed. Even during Paul VI's own pontificate, the signs emerged when the first ordinations of women took place in the Anglican Communion. Nor have prospects been improved since by the ordination of a homosexual bishop in an openly "gay" relationship by the Episcopal Church USA and the approval of a "blessing" of homosexual unions by the Anglican Church in Canada. These latter actions, of course, have brought upon the whole Anglican Communion the kind of disarray that, from a Catholic point of view, shows why a primatial see with true jurisdiction is so *necessary* in the Church (if only the archbishop of Canterbury *could* settle the matter!). In the meantime, some Vatican officials now politely refer to the Anglican Communion as undergoing a period of "discernment."

Dialogue with the Eastern Orthodox, which, after an earlier very favorable start, was unfortunately broken off for five full years after the year 2000 over such issues as "Uniatism," was again resumed in 2005, following an appeal by Pope John Paul II prior to his death. The Orthodox today, in spite of many doubts and even some expressed hostility towards contemporary ecumenical dialogue (they believe *they* constitute the one, true Church of Christ!) nevertheless seem to believe, like the Fathers of Vatican II, that ecumenism must be pursued in response to Christ's prayer, no matter how little *we* might think it should be necessary or helpful. It never was just a question of the pope coming to an agreement with the ecumenical patriarch, after all, as many may have imagined back in 1964, when Pope Paul VI and Ecumenical Patriarch Athenagoras I issued their Common Declaration officially lifting the joint excommunications of the year 1054.

The ecumenical patriarch is not the head of a single communion, as the pope is; rather, he is the *primus inter pares*, or "first among equals," of the heads of some fourteen different national Byzantine and Slavic Orthodox Churches in communion with each other, but each with its own patriarch or metropolitan. According to Orthodox doctrine, these independent, autocephalous (single-headed) Churches in communion with each other constitute the true model of the one Church of Christ.

The Catholic doctrine is that these national or independent Churches, while indeed they should enjoy autonomy along with their doctrinal and sacramental communion with each other, should nevertheless also be in communion with and under the successor of the head apostle, Peter, the bishop of Rome, the pope. In the Catholic view, the Orthodox model of the true Church fails to reflect the apostolic Church completely in that it lacks, precisely, any successor to the head apostle, Peter. The original apostles formed a college headed by Peter. Their successors, the bishops of the Church, need to be united with the successor of Peter.

The question of the primacy of the successor of Peter over the whole Church remains, in fact, the outstanding major and unresolved ecumenical issue today. In spite of all the various surprising and even heartening ecumenical agreements that have been concluded, one interesting fact about post-conciliar ecumenical dialogue is that there have been *no* agreed statements produced anywhere on the primacy of Peter, the one subject that nearly everybody agrees remains the greatest single obstacle to Christian reunion. There have actually been Anglican, Lutheran, and Orthodox voices agreeing both that a center of Christian unity is necessary and that the bishop of Rome is the most likely candidate to serve as that center. Unhappily, however, the terms upon which each of these communions might apparently accept such a Roman primacy presently fall far short of the Roman "primacy of jurisdiction" solemnly defined by the First Vatican Council, which it is hard to see how the Catholic Church could ever renounce.

Thus, in spite of the hopes and wishes of the Fathers of Vatican II, there has been no breakthrough – no significant Christian reunion (with only a couple of very minor exceptions) forty years after the Second Vatican Council ended. Nevertheless, when we ask the question whether Vatican II's decision to adopt a policy of active ecumenical involvement was a providential turn or a historic mistake, I believe we have to opt for the former and reject the latter. Blessed Pope John XXIII was basically right. The quest for Christian unity was at a standstill and this was intolerable. Christ's prayer "that they may all be one" was being steadily disregarded on all sides and, indeed, in certain ways, was virtually *forgotten*.

If we ask what Christian body should have taken the lead in trying to provide a remedy for this situation, we cannot neglect or ignore the idea that it should have been the Christian body which continues to claim to possess the fullness of the Christ's truth and grace, namely, the Catholic Church. The decision of the Fathers of Vatican II to adopt the new ecumenism was thus altogether fitting and proper. Catholics should accordingly embrace the new ecumenism, just as all the popes since Vatican II manifestly have embraced it – most especially Pope Benedict XVI, who has been a convinced and active ecumenist since the long ago days of the service of theologian Father Joseph Ratzinger as one of the more important *periti*, or theological advisors, at the Second Vatican Council itself.

No doubt the continuing lack of tangible results, after so much effort, in the form of any actual Christian reunification anywhere, continues to disappoint. Yet even though the course adopted at Vatican II was surely the correct one, perhaps the expectations of any quick or early success were exaggerated, especially considering the long and deep-seated separations. How much progress can we expect, after all, even after 40 years, concerning separations which have now lasted for nearly 500 years, 1000 years, and even 1500 years? Nobody knows how the ecumenical adventure which began for the Catholic Church at Vatican II will ultimately turn out – whether there will be any significant Christian reunion and, if so, what it will consist of.

Still, it is hard not to think that the very real *movement* generated over the past 40 years by the Council's decision to seek reunion, not to speak of so much genuine good will, is very much preferable to the stalemate and stagnation – and the danger of self-righteousness on all sides! – which prevailed before. Although Christians of all ecclesial persuasions have surely been obliged all along to make the ecumenical effort, nobody should imagine that reunion can or will be brought about merely as a result of human intentions and efforts (as most of the separations originally were). God will no doubt see to that in his own good time.

It was none other than Cardinal Joseph Ratzinger who, nearly twenty years ago, warned us in his book, *Church, Ecumenism & Politics* (New York: Crossroad, 1988), of the necessity of recognizing:

> ...the limits of what one might term the "ecumenism of negotiation" and not to expect of it any more than it can provide: rapprochements in important human fields, but not unity itself. It seems to be that many disappointments could have been avoided if this had been clear from the start. But after the successes of the

early period just after the Council, many have understood ecumenism as a diplomatic task in political categories; [and] just as
one expects of good negotiators that after some time they will
come to a joint agreement that is acceptable to everyone, so people
thought they could expect this of the Church authorities in matters
of ecumenism. But this was to expect too much of the ecumenical
movement.

More recently, the man who became Pope Benedict XVI, in one of
his latest books, *Pilgrim Fellowship of Faith: The Church As
Communion* (San Francisco: Ignatius Press, 2005), has reminded us even
more pertinently that:

> ...We had in fact overrated our own capacities if we believed
> that theological dialogues could, within a fairly brief time span,
> restore the unity of belief. We had lost our way if we got it into our
> heads that this goal must be reachable within deadlines we laid
> down. For a little while we were confusing theology with politics,
> confusing dialogues about belief with diplomacy. We wanted to do
> ourselves what only God can do. That is why we have to be pre-
> pared to keep on seeking, in the knowledge that the seeking itself
> is one way of finding: that being on a journey and traveling on,
> without stopping to take rest, is the only appropriate attitude for the
> person who is on a pilgrimage toward eternity...

Kenneth D. Whitehead is a former U.S. Assistant Secretary of
Education appointed by President Ronald Reagan in 1988. Before that
he served as a career Foreign Service Office at U.S. embassies in Rome
and in the Middle East and he also served a term as Chief of the Arabic
Service of the Voice of America. He now works as a writer, editor, and
translator in Falls Church, Virginia. He is the author of dozens of articles
on political, social, moral, and theological subjects, and of eight books,
most recently, *One, Holy, Catholic, and Apostolic: The Early Church
Was the Catholic Church* (Ignatius Press, 2000). His new book, *What
Vatican II Did Right: Forty Years after the Council and Counting*, is
forthcoming from Ignatius Press. He is also the co-author of two books,
most recently, *Flawed Expectations: The Reception of the Catechism of
the Catholic Church* (Ignatius Press, 1996; co-authored with Monsignor
Michael J. Wrenn). He is the editor or co-editor of nearly a dozen other
books, and the translator of around twenty books from French, German,
or Italian.

Mr. Whitehead was educated at the University of Utah and the
University of Paris. He is the recipient of the Cardinal Wright Award
from the Fellowship of Catholic Scholars and of the Blessed Frederick

Ozanam Award from the Society of Catholic Social Scientists. He was awarded an honorary D.Litt. degree in Christian letters by the Franciscan University of Steubenville. He currently serves on the Boards of Directors of the Fellowship of Catholic Scholars, the Catholic League for Religious and Civil Rights, and the *Review of Metaphysics*, and is a member of the Board of Advisers of the new University of Sacramento. He is married to the former Margaret O'Donohue, a professional parish Director of Religious Education (DRE), and they are the parents of four grown sons.

Remarks Upon Receiving
the Cardinal Wright Award

GERARD V. BRADLEY

I am profoundly grateful to the Fellowship of Catholic Scholars for this award. I am especially indebted to the Board of Directors. They elected me into a distinguished company of faithful Catholic men and women, all outstanding scholars whose published work reflected and enriched their faith. Just considering my immediate predecessors – Sister Mary Prudence Allen and Dr. Elizabeth Fox-Genovese – I am compelled to say that my humility outstrips even my gratitude. These two great Catholic women have recently brought out truly pathbreaking works of scholarship. I have in mind Sister's second volume of her magisterial treatment of the concept of woman in history, and Betsey's huge volume – written with her husband Gene – on the mind of the slaveholding class in the ante-bellum South. Glancing further down the list of previous Cardinal Wright Award winners deepens my feelings of modesty.

Of course, our president, Bernie Dobranski, furthered these feelings of humility by sharing the news that, in my case, the election was hotly contested and carried in the end by a slim margin. But, hey, who remembers that Al Gore actually won the popular vote in 2000? Bush is president and Gore is lecturing in the wilderness. That's all history will show.

I owe a very special debt of thanks to His Eminence Ralph McInerny. Not only did he draw the short straw this evening, and come under an obligation to introduce me. He got me into all this in the first place. It was Ralph who conspired with our founder of such happy memory – Monsignor George A. Kelly – to make me president of our Fellowship in 1995. And it was Ralph who tabbed, or *nabbed,* me to speak at the Cardinal Wright Award Banquet for the very first time, way back in 1994.

I remember the occasion well. I do not as well recall my remarks, which were (I think) a desultory mix of pieties and jabs at Ralph. And no text survives. In fact, there was none – and therein lies the tale.

Our 1994 meeting was in Corpus Christi, Texas. Our host was the servant of Christ, His Excellency René Gracida. Bishop Gracida invited the Board to a reception before the Banquet. I attended because I was then vice-president. The reception was a well-watered one, in the upper room of a local Mexican restaurant. After about two hours of enjoying our host's Latin hospitality, it was time to move on to the Banquet. As I danced my way to the head table, Ralph McInerny – then our President – stopped me short and said: "I would like you to speak after dinner." I stammered something like: "But, er, Ralph, I haven't prepared anything. I don't really know…" Ralph ever-so-cooly cut me short. He assured me that my remarks need not be too long or erudite, just a few remarks would do. I continued with ineffectual resistance to the idea. But Ralph cut that short, too. "There is just one thing," he said.. "What's that Ralph?" "Just be very, very funny."

I tried to be.

The next year was different. No surprises. In the interim I had succeeded Ralph as president. I knew I would host the Banquet, and present the Cardinal Wright Award (to the redoubtable Monsignor William B. Smith, in fact), and say more than a little throughout the evening. I tried to be funny, again, but events nearly overwhelmed the effort. (So much for no "surprises"!)

We met in 1995 in Minneapolis to discuss the condition of Catholic colleges and universities. Then as now there was much to discuss: Catholic higher education is – and was – in a parlous state indeed. That meeting was extra-special for me because my wife Pamela was able to wrest herself from the duties of mothering five children to join at the convention. As we entered the dining room, Pam and I encountered our friend Germain Grisez. We had known Germain for years and we both had come to treasure him as a friend and counselor. Because I had to emcee the proceedings from the main table, Pam had to find another seat. She took one next to Germain, at a table right down in front of the rostrum.

My dinner partner was our host, Archbishop Harry Flynn. It was time to call the assembly to order, then as now a task better accomplished with a bull horn and a German shepherd than with gentle pleas. I was ready to introduce Archbishop Harry Flynn to give the blessing. At that precise moment, our friend Bill May walked up to the rostrum. Within eye-and-ear-shot of the archbishop, he declared (and I quote Bill, verbatim): "A man left this knife in my room." Professor May handed over a menacing-looking weapon. Bill wanted me to make a "lost knife" announcement to the assembled crowd. No one claimed it.

(At the Charlotte Banquet, when I delivered these remarks, Bill May spoke up at this point in the story. In more than a stage whisper, Bill confirmed the story, and insisted that it was "only" a Swiss Army knife. What a member of the Swiss Army was doing in Bill's Minneapolis hotel room that night in 1995 remains an enduring mystery of our Fellowship.)

The Minneapolis banquet went downhill from there. After the knife announcement and the archbishop's invocation, we sat to eat. I then saw right down front that Germain was engaged in animated conversation with a woman I did not know, seated to his left (Pam Bradley was to his right). I later learned that his conversation partner was a former student of his, Jo Harsy, then working for the diocese of Fargo, North Dakota. Now, Archbishop Flynn was also an old friend of Germain Grisez; in fact, Germain holds the Harry Flynn Chair of Christian Ethics at Mount Saint Mary's. I turned to the archbishop at this point and asked him: "Who is that woman sitting next to Germain?" He looked at me as if he were a deer caught in headlights and said, very deliberately: "Professor Bradley, I believe that woman is your wife."

I am grateful to the Fellowship of Catholic Scholars not only for this award. I am grateful to the Fellowship for the great help it has been to me. Because I served this group as its president for several years, that might sound odd. It might seem that I am the one who has given, not received, and it is true that often enough some of you have said thanks for my contributions to our Fellowship's activities. But I am the one in debt, and I am in debt to all of you. The help of which I speak is your example of faithful witness to the truth in your work as scholars. It is more than that, too: in your work as scholars in today's world of higher education and, sadly, even including the vast majority of those institutions listed as college or university in the Kenedy Directory – your work precisely *as* Catholic scholars has been unwelcome, controversial, a grounds for mistreatment or neglect. Your Catholic scholarship is said, even at institutions allegedly within the household of faith, to be "divisive." And your Catholic scholarship is, perhaps most sadly, treated no better by many of those we most earnestly wish to serve – the successors of the apostles, the guardians of the faith in our time, the American episcopacy.

You deserve better. But you understand that all-too-often no good deed goes unpunished in this vale of tears. Still, your work – *our* work – is hard, and is made harder by the icy reception of it among some of those who should know better. For the profound examples of patience and charity and steadfastness which so many of you have set before me, I am and shall forever be most thankful.

Steady. Steady was the key word last Year in Pittsburgh when Monsignor William Smith spoke of our dear Monsignor Kelly. Charity within patience was the key description of our first President, Father Ronald Lawler, when we were privileged to honor him in Pittsburgh, just before his death in late October 2004. Steady have you all been in the face of contradiction. And this has been a great consolation to me.

Our Holy Father Pope Benedict XVI addressed a group of about 140 priests last July 25. They were all resident of the Valle d'Aosta region of Italy, where the pope was vacationing at the time. His main text was the Parable of the Sower. It is, the Holy Father said, a parable of suffering, of courage, of consolation. It is indeed. But as he described the deeper message of the parable it occurred to me that it was about being steady in faith.

"The Lord's work had begun with great enthusiasm. The sick were visibly cured, everyone listened joyfully to the statement, 'The kingdom of God is at hand.' It really seemed," Pope Benedict said, "that at last the sorrow of the people of God would be changed into joy...[T]hey then saw that the sick were indeed cured, devils were expelled, the Gospel was proclaimed."

But the "world stayed as it was. Nothing changed. The Romans still dominated it. Life was difficult every day.". What then are we to make of the power of the Word? It is not a thunderclap. It is not (as Benedict told the priests) a "messenger of God whom they supposed would take the helm of history in his hand." It was instead the "power" of the seed, "a really tiny thing in comparison with historical and political reality." But in the seed, the Word, is the bread of life and thus the life of the future.

So we live in the period of the sowing. But the Word of God seems to be almost nothing; much of it falls on barren or rocky soil, and what falls on fertile ground might take years to bear fruit, and we might all be dead. The parable of the sower enables us to understand, the pope concluded, that we must "be courageous, even if the Word of God, the Kingdom of God, seems to have no historical or political importance."

We must, then, hang in there, be strong, be *steady*. And we can help one another to be strong and courageous and steady. The Fellowship has done that for me. And I shall mention ere tonight just two examples among the many I could cite of the steadiness of our sowers.

One is Father John Harvey. Father Harvey has labored more than most in the heat of the day. In his case it is not the sunlight that burns. It is the heat of criticism, from without and from within the Church. He is criticized even within our Church for his courageous work ministering to homosexual men and women. Some bishops refuse altogether to have Courage in their dioceses. A few of these may simply oppose the group's purpose and goals. More commonly (I suppose) reluctant bishops prefer to avoid stirring the pot of controversy when it comes to this issue – as if one could save souls for Jesus without causing a little commotion.

Most of you know that Father John founded Courage to do precisely that. He remains the Director and guiding spirit of the group. Father John and Courage have done more for the cause of truth when it comes to homosexuality than anyone or anything else in the Catholic Church. It was my privilege to speak to the Courage annual meeting this past August. And then I spent several hours visiting with those attending, most of them being members, and thus struggling with a same-sex attraction.

But these were not "gay" men and women (most were, in fact, men). They were *gay;* that is, well-adjusted and even happy. But that is because they are Christians. They did not identify themselves with their sexual disposition. They understood (because Father John and his collaborators taught them) that everyone has crosses to bear in life. One's struggle with one's particular cross imposed – and not the cross itself – defines the person. And struggling with the cross for Jesus' sake defines one as a Christian.

Father John Harvey was the first person in the Church to identify ministry to homosexual men and women as a distinct kind of calling. But it was not a call of his own making. Father John was trained as a moral theologian and achieved renown as a scholar. Early in his career he wrote an article on homosexuality. He did not intend, or even imagine it, that it would be the launch of a career. Quite the contrary. But then Father John Ford, S.J., perhaps the greatest moral theologian in the Church at mid-century (and also a previous winner of the Cardinal Wright Award) spoke to Father Harvey. As Father Harvey tells it, Father Ford said to him, "John, I hope that you will continue to write on the subject. No one else is doing it. No one else will be able to do it as well as you already do anytime soon. The Church needs it." A few years later another great Jesuit theologian by the name of John Courtney Murray delivered much the same advice to Father Harvey. And then Terrence Cardinal Cooke asked him to found the group which we know as Courage.

The nub of it is that Father John Harvey never wanted to do what he has done. But he always wanted to do what needed to be done for the Church – which means what Jesus wants for the sake of the Kingdom. He accepted the call, and has remained steady in it despite contradictions that would have soured the faith of lesser men and women.

Bill May. The distinguished moral theologian, William E. May, is competent to do more than handle sharp instruments. He is doubtlessly one of the most distinguished and most productive scholars within our membership, and is a very great gift to the Church. The steadiness for which I mean to cite him here tonight occurred at our last meeting, in Pittsburgh. Actually, it was Bill's *unsteadiness* which is illustrative. For our host last year, Bishop Donald Wuerl, was saying Mass on Sunday morning. He was near the end, ready to give the final blessing and to dismiss the congregation. Now, Bishop Wuerl is himself a long-time member of the Fellowship, and he has known Bill May (and others among our stalwarts) for decades, and he had hosted our meeting in 1992, too. I stood not twenty feet from Bishop Wuerl at this Mass, and I happened to be looking right at him when he paused in his progress towards dismissing the assembly. He looked right at Bill May, kneeling there directly in front of him, as Bill struggled to his feet for the final blessing. (Bill's legs are not what they once were, and he hobbles a bit.) I could tell at that moment that Bishop Wuerl was (for lack of a more precise term) much affected by Bill's struggle.

He was. Bill made it to his feet only to be motioned to sit. So were we all. Bishop Wuerl had decided on the spot to say something to us exactly as a *fellowship* of Catholic scholars, and Bill May had triggered this. Those of you who were there in Pittsburgh may remember that Bishop Wuerl then said that Bill exemplified the witness, the spirit, and the steadiness of our group. He was, of course, quite right.

Ten minutes later I arrived at the table to have breakfast with Bishop Wuerl. Before I was even seated, he broke into a narrative of how much it meant to him to see Bill May, a man whom the bishop had known through thick and through thin, and from a time when each was a young man, stay the course. And Bishop Wuerl proved it, in a way: when I returned to my office two days later there was already a check from Bishop Wuerl for a perpetual membership in the Fellowship of Catholic Scholars.

Gerard V. Bradley, a native of Brooklyn, is a Professor of Law at the University of Notre Dame Law School. He holds a J.D. degree from Cornell University, and he was formerly an Assistant District Attorney in New York City. He is the co-editor of the *American Journal of Jurisprudence*, and has himself authored many articles, both in law reviews and in popular journals. He is the author of a book, *Church-State Relations in America* (1987). With Father John Harvey, O.S.F.S., he recently edited the book, *Same-Sex Attraction: A Parent's Guide*, published by St. Augustine's Press in 2003. He is currently recognized as one of the national authorities on the subject of so-called "same-sex marriage," and its implications for law and society. The same thing is true with regard to his knowledge of the Catholic university situation in the light of Pope John Paul II's 1990 apostolic constitution *Ex Corde Ecclesiae* on the Catholic University. He served as President of the Fellowship of Catholic Scholars between 1995 and 2001 (and again briefly in 2003). He and his wife Pamela are the parents of eight children.

Remarks Upon Receiving the Cardinal O'Boyle Award

HELEN HULL HITCHCOCK

My very first encounter with the Fellowship of Catholic Scholars was in 1977, when Monsignor George Kelly visited St. Louis as part of his initial effort to start the organization up. I am pleased to say that I was present at the founding of the Fellowship, and proud that my husband was among its first officers. But I confess that I don't remember much else about those early meetings. My contribution to the foundation of this noble organization was to serve refreshments in our living-room, and to keep our little girls entertained.

I never had the privilege of meeting the man whose name is given to the award that I am honored to receive tonight, Cardinal Patrick A. O'Boyle, the first Archbishop of Washington (1948-73). But I do hope to live up to his motto: "Remain firm in the faith". In his condolence message after Cardinal O'Boyle's death on August 10, 1987, President Ronald Reagan wrote:

> He remained true to that motto throughout his long life of service, and with all of his wit, gentility, and wisdom, it is perhaps for the firmness of his moral leadership that he will best be remembered. Cardinal O'Boyle never ceased to champion the rights and the dignity of all human life, and he never hesitated to take action in its defense.

Those among us who remember the long hot summer of 1968 – in the midst of which *Humanae Vitae,* Pope Paul VI's encyclical reaffirming the Church's perennial teaching on birth control appeared (July 25) – will recall that both Martin Luther King and Robert Kennedy had recently been shot and killed (April and July), and that there had been a constant series of anti-war demonstrations, campus uprisings, protests, and riots (including the famous events at the Democratic National Convention in Chicago in August).

In this dramatic, overheated atmosphere of dissent and rebellion, and only weeks before *Humanae Vitae* appeared, Cardinal O'Boyle had issued a directive that religious educators must conform to Catholic teaching on the subject of birth control. But they publicly opposed him. The cardinal then attempted to discipline the priests who openly resisted. He received little support from his brother bishops, who would soon be confronted with the same open dissent in their own dioceses. For as soon as the encyclical appeared, hundreds of Catholic scholars – faculty of Catholic colleges and universities throughout the country – publicly rejected the authority of the Church in favor of their "right of conscience" to dissent.

But the beleaguered cardinal did "remain firm in the faith." He did not back down or compromise, even if he did not succeed in restoring order within the ranks. Nor did he follow the sheep that were abandoning the fold.

"Remain firm in the faith" might well be the motto of all Christians who live in our turbulent era, where that faith is challenged in almost every venue. This is especially true for those of us who have the responsibility for transmitting the Faith to others – in our families, as well as in our professions as Catholic scholars. These words, "Remain firm in the faith"(Col 1:23), distill to its essence the Apostle Paul's instruction to all who are charged to teach the truth – and to teach the teachers of the truth.

When I was sixteen, my grandfather Hull, a minister, gave me a New Testament, and inscribed beneath his name was this: "II Timothy 3:14-17." This is part of Paul's exhortation to Timothy in which he stresses the obligation to teach the truth of the Gospel of Jesus Christ – and to teach teachers. His letter speaks of the persecutions that "all who desire to live a godly life in Christ Jesus" must endure, "while evil men and imposters will go on from bad to worse, deceivers and deceived." The verses my grandfather singled out for my early instruction are these:

> But as for you, continue in what you have learned and have firmly believed, knowing from whom you learned it, and how from childhood you have been acquainted with the sacred writings which are able to instruct you for salvation through faith in Christ Jesus. All scripture is inspired by God and profitable for teaching, for reproof, for correction, and for training in righteousness, that the man of God may be complete, equipped for every good work.

Paul continues his instruction to Timothy, and it applies to those who would continue this work:

> ...preach the word, be urgent in season and out of season, convince, rebuke, and exhort, be unfailing in patience and in teaching.

> For the time is coming when people will not endure sound teach-
> ing, but having itching ears they will accumulate for themselves
> teachers to suit their own likings, and will turn away from listening
> to the truth and wander into myths. As for you, always be steady,
> endure suffering, do the work of an evangelist, fulfill your ministry
> (II Tim 4:2-5).

Remain firm in the faith! Cardinal O'Boyle, as we know, was faced
with *teachers* "who would not endure sound teaching." He confronted
the "deceivers and deceived." He also endured suffering in attempting to
fulfill his ministry.

Quite simply, he did what he was supposed to do, even though he
failed to convince rebellious priests and professors to turn away from
their errors; nor could he overcome the effects that their dissent would
have on the future of the Catholic faith in the United States. Their influence, as we now know only too well, remains to challenge each of us.
And it is our simple duty to remain firm in the faith.

I am honored to receive the Cardinal O'Boyle Award" from this
organization that I have known and cared for from its very beginnings,
and of which I have been member for twenty years, since I entered the
Catholic Church. I have more reason than most to be grateful for the
courageous witness of the members of the Fellowship of Catholic
Scholars, through these many years, whose faith in Christ and devotion
to His Church and her mission have been an example to me.

I confess that it seems not quite right that I should receive recognition for merely doing what is required of every believer – to serve as best
one can wherever and however one is called. It seems to me that reward-
ing someone for responding to a basic duty is something like being
asked to applaud the choir after Mass, or like the priest thanking the congregation for attending. I cannot even take credit for selecting the various efforts in which I've been involved since 1984. In fact, I did not
choose the kind of work I've been doing, and I would have picked something that I'd be better at, given the choice. But if a baby is left on your
doorstep, you simply have to take it in. You simply must pick up the crying baby and do your best to care for it. It's not a choice. It is a duty – a
responsibility. And it is also privilege to have been called to serve in this
way.

There is one more reservation I have about receiving this award.
Many of you have been my teachers and guides in the faith – and so it is
no exaggeration to say that I was a slow learner! I confess with some
embarrassment that for many years I was unable to see the path leading
to the Church – a path that was well illuminated by some of the best and
brightest Catholic scholars in the country who were founding members

of this Fellowship. They remained firm in the Faith in spite of overwhelming opposition; they protected and defended the Church when she was being severely attacked and cast into a ditch by robbers. Their consistent witness through their words and actions was a great aid in overcoming my own "invincible ignorance." I daresay that the same is true of many, many others whom they taught. For this it is *they*, not I, who deserve praise – along with our gratitude.

Helen Hull Hitchcock is the founding director (since 1984) of Women for Faith and Family. She edits *Voices*, the WFF publication, and is also the editor of the much praised *Adoremus Bulletin*, the publication of the Society for the Renewal of the Sacred Liturgy, of which she is a co-founder and member of the executive committee. She is the editor of *The Politics of Prayer: Feminist Language and the Worship of God* (Ignatius Press, 1992), and has contributed essays and chapters to a number of other volumes. She also edited the WFF Sourcebooks for Lent/Easter and Advent/Christmas. She is the principal editor of the websites for both Women for Faith and Family (www.wf-f.org) **and the** ***Adoremus Bulletin*** **(**www.adoremus.org**). She was a regular columnist for the** ***National Catholic Register*** **(1977-86) as well as** *Crisis* **magazine (1992-97).**

A former Episcopalian, Mrs. Hitchcock was received into the Catholic Church in 1984. She currently serves on the Boards of Directors of the Eternal Word Television Network and Ave Maria University; and she served two terms on the Board of the Fellowship of Catholic Scholars. She has appeared frequently on radio and television and lectures widely, especially on issues affecting Catholic women and families as well as on such subjects as the sacred liturgy. She is married to James Hitchcock and they are the parents of four daughters.

Appendix
Fellowship of Catholic Scholars
Membership Information

For information about joining the Fellowship of Catholic Scholars, contact the Executive Secretary, the Rev. Msgr. Stewart Swetland at:

St. John's Newman Foundation
604 East Armory Avenue
Champaign, Illinois 61820

TEL: 217-344-1184 Ext. 305

E-MAIL: msgrswetland@newmanfoundation.org

Or visit the FCS website at:
www.catholicscholars.org

Statement of Purpose

1. We, Catholic scholars in various disciplines, join in fellowship in order to serve Jesus Christ better, by helping one another in our work and by putting our abilities more fully at the service of the Catholic faith.
2. We wish to form a Fellowship of Catholic Scholars who see their intellectual work as expressing the service they owe to God. To Him we give thanks for our Catholic faith and for every opportunity He gives us to serve that faith
3. We wish to form a Fellowship of Catholic Scholars open to the work of the Holy Spirit within the Church. Thus we wholeheartedly accept and support the renewal of the Church of Christ undertaken by Pope John XXIII, shaped by Vatican Council II, and carried on by succeeding popes.
4. We accept as the rule of our life and thought the entire faith of the Catholic Church. This we see not merely in solemn definitions but

in the ordinary teaching of the pope and the bishops in union with him, and also embodied in those modes of worship and ways of Christian life, of the present as of the past, which have been in harmony with the teaching of St. Peter's successors in the See of Rome.

5.   The questions raised by contemporary thought must be considered with courage and dealt with in honesty. We will seek to do this, faithful to the truth always guarded in the Church by the Holy Spirit, and sensitive to the needs of the family of faith. We wish to accept a responsibility which a Catholic scholar may not evade: to assist everyone, so far as we are able, to personal assent to the mystery of Christ as made manifest through the lived faith of the Church, His Body, and through the active charity without which faith is dead.

6.   To contribute to this sacred work, our Fellowship will strive to:
    *   Come to know and welcome all who share our purpose;
    *   Make known to one another our various competencies and interests;
    *   Share our abilities with one another unstintingly in our efforts directed to our common purpose;
    *   Cooperate in clarifying the challenges which must be met;
    *   Help one another to evaluate critically the variety of responses which are proposed to these challenges;
    *   Communicate our suggestions and evaluations to members of the Church who might find them helpful;
    *   Respond to requests to help the Church in her work of guarding the faith as inviolable and defending it with fidelity;
    *   Help one another to work through, in scholarly and prayerful fashion and without public dissent, any problem which may arise from magisterial teaching.

7.   With the grace of God for which we pray, we hope to assist the whole Church to understand her own identity more clearly, to proclaim the joyous Gospel of Jesus more confidently, and to carry out it redemptive work to all humankind more effectively.

Member Benefits

All members receive four issues annually of the *The Fellowship of Catholic Scholars Quarterly*, which includes scholarly articles, important documentation, book reviews, news, and occasional Fellowship symposia.

All members are invited to attend the annual FCS convention held in various cities where, by custom, the local ordinary greets and typically celebrates Mass for the members of the Fellowship. The typical convention program includes: Daily Mass; Keynote Address; at least six scholarly sessions with speakers who are customarily invited to help develop and illustrate the theme of each convention chosen by the FCS Board of Directors; a Banquet and Reception with Awards; and a membership business meeting and occasional substantive meetings devoted to subjects of current interest in the Church.

Current members receive a copy of the "Proceedings" of each convention, consisting of an attractive volume with the title of the convention theme and containing the texts of the conventions speeches and other material of interest to the membership. Every three or four years all members receive a Membership Directory with current information on Fellowship members (addresses, telephone numbers, faxes, e-mails, etc.).

National Awards

The Fellowship grants the following Awards, usually presented during the annual convention:

The Cardinal Wright Award – Presented annually to a Catholic judged to have done outstanding service for the Church in the tradition of the late Cardinal John J. Wright, former Bishop of Pittsburgh and later Prefect for the Congregation for Catholic Education in Rome. The recipients of this Award have been:

1979 – Rev. Msgr. George A. Kelly
1980 – Dr. William E. May
1981 – Dr. James Hitchcock
1982 – Dr. Germain Grisez
1983 – Rev. John Connery, S.J.
1984 – Rev. John A. Hardon, S.J.
1985 – Herbert Ratner, M.D.
1986 – Dr. Joseph P. Scottino
1987 – Rev. Joseph Farraher, & Rev. Joseph Fessio, S.J.
1988 – Rev. John Harvey, O.S.F.S.
1989 – Dr. John Finnis
1990 – Rev. Ronald Lawler, O.F.M. Cap.
1991 – Rev. Francis Canavan, S.J.
1992 – Rev. Donald J. Keefe, S.J.
1993 – Dr. Janet E. Smith
1994 – Dr. Jude P. Dougherty
1995 – Rev. Msgr. William B. Smith
1996 – Dr. Ralph McInerny
1997 – Rev. James V. Schall, S.J.

1998 – Rev. Msgr. Michael J. Wrenn & Kenneth D. Whitehead
1999 – Dr. Robert P. George
2000 – Dr. Mary Ann Glendon
2001 – Thomas W. Hilgers, M.D.
2002 – Rev. J. Augustine DiNoia, O.P.
2003 – Prof. Elizabeth Fox-Genovese
2004 – Sr. Mary Prudence Allen, R.S.M.

The Cardinal O'Boyle Award – This Award is given occasionally to individuals whose actions demonstrate a courage and witness in favor of the Catholic Faith similar to that exhibited by the late Cardinal Patrick A. O'Boyle, Archbishop of Washington, in the face of the pressures of contemporary society which tend to undermine the faith. The recipients of this award have been:

1988 – Rev. John C. Ford, S.J.
1991 – Mother Angelica, P.C.P.A., EWTN
1995 – John and Sheila Kippley, Couple to Couple League
1997 – Rep. Henry J. Hyde (R.-IL)
2002 – Senator Rick Santorum (R.-PA)
2003 – Secretary of Housing and Urban Development, the Honorable Melquiades R. Martinez and Mrs. Kathryn Tindal Martinez
2004 – Rep. Christopher J. Smith (R.-NJ) and Marie Smith

The Founder's Award – Given occasionally to individuals with a record of outstanding service in defense of the Catholic faith and in support of the Catholic intellectual life. In 2002, the Award was presented to Fr. Joseph Fessio, S.J., and in 2003, to Fr. Ronald Lawler, O.F.M.Cap.

Presidents of the Fellowship of Catholic Scholars

2004 –   Dean Bernard Dobranski, Ave Maria Law School
2003 – 2004   Prof. Gerard V. Bradley, Notre Dame Law School
2002 – 2003   Dean Bernard Dobranski, Ave Maria Law School
2001 – 2002   Rev. Thomas F. Dailey, O.S.F.S., DeSales University
1995 – 2001   Prof. Gerard V. Bradley, Notre Dame Law School
1991 – 1995   Prof. Ralph McInerny, University of Notre Dame
1989 – 1991   Rev. Kenneth Baker, S.J., Editor, *Homiletic & Pastoral Review*
1987 – 1989   Prof. William E. May, John Paul II Institute on Marriage and the Family
1985 – 1987   Rev. Msgr. George A. Kelly, St. John's University

1983 – 1985   Rev. Earl Weiss, S.J., Loyola University
1981 – 1983   Rev. Msgr. William B. Smith, St. Joseph's Seminary
1979 – 1981   Prof. James Hitchcock, St. Louis University
1977 – 1979   Rev. Ronald Lawler, O.F.M.Cap., Diocese of
Pittsburgh